COLD WAR
HOT WINGS

COLD WAR
HOT WINGS

Memoirs of a fighter pilot
1962–1994

by

Chris J Bain

Pen & Sword
AVIATION

First published in Great Britain in 2007 by
Pen & Sword Aviation
an imprint of
Pen & Sword Books Ltd
47 Church Street
Barnsley
South Yorkshire
S70 2AS

ISBN 978 1 84415 541 5

Typeset in Sabon by
Phoenix Typesetting, Auldgirth, Dumfriesshire

Printed and bound in England by
Biddles Ltd, King's Lynn

Pen & Sword Books Ltd incorporates the Imprints of Pen & Sword
Aviation, Pen & Sword Maritime, Pen & Sword Military, Wharncliffe Local
History, Pen & Sword Select, Pen & Sword Military Classics and Leo
Cooper.

For a complete list of Pen & Sword titles please contact
PEN & SWORD BOOKS LIMITED
47 Church Street, Barnsley, South Yorkshire, S70 2AS, England
E-mail: enquiries@pen-and-sword.co.uk
Website: www.pen-and-sword.co.uk

DEDICATION

This book is dedicated to all those friends and acquaintances with whom I flew throughout my 33 years in the RAF, and who lost their lives, for whatever reason, while giving service to their country. If I have missed out any names, please forgive me; it is only because of my terrible memory after all these years:

(Note: the unit names shown below are those in which I knew the pilot indicated, and not necessarily the unit where he died.)

Roger Griffin, Cadet Pilot RAF Sth Cerney – Civil aircraft crash, Leics

Andy Macklen, student pilot 3 FTS – Jet Provost turnback crash

Kenny Tate, 3 FTS RAF Leeming – Buccaneer tailplane fatigue crash

Dennis Hazell, 4 FTS RAF Valley – Red Arrows accident

John Loftus, 8 Sqn – crashed at RAF Valley

Ron Etheridge, 8 Sqn – Hunter T7 crash, Shawbury

Roger Patterson, 8 Sqn – Hunter crash, Oman

Pad Williams, 4, 54 & 20 Sqns – Harrier crash, Germany

Hans "Pet" Larsson, (RDaAF) 810 Sqn Skrydstrup – F100 crash, Denmark

Bruce Cogram, 233 OCU – Harrier T4 crash, Gutersloh

Jim Downey, 3 (F) Sqn – Harrier crash

Steve Beckley, 20 Sqn – Harrier crash

Tony Chambers, 229 Hunter OCU – Kuwaiti Hunter crash

"Martin" Eric Chandler – Strike Wing, Khormaksar

Ken Hayr, 1 (F) Sqn – Vampire crash, Biggin Hill

Keith Holland, 233 OCU – Harrier crash

Joe Sims, 1(F) Sqn – Car crash, 2003

Bill Loverseed, 229 Hunter OCU – Bombardier test flight crash

"Hoof" Proudfoot, 233 OCU – Classic aircraft crash

Pete Bennett, 1 (F) Sqn – Hawk crash

Nick Slater, 229 OCU & 233 OCU – Harrier crash, West Freugh

"Come fly with me, let's fly, let's fly away . . . .."
(Frank Sinatra)

Fate, so cruel to my friends above, decreed that I should survive 36 years of flying and 66 operational missions, and that one day I should be able to tell my father, in my own words, the story of those times. Unfortunately, it was not to be.

Contents

List of Photographs

** ©Crown Copyright/MOD.

List of Maps and Figures

Foreword

HISTORY, n. *An account mostly false, of events mostly unimportant,*
which are brought about by rulers mostly knaves, and
soldiers mostly fools.
(The Devil's Dictionary by Ambrose Bierce)

Although this is a personal set of memoirs from my time in the RAF, no set of stories would be intelligible without some background material with which to convey the setting. Indeed, some escapades would not be understandable without a certain knowledge of the conditions and climate, and the political, military and economic situations pertaining at the time. This is particularly so for my time spent in the Middle East simply because, despite the increase in travel with the advent of fast air transport and the package deal holiday in the past 40 odd years, parts of the world such as the Southern Yemen, are still off limits to the majority of the western population. Hence, despite 131 years of British colonialism in Southern Yemen, there is still an endemic ignorance in the western world of customs and conditions prevalent in those parts.

The rise of Muslim terrorism in the Middle East makes the British mistakes during their time of rule over the vast desert areas, such as Palestine, Iraq, The Persian Gulf, The Trucial States and The Yemen, even more vital to understand today. Indeed, the abrogation of our responsibilities on withdrawal from Empire, overseen by the Wilson Government, is not only a stain on our character, but the main reason why so many in the Arab world no longer trust us.

Though more hospitable, the same applies to areas of Central America. Not many Europeans have worked in Belize, and although backward in parts, it is much more friendly and has more to offer than Yemen, despite the endemic drugs industry. Indeed, it has oft been said that Yemen and South Arabia are being dragged kicking and screaming into the middle ages. It could apply to some parts of Central America, though they aren't screaming as loudly as the Arabs.

It struck me at a very early stage in my air force career, that whilst many books have been written by or about service people recounting their wartime or operational experiences, the reading public very rarely hear about their peacetime exploits. This book is a fund of peacetime stories and experiences, some extremely funny and some deadly serious, only tempered by my poor memory, about air force life in the midst of the Cold War.

My Father spent WW2 in RAF Bomber Command. Flying 54 missions, initially as an air gunner and subsequently as a pilot, he was one of the very few lucky ones to survive all those 1000 bomber raids over Germany. He started as an Aircraftsman, and finished as a Flight Lieutenant in the RAFVR, with a DFM for shooting down a ME109 as a Hampden mid-upper gunner in 1941. He then piloted Lancasters throughout Europe during the Bomber Command offensive and, finished the war as a Dakota pilot ferrying POW's home from Germany. In an era when bomber crews' life expectancy was measured in single-figure missions, his 54 over Europe are quite remarkable, and worthy of a book in their own right. Sadly, he never talked of them, least of all to me. Unlike mine, it's a story of which the whole family could be proud but, unfortunately, those wartime experiences will never be told due to a deep modesty typical of that era. Even more so when you read the standard of RAF advice to pilots in WW2. I quote from an RAF Flying Publication: *"When a prang seems inevitable, endeavour to strike the softest, cheapest object in the vicinity, as slowly and gently as possible."* With that sort of gratuitous advice it's amazing anyone survived, but that was in the days when sex was safe and flying was dangerous! But I wanted desperately to beat his achievement.

I too was one of the lucky ones. With minimal education, aspiring to go nowhere, permanently crippled with arthritic pain in the feet and spine, and the single ambition to be a BOAC Captain without any of the qualifications required, I conned the RAF into making the most of me. Albeit initially reluctantly, the RAF was stupid enough to try and turn me into one of their elite fighter pilots, descendants of the few. But, as I was to learn later, and was often said in the trade, "Flying fighters was better than working for a living!"

I'd figured out that after two tours in RAF Transport Command on a short service commission, BOAC definitely couldn't fly without me! At the tender age of 16, I had already passed the RAF pilot's selection course after three days of trials, tests and tribulations at RAF Hornchurch, and the service had reserved a place for me at pilot training subject to obtaining my educational qualifications. I needed some O-levels to don an airforce officer's uniform, so studied at night school to obtain them. I had managed the three days with exceptional ratings for pilot aptitude, but E's for officer qualities, so offered to go NCO aircrew but, despite the E's, they insisted on making me an officer. Pity . . . . because the NCOs had all the fun without the responsibility! What a misspent youth: exceptional at playing fairground co-ordination machines, thus proving my pilotage ability, but despite a thorough grounding from my strict middle class upbringing I was apparently useless at table manners!

I have to say a big thankyou, though, to the President of that selection board, Wg Cdr E A Fairhurst, who, on 9 June 1961, came down on my side commenting, *" . . . .there is just a spark of potential . . . ."*, and recommended me for Commissioned Pilot Training!

I really was one of the lucky ones. I flew operationally in Aden, Belize, and round the world on covert intelligence gathering/surveillance missions. I survived many airborne emergencies, came home with bullet holes in my aircraft, and was involved in a few campaigns, but in such a minor way that mostly the greatest threat to my life was myself. Looking back, I really have had a very fortunate life. I've been shot at on many an occasion, had aircraft engine failures galore, had constant battles with the medical fraternity to avoid grounding and avoided mid-air collisions by inches, but there was always a feeling of invincibility in the warmth of a fighter cockpit. It therefore came as a nasty shock to find you'd been hit, even if you were back on the ground before you realized it. I *have* been lucky – I've had some good times, and really mustn't complain, even if my mini-walk-on part in the big scheme of things has often felt blurred. But some need the adrenalin of enthusiasm to achieve anything.

Throughout the 33 years I had a ball, and some of the things my comrades in arms and I got up to, will, I hope, enthral you. It is not, I hope, a self-indulgent or a self-seeking memoir but, a word of caution: this is a story of an ordinary, everyday, fighter pilot, warts, mistakes and all – and there were many of those! There is no dashing or daring – nothing brave or exceptional – just a typical life in the career of a military, fighter pilot who was lucky to obtain the job in the first place, lucky to maintain it, and lucky to come out alive. Perhaps one of the motivations for this book is to try and set the record straight for those that thought they knew me. People who described me as moody in my younger days never knew, for instance, that I was in constant pain from my arthritic back. With permanent back-ache and consequent lack of sleep, it was often difficult to rise to the occasion. Popping anti-inflammatories for 25 years to stop the pain took its toll, but you could never tell anybody – it would have been instant endex for one's career. Gritted teeth: *"I'm fine thankyou!"*

Nevertheless, there's always been a bit of a rebel in me. Just tell me that I'm not allowed to do something, or that I can't, and I'll always do it! That's a deep-seated part of my nature, and it was General Olds who stated that rebelliousness is a necessary part of a fighter pilot's make-up! So is a "can-do" attitude to life. It comes with a hatred of bureaucracy, a paranoia about being cuckolded – the services are insular – and the feeling that no one back home in civvy street ever really understands. The hair-tearing insularity of the average serviceman is still prevalent today, though was well summed-up by David Lloyd George's War Memoirs. Under the heading "military mind" are the sub-headings "narrowness of", "does not seem to understand arithmetic", and "regards thinking as a form of mutiny"! So many military autobiographies are mendacious works of self-justification to be used with extreme caution.

I trust and hope that I'm not an immodest writer, but when I think of what we went through and the dangers we encountered, even in peacetime, both while flying and on ground duties, I think we were all so used to the precarious perils that we perhaps carried our modesty too far – shrugging it off in front of ones peers as if it were an everyday occurrence – which in fact was the case! Even so, I'm quite proud of that attitude, but a lot must be ascribed to luck rather than any ability, courage or endurance. My goodness! To think of some of the things we did, and some of the mad and stupid things we did when young . . . and I was being paid for it!

8 Sqn on active service during the last few years in Aden and South Arabia (the best low flying area in the world!), together with 2 Sqn during its Hunter FR10 days in Germany, were two of the very best flying jobs in the RAF. I really was very fortunate to have had such a thorough, rewarding and enjoyable introduction to fighter flying.

Unlike other tomes on the subject, this is written from an air force view-point, without whom the army couldn't operate. The air force is a team made up of pilots, navigators, engineers and our indomitable groundcrew. Fighter pilots are an irreverent bunch, but they would be the first to admit, despite my comments elsewhere in the book, that they couldn't operate efficiently without the others.

Two other reasons for writing it are that no-one after my generation will have had first hand knowledge, good or bad, of Empire, and secondly, my son Andrew may, at long last, understand me!

For those ardent, air force fans who may deign to read this work, I'd like to make it quite clear that originally it was written for my son, Andrew, who dearly wished to follow me into the Air Force. After obtaining an RAF flying scholarship he was devastated to be refused aircrew entry on a minor medical technicality and eventually opted, sensibly, for commercial airlines instead. Hence, this work was to be added in CD form to my logbooks as part of his inheritance. Only then, after I had fallen off my perch, would he know, finally, whom his father really was. The fact that a grossly simplified and précised edition has been published a little early – reports of my demise are most premature – is not necessarily an agreeable idea!

This book is a light-hearted, semi-autobiographical history portraying aspects of my time in the RAF. The stories are all based on truth in my opinion, and as far as my memory serves me, but stories get better with the telling. Only you, the reader, can judge how much hot air has been used to embellish them. *"There I was, 40,000 feet, upside-down, nothing on the clock but the maker's name. . . "*!

Preface

At the end of WW2, British paramountcy in the Middle East was more formidable than it had ever been, but its pillars collapsed like skittles after Indian independence in 1947, and the end of the British mandate in Palestine in 1948. British power declined rapidly as revolutionary regimes took over Egypt, the Sudan, Libya, and Iraq and even Jordan. It lingered on in the only British Colony in the Arab world – Aden.

Three years before our sneak-out from the Aden fortress, British forces, myself included, had won the last colonial campaign in the Empire's long history of battle: the Radfan and South Arabian campaigns. Fought on the wild Yemeni frontier, it demonstrated Britain's determination to rule in the way rebellious tribesmen were deemed to understand best: the law of the gun. It showed Britain could stay in those parts as long as she chose, but a change of government soon afterwards in London to Wilson's Labour, brought a quite inconceivable reversal in policy, which had a monumental and long-lasting effect on Middle East relations.

Wilson protested against the charge that he couldn't think strategically, " I think at least six weeks ahead", he responded. That summed him up perfectly. He chose to leave Aden and all other bases East of Suez, lock, stock and barrel. Our Arab friends now felt themselves betrayed by a British government that sought to wash its hands of the whole dirty business in Aden by complete abdication of responsibility. It was utterly shameful; Britain was unilaterally abrogating solemn treaties of protection that had specifically ruled out any changes without mutual consent, and the Arabs still hadn't forgotten the first time we betrayed them. These were the promises to Sherif Husein in 1916, conveyed by Lawrence, of an Arab empire encompassing Arabia, Syria, Jordan, Iraq and modern Israel, promises which Britain never anticipated having to honour.

Exactly the same happened in Aden in 1966. Once is a mistake, twice is unforgivable. Britain's failure to honour its promises created a reservoir of deep resentment upon which opponents of the West have regularly drawn. Why should we expect the Arabs to respect us ever again?

Furthermore, the hypocritical obfuscation of our Labour ministers of the time beggars belief. In July '65 after numerous discussions, Dennis Healey (then Defence Secretary) stood in Middle East Command HQ, and quite clearly stated to the British High Commissioner, the CinC, and their staffs, that the Aden base would stay. Six months later he reversed that decision, and typically made no mention of it in his memoirs[1]. His memoirs were not only too busy blaming the Tories, but Healey stated that, " . . . *ADEN HAD NO STRATEGIC IMPORTANCE until the RAF started building its largest base in the world at Khormaksar in the sixties[sic] . . .* ", adding that the Aden base

xvii

was only there to defend itself and had, unlike Cyprus, no regional responsibility. Whereas Correlli Barnett in his tome entitled "The Greatest Power in the World", quite rightly states, *"The . . . need to protect the Suez route to India (BEFORE AS WELL AS AFTER the Suez Canal was opened in 1869) landed Britain with . . . Malta, Cyprus, Aden and British Somaliland, and protectorates over Egypt, the Sudan, the Persian Gulf states, and southern Persia. Long-forgotten STRATEGIC needs of the age of sail and modern requirements for coaling stations added islands in almost every sea and ocean.",* Kamaran, Perim and Socotra to name but three. Admittedly we didn't need that route any longer after the loss of India, but quite obviously to anyone, Aden still commanded the southern mouth of the Red Sea, and hence, the use of the Suez Canal. What greater demonstration of Aden's strategic importance did Healey want!? Moreover, denying the area to terrorist organisations over the past 35 years would have stopped Bin Laden and produced a more stable world. (Note the above capitals are mine).

Further in his memoirs, Healey went on to say, *"Our decision* (to leave Aden) *was published in the White Paper of February 1966. Trevelyan took over in May the following year and tried desperately to find someone to negotiate with, so that we could leave a viable government behind. But the nationalists in Aden were slaughtering one another, and the sheikhs of the interior were, as always, fighting among themselves."* What he didn't say was that it was this very decision, and its stupid timing, that contributed between Feb '66 and Nov '68, to so much fighting and, GREAT LOSS OF BRITISH LIVES.

And then, astoundingly, four years later, we did exactly the same thing to Bahrain and the Gulf States after continuous assurances to the contrary. Surprise, surprise, the consequences have been frightening: a power vacuum leading to continuous Russian mischief, instability throughout the region, continuous "war" between Arab and Israeli, the two Gulf wars, and the rise of Bin Laden and Al Qa'eda from Yemeni/South Arabian beginnings into international Islamic terrorism. America is now spending a lot of time mopping up the failures of British imperialism from Afghanistan to the West Bank and Sudan to Iraq; and that's just in the Middle East!

The brutal fact was that the treaties were hangovers from another era, from times when the *Pax Britannica* was a blessing to millions of diverse peoples around the world. But now, imperialism had become a dirty word. The cost of trying to stay in Aden, with an increasingly hostile population armed and supported by Nasser's agents from neighbouring Yemen, was out of all proportion to the gain; regardless of what the politicians said, THAT WAS THE SOLE REASON FOR LEAVING. The sun had set on British global power from the time of the equally shamefully hurried withdrawal from India two decades earlier. Unfortunately, the world had not, and still has not, produced anything to replace the imperial British role of maintaining law and order over large areas of the globe, suppressing slavers, murderers and thieves whether they operated as mere robber bands or as ambitious tribal chieftains. The inexperienced Americans, however, have taken on the role, and are being forced to learn fast.

As the huge ball of red sun descended over the Arabian Sea on 28th November 1967, most of the tribal rulers of the desert hinterland, with whose forebears Britain had signed treaties of perpetual protection, had already screamed "betrayal" and fled their palaces, fearful of the Nasser-backed Marxist mobs. We left behind many other Arabs, including my faithful bearer Hassan, with a greater feeling of let-down – humbler men who had worked to improve the lot of their own people as officials of a benevolent colonialism. For most there was no escape.

It had become a fixed idea in Arab minds that the presence of British soldiers in Aden caused all the horrors, despite 120-odd years of peace and prosperity. So to them the answer was simple: remove the British and the horrors would disappear. Even some of the BP oilmen from Little Aden's refinery voiced such thoughts. It's a bit like saying that policemen create criminals. Yet without police there can be no law, justice or community order. The British military presence was there to safeguard British interests, but it served as the catalyst for agitation. No, it was the Wilson government's ill-founded decision to announce the pull out deadline early that fanned the flames of civil war, in which the British troops were whipping boys for both sides in the internal struggle. On a vastly greater scale, the same thing happened to America in Vietnam a decade later. Aden was Britain's Vietnam.

Belize was the opposite: they wanted us to stay! We can be proud of taking this steamy, tropical country to independence, for once, peacefully.

Yet Germany, during the Cold War, was chilly and serious. Being on NATO's front line close to the Inner German Border (IGB) was fraught, forbidding and farraginous. Were we conventional or nuclear? Were we a defensive deterrent or part of a "first-use" policy? But then, flexibility is a principle of war!

Most of all, as a very young man, my role in Belize, and particularly in Aden, unlike George Orwell's in the Burmese Colonial Police, was most enjoyable and more flexible, being the instrument guarding British colonial law and order. But considering the manner of its execution, it was not necessarily something of which to be proud. Unlike Orwell, I didn't have the benefit of a higher, Etonian education, and while I recognized at the time that actual good work was being done by doctors, teachers, nurses, my MDRT[2] et al, it was decades later before I realized that no amount of it would compensate for the evils of foreign domination. As Orwell suspected, all over the decrepit, embattled Empire there were those of us who felt this way, but were trapped in a bureaucratic military conspiracy of silence. The oppression with which Orwell collaborated in Burma was little different forty years later in Aden, and was just a symptom of an entire world of social domination, as pernicious in Britain as in the Empire.

Notes
1. "The Time of my Life" by Dennis Healey.
2. Mountain Desert Rescue Team (see chapter 9).

Glossary

AAA	Anti aircraft artillery
AAC	Army Air Corp
AAR	Air-to-air refuelling
ac	aircraft
AC	Army Cooperation
ACE	Allied Command Europe (One of three NATO senior commands)
ACM	Air Chief Marshal
ADEN	**A**rmament **D**evelopments **EN**field. Nothing to do with the colony of Aden! By coincidence, it was the name given to the gun by the Royal Small Arms Factory at Enfield which developed captured German, Mauser, prototype, revolver-action, 20mm cannons at the end of WW2, into the ADEN 30mm. The French did the same with their DEFA 30mm gun, as did the Americans at 20mm before the introduction of the airborne Gatling.
ADF	Airborne Direction Finder
ADHD	Attention deficit and hyperactivity disorder
a/f	airfield
AFC	Air Force Cross
AFCENT	Allied Forces Central Europe (a NATO command)
AFME	Air Forces Middle East (an RAF Command with HQ in Aden until 1967)
AFNORTH	Allied Forces Northern Europe (a NATO command)
AFTS	Advanced Flying Training School
AFV	Armoured Fighting Vehicle
agl	above ground level
AHQ	Air Headquarters
AM	Air Marshal (3-star air force general)
amsl	above mean sea level
AOC	Air Officer Commanding
APC	Armament Practice Camp
APL	Aden Protectorate Levies
AS	Ankyilosing Spondylitis, an arthritic disease of the spine
ASI	Air Speed Indicator
ATAF	Allied Tactical Air Force
ATC	Air Traffic Control
AtoA	Air-to-air
AtoG	Air-to-ground
AVM	Air Vice Marshal (RAF 2-star air force general)

AVPIN	Highly flammable rocket fluid used in the Avon engine starter motor on the Hunter
AWACs	Airborne Warning and Control aircraft
BA	British Airways
BAe	British Aerospace
BandN	Britten-Norman (a British aircraft manufacturing company)
BAS	British Antarctic Survey
BBC	British Broadcasting Corporation
BDA	Battle damage assessment
BDF	Belize Defence Force
BL755	A British cluster bomb
BO	Body odour!
BOAC	British Overseas Airways Corporation (predecessor to British Airways)
BofB	Battle of Britain
BOQs	Bachelor officer quarters (US)
BRIXMIS	British military intelligence mission in Berlin during the Cold War
BUA	British United Airways (amalgamated later with Caledonian Airways)
CAS	Chief of the Air Staff
CBF	Commander British Forces (Belize)
CBU	Cluster bomb unit
CENTO	Central Treaty Organisation
CFRP	Centre for the Rehabilitation of the Paralysed (Bangladesh)
CFS	Central Flying School
CIA	Central Intelligence Agency
CID	Criminal Investigation Department
CinC	Commander in Chief
CNN	An American TV news network
CSA	Child support agency
CSE	Combined Services Entertainment
CSRI	Combat Survival and Rescue Instructor
CSRO	Combat Survival and Rescue Officer
DAO	Duty Authorizing Officer (for flight authorization)
DAW	Department of Air Warfare RAF
DBS	Days before Sidewinder!
DEA	Drug Enforcement Agency (US)
DIA	Defence Intelligence Agency (US)
DIAC	DIA Centre
DIY	Do-it-yourself
DFC	Distinguished Flying Cross
DFGA	Day Fighter Ground Attack
DFM	Distinguished Flying Medal
DME	Distance Measuring Equipment
DSC	Distinguished Service Cross
EAF	Egyptian Air Force
EAP	Eastern Aden Protectorate
ECM	Electronic counter measures

EO	Electro-optical
ETA	Estimated time of arrival
ETD	Estimated time of departure
EU	European Union
FAA	Fleet Air Arm
FAC	Forward Air Controller
FADC	Chilean Air Force (Fuerza Aerea De Chile)
FAF	French Air Force
FBI	Federal Bureau of Investigation (US)
FCU	Fuel control unit
FGA (9)	Fighter Ground Attack (Mark 9)
FLIM	Flight line mechanic
FLIR	Forward looking infra-red
FLOSY	Front for the Liberation of Occupied South Yemen
FNG	Federal National Guard (South Arabia)
FR	Fighter Reconnaissance
FR	Flexible response (nuclear)
FRA	Federal Regular Army – Aden
FRI	Fighter recce instructor
FSO	Flight safety officer
FTS	Flying Training School
g or G	Force of gravity
GAF	German Air Force
GD	General Duties
GLO	Ground Liaison Officer (army officer attached to the air force)
GOC	General Officer Commanding
GSM	General Service Medal
HAS	Hardened aircraft shelters
HC	High Commissioner
HE	High explosive
HEAT	High Explosive Anti-Tank. A copper shaped-charge warhead designed specifically to kill armoured vehicles such as tanks. A shaped-charge on detonation develops into a long thin, supersonic stream of molten copper which drills a hole through the armour.
HEL	Hunting Engineering Ltd
HFS	Harrier Flight Simulator
HM	Her Majesty
HMG	Her Majesty's Government
HMS	Her Majesty's Ship
HRH	His(Her) Royal Highness
HAS	Health and Safety Act
HUD	Head-up display
HUMINT	Human intelligence (intelligence garnered from a human being verbally)
Humla	Derogatory term for a little Arab
IAF	Iraqi Air Force
ID	Identification

IED	Incendiary Explosive Device
IGB	Inner German Border (Between the old East and West Germanys)
IN	Inertial navigation
INAS	Inertial navigation and attack system
IP	Initial point (on an attack run)
IWI	Interceptor weapons instructor
IWW	First World War
IIWW	Second World War
INAS	Inertial Navigation and Attack System
INR	Initial nuclear response
IOU	"I owe you".
JFK	John F Kennedy
JP233	A British air-delivered, anti-runway, weapons system
JSTARS	Joint Strategic Targeting and Reconnaissance System
KCB	Knight Commander of the British Empire
KCMG	Knight Commander of the order of St Michael and St George
KD	Khaki drill (tropical uniform)
KOSBI	Kings Own Scottish Borderers (a Scottish lowland infantry regiment)
KTO	Kuwaiti theatre of operations
LBNP	Late-bottled, Nuval Port (A cheap Port drunk in quantity in Belize Garrison Mess)
LGB	Laser guided bomb
Kts	knots
LL	low level
LOX	Liquid oxygen
M25	London's motorway ringroad
Mach/MACH	Mach number (Mach 1 being the speed of sound or 600kts approx at sea level)
MAD	Mutually assured destruction (nuclear)
MASB	Master armament safety break (an aircraft weapons safety device)
MC	Malcolm Clubs (a charitable organisation with clubs on military bases in Germany)
MC	Military Cross
MDRT	Mountain Desert Rescue Team
ME	Middle East
MECS	Middle East Comms Squadron
MET or met	Meteorological
MEXE	Name of the movable metal landing pads for Harrier VTOL
MFPU	Mobile Field Photographic Unit
ML	medium level
MOD	Ministry of Defence
mods	modifications
MP	Member of Parliament
MPI	Mean point of impact
MRAF	Marshal of the Royal Air Force (RAF 5-star general)

MTO	Motor Transport Officer
MU	Maintenance Unit
NAAFI	Navy, Army and Air Force Institute (supplier of cheap goods to the 3 services)
NAFTA	North Atlantic Free Trade Area
NATO	North Atlantic Treaty Organisation
NBC	Nuclear, biological and chemical
NCO	Non-Commissioned Officer
NHS	National Health Service UK
NLF	National Liberation Front (South Arabia)
NOTAMS	Notices to airmen (aviation warning notices)
NPIC	National Photographic Interpretation Centre
NSA	National Security Agency
NVGs	Night vision goggles
OBE	Order of the British Empire
OCA	Offensive counter-air
OCU	Operational Conversion Unit
OPEC	A mainly Middle Eastern oil producing country's price-fixing cartel.
OP/op	OP = observation post op=operational
OTT	Over the top
PA	Personal assistant
PAI	Pilot Attack Instructor (predecessor to QWI)
PaI	Parachute Instructor
PC	Politically correct
PI	Photographic interpreter
PMC	President of the Mess Committee
PNR	Point of no return
POL	Petrol, oil and lubricants
POW	Prisoner of War
PRL	Pressure ratio limiter (monitors jet engine air pressures to ensure correct fuel input)
PRO	Public relations officer
PRU	Photographic Reconnaissance Unit
PSC	Piano smashing competition or Passed staff college (whichever takes your fancy!)
PTO	Please turn over
PTR	Public transport rate (travel allowances)
PVC	Poly-vinyl composite
QC	Queen's Counsel
QFI	Qualified Flying Instructor
QGM	Queen's Gallantry Medal
QRA	Quick Reaction Alert
QWI	Qualified Weapons Instructor
RADFAN	A mountainous area of south Yemen some 60 miles North of Aden.
RAF	Royal Air Force
RAFC	Royal Air Force College
RAFVR	Royal Air Force Volunteer Reserve

RBelAF	Royal Belgian Air Force
RDAF	Royal Danish Air Force
RDF	Rapid deployment force
RFC	Royal Flying Corps
RIC	Reconnaissance Intelligence Centre(successor to the MFPUs)
RIP	Rest in peace
RJAF	Royal Jordanian Air Force
rkts	rockets
rnds	rounds
RNeAF	Royal Netherlands Air Force
RNoAF	Royal Norwegian Air Force
RNF	Royal Northumberland Fusiliers (British Army)
ROAF	Royal Air Force of Oman
Rockape	Slang term for RAF Regiment personnel
RPM	Revolutions per minute
RRhAF	Royal Rhodesian Air Force
RSM	Riyan-Salalah-Masirah (a regular milk-run for the Argosy transport aircraft in the 1960s)
RSM	Regimental Sergeant Major
RV	rendevous
SAA	South Arabian Army
SAM	Surface to air missile
SAR	Search and Rescue
SAS	Special Air Service
SASO	Senior Air Staff Officer
SEAD	Suppression of enemy air defences
SEATO	South East Asia Treaty Organisation
SMO	Senior Medical Officer
SMS	small man syndrome
SNEB	Name of a French air to ground rocket used by Hunter sqns during the 1960/70s.
SOAF	Sultan of Oman's Air Force
Sqn	Squadron
SRBM	Short range ballistic missile
SSAFA	Soldiers, Sailors and Airmens' Families Association
SSB-HF	Single side band – high frequency
SSM	Surface to surface missile
SSV	Soft skinned vehicles (military, as different from armoured vehicles)
STMDS	Short Term Memory Deficiency Syndrome
STOVL	Short take off and vertical landing
SWO	Station Warrant Officer (RAF equivalent for all practical purposes of the RSM)
TACEVAL	Tactical evaluation
TAF	Tactical Air Force
TASMO	Tactical air support of maritime operations
TFN	till further notice
TIALD	Thermal imaging and laser designation Pod (British LGB designator et al)

TOB	The Orange Baron
TOT	Time on target
TP	Turbo Porter (a Swiss Pilatus aeroplane)
TSR	Tactical strike and reconnaissance (as in TSR2)
TWA	Trans World Airlines
UDI	Unilateral Declaration of Independence (Rhodesia – Zimbabwe)
UHF	Ultra high frequency
UK	United Kingdom
UN	United Nations
US and USA	United States of America
USAF	United States Air Force
USAAF	United States Army Air Corp (predecessor to the USAF)
USN	United States Navy
USS	United States Ship
USSR	Union of Soviet Socialist Republics
UTP	Unit Test Pilot
VC	Victoria Cross
VD	Venereal Decease
VFR	Visual flight rules
VHF	Very high frequency
VIP	Very important person
VL	Vertical landing
VSTOL	Vertical and Short Take-off and Landing
VTO	Vertical Take Off
WAAF	Women's Auxiliary Air Force (predecessor to WRAF)
WEC	Weapon Employment Course (or Whitbread Enjoyment Course!)
WO	Warrant Officer
WRAF	Women's Royal Air Force
WWO	Wing Weapons Officer

Acknowledgements

I am indebted to the Ministry of Defence for allowing me to use parts of their publication, AP3431, *"Flight from the Middle East"*, by Air Chief Marshal Sir David Lee GBE CB RAF(Ret'd), whose monologue on the high strategies involved in running our Middle Eastern colonies and protectorates was invaluable in setting the scene for the high jinks of a young fighter pilot engaged in protecting those vast areas of the Empire.

Equally, I am indebted to Colin Richardson for the overview of Masirah Island. His history of Masirah, entitled, *"Masirah – Tales of a Desert Island"*, is unique.

Further thanks must go to Pierre Clostermann, DFC FAF, whose book, *"The Big Show"*, inspired this rendering. I make no apologies for grasping the odd piece of his text as, in flying matters, he has the gift of description of which I could only dream. I too ask the reader not to expect a work of literature. I simply noted impressions, often fleetingly caught incidents, in my logbooks that were an invaluable aide-mémoire, showing where I was flying and the actions of my every day airborne life. Without my scrapbooks, and particularly those logbooks, it would have taken a remarkable talent to reproduce with both truth *and* literary grace the life of an essentially peacetime fighter pilot.

My gratitude also goes to Gp Capt Tony Chaplin RAF(Ret'd), but particularly Alan Pollock and Steve Hodcroft. Al, not only for his constructive readings, valid criticisms and peer group authenticity, but also, and most importantly, for finding me a publisher. Steve – my English 'professor' – for his unbelievable grasp of the grammar and syntax of the language. His many hours of corrections, his running out of red ink, his "see me's!", and his great linguistic discussions were a joy. Steve with his photographic memory, sense of humour, and an astonishing grasp and love of languages and literature, continues to disagree with my preferred plural of the C130 Hercules as Herculii! But at least I now know that the book will stand up to peer group pressure and that readers will understand my abominable English!

My Publisher, Charles Hewitt, Helen Vodden, the superb staff of Pen and Sword, and Malcolm Bates of Phoenix Typesetting could not have made my life any easier. After five iterations and four years of attempting to persuade publishers that a Cold War tale was worth telling – most couldn't see beyond WW2 – Charles and his team made sure that, at last, this saw the light of day.

I must also thank my wife, Jan, for putting up with me during the writing of this book and for the, at times, extremely critical first impressions and editing of the original scripts. She puts up with a great deal normally, never mind the old war stories, and the ranting and ravings of an old veteran that go with them!

Part 1

Take-Off

"... have slipped the surly bonds of earth ... and touched
the face of God"

(From the poem *"High Flight"*
by Plt Off J G Magee RCAF)

Chapter One

The Federation

A Black Moment

They came at me from low on the left, bright flashes out of the dark. I was bloody frightened, probably more so than ever before. It was a black night and the lights had all gone out, but all the time these numerous, vivid white flashes were coming languidly straight up at me. Regular winking specks always appearing to move lazily in my direction, but then astonishingly, at the last possible moment, veering off rapidly and whizzing through in a hurry of whirling motes, momentary darts of fire through that black night, zipping past and just missing with a final incandescent burst. These stunning white flashes were not good news, and I had no idea what the other three were up to or what they were thinking – one in front of me and two behind, diving into this unfathomable murk. That customary feeling of invincibility one felt when in a fighter cockpit had dissolved into something decidedly shaky.

This was no ordinary dive. It was just after dusk, three days after Christmas 1966, and I was at 12,000ft in a single-seat Hunter fighter over Awabil in the Radfan mountains of southern Arabia, extremely close to the Yemeni border. What was I doing at the time? 420 knots, and I'd just learnt the meaning of the phrase: 'The fog of war'!

This was our first dusk scramble. As we took off, the afterglow of sunset had dissipated as it does in lower latitudes, and the dim of night had suddenly crept up on us. Diving now into 7,000-foot mountains at 30 degrees at night in a day-fighter plane, on the blackest night of the year, with 23mm tracer shells coming up and filling the windscreen, was not conducive to longevity. This remarkable, life-threatening event would be incomprehensible but for the fact that just before dusk a British Army patrol had been ambushed by a party of Yemeni dissidents. The patrol's perilous condition required us to improve *their* life expectancy. I was No 2 in the four-aircraft formation responding to their crisis call, and we all certainly earned our flying pay that night!

Unfortunately, on arrival in the target area, the leader, Flt Lt Kip Kemball (now retired as an Air Marshal), called as briefed to switch off all our nav lights, and then throttled back as he tipped into his rocket dive. His lights and the glow from the back-end of his jet pipe went out, and abruptly all went impenetrably black. That hadn't been briefed! I had nothing left to formate on, and couldn't see the ground, the leader or anything, never mind any target.

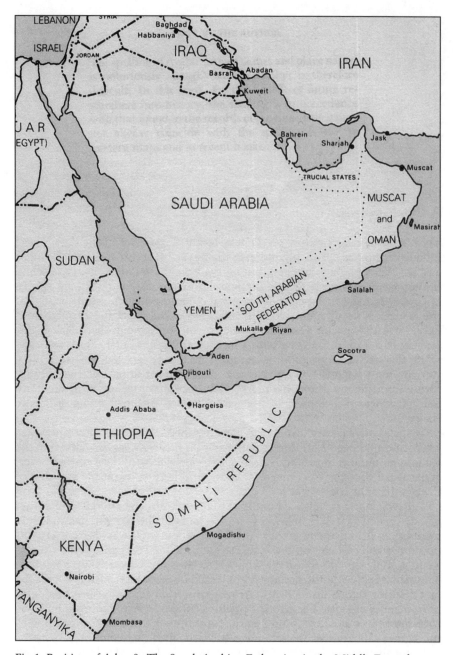

Fig 1. Position of Aden & The South Arabian Federation in the Middle East of 1965. ©Crown Copyright/MOD.

4

The only part of the universe moving outside the warm, red glow of the cockpit lighting was the white-hot tracer coming up lazily from below.

With a flash of passion tipped with the courage of panic, I slanted in behind him. By now I was down to between nine and ten thousand feet with Kip just in front of me, having disappeared into the cold black night below, and the third and fourth aircraft just behind, diving in line astern, rapidly and steeply into the charcoal unknown only two thousand feet from the volcanic mountain tops. I had this panic thought: I'm not paid enough to do something so stupid as this, and whose bloody idea was it anyway? It was turning into one of those situations over which I had no control!

Yielding to a calmly normal, but irresistible impulse, an overwhelming desire for self-preservation, I decided it was time to get out of there in a hurry, so I screamed a radio warning and pulled like mad. It was then that I saw the fireballs of the first of the thirty-six rockets detonate as they hit the target area. Being young and rash, I decided to complete a timed circuit and go in behind No 4. After seeing 3 and 4's rockets go off, I slotted temerariously back in behind them into the usual 30 degree dive and, still completely unsighted, pickled off my rockets and, with an enormous release of tension, headed for home.

These uncontrolled events had occurred in response to the usual army grievance, kicking up a fuss about no air support at night from the RAF's day-fighter/ground attack squadrons. So someone with no day/night fighter experience decided that we ought to be able to do the job twenty-four hours a day: Christmas present 1966: do it at night!

Christmas 1966. I was twenty-one years old and I'd been serving in Aden for just under two years, playing my part in the downfall of British Empire. When I'd appeared at the top of the transport aircraft steps on my first arrival at RAF Khormaksar just to the North of the port of Aden, the wall of hot air hit me with stunning effect. After the initial heat shock, looking at the black mountains and bleak, green-less sand and dust landscape, I knew I had arrived in the Empire for the first time. It was an exciting but unsteady moment, and I felt a little shaky with trepidation, perhaps as seventeenth-century buccaneers did on making their first landfall on foreign territory ready for the plundering.

This is where my flying career took-off. I was joining the one RAF Squadron that could truly be called "The Empire Squadron", having been policing the Middle East since the World War One. And I would soon discover that the British Empire – the biggest empire the world has ever seen – could be magically exotic, decadent, rich with strange places, perfumes and spices, and peopled by every class and creed of the deepest dye.

Seized from the Arabs in 1839 and ruled by the East India Company as a strategic coaling station serving ships trading between Britain and the Raj, Aden was transferred to the Crown in 1858. After the opening of the Suez Canal its importance increased. Latterly it contained the main BP Oil Refinery at Little Aden, a vital air-refuelling stop in the only British colony in Arabia.

Though Aden became a separate colony from the Indian Raj only in 1936, additional territory had been gradually brought under British protection, from 1873 onwards, through some ninety separate treaties with inland Arab

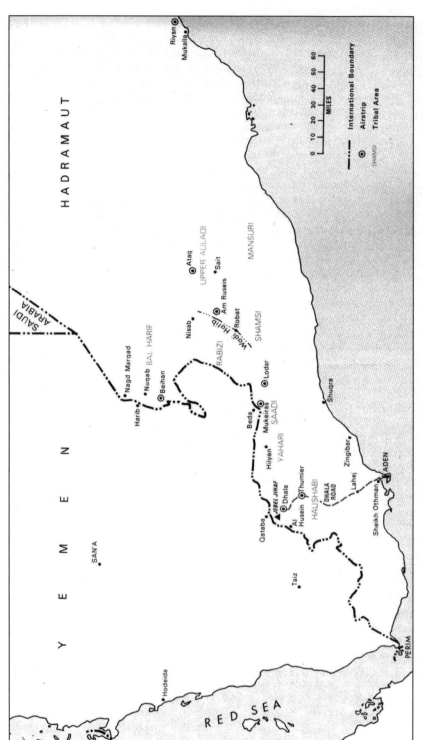

Fig 2. Aden and the Protectorates 1965. ©CROWN COPYRIGHT/MOD.

sultans, forming the Aden Protectorates (renamed in 1963 the Federation of South Arabia). This was nothing more than a loose federation of independent states providing, inter alia, defence in perpetuity for those sultanates and sheikdoms. We were the law in Aden, but not in the protectorates unless requested. This interaction caused most of the ensuing problems and, as with Iraq, the area was too feudal, too medieval, and impossible to govern. The Federation stretched almost 1,000 miles from Aden in the south-west to the Dhofar region of Muscat & Oman in the north-east. As well as the border with Yemen, some of the Federation's borders edged on southern Saudi Arabia, the empty desert quarter. Post World War II, AHQ Aden controlled some thirty small and widely scattered stations, including outposts on Kamaran Island in the Red Sea off the Yemeni port of Hudada, Perim Island in the mouth of the Red Sea, and Socotra Island off the Horn of Africa.

The RAF had come to Khormaksar in Aden, and No. 8 Squadron to the Middle East, in 1919 after the First World War. The Squadron (Sqn) arrived in Aden from Iraq in 1927, and stayed for the duration. As the RAF had been put in sole charge of governing the province and the Squadron was the primary instrument of power, the Squadron Commander was actually the head of the government at one time! The Aden Colony itself was the only territory in the whole Arab world under complete British rule, and the most politically and socially advanced state in the Arabian Peninsula. It was known as "The Little Raj", with a cosmopolitan population in the early '60s of 140,000, all living in reasonable prosperity and ruled by some 4,000 British government bureaucrats. Unlike in the wider Federation, order reigned in Aden, and no one walked the streets in fear, at least not until the 1960s.

Post-1946 efficiency measures reduced Air Forces Middle East Command (AFME) from 20,000 airmen with no squadrons to 7000 supporting thirteen by the 1960s.

RAF Khormaksar, the largest airfield in RAF history, supported 13 squadrons and independent flights in three flying wings (over 80 aircraft of 11 types), with two engineering wings and two administrative wings, sometimes three RAF Regiment Squadrons, a full Maintenance Unit, trooping flights from UK, and a civilian airport including Aden Airways main base. This huge jam-packed airfield with only one runway absorbed a hefty share of the seventy-five square miles of the Aden peninsula with some 6,000 airmen with 9,000 dependants, all there to police the Aden and the South Arabian Federation against terrorism and tribal uprisings.

In early '65, "Aden's Own[1]" 8 Squadron, part of our Strike Wing with a squadron of Shackleton maritime reconnaissance Bombers and two and a half Hunter Squadrons, was tasked both with army support and the air defence of the region. From an Egyptian and Russian-backed government in the Yemen actively supporting fiercely hostile and dissident tribesmen, over 100,000 square miles of rugged mountain and desert (with no red avoidance dots on the map!) were policed by this outfit. It was still a raw frontier area, a mini-version of the North West Frontier. These last raw vestiges of Empire proved the best grounding in fighter-flying anyone could desire with the finest low flying on active service.

This harsh terrain bred a hungry, isolated, savage people living in fortified villages, often on flat mountain tops, their ideas dominated by their rifles and

7

their *gambias* (their traditional curved daggers), always to hand to guard their terraced fields and flocks from covetous neighbours. Sentinels manned rocky watchtowers ready to shoot approaching strangers on sight. Blood feuds were fought for generations, long after the original quarrel was forgotten, and populations were counted by the number of available armed men and boys. Not surprisingly, the inhabitants are some of the poorest in the world, with no natural resources and little water. Pot-shots from neighbours were a normal hazard of travel beyond village boundaries. It added passion to the hard life of survival in an environment cursed by nature.

The Aden Protectorate Levies (APL) – with air support from 8 Squadron – were trying to be umpires, keeping the war games within sporting limits, and occasionally they clashed with raiding tribesmen from Yemen, armed with ancient Turkish rifles. Two decades earlier, the RAF had bombed Taiz, one of the twin capitals of Yemen, but regular ground and air patrols to show the imperial flag had usually been sufficient to maintain the status quo. In the late 1950s and early 1960s, however, the situation was deteriorating. The nature of the age-old tribal disputes had subtly changed as the raiding parties replaced their Turkish arms with modern Czech rifles and machine guns, and were clearly under professional military direction – from the Egyptian army. Soon after his victory in the Suez War of November 1956, Egypt's President Gamal Abdel Nasser had launched his campaign against the British in Aden, sponsoring a New Year's Eve, major incursion over the Yemen frontier with little or no reaction from London. Yet there was something of a dichotomy in operating modern, jet-fighter planes in this biblical setting against nomads and ancient tribes, some of whom had never even seen electricity, but they knew how to use modern weapons. The little known Federation and its tribesmen were fiendish, feral and forbidding, and I was to learn quickly to both love and hate them equally.

In 1961, British action had to be taken to curb 'toll collecting' by the Quteibis, which had degenerated into an unacceptable level of looting and pillaging of the caravans passing through the Radfan. But the action caused a resentment and a bitterness which never diminished. Consequently, the Radfan tribes provided excellent material for Yemeni and Egyptian propaganda. Following the Yemen revolution of September 1962, Egypt took every opportunity to support the Yemen claim to South Arabia by stirring up subversion against the Federation and against British rule in Aden. And a virulent programme of propaganda streamed out continually from Radio Cairo, Radio Sana and Radio Taiz. It was both clever and entertaining, and could be heard, not just in the duty free shops of Steamer Point, but from almost every transistor radio in almost every house and back street in Aden. The subversion increased throughout 1963 and, despite frontier air and ground patrols, and air action against dissidents, the infiltration of arms and money steadily increased. Tribesmen were invited into the Yemen for free training courses at the end of which they were provided with gifts of rifles and ammunition, a currency they very well understood.

Despite the fact that all the Radfan tribes sued for peace and were thoroughly chastened by the successful RADFAN operation in 1964, it did not stop the steady infiltration of Egyptian and Yemeni sponsored dissidents. They maintained a constant harassment, especially in the Radfan area, on our soldiers up-country, who were endeavouring to pursue a 'hearts and minds' policy by assisting the tribes to build schools, roads, wells and other agricultural facilities. But it was too little, and much too late: a great deal of the good work was undone by hostile infiltrators before it was even completed. The exposure to sniper fire of our Royal Engineers while helping the villagers and building roads, resulted in a number of casualties among them. Indeed, I am the proud owner of a 10Field Sqn, Royal Engineer's Tie struck specifically for those who had worked on building the Dhala Road through the Radfan area, simply because of all the top cover missions we had flown in their support. Even so, this new colonial war went almost unnoticed in London, and yet it was turning into a miniature 'Vietnam of the British'.

The beauty of my role as a fighter pilot, though, was that all the problems of life in Aden paled into insignifance once I was airborne and leading a Hunter four ship in battle formation up country. Few Europeans ventured into the wild desert and mountains of the Federation, which covered some 112,000 square miles around the seventy-five square miles of the British Colony of Aden. Inland from Aden beyond the lush oasis of Lahej, the sandy desert ended in a huge, black, craggy rock massif of the Radfan rising above 7,000 feet. It was a natural barrier, closing the way into the Yemen to all but the hardiest of travellers. Yet the ancient Frankincense trail from the south and east ran straight through it. There is a letter in the Squadron diaries written by Air Chief Marshal (ACM) Sir Ralph Cochrane, a 1920s Squadron Commander, stating that in return for some help one day the Emir of Dhala had promised him the freedom of safe travel throughout the land. The Emir controlled the whole of the notoriously savage Radfan area, the biggest hotbed of dissension in the Federation. By the early 1960s no European had ever come out of the Radfan alive: at least not with his balls connected in the right place! Sir Ralph would have been the only European to survive a visit at that time. He said, "Luckily, I never had to hold the Emir to his promise!"

Service in Aden produced curious effects on different individuals. To some the heat, sand and discomfort were anathema; they claimed to have hated every moment of it but, curiously enough, proceeded to talk about it with a kind of reluctant nostalgia for the remainder of their lives. Many were the short-term visitors, and unaccompanied married men, to whom I used to listen in the Jungle Bar of Khormaksar Officers' Mess, moaning into their beers about the miserable place. But for others, especially those of us there for long periods, the desert held a fascination.

The isolation and the vague but irresistible feeling of a link with Biblical times has affected many Britons who have dedicated their lives to serving one or other of the many Arab potentates in some advisory or administrative capacity. It has oft been said that South Arabia was 'advancing rapidly towards the Middle Ages'. But, like Sir Wilfred Thesiger, that quintessential English explorer, the last of the great travellers who sought out the secrets of the deserted areas of Oman, I felt the country provided a freedom unattainable in western civilisation. The up-country Bedu tribesmen had a proud honour code steeped in history, and dipped in the hardships of the harsh environment in which they survived. Even the advent of airlines and package tours has not destroyed the mystery of this part of the world, a mystique and an enthralment that captured the imagination of many of us who served there. Who would have imagined, for example, that an RAF station could have the reputation of standing beside the last incense orchard in the world? But such is the reputation of RAF Salalah in Oman, which we often used as a staging post.

Generally, the weather in Aden and the Federation was very good, with a cool season in the low 80s and low humidity, but the hot season produced high 90s temperatures together with much higher humidity – not as high as in the Gulf at Bahrain, but uncomfortable for all that. It was the Inter-Tropical Convergence Zone moving south in the spring that bought with it not only the temperature variations, but the possibility of severe sandstorms. We had no close diversion airfields for our short range Hunters, only Djibouti 135 miles away bearing 235degrees, and sandstorms were the main weather problem for our operations; the more so because they could arrive with little warning. I well remember seeing my first sandstorm while running the squadron operations one day. By the time we'd got all our fighters down on the ground, it was already half way across the airfield. On ringing the met office to ask how long it would last, I got the reply, "Sandstorm? What sandstorm? We haven't forecast any sandstorm!" "You're too busy looking at your charts," said I. "Just for once take a look out of the window!" Meteorology's marvellous until it comes to predicting the weather!

Besides the storms, it was quite normal to have 'goldfish bowl' conditions, where huge amounts of sand are blown up into the atmosphere, producing low visibilities and blotting out the ground from the air for much of the year. Once we were airborne it appeared from the cockpit that you were flying in the middle of a yellow goldfish bowl, unable to see more than a few hundred metres in any direction, including downwards. But up-country, air-navigation was not in general difficult, except when flying low level, or across the Empty Quarter from RAF Salalah on the southern coast of Oman north to RAF Sharjah on the Persian Gulf, when we could be out of range[2] of any station for a considerable time. As an additional safeguard therefore, it was customary, nay obligatory, for single-engine aircraft to fly in pairs on long, cross-country flights from Aden to any of the staging or Gulf stations.

Usually for training, we headed northeast towards the Lawdah Plain, which meant a one-way ultra-low level trip down the Wadi Hassan. Wadi Hassan was a long, straight narrow Wadi that ran northeast from Zinjibar for forty miles below the Yafa Mountains onto the Lawdah Plain. Its only delightful problem was a wonderfully tight S-bend half-way along which was made for a Hunter with 90 degrees of bank and pulling 4 to 5g, followed instantly by a reverse to regain the next straight, until one day we met another four-ship formation in the S-bend . . . head-on: going the opposite way! Overnight, Wadi Hassan became the first one-way system anywhere in the Federation – air or ground! Further northeast lay the unending vastness of the Rub-al Khali – the 'Empty Quarter', hundreds of miles of empty desert, the largest sand desert in the world, stretching north towards Saudi Arabia and east to Oman.

If navigation was relatively easy, map reading was not. Some areas, notably the two Aden Protectorates, the Trucial States (now the United Arab Emirates) and the interior of Oman were badly mapped, and finding a small target could prove extremely difficult. The Commanding Officer of 6 Squadron recorded that, when his squadron was called upon to demonstrate in the region of the Buraimi Oasis in north-western Oman in 1952, the best maps were those he tore from the *National Geographical Magazine* and which were based upon Thesiger's earlier travels in the area. The official navigation maps were quite valueless for accurate low-level flying. In the Western Aden Protectorate and in Oman, villages were frequently incorrectly shown, and there was always considerable risk of attacking a friendly village or fort. The 50,000 scale maps were called Choccies, as they consisted of little more than varying shades of chocolate-brown hatching showing the different ground heights.

Up in the north-east of the country, due to a complete lack of any survey, the maps turned totally white with nothing on them except the Lat and Long lines. Predictably, white maps equalled the vast undulating sand dunes of the Empty Quarter, the maps showing nothing except, some fifty miles into the Rub 'al Khali, one single solitary mine (had it once belonged to the Queen of Sheba?). It was at the extreme of our range from Khormaksar, even flying high-low-high, and in an area infrequently visited; certainly one to be avoided.

Inhospitable and unfrequented even by self-sufficient Bedouins who eke out a harsh living from well to well and do not venture lightly into this barren land, this was real Thesiger country, an interminably desolate host to scorpions, camel-spiders, heat exhaustion and a constant dehydrating wind depositing its sandy load into every cranny of the body, even when flying above it. This north-eastern quarter formed the edge of the area where we fought the dissident tribesmen of South Arabia for nearly fifty years, and after we failed, where – in the Beihan Sultanate area of the Federation – the fermentation took place of today's Arab terrorism producing Bin Laden and Al Qa'eda.

Navigating accurately in the Empty Quarter was difficult in the extreme. We tested ourselves by trying to locate the mine of the Queen of Sheba. We would fly a northerly heading from the last known mark on the map, for some eight minutes at 420 knots low-level for fifty-six miles and across totally featureless and endless sand-dunes, but only once in three years did we ever see the mine. Evolving dunes made accurate navigation impossible, despite constant additions to one's almost bare map from experience.

On occasions we were firing at positions within a few yards of our own troops, though rarely less than 150 yards and not usually in sand-dune territory thank goodness. It was for this reason that experience and continuity among the aircrew operating in those areas were so essential, and our practice of flying the leader of a projected attack over the target in a transport aircraft in advance was frequently adopted. Many a time we were scorned when we returned from an aborted sortie reporting that the target was not there – scorned, that is, until we were subsequently proved right by photography from further reconnaissance.

By the mid-1960s, the Hunters of 8 and 43 Squadrons were responding more and more to requests from political officers, and the army, to take out suspected terrorist hideouts, often situated in built-up areas up country. A fifteen-minute warning of an attack was dropped over the target by reconnaissance aircraft and the wing soon built up a reputation for being able to destroy a single building in a street without damaging its neighbours; modern parlance being 'no collateral damage'.

Stephen Harper, in his book *The Last Sunset,* beautifully described the dark, often moonless, oppressive and frightening atmosphere of the area on a typical night at the Dahla British Commando Camp, close to the Yemen frontier, where a walled, tented cantonment was manned continuously. Beneath the shadowy silhouettes of great rocky ridges, young British soldiers, watchful, alert, tensed over guns manned the ramparts – a lonely garrison in a fortress cut off by many miles of mountain and desert peopled by lawless, hostile tribes.

As the Yemenis encroached on the border more and more, late in 1966 the wing started practising for night ground attack on our Khormaksar training range on the beach five miles north of the airfield. They gave us a Wessex helicopter from which to drop flares 4000 feet above us to illuminate the whole range area. The range practice was great fun, if not conducive to accurate rocketry. Our rocketing parameters were pretty critical for any precision with the '3-inch drainpipe' – our Second World War, 60lb semi-armour piercing warhead rocket, — and difficult enough to achieve in full daylight. There was no margin for error in a thirty-degree dive at 400 knots, firing at 800 yards range (900 and it went supersonic!), pulling 6g to get out of it, clearing the ground by 100 feet and the target by 300 to clear the rocket debris zone. Now try that in the mountains at night! I know we were paid flying pay, but 30-degree dives into 7000-foot mountains in the pitch dark with no modern targeting or nav aids, no target illumination, and three other invisible aircraft in close proximity, was as close to suicide as one can imagine!

Our first dusk scramble on that night three days after Christmas 1966 did not cover me with glory. The following day, the political officer from up-country came waltzing into our crew room with the words, "Which silly bugger put his rockets 5,000 yards over the border then?!" Welcome to Night Fighter Ground Attack using Day Fighters, inaccurate World War II rockets and no proper rocket sight! A typical cobbled-together RAF shoestring operation, which is probably why we got away with it!

Thank goodness someone quickly came to his senses! Night attack didn't last! We soon went back to our normal daytime war – life was simpler and longer, that way!

Notes
1. The squadron had been there for 40 years!
2. The Hunter only carried a short-range, line-of-sight UHF radio.

Chapter Two

The Influences and the Training

It strikes me that perhaps, despite my best efforts, most of my readers will have no idea what it's like just being a common or garden fighter pilot. There are of course, a lot of misconceptions and ideas about the so-called glamour of the job, but while we often said, "it's better than working for a living", everything has drawbacks. I should explain the training, clarify the medical conditions, describe the man who influenced me the most during my early years in the air force, and enumerate some of the obstacles.

With his WWII experiences, my Father was my first major influence in aviation though he never tried to persuade me one way or the other. Hence, three weeks after my 18th birthday, my initiation into the Empire began. I arrive by train from London and coach from Cirencester station, at No 1 Initial Training School, RAF South Cerney. It was the 24 Apr 62, which was a Monday, and there was a dozen of us. Utter trepidation and nosey interest were the order of the day – none of us knew what to expect. Most surprisingly, that day and overnight, the officer and NCO instructors were all very pleasant and even polite to us – some 50 odd budding cadets comprising No. 175 Course. We were almost tucked up in bed that night with a bedtime story after the staff had fallen over themselves to show us the station, walking us round like estate agents with prospective clients about to buy the whole place.

Come Tuesday, we signed on the dotted line, and the atmosphere . . . , everything . . . , instantly changed! An Officer Cadet was the title, but you were known only by your service number: 4231530. For the next four months, it was all shouting, marching, polishing and cleaning. By lunchtime my hair was shorter than it had ever been, almost non-existent. We'd been kitted out, found our bed space in the barrack-block, double marched everywhere badly, and bawled at so often by the drill sergeant, it was a wonder we had any hearing left at all, never mind good enough to pass an aircrew medical! But never let it be said that our Sgt Sparks wasn't a personable character. Long and wiry, with a face lined from years of screaming at the top of his voice across the parade ground, his favourite expression was, "Cum On, cum On, Stand Up straight, Sir. You look like a spastic turd loosely tied in the middle!"

That was the start of three long years of intensive training designed to turn this loopy schoolboy into an officer and fighter pilot. On the other hand, if it helps to explain a Queen's Commission, the Russian version, from "The Odessa News" printed in 1959 is given below:

13

THE ENGLISH OFFICER

The English officer is least of all an officer. He is a rich landowner, house owner, capitalist or merchant, and only an officer incidentally.

He knows absolutely nothing about the services, and is only seen on parades and reviews. From the professional point of view, he is the most ignorant officer in Europe. He enters the Services not to serve but for the uniform, which is magnificent.

The officer considers himself irresistible to the fair-haired, blue-eyed English ladies. The English officer is a beautiful aristocrat, extremely rich, an independent sybarite and epicure. He has a spoilt, capricious and blasé character and loves pornographic literature, suggestive pictures, recherché food and strong drink.

His chief amusements are gambling, racing and sports. He goes to bed at dawn and gets up at mid-day. He is usually occupied with two mistresses simultaneously, one a lady of high society and the other a girl from the opera or ballet.

His income runs into several thousands, often tens of thousands a year, of which he keeps no account, being incapable of keeping accounts. The pay he receives from the Government hardly suffices to keep him in scent and gloves.

English officers, especially the young ones, do no work of any kind. They spend their days and nights in clubs noted for their opulence.

Extract from the Russian newspaper Odessa News, August 1959, Quoted in Mars & Minerva, June 1972.

If only, If only!

I'd started training, aiming to be a Transport Command pilot flying four-engined jets so that BOAC would finally take me. All my great plans soon went south . . . my instructors had all been fighter pilots and they gradually showed me the light.

After cadet training and gaining my commission at South Cerney, a year flying Jet Provosts at Leeming culminated in my wings parade. Valley flying Folland Gnats got me supersonic for the first time and, eleven months later, saw me arriving at Chivenor. Here, I spent eight months learning to operate what would become my first operational aircraft: the Hunter. After three years of training the Far East had sounded good, but I was posted to one of the far flung corners of the Empire, RAF Khormaksar in Aden to join 8 Sqn.

I was initially horrified: the desert – forget it! Of all the Hunter squadrons' bases, Aden was the last place that I wanted to go, even though I'd no idea where Aden really was. So much so, I even took my huge air force winter great-coat with me!

Alan Pollock had been my first Flight Commander at RAF Valley where I started my swept-wing training. After Valley, he was posted to my Hunter Course at Chivenor, and, subsequently,we spent a further two years together in Aden. He was a long and gangly man with more than General Old's little streak of rebelliousness; Al met him and both had a sparky chat! The some-times startling, but always principled, disobedience of this established fighter-pilot left a lasting impression on me, still 'wet behind the ears' in those days.

I was running the 79 Sqn ops desk at Chivenor when the phone rang and it was Sqn Ldr Phil Champniss, whom I had known as the extremely popular Boss of 43 in Aden. Having been posted home in the same rank, he now called himself Senior Air Staff Officer (SASO) at Maintenance Command HQ, at that time at Andover. His first words were inquisitive: "Got any four-tank Hunters airborne, Chris?" I said, "No, try West Raynham." Our 79 Sqn and the West Raynham wing (1 & 54Sqns) were the only outfits in UK some-times flying four-tank aircraft. I asked why he wanted to know and he exclaimed, "Well one's just flown under my window!" "So what?" I enquired. His response, delivered with emphatic deliberation on each word, nearly floored me: *"I'm on the third floor of the MOD Main Building in Whitehall!"*

Al had flown under Tower Bridge, in protest against the lack of official celebration to mark the RAF's fiftieth birthday! I shall always remember 5th Apr 1968 – my 24th birthday – as the day of Al's "demise". I thought Al had really blown it this time. He'd never get away with it!

It was widely believed that the Air Force handed him over to the RAF doctors to make a case for mental imbalance but, while awaiting disciplinary action, Al contracted pneumonia and was discharged medically on full pension. The story is well documented elsewhere, though some say it was an RAF 'political fudge' to save face – who knows? A great shame, though! Al had the spirit of a top-gun fighter pilot, and was one of the few I'd have gone to war with. I can't say that about many guys I've flown with. In fact I can think of four: Phil Champniss, Ron Etheridge and Chris Golds.

I remember an earlier episode – on New Year's Day 1964 – the day the squadron formed at RAF Valley. Al had used my road atlas to find his way to RAF Training Command HQ at Shinfield Park near Reading, leading three Gnats. They proceeded to 'bomb' the HQ with toilet paper from the flaps and emptied brake-chute bays in particularly bad weather, having bombed Central Flying School (CFS) at Little Rissington en-route – and all in protest at higher policies lacking in support for his new unit. Thus he lost his Flight Commander status for the first time! Unfortunately, some of Al's ways rubbed off on me, as I also tried something similar twice later in my career on similar principles with similar results! Thirty-eight years later he e-mailed me, recalling the incident, and suggesting that only *". . . nine and a half hours of being a Flt Cdr before being stripped must have been some sort of record . . . "* and that he *". . . was not over-enamoured with the minimal amount of help starting that new squadron and thought* [they] *should at least start with something different . . . ".*

About eighteen months after the toilet paper incidents, Al further vexed the authorities in Battle of Britain celebrations at Acklington and Leuchars where he performed aerobatic displays in a Gnat declared non-aerobatic for reasons of intermittent aileron shroud jamming. Typically, he was again protesting on principle about policies with which he disagreed. In an e-mail to me recently, he stated that CFS *". . . were playing serious and fairly political games against Valley and 4 FTS . . . ".* He says, *"CFS cancelled all their aerobatic commitments to lean on Command to try and get aileron shroud mods done faster . . . ".* Thereafter Command would neither let him cancel the BofB displays, nor curtail to a three minute non-aerobatic routine. Rather, they insisted on a full seven minutes of non-aerobatic display, which, Al considered dangerous because, on low level aeros in particular, the aileron pulleys were known to jam occasionally due to tiny particles of grit off the cockpit floor. He angrily asserts that the solution, to strip down *". . . to completely clean out the cockpit floor below the bang seats . . . "*[1] was too obvious for the *". . . daft engineering and flying specialists, right up to the C-in-C."*

In absolute fairness, Al does point out that the C-in-C, Sir Paddy Dunn, *". . . over 30 years later vehemently denied to me that it was anything to do with him and said he was wild how people would invoke shelter below a Commander's mantle, as express instructions etc etc!"*

Suffice it to say that Al had done the aerobatic routine on a matter of principle. He felt that in the event of a *". . . nancy, non-aerobatic Gnat display – [they'd] have been the laughing stock of the whole air force, with the Gnat as its new trainer!!"*

The remainder of Al's e-mail was quite revealing and I leave my readers to form their own opinions:-

"Off I went eventually to do what I considered by far the safest and best solution, a Nelson's blind eye to the ridiculously fatuous orders, which I was made, after a Command signal, to sign for – Hobson's choice literally! All went OK until two most congratulatory signals came in on the Monday, according to Henry Prince's then intelligence, from Fighter Command HQ on the two shows, at which both Flying Training Command and Valley's Stn Cdr slowly smelled a big rat – yet again I lost my flight . . . I'd quickly had enough and rang up my mate at 23 Group and said get me posted – he did this literally within five minutes that very Friday morning – I had to clear, be dined out that night and be down at Chivenor on Monday morning – all went well until I was called in to say goodbye to the Stn Cdr, Roy Orrock, just before midday, who immediately smelled an even bigger rat about what was happening . . . I ran straight down the corridor and managed to persuade the super switchboard girl to go out on a limb for me and ensure that my call went straight through ahead of the then blocked Stn Cdr's – I was thus able to warn Tony Hopkins . . . all went through then like clockwork and that was why and how I ended up (with me) *on 109 Course . . ."*

So on a Sunday evening some six months later, when I arrived back at

Chivenor to start my second course, imagine my surprise to find Al Pollock, my ex-Flight Commander from Valley, sitting at the bar waiting to join me.

Al, you would think from the above, was a real wiz-kid, but nothing could be further from the truth. He was normally totally unassuming when on the ground. However, when he strapped a jet to his back he became a different person. My belief is that he was in the right place at the wrong time – it was quite normal in the '50s to go bombing places with bog-paper, but things had changed markedly by the '60s. But the air force has different requirements in peacetime, and using your "initiative" to break orders isn't one of them. To err is human, to forgive is divine; neither were ever air force policy!

Three years later when Al left Aden, and some six months before my departure, he gave me his half-million flying map of the whole area. It was far better than mine, and I used it exclusively for the rest of my time there. I still have it today in my scrapbook. Often maligned for his antics he was grudgingly admired for standing up for his principles. Some people touch your life, and you are never the same again. I was touched by Al and was turned from a BOAC transport pilot into a fighter pilot and *my* life was never the same again.

But there are other drawbacks to this profession: life and death ones. They are illustrated perfectly by the horror on the day of my first attempted solo during early flying training at RAF Leeming in North Yorkshire nearly a year prior to Al's incidents above. I was taxiing out in a Jet Provost on 20th Feb '63, whilst watching Andy Macklen, one of our course students, take off in front of me with his young, first-tour Flying Officer instructor, Bill Gambold. They had declared beforehand that a practice turnback was going to be flown.

A turnback is a manoeuvre designed to get you back on the ground as soon as possible after an engine failure immediately after take-off. Basically you trade speed for height and turn into wind, flying a tear-drop manoeuvre to land back on the same runway in the opposite direction. For practice purposes, the instructor closes the throttle and the student then completes a turn back but overshoots not below 200feet above ground level(agl).

On this occasion though, at the end of their turnback, Bill told Andy to overshoot, but, by an incredible coincidence, on opening up the throttle they found that the engine really had failed, and the symptoms had been hidden by the closed throttle. By this time it was too late, and they both ejected also too late, just before the aircraft hit the ground. Andy Macklen's parachute had never had time to deploy. He hit the ground and was killed instantly.

Bill, on the other hand, actually got his parachute partially deployed, but, still in his seat, he careered through a large tree, where his parachute wrapped round the branches, saving his life. He was badly hurt, but alive. It was an incredibly lucky escape, but he never flew again. He remustered as an air traffic controller, where he finished up as an Air Commodore with a limp!

There always was a school of thought that said you lose more practising than you do for real, so I'm certain that the turnback is no longer part of the flying curriculum.

Macklen was the first of many! But I had sat at the far end of the runway watching all this with increasing trepidation, when, to my great relief, flying was cancelled and I taxied back in. The tragedy of the loss of a good friend for the first time had to be hidden; life had to go on. It was my first incident of "I'm fine thank you!" Despite a mournful atmosphere, we were back in the air the following day, but the heart had gone out of it for a while. Andy's was the first of many funerals[2], and a sobering one it was too.

Matters of life and death have to be put into little compartments and closed up briskly. Of course, there is an upside, and young guys get up to all sorts of trouble and japes, so it's worth recounting some of them. Perhaps I should be grateful to the designer and builder of the drainpipes and their connections on the walls of the Ripon Teachers' Training College female dormitory building, but that's another story! A better one was the famous Gatenby Lane Run! It was a car race from the A1 to the main gates of RAF Leeming. Gatenby Lane was narrow, dead-straight, and ran from the A1 for a mile and a quarter, after which there were 800 yards with five right angle bends before the main gate, roughly 1.75 miles in total, and nobody had broken the one minute barrier when No 7 Course arrived! Between the last bend and the main gate was the station commander's quarter, Gp Capt Hyland-Smith in residence with his family, including two super daughters in their late teens, the elder of whom was going out with (later to marry) one of our flying instructors, Neil Hayward, who later finished up as OC 6 Sqn.

Four guys on the course, Andy Markell, Rich Rhodes, Mike Bettell and Barry Lee-Smith, had saved up between them and bought a beautiful, old, black and chrome, fast-back Austin Atlantic A90 with no exhaust, but it would do a ton easily. This car became infamous at Leeming for more than one reason.

Firstly, it took and held the Gatenby Lane record for the whole year we were there, and beat its own record on many occasions. I think they got down to something like forty-nine seconds by the time we were posted! But secondly, the police found it one day parked in a lay-by on the old A1 right opposite the camp.

We had all been out in teams of four, on a three night escape and evasion exercise in the Dales to the west of Leeming, and which had entailed evading the Catterick Garrison troops on all three nights, while hiking roughly twenty-five miles each night and making camp at a "safe" rendezvous each day. On the last night we had to get back inside the perimeter of RAF Leeming to be safe. Incredibly, we found out beforehand the position of the initial secret drop off point on the first night, and were able to sortie out the day before and park the A90 half a mile down the road. Hence, the exercise nights were spent initially in the pub, and then sleeping in the car, while everyone else walked and evaded! On the last night we parked it in the lay-by on the A1 opposite the camp and walked the last half-mile home! Then the trouble started!

The following day, for some reason we couldn't get out to pick up the car and the police found it, checked its ownership, and rang the station adjutant. He was a bright boy who put two and two together, and decided we should be thrown out of the Air Force for cheating. Fortunately for us, Hyland-Smith, the Group Captain station commander, in an extremely one sided interview, had a sense of humour, and I remember him saying, "Your only crime is getting caught!"

The sequel is the funniest part! He banned the car from the station, and so we parked it just outside the main gate on the public road immediately outside his married quarter! For the rest of the course he had to put up with an unsilenced car roaring to a screeching halt at the end of the Gatenby Lane Run, at ungodly times of the night on our way back from the pub! Indeed he mentioned the car in his speech at our course dining out, the evening after we received our wings, saying that he was glad to be getting rid of No. 7 Course because he'd now have some peaceful nights! . . . to which we chorused, "Oh no you won't. We've sold it to No.8 Course!!"

The Aviation Medical

Part way through advanced training at RAF Valley, we all went on a commando training course, no big deal but a good couple of days out. This proved, however, a significant event in my career. I developed painful heels, preventing any application of pressure, and ended up in hospital. Many hours of hot wax footbaths afforded but short-term relief, but it got me off marching!

Posted from AFTS RAF Valley to RAF Chivenor onto 234 Sqn of 229 OCU (Operational Conversion Unit) on 26th July 1964, that's where my world started to fall apart, and where thirty-five years of foot and back pain ruined what could have been a satisfying career. It's very difficult to maintain a jolly personality when one's in pain all the time – and stupidly, I didn't dare go to the doctors for a long time for fear of losing my flying category (a classic syndrome in those days – don't trust service doctors, they'll only ground you!). My feet were getting worse and worse from the Valley commando course, until there were times when I just couldn't walk at all. I soldiered on into my first Hunter course not realizing that I was having major training problems. My heels were deteriorating, I could hardly walk, and my lower back was starting to ache so badly that it was obviously affecting my flying. Eventually, I was forced to see the Doc, was grounded, and finished up in Wroughton RAF Hospital under the orthopaedic specialists for three weeks. During this hospitalisation my favourite grandparent died. My maternal grandfather, another big influence on my life, had bravely fought prostate cancer for two years, and I missed him terribly.

After two and a half weeks of Hydrocortisone injections and physio-therapy, the orthopaedic specialists gave up on me. They couldn't find anything wrong and I wasn't responding to any of their treatment. So, one day I found myself outside the office of this Wg Cdr Doc, who turned out to be a psychiatrist! Without saying a word to me, they had decided that I was a waster who didn't want to fly and was 'trying it on' to get out of the Air Force! I spent three sessions listening to him trying to force me to admit that I didn't want to fly! I've never been so mad in my life, and it doesn't bear repeating what I said to the ortho white-coat, even though he was a Wg Cdr! Only a Doctor after all, and a pretty lousy one at that!

19

So what was their solution? Back to flying with a better medical category to fly than on the ground (A1G3Z5)! They paid to have my shoe heels raised two inches so that the weight fell on my toes when I walked! So I spent the next six months with high-heels! You can imagine the taunts I used to get from the rest of the boys!

Secondly, they sanctioned an RAF station bicycle for me so I didn't have to walk around the station! This also attracted much derision and was the subject of a regular jape by the other pilots. Whenever we went out to fly, I would ride my bike to the aircraft, where the groundcrew would look after it and subsequently meet me with it at the end of the flight. But after landing, if I didn't taxi in first, one of the other pilots from the formation would get to the bike before I did . . . !

So on a Sunday evening when I arrived back at Chivenor to start my second Hunter conversion course, from this ridiculous attempt at a psychiatric answer to my broken heel problems, I was beginning to understand why Air Force Doctors were held in such contempt by aircrew in those days.

These heel problems cleared up in the hot climates of the Middle East, but a longer term problem manifested itself: once back in European climates Ankylosing Spondylitis – a type of arthritis – at the base of my spine and sacroiliac joint, all caused by damaging that joint on the same jump that I'd hurt my heels. For the rest of my career, I had constant back pain, wore a specially fitted back-pad for the ejection seat, and swallowed hundreds of anti-inflammatory pills, in order to enable me to continue flying. The fact that I was able to continue to fly fighters is a great tribute to the skill and dedication of the staff during my numerous visits to the RAF Rehabilitation Centre at Headley Court on Epsom Downs, close to the racecourse (see chapter 20). When my back became too sore and stiff, they sent me there for a few weeks. I had three separate four to five week visits over the years, and each time I came out a new man, fitter than I'd ever been before. Even though I was grounded for eighteen months at one time because of my back problems, I was able to continue to fly fighters for the rest of my career: a tribute to the capability of the staff there.

That was just as well because, if the Air Force had known about my other medical problem: Short Term Memory Deficiency Syndrome (STMDS), I'd never have got past the selection board in the first place. Thank goodness the doctors hadn't got their hands on that syndrome when I was younger! A defective hereditary gene, probably from my paternal grandmother, who left this world asking the time of day every ten seconds, and which I passed on to my son, was only identified at my son's primary school. Good, modern, private education was then able to give remedial lessons, but in my day, I had to make do with writing lists for every day's tasks. Hence, surprisingly, a job that was run by check-lists, flight reference cards, constant cross-references, procedures for everything and, almost parrot-fashion learning, was absolutely, and amazingly, ideal for anyone with STMDS!

Finally, I must put the Scottish public medical staff's minds to rest over the Aberdeen Typhoid scare of 1964. I can at last reveal the true cause. For a few weeks at that time I flew Varsities out of Topcliffe in North Yorkshire which were being used for Air Electronics Officer training. Each aircraft had eight crew, and we flew eight missions each day round the North of Scotland. Each member of the crews was always given a white lunch box pack-up which, amongst other things contained a hideous NAAFI pork pie. The Aberdeen navigation beacon was where the aircraft coasted out to sea, and at that point all the pork pies were thrown overboard! Sixty-four rotten pork pies per day rained down around Aberdeen, and the rest, as they say, is history . . . !

Notes
1. Literally with a brush and dustpan!
2. See dedication at the front of the book.

Chapter Three

The Psychology

As you may already have gathered, there is a gallimaufry of personnel in this profession; they are a real heterogeneous bunch, but they do have some very fixed traits. I should then try to describe, in detail, what actually makes a fighter pilot tick, his psychology, what makes up his day, and how it all gels together.

On the humorous side, here's a good place to start:

The Day Fighter Pilot:

BROW:	—	Furrowed from long years of supersonic earth shaking decisions
EYES:	—	Keen as 'awks for spotting other pilots' beer
TONGUE:	—	in cheek, when listening to non-aircrew types complaining about flying pay
BRAIN:	—	Er, yes~
HEART:	—	N/A. Fighter pilots is all heart
FACE:	—	Handsome – a feature of all steely eyed killers
EARS:	—	at standby for the words 'What's yours?'
SHOULDERS:	—	Weary from the heavy burden of responsibility experienced by all Mach men.
FIGURE:	—	Sylph like – vital for fitting inside complicated cockpit of 'all-aloominum' death-tube
SKIN:	—	Thick – necessary for one who is in command from such an early age
HANDS:	—	Delicate, for hauling around fifteen tons of screaming death
ELBOWS:	—	Calloused from continually propping up hop-moistened bars
OUTLOOK:	—	Broadened through sitting long hours on standby
KNEES:	—	Worn, due to grovelling before OC Flying Wing after complaints about low flying and sonic bangs
LEGS:	—	Partially retracted from many applications of high 'g'
FEET:	—	Large enough to play 'Changing the Guard at Buckingham Palace' successfully
HEELS:	—	A clean pair of being constantly shown

TWO THINGS HE ALWAYS LOVES TO HEAR:
> — "No, darling, I'm not pregnant", and "Night flying is cancelled".

THE WHOLE: — Alert, muscular, intelligent, superbly fit, sun-bronzed, lovable, witty, charming, irresistible **and inclined occasionally to gross exaggeration!**

However, to balance the obvious self-congratulationary tone of the above, it should also be noted that SPOILT is an anagram of PILOTS, and 50% of them graduated in the bottom half of their pilot training class!

But the real psychology of a fighter pilot is something quite different. Brigadier General Robin Olds, a WW2 and Vietnam veteran ace, describes a fighter pilot as an attitude. He says, "It is cockiness. It is aggressiveness. It is self-confidence. It is a streak of rebelliousness and it is competitiveness, but it is something else. There is a spark, there's a desire to be good, to do well in the eyes of your peers, and in your own mind." Though the above could be applied to a number of professions, in fighter flying it is the love of that blue-vaulted sky. It becomes your playground if, and only if, you're a fighter pilot. You can't understand it if you're only flying from A to B straight and level, and merely climbing and descending; you're only moving through the basement of that vault.

A fighter pilot is a man in love with flying. A fighter pilot sees not a cloud but beauty, no ground but something remote from himself, something that he doesn't belong to as long as he is airborne. He's a man who wants to be second best to no one. Unfortunately, stupid people start wars, and stupid people run wars, and they very seldom listen to the people who are fighting the wars, such as the fighter pilot on the front line. He wants to be heard because wars are a filthy business.

In peacetime he can, and does, tolerate an awful lot of rubbish on the ground just for an hour in the air. When I see how well the Chileans, Omanis, Swiss, Swedes and particularly the Israelis operate, it becomes obvious that we stomach, in typical British fashion, an awful lot of petty bureaucracy that has become worse as the years have gone by. Surrounded by unfair rules and regulations designed to protect the government and the MOD, ones which wouldn't get the time of day in any civilian organisation, we are governed by a modern mind-set – a civil-service style culture – that is incompatible with efficient fighter flying. It is a constant battle to find one's way round ever-increasing, petty, 'thou-shall-not' style regulations in order to achieve the task. It ruins his love of fighter flying, produces a compensation culture that moves him into civilian flying at too early an age and, contributes markedly against what would otherwise be the best job in the world. Other nations achieve ground-air compatibility without petty interference – we haven't for over thirty years. We should take a leaf out of the Omani Air Force where there's only really one rule: don't f— -up or you're on ya' bike!

An aviation psychologist and accident specialist, Roger Green, who headed the Institute of Aviation Medicine accident unit at Farnborough, and a very personable and clever guy he was too, became well known to us in the fighter world due to his accident investigations. He used to say that no matter what design failings a fighter aircraft had, your average macho fighter pilot would unconsciously compensate for them rather than complain about them. Hence, it was very difficult to adduce those failings in order to design them out of the next generation of fighters. His premise was that the fighter pilot is a constantly compensating machine which, whatever environment it finds itself in, readily adapts. He also applies the same assertion to the nanny culture he has to accept on the ground.

There's certainly a lot of truth in what Roger says. You do whatever it takes to make the machine do what you want it to do and to the accuracy required to complete the task to the highest standard. Although you'd complain bitterly to your peers about "that bloody machine's" idiosyncrasies, you'd never talk it down in public.

This may all be so, but the fighter pilot also has many failings. He is one of a particular type or group of people who are absolutely necessary in order to achieve the aims in a high-speed three-dimensional environment. If he's any good in the fighter business, in my view, there'll always be four traits in his personality:

1 He must be in control.

A measured input produces a measured response: you move the stick to the right and the aircraft turns to the right. It's a stimulus-response relationship, and if it's so good in the flying business, then why could it not be used at home? It is. You do use it! You try to be in control of your children, your family and your spouse, just about everything with which you come into contact – and if you can't be in control, you exit stage left!

Often he'd be the eldest or controlling son when growing up in your family, and he lived under the auspices of the 'old man', who was a little strange and different. Dad didn't say things to us when he needed to. He didn't tell us he loved us after a certain age. Around thirteen years of age seems to be the turning point. He stopped dispensing a lot of that warm loving affection that he normally did beforehand, and started using symbols of affection.

If at the age of sixteen you cut the lawn for him, he wouldn't pat you on the back and tell you what a good son you were. Instead he'd take you with him for cricket practice that evening. That's how he expressed his love and affection. That's how he handled that; how he told you he cared. So now we're always looking for symbols of affection from everyone around us, from our jobs and our sporting activities. What better way than with our badges of rank? They're a control and affection symbol, as are the wings we wear. They also show who we are, but how about our medals? Rarely are they seen during normal wear because we know what little they're worth. But you'd never dream of going down town without them. That's who you are, and those clowns down town don't know what they're worth! With puffed out chest, medals say, "Look who I am, boy. That's me!" They're also symbols of affection that we reach out for to make us feel important about whom we are.

Most fighter pilots are "safety-wired in the pissed-off position"! "How're you doing today?" "I'M FINE THANK YOU," comes the reply through gritted teeth! Everybody's always "fine thank you", but what a bunch of bull that is! Life is not like that, but that's how we always present ourselves. Even when we get highly annoyed, driven up the wall, once down from the ceiling we're "fine thank you". We get over it quickly.

As controllers, we grow up with other controllers. The people we like to have around us are also controllers. Why? Because they're like us. In any situation or encounter we know how they'll react. In a way, they're nearly a spitting image of ourselves.

Most of us have only one, possibly two, and at most only three close friends, people who know us directly and something about us within. Most others only know the fake version. Only one or two know the real you, and they'll usually be controllers from the same fighter world. Only Tony Chaplin ever knew me within.

He likes controllers so much that he marries them! Most are married to first or controlling daughters, but why marry someone who is strong willed when he's trying to control her?

Now there's a good question!

The reason is simply that he doesn't want to take her out in public and say, "Look at my wimp wife." She's got to be a strong lady, even when he's telling her to shut up! He wants someone with strength around him, to show his masculinity through her, but he has to learn when to shut up himself and listen, or he'll be divorced very quickly. If he's been a fighter pilot all his life and is over forty years of age, he'll have a nearly fifty percent chance of being divorced, and that causes all sorts of problems in the fighter world.

He doesn't show his feelings: feelings are for queers and sissies, for people who are weak, people who have strange ideas about life. Hence, his shams and facades: "I'm fine thank you . . . no problems whatsoever!" That's the sentiment he conveys to everybody. Revealing finer feelings is frowned upon in the fighter world. He'll probably even be the last to know when divorce is pending, because everything is "fine thank you!"

2 His male/female interface is characterized by distance, and that is an emotional distance. Emotions are risky to show; he can get crapped on from a great height for showing his emotions. They can be misunderstood, so he takes them as defects and submerges them, gets rid of them from his consciousness. He is also in the group that is the easiest to really annoy, especially if he's in the young pilot category. But guess what? Try and annoy the older ones, and what's their reply? "I'm fine thankyou," through gritted teeth! So, if he's showing no feelings, how does his spouse feel about him? "You unfeeling assh . . . e. You've no idea how I'm feeling, or how the children are feeling!" So in a life crisis, and we all go through at least one in our middle years, when feelings suddenly surface, whom are you going tell about them? There's no-one. No Boss, no padre, no psychiatrist you'd trust, and the old lady's going to show you the way to the door! So we argue, and we argue about the children, sex, money and communication. Not a lot about communication

because he doesn't know how to communicate! Hence, the number one cause of divorce in the fighter business is lack of communication, which accounts for about ninety percent of all divorces.

He will be fast asleep within five seconds of solving a discussion or problem at home, but at breakfast the next morning, the wife will be still yakking about it. What's his reaction? Disappear stage left – go to work so that by the time he arrives home that evening, she's solved the whole thing for him. He likes to deal with problems once, solve them instantly, and never look at them again.

3 He is mission orientated and compartmentalized.

He puts everything inside its own little compartment. So, what makes him so good at the job is that when he gets inside his flying compartment, he ignores all else, and gives it his complete attention. He is 100% committed, using 100% of his time, effort and ability to the detriment of all else. If he's going away on detachment, two days before he goes he's already there in his detachment compartment: the family have already lost him. But again, he uses the same technique for everything else in his life. He has, for example, a getting up compartment that includes all the little details necessary to get him from bed to work. He showers exactly the same way every day, cleans his teeth with the same movements, and shaves with exactly the same strokes. If he uses forty-nine razor strokes today, he'll use forty-nine tomorrow, and forty-nine in ten years' time; it's a science. He has a perfect system for his life, and no-one, least of all the clowns of his family, is ever as perfect. But he's raising them, so they need sorting out because, in his opinion, they don't know how to run their own lives. So he's constantly trying to make them exactly like himself – perfect!

That's the way he sees life, and is one of the reasons the failing aviator has problems in life: his family don't want to be like him. In fact they don't want to come even close in most cases!

Then there's the Get-home-itis compartment. Inside this is the, "Hey, we're good! We've got 500hours flying time. We're really proficient now." And that's when he starts to take little or minor chances. So, despite problems, he presses on and makes it through, and he continues to press on because he knows he's good. He's been around a little, and overconfidence finally backs him into a corner out of which he can't return. On Get-home-itis missions, those missions where he's staging back home, because he wants to get home after a long detachment, there's a much higher accident rate than on any other except Search & Rescue and Casevac missions. Why? Because he takes those chances more and more often, vis: Chapter 15's ferry trip!

Perhaps the best example of a get-home-itis mission was the story told of one WW2 mission by that now famous USAAF aircraft, the B17 Flying Fortress called the "Memphis Belle". Based at Bassingbourn in Cambridgeshire and captained by Colonel Bob Morgan, she was the first USAAF bomber to survive twenty-five missions over Europe. On one of them, on the way home from France in 1943, Bob was forced to put her down at Exeter to repair a faulty engine. However, Bob had had a special invitation to a party back home that night, and he planned to be there. But he couldn't start the rogue engine. So he decided to take-off on three engines and start the fourth using the slipstream to turn the propeller. His nine-man crew, all but the engineer, objected, so he took off without them. The engine was started as planned. He landed again, picked up his crew, and arrived home just in time for the party! That's "get-home-itis"!

4 The failing aviator is extremely predictable!

From all the above-mentioned attributes his predictability must now be obvious. He's systematic and methodical. He's a check-list freak. Check-lists get him through his daily life. Anything he does, he has a check-list for it, including everything at home and holidays. Every outing requires an ETD/ETA[1]. He is going to leave at 0849hours come hell or high water, and little Johnny and the wife had better be ready. And are they ever ready on time? Hell – no!

He lacks spontaneity, and though he is amongst a highly intelligent group with one of the highest IQs, he doesn't free think. He will plan on someone else's ideas, but does not produce new ideas or inventions, because he is trained for automatic response, to react quickly to any stimulus. He shows utter contempt for bureaucracy, and firmly believes that no one at home can ever really understand him: "How many passengers does a Hunter carry?" came from an old school chum on my first visit home after qualifying!

As a sucker for complacency, he believes he is infallible, and then he becomes an accident waiting to happen. Aircraft only kill others, but we all make mistakes, and familiarization breeds contempt. At first he's in awe of a new aircraft, but he soon learns that a monkey can do it. From gross under-confidence to gross over-confidence in one easy stage, and it applies at home as well as in the air! I saw this in myself after thirteen years of Harrier flying. "Their lordships" wanted me to go back to the same thing yet again for another tour, but I held out for another type of aircraft. I had seen it in myself, cutting corners, as the aircraft had so easily become a second pair of underpants to be thrown on and off at will! So, I purposely refused to go for another Harrier Flight Commander job when it was offered, and finally got my choice to fly high level recce with the Canberra PR9, but that's a story for Chapter 23.

Role ritual itself is a trap, because ritual and methodology eventually supersede the goal. His downwind pre-landing checks become such a common ritual that they are not completed correctly, even though he feels he's done them perfectly. He turns Finals knowing he's put the undercarriage down, but fails to positively check the three-green lights because HE KNOWS he's done the action required. Familiarity breeds that contempt that eventually kills him, and he's still wondering why as he hits the deck with no undercarriage!

Hence, the constant training, day after day, keeping fit and ready for any contingency. There's a feeling of invincibility when up there in the air with the jet strapped to your back. It's an absolute must; you have to be the best – always; it could be a matter of life and death. He's not frightened, though he sometimes frightens himself in pushing the aircraft to the limits, but he'd never admit it – the fear comes later, but he doesn't spend his flying career looking for tea and sympathy. Although always practising emergency drills and survival procedures, it never occurs to him that he may not succeed: failure is not an option.

But it's JUDGEMENT that sets the fighter pilot above the rest, and the lack of which is shown every minute on our roads today. It is rapid, immaculate judgement that sets him apart from the masses, but it is positive male feed-back that drives him. This does NOT mean he loves men better than he loves women! The term 'maverick' also comes to mind, but unfortunately it has now been tainted by the film "Top Gun", and there all similarity ceases. But, who gives him his importance? Who pats him on the back? It's his peers, and only his peers. It's also his peers, and only his peers, who can tell him he's a failing aviator.

It also follows that those who are short term fast-reaction thinkers, those who can think fast on their feet, can become good fighter pilots. Unfortunately, although quick reactions can help in difficult situations, it does not necessarily create natural ability in the air. Though there is a place for longer profound thinking, that place is a must prior to flight, having carefully thought through one's reactions to any given set of circumstances so they become automatic. Only then can one be sure that the airborne fast reaction is, perhaps unthinkingly at the time, correct. Many of the decisions one makes are based on a reaction to previous actions by others. One's actions and responses, often while directing all four aircraft in your flight, are continuous processes happening in a very high subsonic or transonic environment, in all three planes. Good co-ordination is a necessity. Its not easy, and comes naturally to very few.

"They get easily upset, these jet pilots,
I think it's the vertical take-off!"

(Ronnie Barker – Open All Hours, 1987)

Notes
1. ETD: Estimated Time of Departure. ETA: Estimated Time of Arrival.

Chapter Four

My First Operational Aircraft –The Hunter

And so, I finally made it through to my first real fighter aircraft – Queen of the Skies – The Hawker Hunter (hot oil & old rope!), my first operational aircraft. Oh, you've no idea how delighted I was to be going to this role and aircraft. It was everything I'd ever asked or dreamt of since giving up the idea of BOAC. The Hunter is the Spitfire of the jet fighter world. As I'd started with a grade E - *"We're short of pilots, so we'll experiment with him!"* – this really was a posting to celebrate.

Posted to 229 OCU at Chivenor, I started operational training on No 107 Day Fighter Ground Attack Course, but what is an OCU all about? Well, an OCU teaches you to 'operate' the aircraft you will fly on your first squadron – the basic art of flying a supersonic jet fighter is taken as read – you have to learn to use it to some effect.

This fantastic six-month course consisted of lots of aerial combat, close and battle formation including formation aerobatics, air-to-air firing against a towed banner using the four x 30mm cannon, air-to-ground strafing, rocketing and bombing, and low-level formation navigation and targeting. It teaches how to fight an aircraft – the sad cowardly art of getting behind a fellow fighter pilot and shooting him in the back before he does the same to you. Contrary to popular opinion engendered by Top Gun and all that, it is often he who flies the slowest, not the fastest, who finishes at the back of the fight and, therefore, in a shooting position. The ability to handle an aircraft at or just above the stall becomes paramount, and hence, the phenomenal success of the Harrier in aerial combat. Learning to fly a fighter for the first time was a schoolboy's dream come true.

When first starting, an aircraft pilot's manual is often a good place to look for some of the idiosyncrasies or "gotchas" of an aircraft, usually given as cautions, warnings or prohibitions. The Hunter has none to speak of. The only real abnormality the Hunter has is misuse of flap at high Mach numbers, which can cause elevator jack-stalling and a potentially irrecoverable dive, but this is only really likely in high level combat manoeuvring.

The Hunter's engine is a fifteen stage Rolls-Royce Avon, and, with the later 207 Series, developed an amazing 10,150lbs of thrust! This was an enormous increase of over 30% on the original 121 series engine. For a power-to-weight ratio of only a little less than one to one, a light Hunter had a sensational performance. It was also most reliable, and would continue to operate in the worst of conditions. For example, a couple of years later I watched a 1417Flt Hunter land at Khormaksar and run off the side of the runway due to hydraulic and consequent brake failure. On taking a closer look, it was found that a four-foot wingspan 'Shitehawk' had gone straight through the starboard intake, peeling the wing root skin back above and below, and mangling the front of the engine, but it still ran for twenty minutes!

Some time later, and this was one of many instances, a Hunter, also at Khormaksar, landed with the engine running after flying for forty minutes without any engine oil, and the engine seized up on the landing run only after the pilot had throttled back to idle rpm. It was a known fact that if you left the throttle and maintained the rpm without change in such circumstances, the engine would run on the hot bearings, but only at the constant rpm. It was a strong but versatile beast.

For an early 1950s aircraft to have a design ceiling over 47,000 feet (I've had one to 49,500ft), a maximum speed of 620kts straight and level with no Mach limit, supersonic ability in a shallow dive (been to M1.2), and a weapons carrying capacity of more than 4,000 lbs, it was an exceptional lady. Used in the worst possible environment in Aden, it became known as a rugged, reliable, highly manoeuvrable and superb weapons platform. Despite being struck by ground fire several times, it never let me down. For its time it was one hell of an aircraft!

Certainly with its 4 x 30mm Aden cannons, it was the heaviest gun-armed fighter in the world, but the use of all four guns together which only ever occurred on operations, produced some dramatic consequences, and not just for the enemy. The first time I used all four, it felt as if the aircraft had hit a brick wall – the recoil was so great. The vibration on the airframe usually popped numerous circuit breakers and the radio would go off line as did most of the electrical services. Not a nice position to be in pulling out of a dive 100 feet above a target who's firing back at you!

There are other quirks though, especially on engine start up. The later Hunter single seaters used an Avpin turbine starter system. Avpin is an isopropyl nitrate, and a very nasty, highly-corrosive and very explosive liquid fuel used in military engine starting systems, but never in a civvy environment. It was just not safe enough, as I found out after spilling some after a show at GAF Memmingen in southern Germany. The spillage not only stripped the paint off the wing, but corroded my flying suit so badly that it needed changing!

Still, this starter system gave you three attempts, after which it was too hot and the liquid might explode, so you had a half hour cooling down time. Also on each start, some Avpin was purged, overflowed and poured over the hot starter exhaust and out of the bottom of the fuselage, often causing fires! Today Health and Safety might put their oar in!

Start procedure, therefore, required the under fuselage starter panel to be kept open and swinging down on its hinges, together with a flight-line mechanic armed with an asbestos glove and a large, universal screwdriver. The glove was obviously to pat out any fires, but the screwdriver, held by the sharp end, was for hitting the starter box with its large wooden handle! This preferred method un-jammed the starter for a second attempt!

Once airborne she was a delight to fly, even when heavily laden with four underwing tanks and weapons. The Hunter was forgiving in the rough aerial combat environment and was a stable weapons platform for ground attack. She has been variously described as *"the most beautiful fighter ever"*, and *"the most graceful fighter ever produced"*. The big Avon-powered Mk 6, and its principal derivative, the FGA Mk9, both of which I flew, were undoubtedly widely regarded as the world's finest all-round fighters.

Each flight starts with the take-off. The pre-dawn take-off and climb to height is perhaps one of those poignant and unforgettable moments in flying. I have always liked this time of day for take off – at least once you've got out of bed! After being partially awakened from an incomplete sleep by a strident alarm clock, you stumble out of bed in the dark, mind still in neutral, to find one's way to the squadron in autopilot mode. Using the single cup of caffeine for any conscious thoughts, one's reward is the pre-dawn take-off. There is a timelessness about it, utter calm and silence and nothing moving, still dark with the day not yet come, the world in limbo, everything a little unreal. As you walk out to the aircraft, only the coloured lights of the runways and the tall buildings twinkling from the floodlights' reflections off the dew, and the stars imitating the scene overhead. And no noise: it is so tranquil and serene. The world is at peace . . . at least until engine start!

You taxi out in the calm, warm glow of your dim red cockpit lights, following the amber/blue, subdued, taxiway illumination. Take-off along the twin lines of flarepath lighting catapults you airborne in the pitch blackness of the twilight hours. The instruments never seem to move as fast in infra-red illumination at night, and you also seem to become enveloped in the stillness of the dark night as you accelerate away from the runway, leaving a slumberous earth behind. All is quiet as you climb on course through the black, keeping a languid watch on the vague phosphorescence of the flight instruments. Then, at something over 20,000feet, as the stars start to dim and without any transition, you burst out of the cloud tops into the full, blinding lemons and gentle scarlets of the rising sun. The wings and nose of the Hunter turn shades of carmine, claret and crimson, and you are so dazzled that you lower your sun visor and are forced to concentrate more on the instruments. The sun emerges on the horizon, like a molten ingot from the leaden skies. Beneath your wings it is still night, most are still asleep, and you have this heaven all to yourself. You are the first to breathe in the warm life of the sun's rays, which pierce the eyeballs like arrows. I can convey nothing of the indescribable quality of translucent unreality during dawn at very high level; the contrast with the pedestrian humdrum banality below, the sense of invulnerability and utter invincibility that permeates one's mind. The scudding dots and puffs of lower cloud obscure the sleeping 'ant-hills' below, and you're totally alone in a cosmos of your own with only the engine's slumberous murmur, a feeling of hanging suspended, as sole possessor of the dawning day. With indolent serenity, the sun is shining just for you.

The horizon is starkly marked in pitch black below, and on the eastern side, a dark crimson line above. This gradually transforms through its reds and oranges and on to the yellows, all only 'an inch' high, as the sky above ranges through all the blues from indigo through ultramarine to cobalt and azure. A single jet contrail bisects the lightening horizon, scything through an

31

otherwise perfect, eclatant horizontal, iridescent rainbow – colours so beautiful they could only be gazed upon by angels in their flight. Before the actual dawn there is this half-an-hour of utter serenity . . . until the rim of the sun suddenly materializes spraying incandescent, wake-up rays of yellow and white, spoiling the calm and blinding the eyes. Turning west to put the dazzle behind you – 'the Hun in the sun' – the tranquillity is regained for a few moments longer. It really is flying closer to the gods, but the magic disappears as another day dawns . . . back to work but with a more spiritually uplifted countenance. You have truly *"slipped the surly bonds of earth and touched the face of God."*[1]

Every sunrise is different, but they all have a certain magic at 40,000 feet. Moments like those are few and far between, and compensate for the sweat, toil, sacrifice and many a danger. Moments like those do not constitute a "normal" working day as they are so scarce. But moments such as those are what the quintessence of fighter flying is all about!

At the other end of the sky comes the real work: ground attack. It is a hot smelly, noisy, high-g, adrenalin-pumping environment. However, a straffing or rocket attack is as simple as doing a circuit round the airfield to land, except for the two seconds of suppressed terror after releasing the trigger as you attempt to pull out of the dive before hitting the ground.

Flying downwind on the range at 400kts and 1500feet, you do all your pre-attack weapons checks while looking back for the target and assessing the wind. Judging where to turn in on finals, check the gunsight and, holding your height to get a 10 degree dive[2], judge the round out point to ensure correct attack direction without being blown downwind, you aim to put the sight an inch above the top of the target and on the 'into wind' side. While holding it there, the throttle is set for the correct firing speed as you accelerate down the dive. You select guns or rocket master switch on and up goes the rocket button safety flap on the stick, pylon lights or the guns master switch are checked on, and for strafing then down comes the trigger from its folded safety position. The sight then settles down, indicating the correct gravity drop and wind deflection for the weapon, so you adjust its position onto the top upwind corner of the target, and start accurate tracking. As you lose height in the dive, generally the wind slackens and the airspeed now accelerates towards 450 knots, so the sight position needs constant adjustment. It's a continuous process until, just before firing range at 600yards (guns) or 800yds (rockets), you've got it right in the centre of the target, but for the slight upwind adjustment for the final wind velocity . . . that's the wind effect imparted to the bullet during its flight time to the target.

Now it all happens at once. In a rapid tap-dance staccato, the trigger is pulled, the guns fire, and the rat-tat-tat doubles the noise level, the aircraft shakes, and the sight goes fuzzy. Half a second later, you simultaneously release the trigger, shove the throttle into the top left hand corner, and pull 'smoothly' to the buffet – approx 6g. As you do, the noise level and buffet increase, your G-suit inflates, you strain like mad to hold your consciousness, and you just have time to see the first bullets hit the ground, giving a fleeting glimpse of your dreaded inaccuracy. But concurrently calling your immediate attention, the ground flashes past 100 feet below you as you bottom out of the dive, mushing like crazy, clambering for height to both attain 300 feet over the target itself to minimize the possibility of ricochet damage, and more importantly to miss the ground. All that happens in a second and half before the aircraft recovers, and with a high nose attitude staggers back into the luft for another go, while all the switches and the trigger are made safe. Having fired approx 15 to 20 rounds from one gun (quadruple that if firing all four guns for real in wartime) you then wait with trepidation for the range controller to give you your acoustically marked score, blaspheme that the scorer is, as usual, underscoring, and mentally adjust your sight position accordingly for your next attempt. It's hard, sweaty but rewarding work, and there's no better playground!

Despite the moans, this life was exhilarating for a young bachelor, above all in hot climates. Particularly in the Hunter, it was the stifling smells on the sun-drenched flight line of sweaty cockpits and flight gear at thirty-odd degrees in the shade, coupled with glowing brake smoke, hot tyre rubber, engine oil, hydraulic fluid, rocket cordite, and a rubber mask full of oxygen – it has a smell of its own! Above all, it was that unforgettable sinus-clearing acrid stink of burning AVPIN[3] from the starter motor which greeted you, and made you feel at home every morning. Add to this heady cocktail the necessary young macho need to push every rule and regulation to its limit, and often just beyond, and you had an uplifting anticipation of the exhilaration to come at the start of every mission.

It was a sign of one's judgement and perfectionism that you could make this amazing machine dance for you, and when it did, as only the Hunter could do, there was immense satisfaction as your reward for taming this beautifully-graceful, aerodynamic eagle of the skies. An original 1947 design, the Hunter is still in service today.

Notes
1. The opening and closing lines of the poem High Flight by Plt Off J G Magee RCAF.
2. 30 degrees for the old 3-inch rockets.
3. AVPIN: the highly flammable rocket fluid used in the Avon engine starter motor on the Hunter.

Chapter Five

A Day in the Life of Fighter Flying

As most of my flying career was spent flying the Hunter described above, and the Harrier described in Chapter 18, most of the descriptions below pertain equally to both aircraft. Fighter flying is usually made up of very short missions with short-term aims and tactics, which change often and fast. It follows that the shorter the range of the aircraft, the fewer flying hours go into the logbook for each brief, flight plan, and debrief. A single brief, flight plan, and debrief can mean a 24hour flight for an AWACs, but only one hour for a Hunter or forty-five minutes for a Harrier. Four x forty-five minute sorties in a Harrier day is four times the workload of a single AWACs mission: four plans, four briefs and four debriefs, but for only three hours recorded in the logbook. When hover testing Harriers, one can be in charge of the aircraft for an hour but have only three two-minute hovers airborne during that period: only six minutes in the logbook. Hence, a retired transport captain can have 20 to 30,000 hours in a single log-book, whereas my four logbooks show only 4000 over the same thirty-year period, but none was on autopilot!

Modern fighters fly around at 400 to 450kts at low level on average, and at 0.8 to 0.85Mach at high level. But most can reach low supersonic speeds of, say, up to 1.1 to 1.2Mach, and as low as approximately 150kts. With the Harrier, we see combat down to zero speed, and even up to 50kts backwards! So we have a flight envelope of -50kts to 1.1Mach, moving backwards through hovering at low level to transonic at 45,000ft, and an acceleration at low level which would make Ferrari delirious.

So what was a "normal" working day in the life of a fighter pilot? Consider firstly that, as all short range aircraft need good diversion airfields close at hand, and you are dependent on the vagaries of the UK weather, there is no such thing as normal, although there is a "normal" daily routine.

So, you're usually up early, reporting for work some two hours before take-off, which can be as early as an hour before dawn. Breakfast in the Mess, certainly in the Middle East, included salt and Malaria tablets swallowed with reconstituted milk with cornflakes, followed by NAAFI eggs, bacon and taste-less sausages, washed down with something brown that could be either tea or coffee, probably combined with bromide, but you were never sure which. This certainly wasn't designed to put you in a good mood at the start of the day!

Weather briefing ALWAYS starts the day. What's the weather like in the exercise area, or conversely, where's the good weather today for us to fly? What's the base weather going to do all day, and what are our diversion airfields likely to do weather-wise, all day? Also included are Flight Safety notices, NOTAMS (Notices to Airmen), and info. on active danger areas. A basic tenet of the fighter world is that if you're late for morning Met brief, you're in trouble, and that means you've started a lousy day.

Usually, you'd be already in your basic flying overalls, straight from bed, but if not, the next thing was to change out of uniform into your flight kit, known in the trade as 'grow-bags' – so-called because they're green and shapeless! Indeed you would spend your whole working day in your 'grow-bag'.

From the Met Office, you drove to the Sqn for your second cup of caffeine, and then you checked out the state of the aircraft with the engineers who had probably been working on them overnight. Next up would be discussion of the simulated "targets" you were going to attack that day, and this was usually decided by the duty flight commander, sometimes in association with your Sqn's GLO – a army major who was your Ground Liaison Officer with the army.

On most ground attack Sqns, you run four waves of four aircraft each day, but it can change if, say, you're flying longer sorties including in-flight refuelling. But on Hunters or Harriers, your sortie length is around one hour to seventy minutes. So the Sqn's day would revolve around four aircraft taking off every two hours from 9am onwards. Take-offs at 0900, 1100, 1300, and 1500 mean they are all down by sometime after 1600hrs, by which time in the winter it's getting dark. In the summer months this plan also allows for slippage to 1700hrs, and gives the engineers some time to repair any problems with the machine.

Once you've got the target details, you gather your formation round you. Assuming you're planning to lead the first wave for a 9am take-off, you will Met Brief at 6.45am, start planning around 7.00am, brief at around 8.00am, authorize and sign out the aircraft at 8.20am and walk out to the aircraft at 8.30am. Donning all your flying gear, walking out to and checking the aircraft, strapping in, completing the pre-start checks, starting engines, checking in with the other three on the radio, and taxiing in formation order to the take-off point takes about thirty minutes.

To start the planning process, you get your third cup of caffeine and you usually give one of the three targets to each of the other three pilots to plan. They will plan the target runs and attacks on their target, and the target egress, and provide each of the other members of the formation with copies of the maps and details for that target. You, as the leader, then plan the route from base to the first target, between the targets, and from the last target home. You also work out mission requirements for fuel states, diversions and all the procedures for flying in cloud and in the clear, flying formations, bad weather contingencies, enemy dispositions, anti-missile warnings and strategies, enemy aircraft sightings and combat tactics, electronic warfare info. and procedures, and basic weapons employment and sighting solutions for each of the targets.

Once planning was complete, your fourth caffeine cup would be taken into the ensuing detailed briefing on the mission. You conduct this before the duty authorising officer (DAO) authorises the mission. The DAO is one of the senior pilots on the Sqn, who ensures that all procedures and orders have been adhered to, and any updates since Met Briefing are passed on.

The cockpit would already be smelly, never mind from your own grow-bag and flying kit, which probably hadn't seen washing powder in months. By the time you'd been flying in hot conditions, in the same flight suit, G-suit, harness, Mae-west, helmet and oxygen mask for a week or two, they stank. After start-up, unlike the deep roar and blue note of the Hunter, the Harrier generates a high whine from the intakes. This whine superimposes itself on the deep unceasing surging growl of the turbine efflux which, in crossing the tail-plane, vibrates its way throughout the whole airframe, spawning an orgasmic sensation in the cockpit. If the tail's vibrating heavily at one end, you're doing the same at the other! The engine noise coming from the intakes, which are strategically placed just behind each ear, deafens you. Add the cockpit air-conditioning that doesn't compete with hot weather and can't work on the ground anyway, ensuring a steady trickle of sweat, drenching your kit long before chocks are moved, and you have one of the better working environments in life! Health and safety: eat ya' heart out!

And so you take-off, allow the formation to join up, and fly your mission. Normally this would entail flying formation at 450Kts at 250feet from base around the UK taking in the three targets, and maybe a pass onto an air firing range or through the simulated electronic warfare range. For all targets, an Initial Point (IP) must first be found.

An ideal IP should be a clearly identifiable tall structure about one/one and a half minutes flying time from the target, and preferably on the reciprocal of the ideal attack direction. The target's acquisition then becomes elementary as navigation errors have had no time to build up . . . in theory!

The well-flown IP to TGT run is the mainstay of accurate weapon delivery. It provides good and early target acquisition, which is the most basic of requirements for a good weapons delivery run. Once over the IP, map reading reverts from the half-million area map to the 50-thou. Ordnance Survey, and a pre-planned heading and stop-watch time is flown, culminating either in a pull up attack for rockets and strafing, or a straight through attack for low level bombing or a recce pass.[1]

Once past the third target, there is often a climb to height for the return to base. This is because, of course, in a jet the higher you go the less fuel you use, and therefore, the longer the range. In a Harrier, for example, using 200lbs of fuel per minute at 450kts at low level, it reverts to approx 40lbs/minute at the mid-30,000s of feet. So a climb to that level will often save fuel or give you a longer range. Having previously checked its weather, arrival overhead base for a formation-descent and possibly a radar-approach, or a fighter-arrival if the weather's good, running-in fast and breaking downwind in an ever-continuous turn to land, completes the mission. Though, if you've any fuel left, you can then practise a few more varieties of take-offs and landings, before taxiing back to dispersal. The exterior appearance of a hot smelly grease ball that stumbles out of the aircraft has little bearing on the exhilaration felt internally for a great job, well done, in an exciting atmosphere yet again. You have battled round the mission, taking on everything man and nature can throw at you, and returned in one piece with aplomb!

With both exhilaration and relief, you stumble into the crewroom lighting a fag as fast as you can with the adrenalin still going round at Warp 9, grab yet another can of caffeine, your fifth of the day, and debrief the mission together to try and learn any lessons for next time. This usually takes around half-an-hour excluding any gunsight film debriefing.

This cycle of planning, briefing, flying and debriefing continues throughout the day, and a single pilot could be involved in three out of the four waves each day, though two is probably more normal. Usually a quick sandwich lunch ensues, with another intake of caffeine. I have flown eight missions on exercise like this in one day, albeit after the first mission I never left the cockpit. Planning and maps were drawn by others, and passed to you between missions while the aircraft was refuelled and re-weaponed. If you were lucky, someone would give you a pint of orange juice, and the odd biscuit.

Time between missions was taken up with paperwork and secondary duties, and Friday afternoons were usually spent ground training when various lectures were given by specialists on related subjects such as intelligence, aircraft systems, weapons, electronic warfare, reconnaissance training, exercise briefings, and weapons cine-film debriefing. Also of course, as a senior pilot, you spend much time actually running the sqn operations and authorising flights. This could take up two or three half-days per week. Finally, if you were an instructor, be it in Flying, Instrument Rating, Weapons, Recce or Tactics, you spent some time making up and giving briefings on your specialist subjects to the others every week.

Aside from the four waves of aircraft each day, each sqn had one two-seat trainer version, the underpowered T7 Hunter or the heavier T4 Harrier, both without the same performance as the single-seaters. Never popular, the two-seaters were used not only for check rides with the Boss, the QFI, the QWI, and your annual instrument rating renewal, but also sometimes as a 'bounce' aircraft. The 'bounce' was the term given for a simulated enemy aircraft used to attack, or 'bounce', one of the four-ship formations, thus provoking an unscheduled aerial combat on their way to a target.

So the cycle from Met brief, through planning, briefing, flying and debriefing usually takes three and a half hours, and at the end of the fourth wave of the day, the authorising officer will plan a programme for the following day, and each day or week could be something different. This could be air-to-ground firing on a local air firing range at Holbeach or Wainfleet. It could be 2v2 aerial combat; it could be simulated low-level attack missions anywhere in UK, sometimes using army Forward Air Controllers on the ground to direct you onto army targets. Or the sorties could be long range bombing or recce, and include in-flight refuelling practice. Then there was instrument and night flying to keep up with, aircraft air tests to complete after an engine change, and basic essential solo exercises of practising take-offs and landings and various approaches at different diversion airfields, from visual through radar. Also, on the Harrier, there was essential practice of the slow speed environment from hovering to normal flight, including VTOs and VLs, which always took place at the end of every mission.

At the end of the flying day, there's often a short, full sqn debrief on the day's flying, and replenishment of the coffee bar stocks which has dispensed some sixty-plus cups of coffee, before you all repair to the Mess bar for a fag and a few pints. Home by 7.30pm to 8pm was more often the norm, having worked a good fourteen-hour day each weekday, and falling into bed early, pleasantly tired around 10.30pm, for an early start the next day.

The grow-bag becomes your status symbol, your symbol of affection: it puts you apart from all the 'ground wallas'. When I first joined up, flying kit was strictly forbidden outside the aircraft, the flight line, and the squadron buildings, but over the years and into the mid-'70s, it became increasingly seen as a morale boosting status mark. Eventually, the final bastion of correct dress, the Officers' Mess, also fell to the growbag. The Geneva Convention accepted flying suits as a form of uniform, but it took the RAF until the late '70s to catch up with this enlightenment and allow their use anywhere throughout the day until 7pm, which saved many changes of clothes, and therefore time, in a busy environment.

Not only that, but the Air Force seemed ashamed of its proper uniform. You weren't allowed off base in it unless you covered it up so nobody could see it. This was on dubious security grounds, so you crept to and from work with a flasher's mac over your uniform. Moreover, when they abolished the much-loved No 2 battledress, and substituted a silly looking pullover on cost grounds, we never ever looked smart again anyway. I must say, I wore my old battledress until it was threadbare. It was still smarter than the woolly-pully at the very end. Not only that, you could wear your badges and medals with pride, which you could not do on the pully.

I could never help comparing our attitude to our uniforms, with that of the proud Chilean Air Force (FADC), with whom I spent some time later in my career. They not only had very smart battledresses, but peaked hats, leather belts and pistols, and wore them all constantly, everywhere, and with pride. The public also revered them as guardian angels and men of good standing. It was a wonderful culture shock to watch them being admired by all and sundry while walking along the main streets of Santiago, compared with us skulking around in flashers' macs because of some minor threat from IRA thugs! What a change from the days of the gay young Battle of Britain pilots during WW2! We had become a laughing stock! Indeed it was often stated that we needed another war to regain our pride.

Always a matter of pride, you were strapped in, checks complete, and ready faster than the rest, and your wheels came up less than an inch after leaving the ground. Flying lower and faster, while flying over mirror-like seas, you had to see a wake in your own rear-view mirror from your jet exhaust. You would deliberately black out over the top of a loop to savour the sensations of grey-out, black-out and the churning return to full consciousness with the aircraft in full control of itself, properly trimmed, while sliding down the far side of the circle. Or make a curved approach to land with the inner downward wing tip just levelling off as the main wheels touched down, ever so gently, and this while judging to the foot, the height at which to deploy the brake 'chute while still airborne, so that its initial retardation would put you on the runway, right on the numbers, firmly and gently whilst holding the nose-wheel up for as long as possible to take advantage of aerodynamic braking, thus decreasing the landing run and sparing those wheel-brakes from becoming incandescent.

That was a typical day in the life of a fighter pilot during the period 1964 to 1982. That's what made fighter flying a fascinating job, but within such addiction there has always been a fine line between under and over-confidence. Someone actually pays you for the privilege, but there's no such thing as an old bold pilot!

> "A *superior* pilot is one
> Who uses his *superior* knowledge,
> To keep out of situations,
> That may require his *superior* skill"
>
> (RAF Flight Safety Poster)

Notes

1. Of course, more modern, radar-equipped aircraft can fly completely blind to a target, and attack without ever seeing it.

Part 2

Aden and South Arabia

"In all the trade of war, no meat
Is tougher than a sheer defeat.
In all the urge for peace, no feat
Is nobler than a brave retreat.
But nothing's worse than the sour fodder
of withdrawing in appalling order."

(with apologies to Samuel Butler,
"Hudibras Pt 3" 1680)

Chapter Six

Khormaksar Ops

My first sqn, 8 Sqn, was quite famous throughout the Middle East, having often been the ONLY Sqn in theatre. The "Aden's Own" Sqn finally left the colony in 1967 after forty years of continuous service there, but not before they had left their mark on the place. Formed in 1915 at Brooklands as part of the RFC, 8 Sqn saw service in France where one pilot won a VC. During WW2, it played a valuable part in the East African campaign, flying over 800 sorties. During 1943–44, it also sank two German submarines. Italian planes bombed Aden, and Perim Island at the mouth of the Red Sea, during WW2, but otherwise it was an oasis of peace, remote from the main battle areas, continuing its prime role as a refuelling and re-supply port. However, up-country the usual inter-tribal rivalries continued. It took part in the ill-fated Suez campaign in 1956, and participated in the operations against the Mau-Mau in Kenya. It was THE Squadron that had gone into Kuwait with 42 and 45 Commando during the first crisis in 1961 and stopped the problem dead in its tracks; if we'd been there in 1991 and 2003, we'd have stopped two more wars, and the Middle East would be a better place today. So much for pulling out of 'east-of-Suez'.

During the emergency operations from 1964 to 1967, we fought two distinct and separate campaigns: security operations against terrorism in the Aden State, and guerrilla warfare in the mountains of the Federation. As we were based in the Aden State, the former affected our daily lives, but it was the latter to which we, the RAF fighter force there, were intimately involved. Air surveillance with its threat of punitive bombing, the flying gunboats of the overlapping colonial and air ages, was a swift, easy answer to control of the up-country tribes.

Sqn operational reports from the 1940s all said much the same thing and the *modus operandi* had not changed by the mid-'60s:

"The Quatari tribe of the village of Al-Qradi owed HMG £200.14s.9d. in unpaid taxes. They had been warned twice to no avail. Therefore on (date), leaflets will be dropped warning them that their village is going to be bombed on (the following day)"[1]. The report would then go on to dictate a full bombing operation, the rules of engagement, and the results including a political officer's report.

On the following day when, surprise, surprise, the tax had remained unpaid, the sqn would simply bomb the village while the villagers looked on from the hillsides around. They would then rebuild their village and carry on

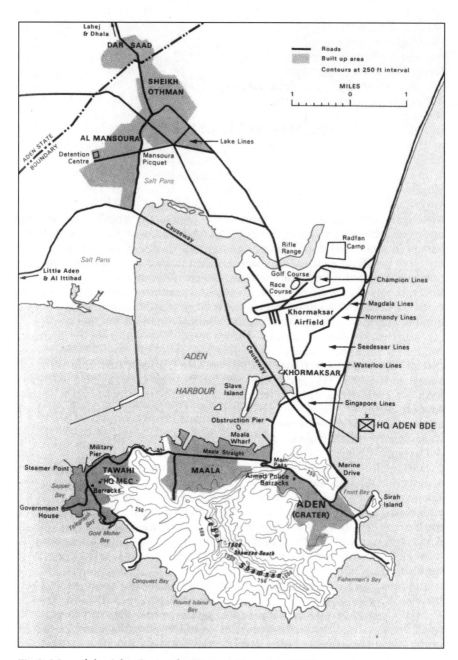

Fig 3. Map of the Aden Peninsula ©Crown Copyright/MOD

life as if nothing had happened – but I don't think it endeared us to them. Any blood spilt instantly produced a blood feud. Hence, we were often cleared to fire but told not to hit! Typically British – fighting with one hand tied! Nevertheless, the South Arabian Arabs only took note of excessive power; it was the only thing they really understood.

Remarkably, many parts of our Empire were policed that way earlier in the last century. Indeed, the RAF governed Iraq in a similar manner at one time. Its base at Habbaniya in 1941 was besieged and the RAF was forced to use its flying training school Audaxe planes there to strafe and bomb the Iraqi infantry divisions. In order to quell the coup, reinforcements from Egypt were sent to relieve Habbaniya and the Iraqis immediately surrendered. Surrendering without a fight seems to be a habitual national trait in Iraq. Is it any wonder, though, that we were unloved by so many colonies, perhaps sowing the seeds of organisations such as Al-Quaida today? After all, Bin Laden and Al-Quaida had their roots in the Yemen and South Arabia (now part of Yemen), and those tribesmen are just as hostile now as they were in my day. We never did succeed in subduing the Radfani hill-tribes, and we finally pulled out in 1967 with our tails between our legs. The subsequent deterioration there has a direct bearing on the terrorist attack on the USS Cole in Aden harbour in 2001 and the French tanker attack off Aden in 2002, never mind the many up-country terrorist incidents in the intervening years.

No. 8 Squadron Operations 1964 –1967

RAF Khormaksar's Strike Wing was not only tasked mainly with army support work, but was responsible for the air defence of the whole region. It also had the best working shift system ever devised, and all because we had so many aircraft and personnel available by today's standards.

Despite two large fighter squadrons, 8 and 43, both needed their rest periods, and one Sqn alone was usually adequate to maintain the operational task and complete our necessary training flying. Hence, uniquely to my knowledge in the RAF up to that time, all the wing aircraft had both Sqn badges on them and were shared by both Squadrons. On the forward side of the fuselage roundel were the three yellow, red and blue horizontal stripes of 8 Sqn, while at the back (of course) were the black and white chequers of 43. It was oft quoted that the three 8 Sqn colours were those of Aden: yellow sand, blue sky and red for the blood! Well the Sqn had been on almost continuous operations there for some four decades, so there's probably some truth in it.

To complete the picture, besides our two Hunter Squadrons, a separate small flight of FR10 Fighter Recce Hunters called 1417 Flight were also part of the wing. This was the Flight I was to command later in my career.

The Sqns were organised very simply: twenty-four aircrew: One Sqn Ldr Boss, four Flt Lts, two of which were flight commanders plus a Sqn QFI and a Sqn Pilot Attack Instructor (PAI). The other nineteen were first tour flying officer bachelors, average age 22, and I was the youngest. What a recipe for some high jinks! Never a moment went by when somebody wasn't up to something, and I'm glad I wasn't the Boss during this period. I was still only 20 when I started here on my first operational tour, and my 21st was a few drinks in the mess bar soon after I arrived. Well, a few more than a few!

In operational terms, every pilot had a rating that decided how many aircraft in combat you were qualified to lead. You started as a non-operational pilot usually taking six months training to arrive at full operational status, allowing you to man the standby pair as the wingman and fly on operations up country. You then progressed to Op2 (leader of a pair), Op4 (leader of four aircraft) and so on. Everyone made Op2 on his first tour, and the good ones made Op4. Only the Flt Cdrs could lead eight, and notionally the Boss had all sixteen, if there was ever that number serviceable! But the standard battle routine was pairs, and four-ships, and that's how we trained.

We only had one Sqn on duty at any one time and we worked a 24hrs on/24hrs off shift, from lunchtime to lunchtime, handing over to the oncoming Sqn at midday. A pair of aircraft and pilots were always kept on fifteen minutes stand-by; sometimes this became four if the alert state increased. This system continued seven days per week, though with minimum manning at weekends. This meant that every 24hrs you finished work at lunchtime, went down to the beach for the afternoon, got pissed in the evening, slept it off the following morning and at lunchtime stumbled back to work again! And they paid you to do it!

We were equipped only with WW2, 6 inch calibre, HEAT[2] rockets, and the four internal 30mm ADEN[3] cannons, no napalm or bombs, (traditionally, the four-engined Lincoln aircraft had done the bombing role, subsequently taken over by the Shackletons), our usual fit being twelve x 60lb rockets under the outer wings, and 120 rounds of 30mm HE ammo in each gun. So armed, the stand-by pair, on fifteen mins readiness dawn till dusk, was manned by two pilots, the leader of whom had to be a qualified Op4, with an Op2/Op as a wingman. This quick reaction alert was not only for army support up country, but also for air defence if required. Our main task was army support, but few and far between as they were, we used to enjoy the air defence scrambles.

There were two reasons for this taste, the first being that with both ends of the runway ending in the sea, whichever way you took off, and as soon as the wheels were up, it was standard operating procedure to jettison everything under the wings into the ocean on air defence scrambles. This was thought crucial to lighten the aircraft load for the fastest possible climb to height. It didn't happen often! But two full 230gall fuel tanks and twelve rockets going off together into the sea was a sight worth watching.

The second was that an air defence mission usually meant climbing to high level which, in turn, meant you found the only cool part of South Arabia for once. As 90% of our flying was low level army support and ground attack, we spent most of our flying drenched in sweat, since it was desperately hot in the cockpit at low level throughout the year.

The task, both then and today, of bringing fugitives, dissidents or terrorists to justice, was complicated by a daunting combination of factors from the country's complicated social and tribal composition, to the sheer in-hospitability of the geography of the place, which is both huge and unforgiving. The inhabitants are some of the poorest in the world, with no natural resources and little water. Three-quarters of a million of them in a country the size of France. Of course, it didn't help matters that, with the exception of the tarmac Aden-Dhala Road being built by our Royal Engineers, there wasn't a single metalled road in the whole of South Arabia outside the Aden Colony. From the 7,000foot sheer escarpments of black granite rising above the Lawdar Plain, to the unending vastness of the Empty Quarter, with only a few sand-graded airstrips able to accept a Dakota size of aircraft, it's an impossible world for all but the toughest.

It is hard to conceive in the modern world of the communications' problems prevalent throughout the Arabian Peninsula; lack of landlines between RAF bases, no satellites, inefficient short-range, radio-telephones and dependence upon time consuming teleprinters, morse code and tardy air-mail. Communications throughout the Arabian Peninsula were totally inadequate and would have been severely tested if ever any major operation had had to be carried out. We fell foul of this problem during a fighter transit of Turkey on the way home in late 1967[4].

The variety of airfields and landing grounds that had to be used by the force was almost unlimited, though only the international standard of Khormaksar could take fighters. For the rest, every conceivable kind of surface, length and gradient could be found, down to rough, short and precipitous landing grounds like Dhala in the Western Aden Protectorate. Hard, natural surfaces were usually stony with a great danger to tail-planes, main-planes and under-carriages from large flying stones. The wear and tear on tyres and on nose and tail wheels from these conditions was excessive, and a significant number of unserviceabilities could always be attributed to the landing and take off conditions to which all aircraft were subjected. We were constantly being asked to operate from airfields which had been adequate for the old Vampires and Venoms but which were no more than marginal for Hunters such as Beihan, Riyan and Salalah. It is understandable that our overall accident rate tended to be higher than the RAF average[5], not because of any lack of skill, but because of the greater hazards up-country with which pilots had to contend.

In typical Arab fashion – waste not, want not – most of the curved *Gambia* dagger blades locally fashioned in that part of the world, and worn by every self-respecting tribesman, were formed from old broken down Land-Rover or Bedford three-tonner steel springs. It wasn't only the Mitla Pass of the Sinai Desert and the Kuwait City-Iraq border road that were littered with old wrecks, our desert was also plagued with the disarticulated skeletons of these ex-military vehicles, all ripe for the plundering, with spring steel of the highest Sheffield quality.

All the same, this appalling corrosion was worsened by the lack of rain and good supplies of fresh water with which to wash the salt and sand off our aircraft and vehicles. It rarely rained in Khormaksar to my knowledge, only once in 52 years[6], but that's a story for Chapter 8! The Middle East must have been the only theatre in the world where aircraft washing plants had to be installed, and even with these much of the water had to be purified before it was sufficiently free from salt to be usable. One good reason why Eastleigh airfield at Nairobi became our major servicing base was that corrosion could be tackled there much more efficiently than anywhere in the Arabian Peninsula, as aircraft could be washed thoroughly in rain water.

Besides corrosion, occasionally while flying low level, we had to contend with the massive, black four-foot wingspan Kites, or 'Shitehawks' as we colloquially called them, which being the largest birds in the region and therefore queen of the local skies, didn't give way to anything. The usual strikes on the leading edges of our main-planes and engine intake areas usually meant the loss of the aircraft for many months for major repairs, though, thank goodness, the Avon engine withstood enormous damage without coughing and aircraft were rarely lost for this reason. The Hunter was so sturdy that even after ingesting a Kite with enormous intake damage, it generally flew, sometimes long distances, home safely.

In 1966 we had a remarkable Hunter incident which totally vindicated our problems with corrosion in the eyes of the powers back home. Dick Wharmby was trying to land his Hunter one day after experiencing a hydraulic failure. The Hunter's back up system was a compressed air accumulator used to blow the undercarriage down after any loss of hydraulic pressure. A simple, mechanical pull lever in the cockpit controlled the accumulator and, having lost his hydraulics, Dick pulled the lever. It just came off in his hand, the heavy steel cable attached to the lever having corroded right through since its replacement less than three months earlier. Dick finally landed the aircraft wheels up, on its empty under-wing 230 gallon drop tanks and, keeping the runway clear for other aircraft, skidded down the taxiway in a shower of sparks, damaging nothing but the drop tanks. A measure of how robust an aircraft was the Hunter is also proven in this incident, in that the aircraft was jacked up – drop tanks changed, a hydraulic valve substituted, the handle replaced – and was flying again the following day!

Indeed, back in 1957, the latest marks of Hunter were given their initial, very successful, hot weather trials in Aden. Hardly surprising then that a few years later, our new squadron Hunters stood up to these extreme conditions better than any other fighter before or since, as our operations showed.

Operating continuously in this environment posed us many problems which, at times, demanded the highest standards of airmanship. Not least of the problems was that of combating intense heat, glare and sandblasting. The perspex cockpit canopy tended to focus the rays of the sun onto the head of the pilot, and prolonged exposure to this concentration could induce headaches and sunstroke. In this type of aircraft, however, we normally wore protective helmets, or 'bone-domes' for safety in ejection, but astonishing as it may seem today, just ordinary desert shoes on our feet!

Cockpit windscreens suffered most. Constant sand-blasting etched a six-month life into a screen which lasted years in a European environment, and progressively aggravated the sun's glare. Squinting into the small quarter light on each side, the only recourse, did little to facilitate landing on a runway ill-defined in full sun.

Spending over fifteen minutes on the ground in the cockpit where temperatures often exceeded 150degF was precluded by an air-conditioning system unusable prior to engine start, and certainly not designed with Aden in mind; it couldn't cope with normal low-level flying which were always hot, sweaty affairs. The inviolable 15-minute rule then was to cancel the mission to avoid heat exhaustion; the subsequent recovery seated in air-conditioning included much "jungle juice" (powdered orange-juice) consumption provided by the ground crew. Only in Aden were two plates of pills kept permanently on all mess dining tables: one of vitamins and, by far the most important, one of salt pills which we all took religiously to avoid the vertiginous effects of sodium deficiency.

Although a tubular-framed, mobile canopy reduced cockpit ground temperatures, it was insufficient to prevent spending the ensuing hour or so at high level, strapped into a refrigerated cockpit, soaked to the skin in our own sweat. Notwithstanding some acclimatization, avoiding pneumonia was miraculous!

Back on the ground, if the technical problems were trying, the conditions under which our airmen had to solve them were even more demanding. Conditions for servicing aircraft could hardly be worse than they were at Khormaksar. Salt and sand posed alarming problems for the maintenance of metal-skinned aircraft, engines, vehicles, equipment and buildings, often necessitating complicated and difficult repairs. Almost all work had to be carried out in the open and exposed to incessant heat, sand and dust. It was oft said that the humid, dust filled, salt-laden atmosphere of Aden produced the finest grinding compound in the world, with immense patience needed to reassemble components with bearing surfaces free from these harmful agents.

In Fighter Command our ADEN 4-gun packs were serviced and stored in special air conditioned armouries. Not so in the Middle East. If a suitable building was available, it was fortuitous. Often a square patch of sand denoted the armoury, and ADEN guns were destined to swallow their allotted portion of sand like everything and everybody else.

The extraordinary thing was that, though the rate of wear was fairly high, the guns worked extremely well with stoppages happening but rarely. This caused many an eyebrow to be raised at the luxurious accommodation being provided in the UK, but at Khormaksar the choice between stifling heat but reasonably clean conditions inside a hangar, and salt-laden, blowing sand but cooler air in the open was often a difficult one to make. After an incident occurred in which an NCO died of heat exhaustion while working behind one of the engines *inside* the main wing of a Beverley, some change to working practices had to be made. He collapsed and was not found in time to revive him, which immediately caused a standing order stating that they had to work in pairs, causing some bemusement in new arrivals.

As pilots we each had to do our stint as part of the standby pair on the fifteen minutes readiness. This meant all the pre-flight checks had been completed on the aircraft, which included two x 230gallon underwing tanks inboard, the twelve rockets and the four integral cannons in the nose, with one's cockpit set up to personal requirements when taking over the duty. As usual we then lolled around the crewroom in air-conditioning, hoping that something might happen, having been ready either half an hour before dawn for duty until lunchtime, or lunchtime until half an hour after dusk.

Khormaksar was the largest and busiest RAF station anywhere, housing not less than three wings of nine squadrons. Security was a constant cause of concern as Aden was at that time being subjected to a mounting wave of terrorist attacks, some 286 in 1965 and almost double that number a year later.

Although most fighter patrols were flown at low level to ensure the dissidents on the ground heard us and knew we were there, occasionally, high level patrols were flown in the fond hope that their air force would know we were around and make them think twice about coming across the border. In any case there were many transit flights to and from the Gulf, and ferry flights to and from UK, all of course flown at high level. It is difficult to describe sensations during high-level, long distance transit flights or border patrols in that part of the world. As the patrol pair, we were usually up at 36,000ft in wide battle formation, some two miles line abreast, flying slowly at 0.75Mach along the border for endurance. The cloudless sky was so vast and limpid with patches of dissolving fleeciness and usually no horizon. One felt stunned by this cavernous airspace we, alone, inhabited, while below, the ground was barely discernible, hidden by the dreaded 'Goldfish Bowl' conditions. This yellow haze made orientation difficult, made possible only by frequent recourse to instrumentation!

You knew that the hostile, granite South Arabian mountains were some-where below and, despite the minus 40degC of cold outside the canopy, you could still feel the sun's rays burning through, blinding your vision, and impairing even further your capacity to make visual sweeps of the sky. Instead of breathing the usual air/oxygen mix, the system was often turned to pure oxygen, especially if you'd had a few pints too many the night before! Breathing pure oxygen always gave you a lift and put you on a 'high'. It increased the curious but satisfying sensation of being isolated and totally detached from reality. You couldn't hear any engine noise at that height, just a slight swish of the airflow across the outer skin, and the constant minor static from the radio. There is little relative movement to show speed, only what's on the dial. Time appears to go so slowly that everything seems unreal and remote. The cockpit environment gradually becomes a sort of low, noisy growl in your earphones, blocking out everything else and forming a neutral back-ground that ends up by merging into a profound, vague, and dreamy silence, threatening to break the ingrained discipline of constant scanning.

At the other extreme of our ops were the many frantic, frenzied scrambles that found you airborne within minutes, still trying to strap into the ejection seat whilst already half-way to the target area. On occasion the target area came into view before my seat safety pins came out! Such was the hurry to help the army guys, especially the 10 Field Sqn Royal Engineers who were being sniped at on the Dahla Road. It was a matter of pride and profession-alism that you got airborne as fast as possible; after all, "health and safety" hadn't been invented in those days, thank goodness. If it helped to save lives up-country, you risked leaving the strapping in and safety checks until you were on the way at full throttle, and the hell with the consequences if some-thing went wrong on take-off!

The Yemenis were always encroaching upon the border in the Beihan area, which was round the corner of an S-bend in the border some 150 miles NE of Aden (See Fig 2). It was right on the edge of the Rub-al-Khali (the Empty Quarter) – probably the most far-flung, desolate outpost of any British forces. We had traditionally provided exorbitantly expensive, standing airborne patrols in the area three times per day. Beihan stood some 2,500ft above sea level in a natural, narrow rock and sand wadi running NE-SW, and surrounded by escarpments along its 40 miles length. A main natural surface road ran along the centre of the wadi and through Beihan town. About half a mile southwest of the town, that road had been turned into a short concrete airstrip, but with a large hill at the south-western end. Back in 1957, a mixed force of 500 Yemeni irregulars and their regular army had crossed the Beihan border and ambushed a dawn patrol of RAF armoured cars, forcing them to fight the first pitched battle of the frontier troubles. Indeed, an attack by two Mig fighters in June 1965 on the village of Najd Marqad (see Fig 2) and a nearby Frontier Guard post near Beihan caused the death of two Arab women and injury to three other villagers. This incident necessitated the re-introduction of our Beihan Air Defence Patrol, a wasteful and time consuming commitment. By 1966, the problems in the area had become insurmountable without air support, but Beihan runway, only 1,440yds in length, was too short for Hunters. Consequently, after one Yemeni incursion in July, in which Mig 17s[7] shot up the nearby village of Nuqub (see Fig 2), it was decided to lengthen the runway to 1,800yds for Hunters, much to the delight of the Sharif of Beihan, the local Marib Sheik.

Having to transit each way round the corner to and from Beihan created a 360 mile round trip, instead of the direct line across Yemeni territory of only 300 miles, which further decreased the short time we could stay on patrol there. Maintaining diversion fuel for Djibouti on the African coast, a further 135 miles in the opposite direction from Khormaksar, didn't help. As a result, many were the occasions we ran short of fuel and had to return across Yemeni territory as the crow flies. Fortuitously, the artificial, vaguely-defined and un-patrolled borders on the edge of the Empty Quarter were pretty meaningless.

To land on the newly lengthened Beihan runway, a very tight left turn had to be flown around a tall, narrow spit of rock jutting vertically upwards to a pointed-top that was positioned almost in the middle of the desired approach to the runway. This circular Jebel called J.ash Sha'bah was a phallic symbol shape on short base leg, requiring a tight S-bend to be flown on short finals. If your speed was exactly right, a landing attempt could then be made north-eastwards towards the village. Of course, in order to stop safely on such a short, "hot and high" runway, you had to have no more than the exact minimum fuel state with empty drop tanks on board with which to fly back home to base. There, at 2,000 feet amsl, you were committed to stay until the temperature reduced sufficiently around dusk for a safe take-off, otherwise you'd have still been on the ground rolling down the main village street. Committed for take-off, the aircraft was launched in the same direction regardless of wind conditions, and an operation 'hairy' to say the least. I was reminded of this commitment by a saying of General Schwarzkopf after the first Gulf War. On being interviewed by a UK reporter about his troops' involvement and commitment, he answered by saying, "It's like your Limey breakfasts . . . you know, your eggs and bacon!" He went on, "The chicken's involved but the pig's committed!" At Beihan, we were the pigs!

The more senior pilots flew a pair into Beihan at dawn each day and main-tained a ground standby until dusk when they took off, did a very short patrol, and returned to Khormaksar for the night. With the new part of Beihan runway being at the southern end, the further down the take-off run, the bumpier the ride, until at about 20 knots below flying speed, a particu-larly bad bump could throw you into the air. The next few seconds were spent, nose high in the air, half stalled and desperately clambering for speed and height, mushing down the main street of the village. Happily, the wadi and the road were dead straight, although I wouldn't like to have been walking down the main street minding my own business at the time!

It is long enough ago to now admit it! Although I wasn't one of those chosen to land at Beihan, I certainly used to do "touch and go approaches" there, just to relieve the boredom of desert patrols, and I know I wasn't the only one! The wing flew an enormous number of these Beihan missions: 186 in August, 98 in September, and 151 in October 66. I alone flew seven Beihan patrols in the month of August '66, having flown none in the previous 18 months, but this patrol level was not to last. Beihan was too difficult logistically and, in any case, how were we going to obtain an alert to get airborne anyway, even if the heat had allowed it? It appeared to be nothing more than a show of force to keep up the locals' confidence.

We were kept busy operationally during 1967 and ACM Sir David Lee is quoted as writing, *"The accuracy of 8 Sqn's rocket attacks proved excellent, and the Sqn became one of the most accurate and experienced rocket firing squadrons in the RAF, with average errors measured in feet where others were measured in yards!"* I was always proud of my rocket average, which for the whole three years was less than 20feet, and during one four month period, came down to less than 14feet. This may not sound too accurate to the un-initiated, until it is realised that this was accomplished with very inaccurate, WW2 rockets developed for Typhoons. But 960lbs of explosive in a full load of sixteen[8] rockets detonating five or six yards away was more than enough to make you blink!

On the other hand, our use of this rocket was one of many weapon-to-target mismatches, for which the air force is infamous. The shaped charge warhead was designed to put a small-diameter hole into WW2 armour-plate; single rocket use against soft targets such as Radfan mud forts, at low attack angles, produced a small hole in the side of the fort, another small hole on the other side of the fort as it exited, little change in between, and the rocket disappearing stage right! A full salvo solved that problem, but by far the most effective were the four 30mm cannons.

Each gun fired 1200 rounds per minute of 30mm high explosive shells, putting down 4800 rounds/min, an enormous amount of firepower with all four guns firing, and as good as any Gatling gun. Indeed, at the time it was the heaviest gun-armed fighter in the world. When practising on the range, short half second bursts from a single gun opening at 500yds down to 350yards, were the best for greater accuracy producing less time of bullet flight and a small bullet spread. However, operationally it was usual to fire one to two-second bursts using two or all four guns, thus putting between 80 and 160 rounds on target on every attack pass. For the uninitiated, a low angle, 10degree attack dive at 420 knots meant you moved 1400 feet (466yds) across the ground during a two second burst. Having to pull out of the dive at 350 yards to clear the target safely meant opening fire at about 800 to 900 yards. At that range the bullet spread was too large for accuracy, so a 1 to 1.5-second burst was about all that was operationally possible as a reasonable compromise.

Despite the heavy armament, the use of all four guns together, which only ever occurred on operations, produced some dramatic consequences, and not just for the enemy. The first time I used all four, it felt as if the aircraft had hit a brick wall – the recoil was so great. The vibration set up throughout the airframe usually popped numerous circuit breakers, and the radio would go off line as would most of the electrical services. Not a nice position to be in, pulling out of a dive 100 feet above a target who's firing back at you!

Surprisingly, one aspect of the ADEN cannon was used as currency. The two under-fuselage *SABRINAS*[9] were a late addition to collect the ammo belt-links which otherwise would have damaged the fuselage's underside on ejection. However, the 30mm brass cartridge-cases were ejected. The locals whom we used on our air firing range as a maintenance party were not paid except they were allowed to pick up the spent cases which fetched a premium downtown! Moreover, 41 Commando personnel told me that after firing in their support up-country in the Dhala region, the guns' brass cases were so valuable that the dissidents would down arms and break cover to collect them. Once collected, they then recommenced firing at the marines! Indeed, it is thought that they only fired on our troops to get us called in to provide them with brass currency! In effect we were paying them to fight us!

However, Heath-Robinson had nothing on our drainpipe rockets. They were propelled by long sticks of cordite, some of which would inevitably be ejected unburnt out of the rear-end during the rocket's flight, producing peculiar flight patterns and most uncertain impact points. Indeed, when acting as Range Safety Officer on our training range at Khormaksar Beach, we would walk the range and pick up the cordite strips after a mission had finished. When ignited together in a pile, these would boil a billycan of water for our tea exceptionally rapidly!

Together with the lack of a proper rocket sight in the aircraft, the subsequent inaccuracy of the rockets, sometimes with twirling flight paths, could only be overcome by considerable skill! It is said that a fighter pilot is an infinitely adaptable machine that can make allowances for the most impossible equipment designs to make them work regardless, but there is a limit! By and large, when we did hit the target, all the errors had likely cancelled each other out! Even so, when we came back from missions with empty rocket rails and soot round the gun ports, both armourers and our ground crew were happy; they knew then that their efforts had been rewarded.

In order that our operations can be better understood, and the way we trained for them, listed at Annex A is a table showing my operational missions. Please bear in mind that there were forty-odd[10] operational Hunter pilots on the Wing, and this was only my contribution. If you take my 66 as an average, and multiply by the number of pilots, there were somewhere around 2,600–2,700 operational Hunter missions flown during the last two years of occupation, at a rate of roughly four per day. Compared with the 642 missions flown during the two month Radfan campaign in 1964, our 2,600 were flown at a more leisurely pace, but they were sustained over a longer period with the enemy becoming stronger throughout.

To take just one of my missions, the strike in the Radfan area of Wadi Tiban on Wed 4 May 66, the Boss (Des Melaniphy RIP) and I were scrambled from standby after a party of approximately twenty armed dissidents had infiltrated from Yemen into the Federation. On the Tuesday night, 3 May 66, using explosive bullets, they attacked a British Army patrol operating in the area twenty miles west of Habilayn (45 miles North of Aden and five miles from the Yemen border), under the command of the FRA.

At first light, the Boss and I did an armed recce flagwave over the area, but that didn't deter them. So later that morning we were scrambled with full firing permission. I say that because we needed GOC or AOC's express permission before being allowed to fire, and many was the time we were overhead obvious fire-fights, and couldn't find either of them because they were otherwise engaged with matters clearly more important than the up-country lives, and no delegation of responsibility was ever given.

This was to be my first live firing mission, and I was initially very nervous. I was curious and anxious at the same time to know how I would react, not to the danger, because I never once doubted our invincibility, but to firing weapons at live human targets for the first time. On this occasion, with full firing permission, we went on to direct all our rockets and ammunition at the dissidents, whom we found patrolling down the boulder-strewn, palm tree-lined wadi Tiban. On my first, steep, rocket attack I caught glimpses of the dissidents running away down the wadi through the trees and boulders, but despite repeated attacks thereafter, there were no further sightings.

We were told later that thirteen of them had been killed, and five wounded, out of a party of twenty, whilst no British soldiers or locals had been injured at all. We considered that one of the few successes after all the flagwaves and armed recces we'd flown while not being allowed to fire.

On the ground afterwards, we were quietly excited, not quite grasping what we had done. I had completed my first real mission, not made a hash of it, and a great weight had fallen from me after years of training. It was the first time I'd experienced that strange exultation that often accompanies hard fighting, and I had come of age that day. This was the first time I had knowingly killed anyone, and I have to say that whereas it has preyed on my mind over many years since, I have no conscience about it. I was doing my job, the job I had been trained for, without which it would have been British soldiers' lives, and I'd certainly do it again in the same circumstances. That's all there is to it.

Notes
1. Names and dates are fictitious here, it is only showing a typical example of the wording.
2. HEAT – High Explosive Anti-Tank. A copper shaped-charge warhead designed specifically to kill armoured vehicles such as tanks. A shaped-charge on detonation develops into a long thin, supersonic stream of molten copper which drills a hole through the armour.

3. ADEN – Armament Developments ENfield. Nothing to do with the colony of Aden! By coincidence, it was the name given to the gun by the Royal Small Arms Factory at Enfield which developed captured German, Mauser, prototype, revolver-action, 20mm cannons at the end of WW2, into the ADEN 30mm. The French did the same with their DEFA 30mm gun, as did the Americans at 20mm before the introduction of the airborne Gatling.
4. See Chapter 15.
5. The rate was that for all AFME aircraft; our Hunter rate by itself was surprisingly lower.
6. Though this was not true of the mountainous areas up-country where flash floods were common.
7. A Soviet jet fighter aircraft of 1950's vintage, similar to a Hunter but not quite as powerful.
8. Only 12 carried by the QRA aircraft.
9. SABRINAS: Sabrina was a busty celebrity in the 1950s when the Hunter entered service. The two front, under-fuselage oval tanks used to collect belt-links on our old lady Hunter were, therefore, called SABRINAS by the troops, and subsequently were known as that officially.
10. 19 pilots operational on each Sqn plus 6 on 1417Flt. "Non-op" pilots per sqn are not included.

Chapter Seven

The Last Colonial War

Between 40 and 60 miles north of Aden, the Radfan consists of a complex of jagged peaks and sheer-sided cliffs rising to over 6000 feet with tiny villages perched precariously on the flat mountain tops and deep wadis in between. Our targets were often in these wadis most of which were cul-de-sacs ending in a sheer rock face. In this razor-toothed, granite, mountainous area, the tribes had a very uncertain allegiance and intelligence reports indicated that Egyptians in the Yemen had trained many of them as terrorists. Egyptian propaganda was rife. There's nothing new about the present situation there with an Al Qaeda presence, as terrorism bases were endemic throughout the region long before the turn of the 19th century, never mind the last one.

My first KD uniform and dinner suit came from "Smart Tailors" of Steamer Point. A tall Pakistani, "Mr Smart" and I laughed together at the Egyptian English propaganda pouring from his transistor while he was measuring me. Thank goodness it wasn't for a coffin as happened for many during the mid '60s in South Arabia, though that DJ, tailor-made for fifteen Dinars(£15), did last me over thirty years!

Up country, the tribes of the hinterland were even more susceptible than the inhabitants of Aden to those radio-delivered blandishments and exhortations. Their very existence had always depended on fighting, either among themselves or against some form of authority. In particular, the 'wolves of Radfan' had for centuries relieved their poverty by carrying on extensive raids and protection rackets at the expense of the caravans which wound their way through the mountains to the Yemen and on to Mecca, Petra, the Levant and Europe, along an ancient trade and pilgrim route. The Radfan area, on the only cross-border route, was ideally situated for fomenting terrorism against the British: problems had occurred here regularly throughout the British tenure. The 1964 Radfan operation was to be the last colonial war[1], though this considerable little campaign went virtually unnoticed in Britain. Most have never heard of the Radfan, despite there being a Radfan bar issued for the General Service Medal.

The part of this ancient route that ran through the Radfan was known as the Dhala road after the major border town, where, of the five tribes numbering some 40,000, the Quteibis had always laid first claim on the traffic. Many of our operations were concentrated along this sole major route through to the Yemen at Qa'tabah, some 10 miles north of Dhala itself. Here, 10 Field

Sqn Royal Engineers spent many months, indeed years, turning this desert wadi track into a metalled road. The Sappers were under constant sniper fire from the hills above them, and we spent many hours overhead keeping snipers at bay. I well remember the operation where, after days of both Sqns trying, Dai Heather-Hayes put one of our infamously inaccurate rockets straight into the mouth of a cave, half-way up the 2,000 foot rock face above the road, from where snipers had been sheltering and firing for some weeks in apparent safety. We had no more sniping for many weeks after that! Indeed, I am the proud owner of a 10Field Sqn, Royal Engineers' tie struck specifically for those who had worked on building the Dhala Road, simply because of all the top cover missions we had flown in their support.

Dhala, the principal town in the area, was a huddle of three to four-storied square, fortified houses of mud and rock, crowning a hillock in the middle of a narrow plateau just five miles south of the frontier. The Dhala Garrison must have been the most isolated, lonely and hostile outpost of the British Empire ever, surrounded on three sides by Radfani tribesmen and, on the fourth by the Yemeni border with its safe haven for the Egyptian backed dissidents. This most forward of outposts was beleaguered except for brief supply visits. Monthly columns coming up the Dhala Road from Aden through the twisting passes ran a gauntlet of mines and sniping, despite a ground escort of battalion strength and ourselves providing constant overlapping air patrols in our Hunters. The tribesmen saw no reason why British military convoys should not pay the same tolls to them as any other caravan passing through their territory!

The Emir of Dahla was a real eccentric, especially in his modern garb, which was a tribute to the generosity of various British advisers. Spindle-legged like most of his ilk, he was often seen in a green blazer, wine-coloured pullover, long blue shirt, a multi-coloured turban, brown brogue leather shoes with patterned ankle socks, and a gold and ivory *Gambia* dagger stuck in the folds of a silk cummerbund, while riding a fine chestnut Arab stallion. One of his bodyguards wore a WAAF officer's jacket – don't ask! Although the Emir was the nominal head of all the tribes in this area, his control and authority over many of them was negligible.

Similar to the NW India in Kipling's day, only the quality of the rations, the weapons and the speed of letters from home had changed, though not a lot. But the enemy around this last outpost of "the mini-north-west frontier" was hard to distinguish in daytime. Every tribesman older than fourteen carried a rifle, and machine guns were common. The child has a gun, and in the Radfan that makes him a man, even if he wasn't yet bonking the ladies. We were powerless to stop anybody carrying any kind of weapon by day but by night anybody moving outside the villages was undoubtedly an enemy. Particularly intransigent were those who occupied the high Radfan, experts in guerrilla warfare, courageous even under air attack, and competent snipers with any firearms they could obtain. It is a pitiless region where the accepted rule was 'an eye for an eye', and where feuds and vendettas passed on from one member of a family to another, for generations, until honour was satisfied.

The constant support given by Egypt and the Yemen to dissident factions in the Protectorate revealed a clear determination to provoke the maximum internal opposition to the Aden Government. By 1963 it was obvious that a deliberate insurgency campaign was being waged against South Arabia. This support was particularly troublesome in the frontier areas of Dhala and Beihan. It was accentuated by the deployment of a number of field guns, which the Yemenis concealed close to the border, and which fired intermittently at targets in the Protectorate. Whenever our Hunters located them, these guns were attacked but remained constant irritants. These field guns were often protected by anti-aircraft guns which themselves proved very effective against us. It was also known that Egyptian Air Force pilots flew the Yemeni Mig jet fighters.

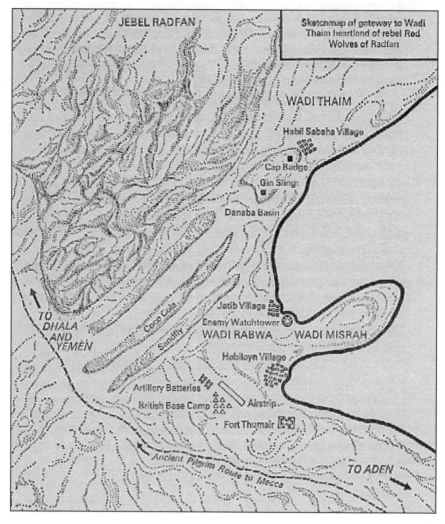

Fig. 4 Map of Habilayn and Wadi Thaim at start of Radfan campaign 1964
(© STEPHEN HARPER 1978)

On 4th January 1964, a limited three battalion strength Federal Regular Army(FRA) force entered the RADFAN area as the British answer to the insurgency campaign. The requirement was to show our determination to put an end to this subversion, to demonstrate that we could enter the area at will, to compel the withdrawal of the dissidents, and to reopen the Dhala Road. This later was achieved with Hunter support on 31st January, but by March their garrisoning of the area was becoming untenable and the FRA was withdrawn. Immediately the dissidents reoccupied the passes, destroyed the road,

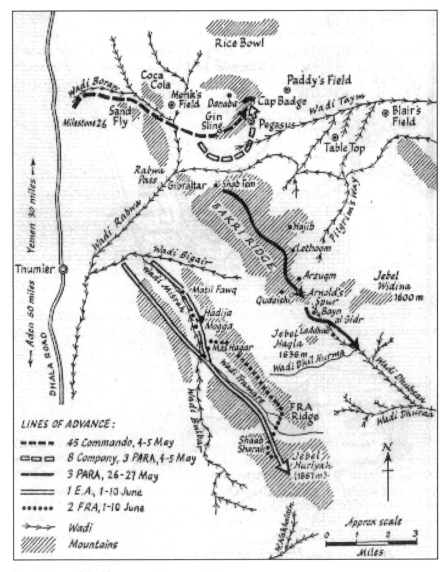

Fig 5. Map of Radfan operations area.**

59

and became increasingly active and aggressive including use of Yemeni aircraft bombing and strafing.

Our answer was to send in a British force to quell the insurgency before things got out of hand. The military aim was to end the operations of the dissidents (some 500 in total) within a defined area. In May, at the beginning of the main Radfan campaign of 1964, one particular enemy watchtower, a large fortified house just to the SE of Jatib village overlooking Habilayn and Thumair, had become a major problem; it could monitor every movement by air and road into and around the main army camp and airstrip. It was decided to take out this enemy OP using our Hunters as the starting point of the Radfan campaign but, unbelievably, just before the air strike was due on the afternoon of 4th May, the political authorities in Aden vetoed the whole show.

Once more we had become victims of the British "minimum force" policy, which would leave more dead British bodies later in the confrontation. Conduct of military operations in support of the civilian power forbad firing on habitations, and the only exemption was for buildings from where hostile fire had been seen. The fact that tribesmen who had fired on British patrols had been seen coming from the building beforehand was insufficient. We were, therefore, constantly fighting with one hand tied behind our backs, typical of British colonial conduct in the Empire's latter days in maintaining the rule of law. The policy of forgiving conciliation was taken to extremes of cynical hypocrisy at times, as was the habit of dropping warning leaflets.

Nevertheless, later in the campaign, occupants of the original watchtower at Jatib were seen firing on passing aircraft, so at long last it was now fair game. Two of our Hunters blew it to pieces with rockets and 30mm ammunition, to the delight of our local garrison.

During this period, 37 Sqn Shackletons dropped the odd 1000lb bomb and, flares to allow night operations. This would be the last time the RAF used propeller aircraft to drop bombs, at times a spoiling tactic to disturb dissidents' sleep at night to reduce their fighting fitness during the day.

While the Paras and Commandos were attempting to capture various Jebels dominating the main Wadi Thaim, our Hunters strafed rebel positions interminably, often firing within 150 yards of our own troops, and sometimes much less. So close and accurate were they that soldiers were injured by falling 30mm spent cartridge cases ejected from the Hunters. Hunters were airborne almost throughout daylight hours and often fired while flying level and sometimes while climbing along the wadi beds, only feet above the ground. The terrain being so difficult it was often impossible to dive steeply into the mountainous areas where the dissident targets were situated.

Many of the Hunter strikes were conducted using what is now an old fashioned Forward Air Controller (FAC) technique, in which a suitably trained army/airforce officer on the ground with the troops would direct the aircraft visually onto the target. The FAC would use track and distance from an easily found local point, or adjust the fall of shot from one of their guns, and describe the nature of the ground to the pilots by radio. The use of the "bushy-topped tree" as a reference point by an FAC is legend in the ground attack force, as in temperate climates one looks just like the other billion or so. In the Radfan, bushy-topped trees were so rare that they were actually useful for target finding!

60

The campaign lasted four months (May to Aug '64) before the tribes were brought to heel, but even then the tribesmen had dispersed into bands, laying mines, sniping, and generally harassing using guerrilla tactics. Some hardcore groups were eventually flushed out by Hunter strikes as late as November, but August had seen the tribal leaders submitting and agreeing to keep the iron-fisted peace that Britain's last show of old-fashioned imperialism had brought to the Radfan. For their support to the Radfan Campaign, the Hunter Wing received one Distinguished Flying Cross and six Mentions in Despatches.

Indeed, soon after Radfan a pair of Hunters near Beihan almost dealt with a Mig 17 intruder, saved by the leader's intermittent r/t reception as the Mig raced for the border and safety. Although the main campaign took place during the summer of '64 just before my arrival on the scene, the Radfan, together with Beihan at times, remained the main area for our up-country operations throughout my time there, and until we finally withdrew from Aden altogether.

So started the terrorism campaign in Aden itself, backed by Cairo with Moscow and Peking undertones, not helped by the change of government in London, and the utterly contemptuous, un-thought-out "East of Suez" policies being pursued by the new Labour government. Paradoxically, at the same time, the locals were far from sympathetic towards the terrorists. They were aware that we, the RAF, daily brought Arabs from their up-country, remote villages for treatment at RAF Khormaksar Beach Hospital, the only military hospital in the world built solely for the care of a backward in-digenous population. We had actually "won" their hearts and minds in this manner over many years but, due to the new policies from London, we very soon lost them again.

In this forgotten last-colonial campaign of Aden and the South Arabian Federation, between the 1964 Radfan conflict and our final withdrawal three years later, I flew 66 operational missions against an illusive enemy. So illusive in fact, that even when B Squadron of 22 SAS arrived in 1965, Major John Watts,[2] their CO, was unable to conduct disruptive ops due to lack of hard intelligence. Only by predicting the insurgents' movements after studying the terrain and placing himself in their position, were any successes achieved, and usually with air support from us on the Hunter wing.

From the Radfan conflict to the withdrawal, the army was always well impressed by our support, but it was during the original 1964 campaign that our Hunters won their well-earned reputation for the accuracy of their strafing and rocketing in support of the army. Indeed, when army artillery had to cease firing because their shells were falling too close to their own troops, Hunters were called in many times a day.

To quote Julian Paget (The Last Post – Aden 1964–1970), "*The strike aircraft of the RAF were superb, brilliantly handled and always on the spot within minutes . . . the ground forces, who had complete confidence in the air support provided by the Hunters.*" . . . "*A significant factor in all operations up-country was the very fine support given to all our forces at all times by the RAF fighter aircraft. The intimidating effect that they had on the enemy was considerable, and it did much to prevent them from operating at all by day. It was an important factor in the morale of our own troops, and influenced their techniques.*"

We may have been the most accurate in the RAF, but we'd had a lot of practice! However, the opposition was almost as good as well. Before my time they had shot down a squadron Venom, while the recce Meteors and other slower transports were always coming home with bullet holes in them. Our slow, lumbering Shackle-bombers also landed quite often with bullet holes in them. But it was during 1967 that the wing had seventeen Hunters returned from operations with battle damage, and one was shot down. The pilot of the latter, Sid Sowler from 43 Sqn, did manage to get the aircraft nearly home while a fire raged down the back end after a bullet had nicked a hydraulic line. By the time he ejected, some ten miles from base, the whole rear end of the aircraft was on fire. He was picked up safely near Sheikh Othman, with nothing more than a bruised back and a broken ankle.

Such was our keenness to do a full support job for the army and the locals that, on a number of occasions after long or distant patrols, the engine would wind down, having run out of fuel while taxiing after landing. Pushing it a bit you may think, but it happened occasionally to Mike Webb, who as a flight commander should have been setting a better example. Perhaps he was! Though it was a bit ignominious to have to walk the last few hundred yards in full flying kit to tell the crew chief his aircraft was parked half-a-mile down the taxiway, and could he move it please! Especially as the Wing Commander was usually on the blower by then, wanting to know what in hell was happening!

Flying daily over this astonishingly hostile territory, the most important document we carried on all our Hunter flights was our "goolie" chit. This promised the finder 100 Dinars (£100 sterling), a huge amount of money to a Radfani in those days, for a pilot's safe return IN ONE PIECE! In'sh Allah! But at £50 per ball, I thought the MOD were penny pinching again, much like Neil Armstrong's trip to the moon. When asked how it went, he said, "How would you like it on the cheapest tender!" Use of the Goolie Chit was not something we practised often, although there were stories from bygone days. I heard, but have no evidence, of an Army Air Corps helicopter pilot who had crashed up country before my time, and was later found, still alive, with his goolies sewn into his mouth!

For my tiny part, my aircraft was damaged twice. The first was minor, but on the 16 Aug 67, I was leading the standby pair on the usual fifteen minutes readiness and, as normal, was lolling around the crewroom waiting for the next scramble, having been ready since half an hour before dawn. On this occasion we were scrambled for an armed recce to Al Kirsh near Dhala in the Radfan region, where we found a large party of over forty dissidents in a Wadi, ambushing some locals and our troops. We had evolved one golden rule for operations of this nature: no-one flew below 2,000ft above ground level in op areas unless engaged in an attack in order to reduce the likelihood of any damage from small arms fire.

We flew over the area at 2000ft agl showing our presence for thirty minutes, used up all our ammunition and returned to base. As we were climbing out of the aircraft, my crew chief was looking at something under my port wing, and subsequently I was staggered to find two 0.5inch machine gun shells had passed through the aircraft, one of which had come rather close. The second shell had come up through the gun pack, which is situated immediately below the pilot's ejection seat. It had hit the top of the 30mm ammunition tank, which must have been empty by then, and I was only six-inches from a good goosing! The tank top had then deflected the shell horizontally out through the port side of the fuselage, where it had scored along the port wing underside and hit the inboard pylon. At this stage, it had deflected downwards through the underwing fuel tank (which also must have been empty by then), and had come out of the bottom of the tank never to be seen again! No fire, no explosion, just a lot of damage, and a very close shave for what turned out to be my penultimate operational mission in this theatre!

Notes
1. Arguably, the Falklands War could be considered colonial, though to my mind, not in the accepted sense at all.
2. Later to retire as Lt Gen Sir John Watts, ex Director of the SAS.

Chapter Eight

The Pomp, Ceremony and Personalities

Besides the serious side to our lives, the up-country operations, there was a lot of hard playing, and much pomp and ceremony, only curtailed by a militarily imposed curfew requiring all to be off the streets by midnight until 6am. Outside the base, the only really safe place for relaxation was the Officers Beach Club at Tarshine, just round the corner from Steamer Point. This South-facing bay, together with Goldmohar Bay next door, were the centres of afternoon social life during those times off duty. An excellent swimming beach, Tarshine Bay changed its nature totally as the weather changed every six months in and out of the southwest monsoon[1]: south-westerly prevailing winds during the summer, and north-easterly for the winter. For half the year Tarshine was a long, shallow surfing beach, but within a couple of weeks of the monsoon change, it became a steeply shelved bathing beach; you were out of your depth within 25 yards of the shore. In these latter circumstances, an anti-shark net was erected for safe swimming, as much against sharks as Portuguese Men-o-War, which were more prolific.

Many were the warm evenings we would spend at the beach club, where one could also meet most of the European girls in the Port – all 54 of them. However, those long, languid evenings of drink, club sandwiches and chat-up were always followed by a mad dash across Aden to be back inside the base main gate by midnight. Eight minutes was the record for the six miles on a 50cc Honda bike, unless you had a pillion passenger, when you had to leave three minutes earlier, but only if you took the forbidden short cut through the no-go Arab quarter at the Crater end of the Maala Straight! Well, it cut over half-a-mile and thirty seconds off the journey, and no one to my knowledge had ever been caught!

The other arduous task while on standby entailed maintaining two secret squadron files entitled BOAC and BUA respectively. Both airlines ran regular twice-per-week VC10s through Aden, BOAC on scheduled services to India and the Far East, while BUA provided our trooping flights, and both maintained a slip crew in the old, peeling, colonial Crescent Hotel.

The hotel receptionist was the brother of our squadron cleaner, and so our relationship with two crews of stewardesses, changing twice a week, began! If you were a BOAC or BUA stewardess on VC10s in the mid-'60s, we knew everything about you! Each enclosure on the files was the name of a stewardess, and all everyone on the sqn knew about her, together with her promiscuity rating on a scale of one-to-10! An hour after each VC10 landing, we would receive a call from the hotel receptionist with the names of the new crew, and you can guess the rest! That's how I met Rita, a lovely little Glaswegian redhead, flying with BUA out of Gatwick on trooping flights to Aden, and her rating is my business! It was a necessary outlet for us because with 8,000 troops in the colony, and only fifty-four girls, there was a slight element of competition! My Sqn tankard however, presented by the aircrew as I left Aden three years later after only this single liaison, has the inscription, "Contact thro' BUA"!

Today, forty years later, there is still an English Bookshop on the pier behind the Hotel where the liners tied up at Steamer Point, and not far from the beach club. The pier was named, and still is called today, "The Prince of Wales Pier". The Crescent Hotel is the hotel where the Queen stayed on her last visit to Aden. Fifty-three years later, the Crescent still keeps a room set aside for the Queen in the hope that she might once again deign to stay! Her one and only visit was in 1954!

As was typical of any ex-pat community of the time we had very little social contact with the locals, although in late '65 there was one extremely generous Arab fahdal to which the whole Squadron officer contingent was invited. The local sultan, The Sultan of Lahej, whose summer palace was in Crater, also had a winter house in the comparatively lush wadi of Zinjibar some thirty miles Northeast up the coast from Khormaksar. One Sunday lunchtime at Zinjibar all around this mud and white painted three-storey fort, biblical in its setting, goats nibbled in the sand at non-existent grazing, camels grunted and farted, veiled women chattered while children hid and whispered. A warm welcome was extended to us in the richly carpeted dining room with cushions round the periphery, and its floor centre table-clothed under plates of fresh food.

In this moderately sized room, we found ourselves sitting cross-legged around the walls on the cushioned floor along with a dozen local Arab dignitaries while servants poured green tea into diminutive cups. There was fresh cous-cous, dates, figs, olives and every variety of vegetable with a central,colossal, flat,silver-bowl, piled high with congealed, spiced brown, steaming rice, and atop of which was a beautifully presented and decorated whole roast lamb. It had been killed especially for the occasion and been slow roasted over a spit outdoors for nearly 48 hours: its smell was delectable. Torn off the hide using the right-hand only, and mixed with a handful of the olive oil and spice-soaked rice, that lamb rates as the best meat I've ever tasted. Indeed, the whole affair was an epicure's dream: pity about the lack of wine!

During the meal we could hear, but never saw, the women of the house chattering upstairs. They had lovingly prepared this meal for us, taking days to complete the task, and were then hidden above waiting for us to finish and depart, when they would have their turn at the left-overs. I know it's their custom, and I saw the same in high Bangladesh society years later, but it was such a shame that they were not allowed to mix with us infidels. It was indeed, an honour for us to even be there, and the roasted lamb was a tribute indeed.

On the Squadron, my first Flight Commander was a tall, dark New

Zealander called "Kiwi" Hounsell. He had a rough tongue, and his favourite expression when you were getting the regular, weekly dressing down was, "If you had a second brain, it would be f . . . . . lonely!" Needless to say, I heard this expression on many an occasion!

Conversely, we had a lovely, very experienced and worldly-wise, flying instructor whose name was Ron Etheridge. Together with his lovely wife Linda, they became Mum and Dad to the young bachelors of the squadron. We could turn up at their place at any time of the day or night, and it was often the latter, and know that not only would we be welcome, but that eggs and bacon would be on the table asap, and either a friendly ear would listen to our problems, or a game of crewroom Bridge would ensue. He taught me the game of Bridge, for which I shall ever be grateful. Without Ron and Linda we would have been headless, and it was to my utter disbelief that, some years later, he was killed in a Hunter crash at Shawbury. Ron was a wonderful man, Linda, sorely missed by all.

Soon after I arrived, Tammy Syme, our Boss, was posted and replaced. Again, I couldn't believe it, but the man who came through the door as our new Boss was Des Melaniphy, my unloved, ex-cadet instructor!

As a cadet I spent 5 months living in and cleaning a barrack block, after which we moved up to, wait-for-it . . . wait-for-it . . . No. 2 Officers' Mess! This was a ramshackle collection of black, wooden wartime huts, but at least we each had a single room. Here was where I got my first punishment – three days confined to camp from Flt Lt Des Melaniphy, who found some dust behind my wardrobe on one morning's inspection! He was a hard, not too popular individual, so much so that, during our week's camp on the Brecon Beacons, we got our own back – he broke his leg during a night escape and evasion exercise. How was I to know he'd become my first Sqn Cdr? Though if I had, I'm still not sure it would have saved his leg! I'm sure he never forgave us for that escapade in Wales!

When Al Pollock and I were posted together to Aden, Al went to the other Hunter Sqn, No. 43, who had a Fighting Cock as their emblem. They were the proud owners of four beautifully coloured fighting cocks kept in cages outside the rear of their Sqn ops building. When we were bored on standby, and 43 were off duty, many was the time we used to sneak round there and put two cocks together in the same cage to watch a fight. Well, after all, they looked more like mangey chickens, and what the hell were fighting cocks for anyway?!

Phil Langrill was our Sqn QFI. He had reason to be more than a little grateful for the robustness of the Hunter. He had an incident, repeated here in his own words:

> . . . *you might remember that I have reason to be grateful for the sheer strength of the Hunter airframe. On 16 Nov 65 I was programmed to be No. 4 on a practice Dawn Strike led by the late Dick Wharmby. Nick Kerr RN was in the section, too. Being the new boy, I was number four, and when I tipped into the 30degree attack dive, the three preceding aircraft had already done – or were doing – their stuff. At the customary 800 yards range I pressed the RP 'fire' button to mark the cine firing*

frame whereupon the Hunter flicked well over 90degrees to the right and then did the same to the left. I had flown into the jet-wash of the three aircraft ahead of me. The windscreen was full of very adjacent Arabian sand, so once the wings were fairly level I snatched the stick fully back and promptly blacked out. As I held the stick back against the stops I heard someone call "Number four has gone in" – but I hadn't. What he had seen was the sand blown up from my jet-wash – that's how near a thing it was. Of course, when I regained my vision, going straight up through seven thousand feet or so, the first thing I did was to look at the accelerometer reading. The gauge was calibrated up to $10G^2$, but the needle had gone well beyond that, right off the clock, so XG256 'N' had sustained at least 12G. I flew back to Khormaksar and landed very gently, in case anything fell off. I was sent to Steamer Point hospital for a once-over, to determine whether any of the internal fleshy bits had come adrift and the aeroplane was thoroughly checked. The engineers reckoned that although the maximum G-pull was probably 14G, the Hunter was perfectly fine. They demonstrated their faith in their judgement by promptly selling it to a foreign air force. I subsequently found that I was the co-holder of the RAF Massive Overstressing Record. My co-holder also did it in a Hunter. Hawkers built them strong. Really strong.

But the story didn't end there. As I was walking in from my greatly abused XG256 'N' for November, six pilots were walking out for a ceremonial flight, escorting the Britannia aircraft in which the outgoing colonial big-wig[3] was taking his final leave of Aden. All went well enough, with three Hunters in echelon off each of the transport's wingtips until one of the Hunter pilots called, "Who is flying 'N' for November?" No reply. Another pilot called, "It's Mike Flynn." "No, it's not," replied Mike, "I'm in 'O' for Oscar." Short pause . . . then another pilot called, "Do you want a bet about that?" Sure enough, my grossly abused Hunter had been refuelled and Mike had taken the wrong aeroplane. What a Hunter to choose in error!

Despite the white hairs obtained from night ground attack, it is an obvious fact of life that when it comes to picking a young officer to parade the Squadron Standard[4], the one who gets the nod is the tallest, blondest and most attractive! This is one interpretation of how at dusk on the 25th Feb '67, exactly 40 years since 8 Sqn had arrived in Aden, I came to be on parade as the Senior Standard Bearer with eight Standards on display – a record for any RAF Station. I was the only guy on the squadron who had a full-scale No.6 formal, tropical day dress uniform, bought specially for the occasion! It cost a fortune in those days: sixteen guineas from the local Arab tailor, and it was only worn twice, the first time being the dress rehearsal. Forty years later I still have it looking brand new, though I'm not sure if it still fits!

There were Nos. 8, 21, 37, 43, 84, and 105 Squadrons, plus Nos 2 and 16 Field Sqns RAF Regiment on display, and as the senior, I was at one end of the parade ground with the others in line abreast up to 100yards away. I felt sorry for the one at the far end who, over such a distance, had to react to my parade ground orders screamed without Sergeant-Major voice training!

We were there because my outfit, 8 Squadron, was receiving its second Standard; the first ever RAF squadron to have two! The official reason was simply that the old one had deteriorated badly with the climate in that part of the world, but we knew that it was really because there were too many beer and cigarette stains on it from too many raucous parties in the past! Still, it was an excellent excuse for a weekend's party, with 8 Sqn, the senior sqn on the base, at the centre of things.

The much liked CinC, ADMIRAL SIR MICHAEL LE FANU KCB DSC RN[5], later to die tragically as First Sea Lord, presented the standard to me in the twilight. Simultaneously, a diamond-nine formation flown by our Sqn pilots, flew past out of the setting sun.

Two previous Sqn Cdr's were invited from the UK: ACM SIR RALPH COCHRANE GBE KCB AFC RAF(RETD) OC 8 Sqn in 1929, and AM SIR HUGH WALMSLEY KCB KCIE CBE MC DFC RAF(RETD)[6] OC 8 Sqn in 1935. On the previous day, Friday the 24th, it was by a wonderful coincidence, SIR RALPH's 73rd birthday, and what better excuse for yet another celebration Sherry Party that night to start off the weekend's proceedings.

They were two lovely old codgers with many a story to tell, especially about Station Commanders. At the time, our Stn Cdr was Gp Capt Browne with an "e", and God help you if you spelt it any other way! He was an ex-bomber pilot, as had been his predecessor. Both were disliked intensely by the fighter boys in Aden, and so it came to pass that within 24 hours of arrival from UK, Sir Ralph had picked up the vibes! At the ensuing formal dinner, during his speech, he alluded to the fact that the first of every new type of aircraft arriving on the Sqn during his period, the 1920s, had been piloted by the Group Captain Station Commanders, and he had been forced to fly with them on those delivery flights. Apparently, in those days, it was difficult to land at Khormaksar due to the near permanent wind-shears on both ends of the runway, as the prevailing winds were forced to curl round the barren rocks of Aden close by, and the first of each new type had finished upside-down in the mud of the undershoot. The final words of his story were, "and that is what comes of flying with Group Captains!" It brought the house down, and he was chaired out of the dining room to the bar for an early start to the Sqn's 40th Anniversary [in Aden] Ball in the Officers Mess that evening, with continued celebrations lasting the whole weekend.

The following week, we all flew home to the UK for the laying up ceremony of the old Standard at the RAF church, St Clement Dane's in the Strand. I spent a gruelling week at RAF Uxbridge, being taught how to parade a Standard "properly" by a youngster of the Queen's Colour Squadron, who'd never been on parade with so many Standards in his life as I had recently!

Accordingly, it was an excuse for another party. As the Sqn had been in the Middle East for 40 years, it had never ever had a reunion, but with so many back home for this ceremony, what better excuse for the first ever 8 Sqn reunion, held at the RAF Club in Piccadilly on 12 Mar 67, to mark the Sqn's 50th Anniversary? Another lost weekend partying with over a 100 in attendance, but after having marched down the Strand into St Clement Danes with this tatty old Standard, I felt we deserved a bit of partying! Unfortunately,

2. The Author, 1(F) Squadron RAF Harrier Detachment flight planning tent on the airfield at Kirkwall, Orkney Islands, 5 Sep 78 for Exercise Northern Wedding.

3. Sandstorm halfway across Khormaksar airfield. (Photo looking North across the runway)

4. Al Pollock immediately prior to his Tower Bridge flight, Tangmere 5 Apr 1968.

(© No 1 Sqn archives)

5. Real Low Flying! Really the Thumrait Gate Guardian.

6. Hunter close to Thumrait, Oman – 1990.

7a & b. The Strafing Dive. *Above*: Swiss Hunter Firing all four 30mm Cannon. Muzzle flashes and the expended shell cases can be seen falling away below the aircraft. *Right:* Effects of 4800 rnds per minute of 4 x Aden 30mm.

(© Swiss Air Force)

8. The Aden Colony Peninsula – 1965. RAF Khormaksar runway in the fore-ground, Steamer Point – top right, Crater Arab quarter – top left and the curve of Khormaksar Beach – left central. The black, barren rocks of Shamsan Mountain, Aden, with rare cloud cover – top centre with the Maalla Straight in front.

9a & b. *Above*: Wilan – a typical Radfan village, 2000 feet above sea level.

Right: A typical Radfan landscape.

10. 1417 Flight print of Lamitar – a typical South Arabian wadi – Mar 64.
(© *Crown Copyright/MOD*)

11. 37 Sqn Shackleton and 4 x 8 Sqn Hunters, all of Strike Wing, Khormaksar, with the 6000 feet massif in the background.

(© *Crown Copyright/MOD*)

12. Presentation of the 8 Sqn's second Standard – RAF Khormaksar 25 Feb 67.

(© Crown Copyright/MOD)

13. 8 Sqn Standard laying-up ceremony – St Clement Danes Church – The Strand – 12 Mar 67. The author handing the standard to the Squadron Commander, Sqn Ldr Des Melaniphy, for laying on the altar.

(© Crown Copyright/MOD)

14. RAF Middle East Mountain Desert Rescue Team, somewhere between Mukalla and Khormaksar, on the way back from RAF Riyan, changing yet another tyre, checking yet another boiling radiator and/or looking at another broken spring. Christmas 65.

15. Flat topped hills of the Hadrumaut, and the one cobbled road, near Say'un 67.

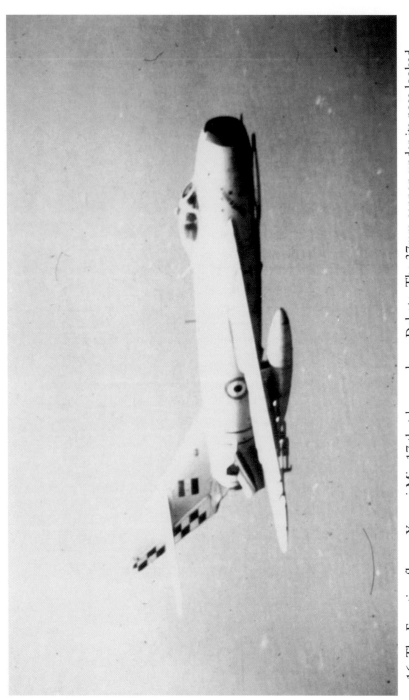

16. The Egyptian-flown, Yemeni Mig 17 that bounced our Dakota. The 37mm cannon under its nose looked enormous at the time!

it was the wrong way round; the party was on the Saturday night, 11th Mar 67, followed by the laying up ceremony in St Clement Danes on the Sunday morning, the 12th March. Of course, all the others had to do on the Sunday morning was sleep it off in the back rows of pews, while muggins here tried to act smart and sober in charge of the Standard party!

Twenty-five years later, the Sqn was the first to receive its third Standard. Now at RAF Waddington, as the RAF's AWACs Sqn, 8 Sqn invited me to be the reviewing officer at the parade where "my" old Standard received in Aden in 1967, was paraded off and laid up for the last time on 28th May 1992. The Duke of Gloucester was hurriedly asked to present the new Standard when Princess Margaret cried off at the last minute, apparently due to illness, but I shed a tear as I saluted from the dais while my Standard was marched off for the last time. Here, truly, we were losing a symbol marking the end of Empire.

1967 was certainly the year for formal occasions, as three weeks later the Sqn was heavily involved in another exclusive formal ceremony. On Saturday, 1st April . . . yes on April Fools' Day, and the RAF's birthday, one of our pilots, John Hill (or JB to his friends), was getting married in Aden: the only time in the forty years it had ever happened. All was arranged at the beautiful old colonial-style church at Steamer Point, with the reception at our Mess at Khormaksar, for the wedding of Fg Off J B Hill to Christine Brokenshire. Christine was the dark-haired, ebony-eyed daughter of our OC Accounts Sqn, and I had actually introduced her to JB: a real mistake!

Being April Fools' Day, the gods just had to intervene in a big way. We awoke that morning to find the heavens had fully opened, and it was bucketing cats, dogs and even camels! It hurled thirteen inches into Aden in three hours, carried on pouring for two days, and left the whole colony flooded and in complete chaos. Although it rained around Crater and the Shamsan mountain roughly once every two years, it rarely rained at Khormaksar. Nevertheless, this amount of rain was unheard of in fifty years, but it seemed not to bother the gods. Out of the blue and without any warning, over a century of rainfall deluged the place that Saturday morning. The whole airfield was under two feet of water; the aircraft operating areas were completely flooded, and the power station's flat roof collapsed, resulting in a complete loss of all but emergency power for nearly three months. Huge amounts of water built up on the lower slopes of Shamsan Mountain behind various security walls, which were then pushed over, pouring gallons of mud into the married-quarters area on the Maalla Straight. People were drowned and cemeteries washed away and, once the water had subsided, it left two feet of thick stinking mud, human remains and other odious detritus. Over 50years of wind-borne and human debris had swept down from the higher slopes of Shamsan, the black hill of Aden, and was deposited on the lower areas of road and surrounds. Later, once the sun got to work on this accumulation, the odour became invasive and utterly abhorrent.

But out of this mess rose one of the most beautiful sights ever seen in Aden. Two to three days afterwards, the black, granite, gaunt hills of Shamsan came alive with all the colours of the rainbow, and the desert turned green with grass. The windblown seeds, spread throughout all the rocky crevasses for more than fifty years, suddenly sprung to life, and for a few days the barren rocks produced every type and colour of flower in the book. It was almost miraculous, but as is the way with tropical plants, they didn't last: the intense sun and dry salt-laden atmosphere soon brought the hills back to their usual stark, satanic state. All the same, for those few days, the centuries of barren rocks were transformed into a tropical garden.

Longer term, constant cold food and no warm water for washing and shaving were the major results of this extraordinary weather, but the army did a sterling job in clearing up after the water had subsided a few days later, although it took over three months to restore everything back to a semblance of normality.

Meanwhile we had a wedding to reorganise! Because of the dreadful behaviour of the UN Team in residence at Crater, the locally employed personnel had gone on strike. This included the mess waiters. That Saturday lunchtime, as the rains subsided, we were running around rear-ranging things, the outcome of which was that the ceremony was moved hurriedly from the colonial church to our own little Nissen-hutted chapel 150yards behind the mess at Khormaksar. Four of us, wading through two feet of water, carried the bride to and from the chapel!

The reception went off without a problem with a cold buffet, despite our having to serve the food and drinks ourselves. However, we did succeed in launching the SAR Chopper, which flew over to Steamer Point, collected the marriage register from the church, and winched it back onto the flat roof of the mess during the reception for the signing ceremony. A little late maybe, but now they really were legally married! I'm sure that was a day of pomp and ceremony neither of them will ever forget.

Notes
1. Monsoon in an Aden context means a change in temperature, humidity and wind direction – not rain!
2. Maximum g allowed was 7g
3. Sir Kennedy Trevaskis
4. An RAF Standard is the equivalent of an army Colour, it includes the Squadron's battle honours, and is treated with the same respect.
5. His Excellency the High Commissioner, Sir George Turnbull KCMG should have been the reviewing officer, but had been unavoidably detained back in the UK, and the Cin C stood in for him.
6. Air Marshal Sir Hugh S P Walmsley retired as the RAF's last AOC-in-C India.

70

Chapter Nine

Up Country

Arriving in Aden for the first time, the majority would never step foot outside the tiny colony. They would spend their entire time, both work and play, on the Aden isthmus with only the black rock of the Shamsan mountain for a view. My main secondary role, pitched at me soon after joining the squadron, was the command of the RAF's Middle East Mountain Desert Rescue Team (MDRT). Of all the rotten duties that could have come my way, this one was an incredibly lucky dip. On the ground it was only a lucky few who saw even the Radfan and Dhala Road areas, never mind the soaring majesty of the escarpment above the Lawdar plain, or the beauty of the Sultan's Palace at Say'un, and the amazing walled city of Shibam in the Wadi Hadramaut. A unique opportunity to see the country, the whole of South Arabia and its people, was something no other Middle East fighter pilot managed, due to the terrorist dangers, during my time there.

MDRT was the only RAF unit allowed up-country on the ground on a normal, regular basis from Khormaksar. It was manned by 15 full time staff, plus a few part-time volunteers, and topped by a Sergeant: Sgt Pibworth, or Pib to us all, and I was to command it. Its main task was to be ready, at a moment's notice, to rescue any downed aircraft crews anywhere within the Middle East. Its complement was six short-wheel-based Landrovers, which included an ambulance vehicle equipped with mountain climbing, first aid and rescue equipment, and a radio vehicle with both U and VHF, and Single Side Band short wave radios.

Nevertheless, ground-to-ground radio communications in those days were extremely tenuous; there were no satellites in the mid-'60s. The Team, while up country only forty miles from Command HQ at Steamer Point, had to send radio messages using short wave, single side-band sky-waves via the military rescue coordination centre at Preston in Lancashire, who relayed them back to Aden. There was no way we could communicate directly with anyone in South Arabia who wasn't line of sight, and that was often only a few hundred yards in the mountains.

Our aim: *"To boldly go where no European had gone before!"* (with apologies to Thesiger!) Once out of the Aden Colony up-country, we could and did go almost anywhere we chose. Our various training exercises included mountain climbing, desert survival, first aid, rescue techniques and, of course, desert navigation, while helping to win the hearts and minds battle with the up-country tribes. It was the original mini-Lawrence of Arabia masquerade but, by the time I finished with the MDRT, I had a real love/hate relationship with the desert and its people in much the same way as did Lawrence.

Despite the troubles up-country, we in the MDRT were never hindered or threatened at any time. Quite the opposite: the locals fell over themselves to help in any way they could, as some of the next few stories will illustrate. It was always our belief that this was because all our vehicles were painted with the sign of the Red Crescent – the Arab Red Cross. Additionally, all vehicles had the team title in Arabic displayed. Indeed, we often dispensed first aid to the locals and brought back the odd one for treatment at RAF Khormaksar Beach Hospital, the only military hospital in the world set up specifically to treat the local people – hearts and minds! Yet, it had always struck me as a typical British dichotomy, in that I was attacking the dissidents in my Hunter dawn 'til dusk, Mondays to Fridays, then dispensing first aid through the MDRT for their hearts and minds at weekends. I was grateful that not a lot of locals knew that!

This was especially so during the occasions we were forced to drive through Sheikh Othman, one of the few routes into the desert but one of the hotbeds of dissident activity. On one occasion with three Landrovers, we were stopped in the Sheik Othman market place and surrounded at a distance by numerous tribesmen waving their rifles in a menacing manner. It seemed as though we had driven straight into an NLF meeting. At this point Sgt Pib muttered, *"I think we should f . . . -off back the way we came, Sir!"* . . . and it wasn't a question, *"I'm not sticking around here for tea!"* Without thinking, we took off our pistol belts, laid our arms on the seat and unarmed, slowly climbed out and walked round to the front where we pointed to the vehicle's Red Crescent sign. After what seemed an age, and to my utter relief, they slowly backed off and evaporated into the surrounding narrow streets, stalls and buildings letting us through. This was probably one of the more foolish of my actions, but it certainly produced a sublime moment! We didn't do much climbing that weekend!

Never called out in anger during my time there, the team spent most weekends training in the desert. Taking a retrospective view, the introduction of permanently based helicopters into the Aden theatre of ops in the mid-'60s, had made the MDRT a trifle redundant, though surprisingly we never practised rescue insertions using our helicopters, which with hindsight, would have been a good idea. Although we had a dedicated marine craft unit for sea search and rescue (SAR), none of our choppers were dedicated to SAR and, with so few available for the tactical transport role for the RAF Regiment and army units, they were really busy and we didn't exactly have any priority. Hence, having the capability to rescue in mountainous areas and conditions forbidden to rotary wings, we never queried our existence at the time.

Climbing soft, crumbly rocks of the forbidding Federation mountains of the rebel tribesmen was an extremely dangerous, yet vital skill engaging constant training. From regular, hard, black granite outcrops, through a 7000foot, almost vertical escarpment from the Lawdar Plain up to Mukeiras, via extremely rutted tracks, to the interminable, rolling sand dunes of the Empty Quarter, the MDRT had to be able to negotiate them all.

The Team's old Landrovers, though tough in themselves, were not up to the punishing conditions, the main problems being with *tyres, wheels, springs,* boiling *radiators,* and sand in the *air filters* (the *"flirty-five"* as they were known – flirting with one's destiny!). When tracks were available for driving, they were usually extremely rutted but, from experience, one's progress depended on the rut-frequency. A constant speed of 40 to 45mph was usually the best across the ruts when the track was straight enough or the desert level enough. At this speed the Landrover skimmed along on the ragged rut tops, keeping out of the ruts, and minimizing the vibrations, while keeping a "cooling" wind moving through the radiators. Unsurprisingly, we spent many hours crawling in high gear and four-wheel drive either because of the soft sand, or the regular rocky outcrops that had to be negotiated, and surprise, surprise, the radiators at these low speeds were always boiling over.

Travelling at high speed across any desert terrain during the day for any length of time brings further discomforts. Without goggles, one is prone, like snow-blindness, to sand blindness. Everything is shades of yellow and all perspective disappears. All potholes, ruts and rocky outcrops are unseen, at which point the journey abruptly halts as the apparently beautifully level track ends in an unseen pothole and another puncture or broken spring. Moreover, in order to minimize sand-blasting of the skin, each grain causing pin-point stings as it impacts at 40 mph, windscreens have to be kept up, thus losing the cooling ram-air effect. Even in good weather, the incessant wind produces continuous sandblasting. Ears, eyes and nose are particularly prone, and don't even think of opening your mouth! In this sand blown, featureless, arid, dusty, pallid-yellow atmosphere, slow progress is made in a continually irritable uneasiness.

The lack of rock climbing gave rise to one long detachment to the Eastern Aden Protectorate in December 1965, the story of which, when up country on the ground, well illustrates all these problems. A Beverley aircraft airlifted three of our vehicles including the radio vehicle to RAF Riyan, just east of Mukalla, the EAP capital. RAF Riyan was our nearest RAF staging post along the south Arabian coastline, some 400 miles from Khormaksar, and half-way between Aden, and Salalah on the southern Omani coast. It was the only one permanently manned and available to RAF traffic in the protectorate, though there were sand strips available up-country in the Hadramaut and also at Al Ghayda near the Omani border to the east. Riyan existed as the gateway to Mukalla, some 25kms to its west, and consisted of a short, rolled sand airstrip close to and parallel to the coast. It was manned by twenty men and two Flight Lieutenants, all unaccompanied and living in old wartime huts, with an Officers' Mess complete with an unused pink ladies' toilet, though no one could remember the last time it was used. Mike Kelson and his adjutant tossed a coin each day to see who would be the barman and who the customer for that evening in the Mess!

There, the MDRT was to spend three weeks rock climbing on a familiar-ization tour of the Wadi Hadramaut region, an area which fascinated me and I had longed to explore ever since my arrival in Aden. About a hundred miles from the Indian Ocean and below amazing flat-topped mountains, the Hadramaut was an exceptionally fertile sunken valley with an abundance of sweet water and miles of cobbled road along the wadi. In this most civilized part of all South Arabia, many houses had a downstairs room full of cool water for bathing, which afterwards flowed out to irrigate the gardens: early indoor pools!

Think of the flat-topped hillocks with sloping piles of shale around the bottoms, often shown as being features of the USA's Arizona desert, and that's the Hadramaut region. The wadi itself, is very wide, running roughly east-west for 150 miles and surrounded by these camel coloured hills. It is connected to the coast by two wadis running north-south from the coast either side of Riyan, known as the eastern whadi via Raydat, and the western wadi over the Jebel via Sadat. Despite the crumbling terrain, the guys had a unique series of exhilarating climbing experiences there.

On 28th Dec I flew into Riyan and met up with the team on their arrival back from the Hadramaut, where, after the fantastic journey including Christmas up-country, and raving about the area and the hospitality of the fiercely proud but independent tribesmen, they were ready for the air-lift back to Khormaksar.

The following day, as so often happened, the Beverley, flying in from Salalah to collect us, went u/s. Leaving us high and dry with no possibility of another aircraft in the near future, and away from home for the New Year celebrations, the Beverley overflew Riyan on a direct flight for its base at Khormaksar. This was a leadership moment! To the fore, and after a long discussion with Sgt Pib, I made the decision to drive back the nearly 400 miles along the desert coastline to Khormaksar, in order to be home in time for New Year's Eve, a journey we expected to last only two days: a classic case of "get-home-itis". In the aviation world, they are the type of flights that have the most problems. Why should it be any different on the ground? The MDRT was singularly unprepared for long desert crossings due to lack of training and decent equipment. This was not about to deter us! If you've ever watched Michael Caine in the film "Play Dirty", he and his band portray the Long Range Desert Group's problems in the Sahara during WW2. They were some-what similar to ours in the Arabian desert. Who says we learn the lessons of history! Hence, the decision to drive home set up another epic journey over which none of us had any control, least of all the CO!

Expecting to be home on the 31st, we left Riyan on the 30th, topped up to the gunnels with petrol, full spare jerry cans, and as much water as we could accommodate. But, there being no extra spares at Riyan, we had only one spare wheel and tyre per landrover.

An hour out from Riyan, and only twenty miles driven, Mukalla was a disappointment for the equivalent of a county town, with very rough, rocky, muddy and potholed main streets, and nowhere hospitable to stop for a drink or food. So we pushed on through the hot afternoon, taking a long time to negotiate Ra's al Kalb, the rocky headland just to its west.

The track lurched through overhanging rock at the top of the pass, while a white wayside Muslim pilgrimage icon glared at us as we stopped to take in the coast. From 500 feet above the never-ending curve of the white beach and breakers below was a splendid view. It was the one real moment of beauty, for by the time we had negotiated the rough rocky track around the headland, and were back on to the beach, we had changed two tyres, lost one spring on the third Landrover and were already half-way through the first stifling after-noon. At this stage, passing the village of Bir'Ali, close to the ancient incense route, which is surrounded by bubbling black volcanic rock terminating in an astonishing line of contrast with the pure, white sand of the beach, we had only driven some 60-odd miles, so a camp on the beach near Bal Haf was in the offing. So as Black and White Minstrels, we celebrated New Year's Eve under the stars, with little to help except a couple of Tiger Beers each!

By nightfall we were all completely exhausted and uncomfortable from the long, hot, noisy, bumpy, sandblasted journey. Meanwhile, there was more to worry about as we made camp. Whilst we had enough water for the Landrovers and our own needs, we had already used up two of our three spare wheels and tyres, and had lost three of the twelve springs between the three vehicles, with no chance of repairs. Worst of all, due to much time spent at low speed in high gear and 4-wheel drive, traversing more rocky ground than we had expected, we had used half our petrol, and were only a quarter of the way home. The expectation of better ground had come from the fact that the more familiar coastal area nearer to Khormaksar was a well-known long, shallow, smooth and hard, sandy beach that could be traversed at high speed safely, but this wasn't the case on the unknown eastern stretch.

This was my first close look at the desert of the Eastern Protectorate: my first real sight of the problems. Coming straight from England, where nature is hedged, ditched and drained into the perfection of submission, I suddenly discovered the insignificance of man! For three days we would crawl along unfrequented tracks and virgin desert where man was as scarce as a rare butterfly; outside Mukalla and Aqwah, man was indeed a rare animal, having but a precarious hold upon this land.

We pressed on, initially in the cool of the dawn next day, having decided to make for the village of Ahwar, just about two thirds of the way back, where we knew there was a Federal Army Fort. That second day of hot, dusty desert driving was fraught with problems and many stoppages, not only for the "flirty-five", but also on one occasion for Dai Rastall.

Dai was the only Welsh 8 Sqn pilot, and he'd flown out to Riyan with me for the ride, and I think he was beginning to wish he hadn't. What none of us knew was that he was prone to sodium deficiency, and part-way through the second day with the sun beating down from overhead, while we were having a drinks' stop and filling the radiators, Dai literally fell over in a dead swoon.

We had all trained thoroughly in desert first aid, so after forcing salt down his semi-conscious throat and almost drowning him in water to get it down, unbelievably he struggled up and within seconds made a complete recovery. As I've seen since, recovery is instantaneous on salt ingestion. Although he gave us a bit of a shock, Dai was as right as the rest of us within minutes. I have since come across this same problem in the Sahara desert at 51 degrees in the shade, and again recovery is immediate once some salt has been forced into the stomach.

By just over half-way, we were in a sorry state: there wasn't enough petrol to complete the journey. We had now used all our spare wheels and tyres, and indeed had mended numerous punctured tyres in an inch or two of precious water. But the worst problem was the loss of every single spring on all three vehicles; every one of them had snapped. We were now running on teeth-rattling hard bottoms with no protection from the vagaries of the desert. Eventually, through red-raw, squinting eyes, late that day the village of Ahwar eventually hove into sight, and engendered an unbelievable three month saga.

Driving into the FNG Fort, we found the diminutive but welcoming Arab Captain in charge, one of three little officers of the fort. All these people are small in stature, averaging about 5foot 2 or 3 inches. On being asked for some petrol, he directed us to drive round the corner into the village square, where we'd find a Shell pump. Now this is a dry, sandy little village of a dozen hovels, more a hamlet really, in the middle of the desert, 200 miles from anywhere of consequence with no roads except a couple of desert tracks, and we're being told there's a Shell garage!? It really didn't compute, and initially we all thought that the Captain was certainly fobbing us off with a story to get rid of us, albeit in the very friendly and pleasant manner of the hospitable desert Bedu.

But five minutes later, when we turned the corner into the "square", there in front of us was a large area of sand about 100yards square, open to the North and surrounded on the other three sides by low, single-story, white-painted, rock and mud houses. To my astonishment, right in the middle was a little Arab with an ageless, furrowed face, sitting and leaning apparently fast asleep against a single fuel hand-pump with the clam-shell insignia of the Shell Oil Co on top. As Michael Caine would say, "Not many people know that!" "Our saviour," I thought, and I've been a big fan of the Shell Oil Co ever since!

Of course, there was no electricity of any sort. It was only a hand pump, but that was no hinderance; we filled landrovers and jerry cans to capacity without a problem, until it came to the payment. When we didn't have enough Dinars between us for all that fuel – and I didn't foresee a need to carry a chequebook around in the desert – this little man's trusting and smiling acceptance of an IOU, on a McEwan's Beer chit, completely stunned us all. You'll never find this sort of trust again in the modern world!

I was minded of a W C Fields quote, "It took us a week to cross the desert. Things got so bad we had to drink water."! We then spent the night camped at the Fort, and left at first light to try and complete the drive to Khormaksar the following day, 2nd Jan 1966. As luck would have it, the going got better the further west we jolted until reaching Shuqra when, with seventy miles to go, we were eventually able to drive at a comfortable speed along the beach. This better going was an immense relief, not only from the bone-shaking vibrations, but also because we had no more spare tyres and had also run out of puncture kits! Trust me, not another tyre or wheel failed us all the way back on that last day.

The journey had two happy endings. Firstly, all our old, short-wheel-based Landrovers were subsequently written off without a fight with the MTO or Accounts people, a minor wonder in itself. Even better, they were replaced within a couple of months by five brand new, mine-plated and roll-barred, long-wheel-based versions, which though a little heavy for the desert, were an absolute luxury in comparison.

Secondly, three months later and just before Easter 1966, I was summoned to the office of Sqn Ldr Brokenshire, the OC Accounts Sqn at Khormaksar. He was pondering upon the claim he'd just received – on the desk was the tatty McKewan's chit, and in the corner of the office, to my amazement, there was the little pump attendant from Ahwar, sitting on his haunches!

As I walked in, the little Shell Agent's face broke into the biggest grin you

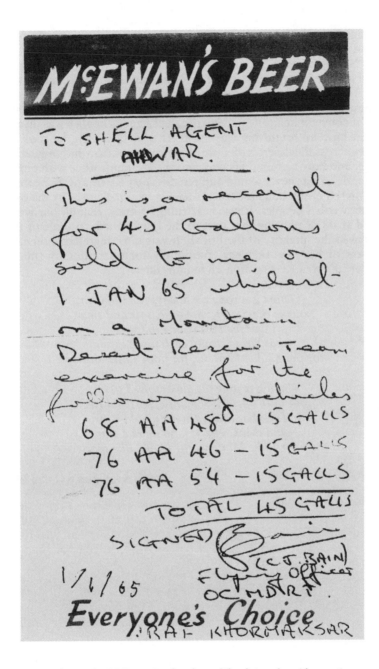

Fig 6. This is the IOU receipt for the uplift of petrol at Ahwar, 1st Jan 1966 (I know it says '65 twice on the chit, but these were mistakes at the time, having just changed years the night before!), redeemed at Khormaksar some three months later by OC Accounts.

can imagine, and he leapt up and pumped my hand vigorously for what seemed ages. I think it was only on seeing me that he believed he'd receive his money. Needless to say, I confirmed the chit's validity, he got his money, and I was able to retain the chit where it has remained in my scrapbook for 37 years[1].

Although I had picked up a smattering of Arabic to get by up-country, I could not converse in any depth, and the Shell Agent's English was on a similar scale. So how he found his way from Ahwar, how long he took for the 200miles across the desert with little or no transport, how he got himself onto the base, and how he found his way into the accounts office with our heightened security, I was never to find out. But this story is perhaps the best example I encountered of the immense trust placed in us, the British, by the ordinary, up-country tribal peoples. It was heartening to know that all our work over 130-odd years of policing that part of the Empire had, to some of them, at least proved the integrity of the British. It was most regrettable then, that all our years of hard work were completely torn asunder by the Wilson Government's treaty renegation 18 months later.

"There is a song we always used to hear,
out in the desert, romantic, soft and clear.
Over the ether came the strain,
that lilting strain, each night again,
for poor Lillie Marlene, for poor Lillie Marlene.

There is a song we always used to hear,
out in the desert, romantic, soft and clear.
Then back to Aden we would steer,
and drink a beer, with ne're a tear,
for poor Lillie Marlene, for poor Lillie Marlene."

(with apologies to Lillie Marlene)

Notes
1. 10 years later in 1978, after that epic journey, a tarmac road was completed by the Chinese joining Aden with Mukulla. Though it doesn't follow the coast in its central section, it is now 662 kilometres (415 miles) long.

Chapter Ten

Masirah

The RAF began to take an interest in the desert Island of Masirah in 1929, but the first flurry of activity came in the WW2 when Masirah played its part as one of our major staging posts on the wider stage of the Middle East. The RAF tenure lasted until 1977 when the airfield was sold to the Sultan of Oman's Air Force (SOAF), later renamed the Royal Air Force of Oman (ROAF).

Colin Richardson, Sqn Ldr (Ret'd), spent fourteen years on the Island, and is still sane! His descriptions in his book, *"Masirah, Tales of a Desert Island"* are well worth reading as they also cover the wider arena of Middle Eastern history. Masirah, part of the Sultanate of Oman, is a rocky offshore island in the Arabian Sea about ten miles from the low-lying mainland coast, and just southwest of the outlet of the Persian Gulf. It is a little larger than the Isle of Wight or the Isle of Man, though narrow and approximately forty miles long, and consists entirely of infertile, sandy plains and dark hills of crumbling, igneous rock rising to about 750 feet. A rather desolate place, the airbase still used is at its northern point.

Masirah has little, and in some years, no rain. Winter storms are usually responsible for any rain, not the southwest monsoon of the summer months. The summer monsoon here is a comparatively cool, southwest wind which persists for days on end. The rough sea is quite cold, and the murky air is salt-laden from sea spray. Vegetation is sparse and very hardy, despite only heavy dews supplying most of the water for the odd plant.

Animal life is also similar to that in Aden, with mostly small lizards, geckos, snakes, spiders, scorpions, and the occasional, inebriated RAF pilot! There is a small population of mountain gazelle, which were introduced by the grand-father of Sheikh Khamis bin Hilal, the latter being the sheikh of the island throughout the RAF tenure. Now that the local people possess Toyota Land-Cruisers and pickups, their domestic donkeys, camels and goats have been turned loose to fend for themselves as best they can, and often stray freely across the runway.

The vast majority of the local people live near the air base at the north end of the Island. Their historical status symbol is the camel, but their "bunga-lows" are generally made up from 40gallon oil drums, corrugated iron sheets, and cardboard, with the paradox of a modern Land-Cruiser parked outside. Some of the most impressive evidence of corrosion was to be seen at Masirah where all fuel shipped in was contained in these 40gallon drums. Ships had to

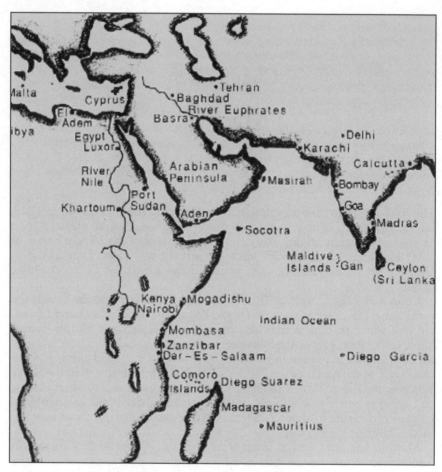

Fig 7a Sketchmap of Masirah Island (© COLIN RICHARDSON)

stand offshore in the shallow coastal waters for a difficult off-loading, and petrol drums were, therefore, non-returnable. Hence the empty drums were dumped in great stacks in the open desert, away from the station, and within a month these would have rusted away to dust.

If the land is barren, the sea is bountiful. The rich fishing grounds are only now beginning to be fully exploited, though even in the '60s large Russian fishing fleets, headed by enormous factory ships, were prominent. Almost every known turtle nests on the ocean coast, the northern coast being dominated by the extremely large, inedible omnivore, the Loggerhead Turtle. Over 35,000 nest here every year, and many were the BBQs on the beach while watching the turtles laying their eggs. The poor turtles always caused some dismay in that they were often so exhausted by their egg-laying that they needed help to reach the sea and freedom again afterwards; turtle carcasses were often to be seen.

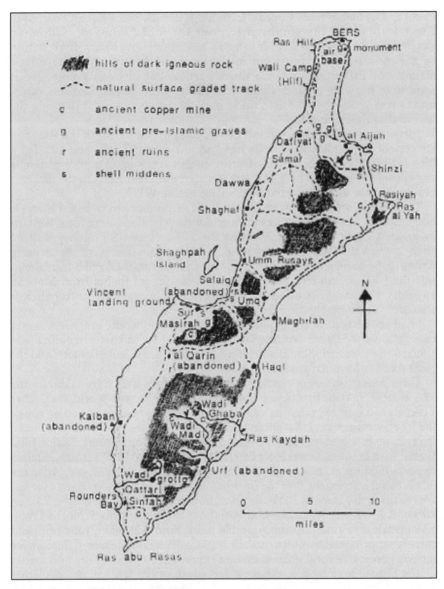

Fig 7b Sketchmap of Masirah Island (© Colin Richardson)

It was here I learnt to drive the backbone of air force logistics support, the three-ton Bedford truck. A truck was necessary to carry all the BBQ gear the fifteen or so miles to Turtle Beach just south of Ras Al Yah on the east coast. The good old Bedford with its four-wheel capability was ideal for heavy loads in the sand and desert conditions. For a Sqn of approx twenty officers, the wine cargo alone was quite heavy, often coming in Jerry cans, being full of cheap Cochinelli from Cyprus! In those days with every Kebab ordered in any restaurant in the southern Cypriot town of Limmasol, unlimited Cochinelli was provided free! It came in bulk, therefore, to any RAF station on the main transport route out to the Far East! Accordingly, I have little memory of driving back from those parties, but obviously managed it somehow, notwithstanding there were no metalled roads, and our three-tonner was probably the only vehicle moving anywhere on the Island in the '60s at that time of night!

Forty years ago the tiny, indigenous population subsisted on the fish, and ate very little else. Brackish wells supplied just enough water and they led a life of deprivation and squalor, their mean diet resulting in a poor physique and chronic ill-health. These days life is better, due completely to the facilities available at the airbase started by the RAF before WW2.

The island's airfield, remote and isolated as no units were based there, is often used for covert operations throughout the Middle Eastern area. Perhaps its greatest claim to fame was during the 1980 "Iran US Embassy hostage crisis", when the Americans organised an air rescue that went disastrously wrong in the Iranian desert. The USAF Hercules that crashed and burnt, along-side the USN helicopters, had all begun those fateful flights from Masirah airfield. Of course, British and mainly American transports and tanker aircraft also used it extensively during the Gulf Wars.

I had six visits to Masirah, and the Sqn spent two weeks every four to six months on the Island, from where some excellent intensive training was effected over the forbidding, almost deserted southern Omani desert, and the Jebel Akhdar Mountains to the west of Muscat.

These mountains were the 8,000 foot high Jebels that were taken by the SAS in 1958, in their first desert campaign since the Second World War. After a communist inspired uprising amongst the village tribesmen in and on top of the Jebel, we supported the Sultan by putting D Squadron of 22SAS in to quell the trouble in a "secret" war. In one of their boldest operations, Major John Watts[1] with Lt (later, General Sir Peter) de la Billiere and No.18 troop, climbed some forbidding, vertical, rock-cliffs at night, with full bergens, surprising the rebels to such an extent that the uprising was crushed. Having flown over the area many times since, it looks similar, though smaller, to the hostile Radfan area of Aden, where we used whole battalions to quell uprisings. No.18 Troop SAS managed to climb the inhospitable Jebel Akhdar at night, fully equipped carrying approximately 80lbs on their backs, which must be one of their major unsung heroics, beyond normal human experience.

The Omani mainland to the west and south of the Jebel is an undulating desert strewn with great forts that dot the old trade routes and wadis. These forts, surrounded by wind-blown baked scrub, are thick-walled, mud-bricked organic edifices that were (probably still are) the basis of clan thuggery and dynastic intrigue. Together with the Sheikhs of up-country Aden, and indeed those throughout the Arab world, they welcomed us all but trusted none. The desert nomad throughout southern Arabia is a wanderer following his flocks, responsible to none bar his family, but governed by an unwritten law of steely formality, never forgiving, never forgetting, preoccupied with long-standing feuds, and bowing only to his God and the crescent moon.

Still, our main reason for being at Masirah was to show British support for the Sultan of Oman. We mostly operated 4-ship formations at low level throughout the country making as much noise as possible to ensure the local tribesmen were aware of our policing presence, and reminded them that terrorist activity would not be tolerated here. These detachments also gave us continuous familiarity with the Gulf stations at Sharjah and Muharraq (Bahrain), then considered a necessity in case of another Iraq/Kuwait crisis. How considerations have changed.

Masirah was also the only RAF base where beating up the runway on arrival from any mission was officially allowed. This was simply because it was the best method of clearing any goats, donkeys or camels off the runway before landing. But equally, it was the only place where I've stood in the air traffic control tower and looked down on to the upper surface of the wings of an airborne Vulcan V-bomber doing at least 350 knots below me!

A whole Squadron detachment, away from its main base with all its rules and regulations, needed no excuse for bonding and partying and RAF Masirah was the ideal retreat for this. A lot of effort was put into drinking the Mess bar dry before we left, and the high-jinks were plenty and noisy!

For example, there was a short, narrow-gauge railway line from the base to the pier used for transporting the heavy cargos from the supply ships. Newcomers were always told, as the Mess bar closed for the night, that if they wanted to carry on drinking, just follow the railway line and at the other end was a night club called "The Golden Flip-Flop"! It was amazing how many guys fell for this tale, and could be seen weaving their boozy way down this railway line looking for this mirage in the desert!

But our high jinks ended abruptly, part way through our February 1966 detachment, due to that great military banger: the Thunderflash. Used for peacetime exercises, this massive firework, the size of a stick of dynamite, was designed to make an loud explosive bang simulating a grenade going off. It can be very useful for fishing, but more normally you light the touch-paper, throw it as far as you can, and run.

Outside the Officers Mess at Masirah were two old ship's cannon, the calibre of which fitted a Carlsberg beer can with a toilet roll wrapped round it! If you put a Thunderflash down the barrel first, then rammed in your beer-can, they would fire the can at or just over our two accommodation Portakabins, fifty yards away, where we all had our bunks! Inevitably, this became too tame, and the two flights would thrash out the fight between their huts using Thunderflashes thrown through the windows and doors.

My part in these games can now, for the first time, be freely admitted. After creeping round the side of the other flight's hut late one night, and succeeding in getting a lit Thunderflash inside, I watched, when after the ensuing bang, an unfortunate Dai Heather-Hayes staggered out with blood streaming from what was left of his nose. A large piece of the flash had taken half of it away! Sobering up rapidly, we rushed him to sick quarters as fast as we could and called the Doc.

Being almost uninhabited, Masirah was the easiest place for everything to be completely hushed up! Dai was casevaced back the 1000 miles to Steamer Point RAF Hospital in Aden the following day on the RSM² Argosy, and a fantastic plastic job was duly performed on his nose. Today you'd never know he'd ever had a problem. Meanwhile, the Boss and the Doc submitted reports to the effect that he'd tripped in a drunken stupor over the concrete steps outside the Portakabins, and I bought Dai beers for the rest of his time in Aden! Indeed, one memorable evening in his bedroom at the hospital, we managed to get the empty Tiger beer cans ten abreast piled up to the ceiling!

Joking apart though, after this escapade I was a very worried man for many days, only returning to normal once it was obvious that Dai was going to make a complete recovery. We were both very lucky: it could have been a career-ending incident – for both of us!

For once I didn't fly my aircraft back from Masirah, but flew home on a Beverley transport aircraft of 84 Sqn with our groundcrew via Salalah, my first time there. Our two-seater trainer Hunter T7 couldn't make the 1000-mile trip in one hop, having smaller 100gallon underwing tanks than the FGA9, and had to refuel at Salalah. Salalah was only a rough oiled-sand strip then, so the Beverley was used to support this refuelling. Landing and taking off from that surface in a modern jet with high-pressure tyres was bone-shaking and teeth-rattling. However, in the Beverley en-route I was allowed up to the flight deck where the pilots let me fly this enormous beast. A rude note was very soon passed down from our groundcrew sitting in the tailboom, impolitely requesting that the crew kicked me out of there, ". . . 'cos he's making us sick"!

The final escapade could also only have happened at Masirah in those days. I've mentioned the peer group pressure to drink the bar dry before we left each time. Well, on my last visit in June 1966, the whole Sqn was due to fly out to Khormaksar on the Friday July the 1st. So, on the Thursday, when we had finished flying at lunchtime as usual, we all repaired to the Mess bar in an attempt to drink it dry before departing early the following morning.

At about 3pm, after some two to three hours boozing, the phone started ringing in the bar, and eventually someone collared me and said the Boss was after me. Worrying what I'd done wrong this time, I picked up the phone and the Boss said, "Get your kit on. You and Mac are flying to Bahrain ASAP to collect some spares!"

I said, "But . . . but Boss, I'm pissed!"

"Get your kit on. Ya going!"

"But . . . but Boss, I'm pissed!"

"Get your kit on. Ya going!"

Numerous repetitions later, I finally got the message, found Mac, also inebriated, and off we went – the only time in my whole life I've ever know-ingly got airborne pissed! Apparently, one of our aircraft was u/s and needed a spare part, available from Bahrain, before it could fly back to Khormaksar with the others the following day, and this started another train of events over which I had no control!

Ordered into the air, in a somnambulistic trance, Mac and I took off gasping pure oxygen. We had briefed to climb as a pair (never send a single engined aircraft across the empty quarter on its own) in battle formation 2000yds line abreast, at flight level 360 (36,000feet), and all went well 'til we got to 30,000feet. At that point we entered what looked like a very thin layer of cirrus cloud, lost visual contact with each other, and made the decision to climb above it.

Fifteen minutes later, and by now hardly climbing nearly at max altitude, I broke out of the top of this "thin" layer at FL460 (46,000feet), but no Mac; he never made it! We then decided to descend below it, and finally broke cloud some twenty minutes after losing sight of each other. I looked round for Mac and, to my surprise, found him in perfect battle formation – BUT ON THE OTHER SIDE! Somewhere up there in that cirrus we had crossed over, probably missing each other by feet. With the help of the 100% oxygen we were breathing, this shock sobered us both up instantly.

Unfortunately, these incidents don't end that simply! Sober now, we landed uneventfully in the early evening at Muharraq, Bahrain, picked up the spare part, ordered transport for the morning, put in a flight plan, turned the aircraft round ready for a dawn take-off the following day back to Masirah, and went to the bar. The first one went down without touching the sides!

We both slept rather soundly that night, but were ready at 5am out at the front of the Mess, waiting for transport to take us to our aircraft. Typically the transport never arrived, but there just happened to be a very inviting RAF police Landrover parked nearby with, would you believe, the keys in it, begging to be borrowed! We left the Landrover on the aircraft pan as we taxied out, and then legged it at full throttle back to Masirah with our spare part. The whole Sqn subsequently took off on time later that morning for Aden. Job well done, we thought!

Three weeks later, a police report from Bahrain landed on the Boss's desk complaining about a random ghostly movement of an apparently driverless RAF Police vehicle which, at dawn one Friday morning, had been found abandoned with the keys still in it next to the Hunter dispersal area at Bahrain, – all of which, of course, "we knew nothing, Que!" Mac and I in trouble again, but he was from Barcelona!

I was never to return to Masirah after that!

Notes
1. The same officer who commanded D Squadron in Aden, mentioned in Chapter 7.
2. Riyan, Salalah, Masirah.

Chapter Eleven

Desert Islands and Twin Pistons

No. 21 Squadron, known as the Middle East Comm Sqn (MECS), with a motley collection of Twin Pioneers, Dakotas and Andovers, was the mainstay of the local short-range transport fleet, whose role was supporting the troops up-country from Khormaksar. Their two Dakota Mk IVs were the real work-horses, as this type of aircraft, the DC3 in civilian parlance, had been used in vast numbers worldwide for many years – and some still fly today. They were the backbone of short-range air transport the world over, and a symbol of frontier resupply – not fast but they covered a lot of ground.

Due to paucity of space with so many aircraft on base, the Daks were usually parked on the civilian apron outside the military barbed wire area, but adjacent to the Hunter fighter dispersal area which had a common barbed wire boundary with the airport. This lead to my eventual qualification as the only fighter pilot to qualify as a DC3 co-pilot, the lowest form of life on a flight deck, during an operational fighter tour! It was also my first attempt at flying tail-wheelers, my first ever piston-engined aircraft, and my first ever twin-engined aircraft. But what an exhilarating way to learn those skills! No cushy training course – just get in and fly it, and learn on the job in an area akin to the North-West Frontier!

Towards the end of '66, one of the Daks was being prepped on the civvy pan to take some army brass up country. Just before boarding, the Captain found something wrong with the aircraft and proceeded to board the second machine which subsequently took off with the brass on board. Just after take off, the first unserviceable aircraft still on the pan blew up. Apparently, earlier, a local civilian airport employee had delivered a bomb onto the flight deck. Fortunately, due to a simple magneto drop during pre-flight checks, the aircraft wasn't used and no loss of life ensued, although the aircraft itself was a complete write-off.

At that time, MECS had two Dakota crews, but after the bomb incident they posted three of the four pilots home, leaving Flt Lt Mike Bennett as the only qualified pilot and captain. I soon heard about this shortage while talking in the bar to Alan Barker, a short, blond, friendly guy who was the Dakota Nav, and I volunteered to act as second pilot to give Mike some relief. As I had every alternate 24hrs off from Hunter Ops, I was often able to fill in and had many happy and adrenalin generating times flying this venerable dog-eared machine.

My Dak pilot's notebook was promulgated by the US Army Air Force, dated Feb 1941, and had actually been updated and amended to Feb 1942! What I didn't know until 40 years later was that my father had had many hours on Daks at the end of WW2, flying, inter alia, POWs home from Germany. He probably used the same set of pilot's notes!

Flying the Dak I was able to see on the ground for the first time all the distant, up-country towns, villages, forts and airstrips, the general desert and mountains, and meet the people over which I'd flown my Hunter so many times. Even the Desert Rescue Team didn't get into all the places one could land in the very versatile Dak.

No one was allowed up-country outside the Aden State unless on operational duty, and flying Hunters over the same country, day after day, gave a different perspective as there was only one place to land – Khormaksar! Indeed, our only diversion airfield was Djibouti on the African coast at a range of 135 nautical miles from Khormaksar – a long way across the Gulf of Aden in a single engined jet, short of fuel after a long-range, low-level desert mission! So the Dakota was the only way to experience the far flung corners of this desert empire.

Besides the up-country resupply to local army units, the Dak was used for numerous longer range supply missions, which were either too far for the small Twin Pioneers, or too small for the larger Beverleys and Argosies. Amongst others, we had a monthly task to supply the High Commissioner on Kamaran Island. This small island was some 150 miles up the Red Sea, and about 8 miles off the Yemeni coast but inside their territorial waters, some 40 miles North of the Yemeni town of Al Hudaydah where the Egyptians had based a few Mig 17 fighters. An island of approx 80 square miles, Kamaran had one heavily bearded Scottish High Commissioner, and an indigenous population of 3000, swelling occasionally to three times that during the Haj pilgrimage, being only a short flight south of Mecca. Once a staging base on the far eastern route for short-range British fighters such as the venerable Venom, it had a short, rough sand, landing strip. On each visit, two crates were supplied for the High Commissioner: one of food and one of Whisky!

We'd passed abeam Al Mukha (Mocha of coffee fame) and were approaching abeam Al Hudaydah when, proceeding to do mock quarter attacks on us, two Yemeni Mig17 fighters, each with a vicious looking 37mm cannon under the nose, bounced us on our first trip into the island. Of course, from our perspective, it was quite frightening being in a lumbering old Dakota, and not knowing whether each was mock until it was over!

Meanwhile, our radio operator, Master Signaller Richards, quickly tapped out a W/T emergency call to Middle East Command, while I assured the rest of the crew that, naturally, our standby pair of Hunters would quite obviously turn up before long, and we'd be entirely safe! But eventually, after four or five attacks, the Migs, tiring of the sport and peeling off and departing, left us alone to land safely on the island strip.

A couple of hours later you could have knocked me over with a feather when, instead of the Hunters, our dear, ancient, 37 Sqn, standby search and rescue, four-engined, maritime patrol aircraft, the Shackleton, pitched up overhead . . . with a Mig 17 on each wing!

Outside the corrugated-iron hut that masqueraded as the Kamaran airport terminal building, stood probably the most unusual of "airport" notice boards (see photos). Giving basic Island statistics on the front of this 8ft x 5ft board, it showed the destinations, via Aden Airways in 3 directions from "Kamaran, Land of the Two Moons", followed by the letters PTO! On "PTOing" round to the back of the board, the following could be read:

THE REAR OF THE BOARD REPEATED:

Established 1882
Your Questions Answered:
LAND OF THE TWO MOONS
KAMAR: MOON – KAMARAN: TWO MOONS
STANDING ON NARROWEST POINT OBSERVE:
MOON PROPER RISING IN EAST
And
REFLECTED ON SEA WEST
*

I	Yes, it is very hot in summer – humidity high.
II	Yes, it rains sometimes.
III	Yes, plenty of water: 200 brakish[sic] wells. We drink distilled water and prefer it.
IV	Europeans: Normally just one. Quite normal.
V	Lonely: No.
VI	Fishing: Marvellous. Non-expanding variety.
VII	Cinema. Yes, but no films.
VIII	Trees: How many? Both are flourishing thank you.
IX	Name 3 people we would take with us to a desert island: Impossible, don't know what a desert island looks like.
X	You are now standing 51ft above sea level. On the level!

Its position in the very mouth of the Red Sea, 150 miles south of Kamaran and 100 miles west of Aden, also gave Perim Island its strategic importance. Previously a site of an ex-Empire radio and broadcasting station, it was also on the extreme SW corner of both the Aden Protectorate and the Yemen, and just south of the Yemeni port of Al Mukha (Mocha) from where the rich coffee crop used to be exported, along with its anti-British sentiment against the Aden colony. This particular anti-Britishness was all due to the trade competition in the 1800s, because Aden was actually closer to the coffee fields than Mocha itself. Whichever port charged the lowest duties kept the trade, and eventually Aden won after a touch of commercial genius in 1848 when it introduced the first ever free port. Within 5 years Aden became the main port for Yemeni Mocha coffee exports, and Al Mukha became a ghost town when 4000 of its inhabitants moved to Aden, though, of course, the coffee variety's name has always remained Mocha.

With total command of the southern entrance to the Red Sea, where a British presence, as well as ensuring no one else's, was an obvious strategic necessity, Perim Island also had a small, rolled sand airstrip capable of taking our Dak. Accordingly, despite the radio station having been withdrawn and the Island now uninhabited, we used to fly in there as a flagwaving exercise periodically to show a British presence and to curtail any Yemeni thoughts of taking it – such was its strategic importance. This also provided the crew with yet more totally deserted, beautiful tropical beaches upon which to laze away one's crew duty time while our presence was noted on the mainland![1] It is now a no go area to foreigners, along with the whole Yemeni south-western corner – a Yemeni acknowledgement, and teaching Denis Healey, of its obvious strategic importance.

Undoubtedly though, Socotra Island, off the Horn of Africa, was the jewel in the crown of re-supply islands, where, besides a tiny, indigenous population and a small platoon of troops, there was often a seismic survey team working at that time. This was the largest and most beautiful of untouched islands, with not only unique flora and fauna, but also an inland mountain range surrounded by stunning blue lagoons and totally deserted, white coral sand beaches, yet a third holiday resort just waiting to happen. Here at Hadibo on the Northeast coast, the gravel and stone runway ran downhill at right angles to, and directly onto, the beach. Such was the gradient that you could only land up-hill from the beach end, and take-off downhill onto the beach. It made for an exciting take-off, running steeply downhill towards the sea, which seemingly filled the windscreen before flying speed was attained, and the aircraft yanked into the hot, heavy air at the last possible moment. Uniquely, at the inland end of the runway, was the wreck of an old Aden Airways Dakota with Royal Mail insignia on the fuselage. What made it significant was its registration code: VR-AAA (see photo), the first registered aircraft on the Aden register, and one of the oldest. Although it hadn't survived its final landing, no accident details have ever been found, but it was very useful for marking the very end of the runway which, from above, looked little different from its surrounds.

Despite the undoubted privilege of witnessing some uniquely isolated scenery and vistas not normally available to the majority, flying this old rattle-trap was not always pleasurable. The old girl was occasionally quite temperamental, and certainly kept us on our toes. More engine failures were experienced in a few flight hours on this Dak than in a whole flying career put together. These included one memorable double engine failure on final approach to Khormaksar, when, after a 150-mile flight on one engine from Ahwar, the second failed just before touchdown at Khormaksar, and though it landed short, it did so without damage.

If that was scary, then even worse was the Dakota participating, strongly, in my only fully-out-of-control ground loop! On 29 May '67, while landing on a rough up-country strip on top of the escarpment at Mukeiras on the Yemen border, some 6000feet above sea level, just prior to touchdown we observed on the two large, white hydraulic pressure dials, two big round zeros! Total brake and pneumatic pressure failure, and total panic ensued simultaneously. Managing to miss the drainage ditches that ran down both sides of this narrow, rolled oiled-sand runway, the Dak ground looped to starboard off the strip, around the central, rolled-sand semi-circular dispersal area – twice, before coming to an ignominious but undamaged halt. Being committed to land, utter alarm had erupted in the cockpit with totally crossed joystick, throttles and pedals giving a minuscule semblance of aircraft control, fear emanating from the passenger cabin, and right in front of the now apprehensive passengers we'd come to pick up! I don't think they were amused by our novel and untried, express parking method, and if I said we were in total control for that last minute, I'd be pushed to put my hand anywhere near a Bible. But, missing all the drainage ditches surrounding the runway and dispersal, Lady Luck was with us that day!

In early '67, the United Nations sent a delegation to try and provide answers to the political and security problems facing the colony and the protectorate. That mission turned into a complete farce and only made the situation worse. In an attempt to put the colony back on track, Lord Shackleton was sent out by the British Government. As part of his fact-finding mission, the Dak was chosen for its famous, worldwide ability to carry a reasonable load unsupported over long distances, and its capability to operate from almost any of the extremely rough airstrips in the Eastern Aden Protectorate. We took the good lord on a three-day trip round the Hadramaut Area of the Eastern Aden Protectorate to talk to the local sheiks. On the 25th May '67 we flew him to RAF Riyan, close to the Qu'aiti state capital, Mukalla, where he talked to local chiefs and the young, 18-year-old, Qu'aiti sultan, and where we spent the night. The following day, we took him, together with James Ellis, the resident adviser to the sultan, on to the extreme eastern airstrip and FNG Fort at Al Ghayda, the capital of the easternmost Al Mahra province on the Qamar Bay coast, and just 60 miles from the Omani Dhofar border, for more talks with the Mahra tribal leaders. We then flew Northeasterly inland to the Hadramaut and landed at Al Ghuraf at the mouth of the Wadi Adim. We were driven round Tarim, a city of Palm trees and Baroque palaces, before moving on to Say'un, the Hadramaut capital, site of the Sultan's Palace (see photo), and largest town in the area. Here Lord Shackleton spent some hours at each stop and town, talking to the sultans, sheiks and the local people and dignitaries, before returning to Riyan for the second night.

In the Hadramaut, we could have been in Arizona except for the heavily fortified, multi-storied, sometimes highly decorated, mud houses of the villages and towns of the area, the most auspicious being the city of Shibam in the mouth of the Wadi. Shibam is an astonishing, 400 year old, walled city of only 500 metres square into which are packed 500 skyscrapers of some five to seven storeys high (see photo). In between, there are only extremely tight, narrow alleyways where it doesn't do to loiter, not for the usual reasons, but because the little chutes projecting from the upper stories are the only toilet exits, and are as likely as not to pour human detritus into the street from a great height at any time! It is now a UNESCO World Heritage site!

On the 27th, after spending three days both in the air and on the ground,

90

meeting people and showing the lord the fantastic, flat-topped mountain scenery of the Hadramaut Wadi and Shibam, we flew him back to Khormaksar. I have never been sure whether we did any good on that trip, especially mindful of the way the conflict ended, but at least he got a feel for the place and the people to help him make any decisions, even if the sheikhs no longer trusted him and his government; he was, after all, very left wing.

The Hadramaut was cut off from most modern day conveniences by the mountains and long distances, and it was too far for the Hunters to patrol regularly. With the exception of the DRT, it was to us a relatively unknown area, ripe for infiltration from Oman and Yemen, as has since happened on numerous occasions. To its north was the Empty Quarter, The Rub 'al Khali, endless rolling sand dunes and an almost completely unmapped wilderness for over 1000 miles in every direction. This, mentioned in chapter 1, was Thesiger country. The fluctuating contours of this land ebbed and flowed with dunes up to 100 miles long and sometimes up to a 1000 feet high. After two long, lone explorations in the 1940s, learning about the Bedu, who themselves didn't travel well through the area, Sir Wilfred had probably come to know more than any other European about this barren quarter. Even we didn't fly into that area by Hunter, or Dakota, on our own.

Further East, RAF Salalah, the next route station beyond Riyan along the South Arabian coast, was the main base for SW Oman, until Thumrait was built inland. Known colloquially as 'Midway' because it was the midway point between Aden and the Gulf stations, Thumrait was built high on the Jebel, 40 miles North of Salalah, and it too had its share of bizarre terrorism. The Dhofar campaigns on the Omani-South Arabian border are well chronicled elsewhere and not for this book, but we also ferried support to the RAF contingent at Salalah, where a constant fight was continuing. One comical part of this campaign was such that watches were set by it every evening. This was the 6 o'clock shoot out when the terrorists let loose at the base for 10 minutes, the base returned fire, and all then returned to the bar for another beer.

Because of the MDRT and the Dakota, unlike any of the other fighter pilots in South Arabia, I was endowed by the time I returned home with a more profound understanding for the country and its people. Many was the time we brought injured tribesmen and pregnant Arab girls back to the Aden hospitals from up-country, since we often returned from our supply runs at least partially empty. Hearts and minds again, and for me, it was these aspects that produced the fulfilment of my fascination with this forbidding country and its people.

Of course, there's always a downside. The only concession we made was to have the tribesmen empty their rifle breeches before boarding, but if a pregnant lady came on board for the hospital run, so did her whole family, kids, sheep, goats, Khat[2], their food, the lot! On these occasions we were forced to fly with the cockpit side windows open. The tangy stench of their dried meats, fish and animals, mixed with our Elsan toilet fumes, was one I would not bottle up for further enjoyment; it was utterly obnoxious and unbreathable! At these times, the Hunter's 100% oxygen capability would have been most welcome!

It was during this period that I met Captain Vic Spencer, the well-known Chief Pilot of Aden Airways. Of course, they were flying Dakotas on the same routes also, and if I thought some of the up-country strips we landed on were rough, then Vic's experiences were much worse. Long before I had even heard of Aden, Vic was landing Daks on rough Wadi beds, and indeed, he had "built" – ie: placed stones around – many of the sand and stony strips that we used. In fact, a deluxe landing strip was one in which the stones had been painted white! Today they would have commanded higher landing fees!

The penultimate Dakota to see RAF service[3], and certainly the last in operational service, our old lady – KN452 – was flown home to be sold in August 1967. The old lady took a long, westerly route across Middle Africa, up the African west coast, and on to Gibraltar. Sadly, I missed that trip, as we were extremely busy on the Hunter Wing with anti-insurgency patrols. But they did get Alan's little Fiat 500 in the back of the Dak (just) and flew it home for free. Just as well, because with our imminent withdrawal, the bottom had dropped out of the local second hand car market!

The venerable old Dakota, workhorse of third world aviation and backbone of air transport and supply for decades, was never properly replaced, and when ours left Aden, departing into the sunset for the last time bound for the UK, it surely symbolised the retreat of the crumbling British Empire.

Nevertheless, up-country in all its guises provided an absorbing spectacle of savage splendour that bred a lifelong craving for adventure. What is there to discover behind the next rock, the next sand dune or the next island? Usually nothing, but you never knew. *"The charm of the desert is the absence of intellectual life there, the freedom one's mind gets from anxiety in looking forward or pain in looking back."*[4] I would add to that: and the freedom to prove your skills and capabilities.

Certainly, we had never conquered South Arabia; we lost the hearts and minds battle and, indeed, we lost the campaign due to lack of political will. Today, we are now most certainly paying for that shabby attitude, having left a cauldron within which Yemeni and international terrorism boils.

Notes
1. 43 Sqn and 1417 Flt used the island for desert survival training very, very occasionally!
2. Khat. A Spindle tree leaf, chewed in abundance by the Arabs for its mild narcotic effect.
3. There was still an RAF Dakota based at AFNORTH HQs in Oslo at the time, but it too was soon replaced by an Andover.
4. Lady Anne Blunt of Arabia and Egypt –daughter of Lord Byron – 1837–1917.

Chapter Twelve

Withdrawal Symptoms

Background Events

Due to the unrelenting terrorism throughout 1965–66, the UK government thought to withdraw but to keep Khormaksar as a main RAF operating base, much like RAF Akrotiri later became in Cyprus. This was a wise decision, but was fatally changed to a complete withdrawal after the fall of the Federal Government and its replacement by the National Liberation Front (NLF), who were extremely hostile to Britain. The largest, ever, RAF base was about to be lost.

At Khormaksar, mortar bombs could be fired into the station from the Arab quarters of Sheikh Othman and Champion Lines under cover of darkness in an indiscriminate attempt to damage aircraft. So crowded was the airfield, and so cramped the hard standing areas, that aircraft had to be parked almost wing tip to wing tip, and were thus extremely vulnerable to indiscriminate attack. So all other aircraft if necessary would be dispersed, leaving our Hunter Wing on base where we had to remain for defence purposes. In the event, it never became necessary to put this plan into action, so well secured were we by the Army and RAF Regiment; as the main air force offensive assets, we were well cocooned from the majority of Aden Colony terrorism. Nevertheless, we offered an exceptionally lucrative target. A single grenade amongst the pilots, for example, would have devastated our ability to conduct any up-country operations and would, no doubt, have grounded the wing entirely.

Unlike the HQ's staff at Steamer Point, we were quite remote from local incidents inside the enormous barbed wired area of Khormaksar station, and were rarely bothered in our domestic bachelor quarters. We sometimes had fire directed from the north across the airfield at our aircraft, and our married people living in their four-storey blocks of flats in Maala were in the thick of it but, as for the bachelor-pilots living in the Mess on base, most terrorist incidents passed them by. Indeed, often the first we heard of any local incident was from the UK papers, which at best arrived five days after the event.

Aden State Terrorism

The two main terrorist organizations were the National Liberation Front (NLF), who eventually prevailed, and the Front for the Liberation of South

Yemen (FLOSY). When they weren't fighting us, they were fighting each other. When they were increasing activity, it became necessary for the RAF to increase guarding around the Steamer Point complex which included not only the HQ building but, inter alia, the homes of AOC Air Forces Middle East, AVM Johnnie Johnson, then latterly AVM Sir Andrew Humphrey (later to be CAS), and the Middle East C-in-C, Admiral Sir Michael le Fanu. Sir Michael was an incredibly fit man. Men used to flinch from bodyguard duties with the Admiral, as it was his habit to take very brisk walks up the local mountain, Shamsan, which proved to be a splendid way for the bodyguards to lose pounds. He also used to dress up in Corporals' uniform and go walk-about amongst the other ranks, much to the chagrin of some senior officers.

With the Chief Minister's indirect encouragement, if not open support, terrorism continued to increase, including, for example, the complete destruction of the first of our two Dakotas while standing on the apron of the civil airport at Khormaksar (See Chap 11). In another instance, I had only been in Aden a week when, during a formal dinner, a grenade was thrown onto the dining balcony at the Officers' Mess at Steamer Point. Ducking under the table, the diners, including women, cowered as a Mills grenade rolled down the tabletop and exploded. The one casualty was a WRAF officer who couldn't bend too far and ended up with a piece of shrapnel in her buttock! The bomber was not found straight away.

Some months later, a transformer outside the Steamer Point Mess was blown up. Yet a few months afterwards the whole Mess main building was destroyed and, in the middle of the rubble, was found the Mess night steward, very badly hurt. He was the bomber responsible for all the incidents and had been planning to blow up the Mess during the Air Officer Commanding's luncheon following his annual formal inspection of the base. By means of the down tube below the saddle of his bicycle he had for weeks been smuggling sticks of explosives into the base. The timer he had planned to use was a modified wristwatch with the minute hand removed, the connection being made when the hour hand contacted a wire soldered into the watch glass. It was assumed that as the bomb was set at about 1.30 am, and since it was intended for it to explode at 1 p.m., the bomber had tried to save time in setting the timer by winding it backwards rather than forward. Another lucky escape for the Steamer Point guys, this was symptomatic of terrorist acts throughout the province at that time!

Terrorist acts reached a peak in August and Sep '65, when firstly a British Superintendent of Police was killed in Crater. Secondly, Sir Arthur Charles, the British Speaker of the Aden State Legislative Council, was shot dead while leaving the tennis club in Crater. Even these devious acts brought no condemnation from the Chief Minister, but only protestation at the curfew which the High Commissioner (HC) promptly clapped upon Crater. Demands for Mackawee's dismissal from office became persistent. On 26 September, acting on HMG's instructions, the HC removed him from his post, dissolved the Aden Government and took over its responsibilities. Direct rule had come to Aden at last. Do I detect a similarity to later events in Northern Ireland? Indeed, the curfew, originally imposed upon Crater, was extended to the whole of Aden, which meant all had to be in by midnight. We had to do our stints as guard officer more often than was liked, and our airmen had frequent guard duties. Against extremists, an uncompromising line resulted in the arrests of 760 suspects. In addition, there were two, and occasionally three, full RAF Regiment squadrons (2, 16 and 66), which were almost entirely confined to the defence of our base.

As 1965 drew to a close, Crater was becoming the focal point of terrorist outrages. The dense mass of tightly packed houses, narrow streets and alley-ways made the old town ideal for hit and run tactics, particularly when no householder dared refuse sanctuary to a terrorist on the run. Because of the particular dangers of Crater, a total of 237 flats occupied by service families was given up in October and, with much relief, the families were re-housed in safer areas.

Before the end of the year, the AOC AFME, AVM Johnnie Johnson completed his tour of two years and was succeeded by AVM Andrew Humphrey CB OBE DFC AFC. Famous he may have been, but Johnnie had the only decent garden in Aden, having misused at least one Argosy to bring back 20 tons of Kenyan soil! My compatriot, Phil Langrill, was sent to Kenya with Johnnie's chequebook to pay off all his debts just before he left for UK. As a renowned WW2 ace, "Johnnie" was never begrudged his garden, and on the 20th December, we flew a "J"-shaped formation fly-past to see him off in style.

The beginning of 1966 brought *THE* most momentous new decision from HMG on South Arabia. A Defence White Paper, published in February set out the conclusions of a Defence Review. This stated, inter alia:

> "South Arabia is due to become independent by 1968, and we do not think it appropriate that we should maintain defence facilities there after that happens. We therefore intend to withdraw our forces from the Aden base at that time . . .".

This meant that the Wilson Labour Government intended to abrogate all the UK's defence treaties with the Federation. Unsurprisingly, the shock to the federal rulers was profound. They now saw themselves being left with an independence that was almost unwelcome to them. The whole basis of the Federation had always been that a treaty with Britain would support it after independence, whereby Britain would provide such military backing *IN PERPETUITY*. This they considered sacrosanct. Now they found themselves highly vulnerable to their enemies, never mind the 70,000 Egyptian troops in the Yemen. Conversely, for the nationalists, the Yemen and Nasser, the White Paper came as a welcome surprise and an encouragement. Nasser, who had been on the point of pulling his forces out of the Yemen, which the UK govern-ment should have known, now declared that they would remain there for 5 years, if necessary, to ensure the final liberation of what they called South Yemen. For us, this was an unmitigated disaster engendered by the Foreign and Commonwealth Office, and Defence Ministries, if not the government in general; it was one of the biggest catastrophes ever. If Nasser had pulled the rug in the Yemen, as was his original intention, we may have had peace in our time, an orderly handover, and a continued British presence. This, in turn,

95

would certainly have denied any bases in the country to the present terrorism and Al Qaeda organisations. But the Labour fools were determined to pull out. With East German, Chinese and North Korean influence, only now can it be seen just how utterly flawed was their judgement. We had just lost the last colonial war ever fought by the British!

The reality meant nothing to home grown, untravelled politicians, but I presume that from a London perspective, our shitty little colonial war, which couldn't be won, was a pinprick on the carbuncle of the instant trigger response of the nuclear arms race, and soaring costs apace in the Cold War back home. Moreover, the perception in Britain was that, after its recent long-term, political closure, this vulnerability made the Suez Canal route to the Far East questionable. In addition, with the new CENTO air route proven, using Turkey and Persia for access to places east made Aden superfluous to our Empire's overall needs. Nevertheless, the Wilson Government's decision for total withdrawal was received with such disbelief by the Aden Governor, who baulked at putting long standing policies into reverse and implementing this new disastrous policy, that he was sacked. He felt, rightly, that years of effort coming to fruition were totally wasted. Indeed, the Sultan of Lahej told him, "You British always betray your friends. You have done it everywhere." I would refine that further as "left wing governments always betray their over-seas friends." This has been seen time and time again, but the timing here was little short of tragic, because Nasser was on the brink of pulling out of Yemen in retreat and failure. Now, instead of waiting a few months, we handed it to him on a plate. This was a classic example of HMG once again abandoning its allies, for little more than a tiny monetary gain.

For our Adeni friends and security forces, this announcement was also devastating. It was clear that the tempo of terrorism must increase and meant we could no longer expect any local support. The undoubted loyalty of the FRA, the FNG, the Police and other Arab authorities would be under intense strain. Every indigenous man and woman in Aden would now look to the day — no more than two years ahead —when we had left them to any reprisals and recriminations which extremists might wish to exact.

What else had been forgotten back home, was the type of people with which we were dealing. This is *THE* land of long-term feuds and vendettas; they are built into the Arab mind. For generations our abrogation of sacrosanct treaties will not be forgotten. American diplomatic pressure to reduce our presence and influence did not help matters. Even so, much of Middle Eastern terrorism problems today can be traced back to this disastrous 1966 Labour Government's decision, over which, in typical fashion, not a single head ever rolled. Just what did the Foreign Secretaries, Michael Stewart and George Brown, the Defence Secretary Dennis Healey, and indeed the whole Cabinet, think they were doing? Ensuring the deaths of British servicemen, that's what these purblind ex-union members and international "specialists" were doing!

Predictably in this atmosphere, the acts of terrorism and consequent casu-alties soon began to mount alarmingly — at a rate of about 50% per quarter. In fact, by the end of 1966, there had been 480 casualties during the year. Not only did the frequency of the incidents increase but the methods and weapons used became more sophisticated and thus more effective. Rocket launchers became unpopular as they were difficult to conceal, but mortars were used in increasing numbers. Undeniably, we were subsequently subjected to nearly two years of extreme terrorism simply because of the stupidity of our own mandarins, who'd been caught out trying to save money. Many would lose their lives because of this catastrophic decision. Its consequences would reverberate round the world for many years, and ultimately include 9/11 and its aftermath.

Unsurprisingly, pure Egyptian imperialism now became the root cause of all our troubles. Men were still being murdered, families terrorised and property destroyed, but why? Certainly this was not to get rid of us; we were leaving anyway. It was because orders from Cairo required everything dear to us be destroyed to create the chaos and fear necessary for the country to fall easy victim to Egyptian imperialism from day one of independence. These underhand interventions sabotaged any real chance of a tidy hand-over or leaving behind any continuity of basic law and order.

Nasser's trouble-making was compounded innumerable times by the astonishing Labour blunder of announcing a time limit for our total withdrawal, lock, stock and powder-keg from our commitments bestowed by history. The guilty were those at Westminster who so thoughtlessly dismissed Aden as a mere colonial hangover to be discarded as quickly and discreetly as possible. Narrow-minded left-wing unionists were never going to be able to think strategically, and that applies to most left wing governments. Here, at a strike they threw away every bargaining chip that might have brought the most re-calcitrant nationalists to a conference to iron out a representative agreement. Actions affecting the lives of many thousands were reduced to mere gambling chips, causing the deaths of hundreds, if not thousands.

The British government's bland announcement in Parliament in Feb '66, that British troops would be withdrawn from Aden in 1968, especially the unexpected rejection of any kind of defence commitment to the new state after independence, shook friend and foe alike throughout the Arab world. Britain's numerous admirers, a silent majority in most Arab countries at that time, were incredulous. None were more sickened than those of us who had to police this monster for the next two years. I began to realise what George Orwell had been through years earlier as a doubting instrument of British overseas security policy in the Burmese Police Force.

Now we were to face the wrath of those Arabs whom we could have counted as our friends, people who felt themselves betrayed by a British government which sought to wash its hands of the whole dirty business in Aden by a complete abdication of responsibility. It was utterly shameful! Britain was unilaterally abrogating solemn treaties of protection, specifically prohibiting any changes without mutual consent.

The brutal fact was that these treaties were hang-overs from another era, from times when *Pax Britannica* was a blessing to millions of diverse peoples around the world. Imperialism now had become a dirty word. The sun had set on British global power from the time of the equally shamefully hurried withdrawal from India two decades earlier. Unfortunately, the world had not, and still has not, produced anything to replace the imperial British role of maintaining law and order over large areas of the globe, suppressing slavers, murderers and thieves whether they operated as mere robber bands or as ambitious tribal chieftains. Is it any wonder that today, few Arabs trust us?

How paradoxical too that some American strategic policies from the 1940s to 1960s to diminish overseas British influence have directly led to serious post Cold War predicaments today for both countries. A grim "own-goal"!

After this fiasco, our base became particularly vulnerable to further mortar attacks. A comprehensive system of perimeter patrolling had to be introduced to prevent parties from Sheikh Othman stealing up to the airfield boundary after dark to set up delayed action mortar attacks. Fortunately, many mortar bombs failed to explode — nineteen out of twenty on one occasion — and the base suffered little damage.

Vast quantities of 40-gallon fuel drums had accumulated on the station over the years. These were now used to construct revetments to give some protection to aircraft from shrapnel and splinters. Each such shelter was constructed from a double storey of drums, the height of which depended upon the size of the aircraft to be protected. The drums were then filled with water to lend weight and stability to the structure. Although offering less protection than sand, it was quick and easy to fill the thousands of drums needed with water: for once we weren't fussed about using seawater.

This background illustrates the general atmosphere over the next couple of years in which we lived our daily lives.

The loss of confidence in Britain by the Federal Government was further exacerbated by London after an incident at the end of July 1966. A small number of Egyptian flown Mig fighters crossed the border again from the Yemen on 30th July, and attacked the house of the Sharif of Nuqab, some ten miles north of Beihan (see Map at Fig 2). After a short but intensive attack with cannon and rockets, a number of tribesmen were left seriously injured and several houses destroyed or damaged. The Sharif of Beihan, who had always been one of the most powerful of rulers, staunchly pro-British, demanded reprisals in accordance with his treaty with Britain. Knowing that they only responded to gun power, we on the Hunter Wing stood by for ten days with a full plan to cross the border in force and exact revenge, before being stood down on Harold Wilson's direct order. Yet another stomach-churning appeasement decision, with distinct loss of local face and trust, by that crass, geographically-remote, Labour government!

To the Sharif's and our amazement, we were to take absolutely no military action against this flagrant violation. Instead, HMG referred the matter to the United Nations. This, of course, brought forth no more than a resolution calling upon both sides to keep the peace. This incident and the lack of retaliatory action further disillusioned the Rulers and noticeably weakened their confidence and resolve. Now, even *we* were beginning to ask questions, even though we had immediately re-instituted our Air Defence Patrols along the border and, for the first time, had put a pair of Hunters at five minutes' readiness during the hours of daylight on to the newly lengthened airstrip at Beihan (See Chap 6).

The local loss of confidence in the UK became more and more apparent as the year wore on with more strikes and civil unrest. Even so, we continued our air support to the ground forces up-country throughout 1966, flying strikes and flag waves spasmodically throughout the period but the tempo was slow, as a sort of stalemate ensued.

The majority of internal security incidents in Aden were initiated from

Mosques, and yet we were not allowed to search them. British patrols came under repeated attacks from mosques, particularly those in Crater and at the Al Noor Mosque in the main square of Sheikh Othman. Instead, Federal troops were used, who invariably drew a blank. Federal soldiers, for the first time ever, were called into a joint operation in colonial territory, for the very first assault on a mosque: the Al Noor Mosque. This was a known nest of NLF gunmen. The ensuing gunfight, including heavy machine guns from inside the mosque, was long and drawn out. Eventually, the federal troops stormed the mosque but would not let their British officers inside. They came out with some suspects, but no arms were ever found. The British General commanding the security forces commented: "They must have been firing at us with catapults, then!"

Similarly, during the "Mad Mitch" Crater campaign the only no-go areas were the town's fifteen mosques, yet the pattern of incidents showed that every grenade attack was made within a few yards running-distance of a mosque. The ruthlessness of the Argylls, however, eventually made Crater a no-go area for terrorists. An occasional FLOSY arms store was found, but no one seemed to notice that no NLF terrorists were ever discovered in a mosque. Indeed, nothing is new. Today we are still worrying about the use of mosques in our own backyard, such as the London Finchley-North Mosque, for terrorist training. When will we ever learn – the fundamentalist nature of their religion is an excuse for terrorism, and appeasement does NOT work with Arabs? It's not in their nature.

Our gut-retching policy of appeasement was only justified when it occasionally worked, but the Arabs showed respect for our authority when our guns were wielded ruthlessly without the normal, squeamish, British constraint. Unusually, despite the howls of protest from back home, for nearly three months of Argyll occupation, Crater was an oasis of peace while Arabs fought a bloody civil war all around it.

The security forces were thus compelled to take on more and more responsibility for internal security, which act, in turn, gave the NLF and FLOSY additional material for virulent propaganda against the British. The situation deteriorated steadily and even the announcement that the United Nations was to send a mission to South Arabia in 1967, to try to find a solution, did little or nothing to restore confidence. Even Amnesty International carried out an investigation of the Aden Interrogation Centre into alleged brutalities. The International Red Cross had full access to detainees, and Amnesty's report produced no conclusive evidence of ill treatment. The Foreign Secretary, on receiving the report, pointed out that 115 Arabs were detained in Aden for political or terrorist activity compared with 2,000 in the Yemen, where some had been executed.

HMG asked Mr. Roderick Bowen QC to conduct a similar investigation. He also was unable to find any evidence to support the Amnesty findings and, in his report, made the following statement:

"The main strain of protecting the population and dealing with the terrorist falls upon military personnel and the police. I certainly gained the impression that generally speaking they discharge their onerous duties with great restraint."

This closed the matter as far as HMG and most of the civilised world was concerned, but the investigations had created the greatest difficulties for the Security Forces. The terrorists now knew that they had nothing to fear at the hands of Government interrogators and, from that moment, information for the Security Forces completely dried up. In the field of propaganda and in the denial of intelligence, the enemy had the upper hand and there is no doubt that these policies and events of 1966 dealt the fatal blow to British authority in Aden, from which we never recovered.

Rhodesian Terrorism (My part in UDI!)

Another form of intimidation took our minds away from South Arabia in late 1966. Ian Smith affirmed a Unilateral Declaration of Independence (UDI) in Rhodesia, and the mother of all empires was having none of it. Pity really, because once again a commonwealth country was brought to its knees by the Wilson government, allowing state sponsored terrorism to prevail over a more benevolent, white-dominated system. But for our stance over UDI, Ian Smith would have been running Zimbabwe, and the country would not be in the parlous state we see today. Mugabe and his henchmen should have been hanged long ago for their atrocities! I, for one, decry that we didn't take a firm stance back in 1966 but, after the Suez and Aden debacles, such was the pusil-lanimity of our cabinet ministers.

In November of that year, we – the Hunter Wing – were put on 24hrs standby to retake Rhodesia and unseat Ian Smith's illegal government. It was a solemn period for us. We watched every type of armed unit come through Aden on its way to Zambia where we were forming a forward bridgehead with an air defence system for a push into Rhodesia. Our Air Defence Radar went south. No. 29 Sqn all-weather fighters with their Javelins came through from Cyprus on their way to Lusaka, together with some of our RAF Regiment boys. But against possible resistance from the Royal Rhodesian Air Force (RrhAF), our transports would have required fighter cover, and Nyerere, despite demanding British action, covertly refused overflight clearance!

Unfortunately, 29 Sqn were having problems with centre-line closure on their Sapphire jet engines at the time, and kept parking damaged aircraft all over our airfield! Centreline Closure is the term used when the compressor or turbine blades expand to the point where they are scraping on the inside of the engine casing. This is pretty catastrophic! It can, at worst, cause total engine break up and was a commonplace problem of their early Sapphire engines. Javelins were chosen, politically, as being less confrontational: they had all the intimidation of the Liechtenstein Navy!

The Javelin support pack-ups were sent to them separately by air from our MU. Unfortunately, at that time, rules for sending kit by air stated that if no available air outlet to the destination airfield was available within the required time, then you were permitted to send it to the nearest alternate airfield. The nearest airfield to Lusaka was Salisbury (now Harare), Rhodesia. Unbelievably, that is where the RAF sent the Javelin spares: straight to the "enemy's" main base!

A cable was later received from the RRhAF to the senders of the spares, thanking them for their kind gift!

A mood of solemnity prevailed among us; we had regarded the white Rhodesians, and especially their air force pilots, as our friends. During WW2 more Rhodesian volunteers proportionately had become casualties than any other allied country. Indeed, they were involved with us in the Kuwait crisis only three years earlier. In fact some of RRhAF Hunter pilots on their No 2 Squadron, had not only trained with us in UK a few years earlier, but some had even finished up on 8 Sqn in Aden before returning to Rhodesia after a secondment tour with us! Hence, we constantly mumbled such mutinous phrases as, "No way am I fighting them – they're our friends; we won't go – wild horses wouldn't make us go!"

I trained with five white Rhodesian pilots, although only two passed out from their cadetship at South Cerney on my course. I've often wondered what happened to them in the longer term. After all, they were white RRhAF Officers when Mugabe came to power, and we've all seen or heard what he's done to that country, and not only to the white population ever since. With ex-terrorists now in charge of the armed forces, any whites should have been over the horizon and away as rapidly as possible. If a white government had caused the present situation in Zimbabwe, the whole world would be up in arms, but this "reverse racism" of Mugabe's appears quite acceptable to the wider world. For doing nothing, South Africa, and Blair and Bush, should be ashamed of themselves. I only hope that the world wakes up to the scale of the human tragedy now consuming Zimbabwe before it's too late.

Delightfully, the story of our part in UDI has an appropriate ending. We stayed on Rhodesian standby until just before Christmas that year, a period of approximately six weeks. Then, as you know, Smith was forced to stand down, and so did we. Well ahead of Christmas, a typical air force Christmas card was sent to No. 2 Sqn RrhAF by 43(F) Sqn. On the front was the embossed squadron badge, in the centre were the usual greetings and all the pilots' signatures but on the back had been written in beautiful black Gothic script, the peacetime rules of aerial combat, concluding with "Cine Only" i.e. NO LIVE FIRING! It rather pleasingly summed up the whole situation to us all!

Trouble with the Fleet Air Arm

Once in a while, some navy boats would haul themselves over our horizon, and of course they became fair game for some inter-service rivalry, but trouble followed them everywhere!

In late 1966, HMS Eagle, commanded by a famous, WW2 submarine captain, Captain John Roxburgh (later to retire as Vice-Admiral Sir John), with a few Fleet Air Arm (FAA) planes, steamed North from Beira, where she was implementing UN sanctions against Rhodesia, into our theatre, displacing a minute part of the Gulf of Aden. We then arranged a three-day air defence exercise with her, and I led a four-ship at low level to attack the carrier. At 450kts we believed we were through her Gannet early warning radar screen but, half-way there, we were spotted and attacked by her Sea Vixens, which came in fast from ahead. A low fast turning 4v2 fight ensued – a good aerial combat session before pressing on to the carrier. The scheme was that she should have been towing a splash target for us to fire upon but, on finding her, we couldn't see any target. On complaining over the radio, all we got back was a series of four-letter words pertaining to our lack of eyesight! So, not finding a target, we proceeded to beat hell out of the carrier – roaring down her deck as low and as fast as possible, before peeling off for home with suitable retorts blueing the airwaves.

The Wing Commander, with a face like thunder, was waiting to meet us upon landing! We had only given the USS Saratoga, who was steaming some twenty miles away from the Eagle, a real roasting! Fancy rowing another boat that size in our pond without telling us! Inevitably two weeks 'duty guard officer' followed!

Always, of course, there was one red dot on our maps – Middle East Command HQ at Steamer Point – the only spot to be avoided at all costs – mustn't upset their lordships' coffee! Returning from the South, an unusual direction as we did very little work out in the Gulf of Aden, leading a pair of aircraft at low level one day, after conducting a mock attack on HMS Eagle, we had to pass by the HQs, and I obviously got a little close for their comfort. Guess what? I was again met by my Strike Wing Commander who let it be known that the wrath of some desk-bound big-wig, "up the hill" as HQ was known, had been incurred as his meeting had apparently been interrupted! Another two weeks 'duty guard officer' re-ensued!

Aden Terrorism Continues: Family Evacuations

Despite UDI, we were still heavily involved in terrorist prevention back in the Aden State. By October '66, the terrorist incidents had risen to their highest level, eighty-four incidents during the month, and the outlook was grim indeed. Casualties among us, the RAF, were mercifully light, largely due to the concentration of our personnel within well-guarded localities on base at Khormaksar and at Steamer Point, but the nine thousand families were becoming an ever-increasing headache. Consequently, from November onwards, no new families were accepted in Aden, and those already in Aden started evacuating from March 1967, the last being out by June. Very few casualties had been suffered by Service families, but the risk was great and the restrictions which had had to be placed upon their freedom of movement were such that life had become difficult for them: schools remained closed, clubs and restaurants were out of bounds and armed guards, escorts and patrols were everywhere and, even our wives carried sub-machine guns!

Britain had announced that her days in Aden were numbered; 'out by 1968' was the official dictum. By the end of 1966, it was clear that, unless some extremely strong and resolute measures were taken, probably involving heavy casualties, 1968 would certainly not see any British forces remaining in Aden. South Arabia would receive no further British backing and, with insufficient time to build up its own Security Forces, had no hope of combating the militant forces ranged against it. We had lost our final colonial war.

The Beginning of the End – 1967 Dawns

At the beginning of 1967, our redefined policy was to withdraw all British forces from the military base at Aden by the end of the year, or very shortly thereafter. For want of more specific information, it was assumed that Independence Day would be 1st of January 1968, but no assumption could be made about the date for the final withdrawal of forces. This date was becoming increasingly important to know in view of the many thousands of personnel and huge quantities of equipment and supplies that would have to be phased out of Aden.

Whitehall decided that the British forces stationed in the Persian Gulf would be increased from those withdrawn from Aden, though the total would be less than half of the Aden strength. It was considered that this force, located at Bahrain and Sharjah, would be adequate to implement the continuing British commitment to safeguard Kuwait against external aggression, and to maintain surveillance over the oil routes through the Gulf and out into the Arabian Sea. Various treaties that Britain still had with the Sultan of Muscat and the Trucial States would also be supported.

With no specific withdrawal date available, the only other preparation for leaving was a thinning out and reduction of equipment. For example, we had thousands of tons of bombs and ammunition in the Explosives Storage Depot in Crater. So further supplies from the United Kingdom were stopped and stocks were transported out by sea to the Gulf stations and Masirah. Obsolete or dangerous items were dumped at sea, and surplus quantities of valuable items, such as 20mm and 30mm ammunition, were shipped back to UK.

In Aden we had more than 3,000 furnished flats and houses which, once the families had left, would have to be speedily emptied of furniture before they could be looted. We, the RAF, were quite determined that no valuable and desirable equipment should be left behind when the final departure took place. Many millions of pounds' worth of new accommodation, technical buildings and facilities would, in any case, have to be left with no prospect of compensation.

As if to encourage the preparations for withdrawal, the acts of terrorism continued to increase during the early months of 1967, with 236 incidents in the first two months, which resulted in 41 killed and 240 injured. Most incidents had consisted of grenade throwing and rocket or mortar attacks, but small arms now began to be used extensively. Incidents were increasingly directed at our Security Forces in the hope that stronger retaliatory action and more repressive measures would provide good propaganda material for the nationalist cause.

The most significant feature of these incidents was the cumulative effect upon the police, who were having greater difficulty maintaining law and order. Furthermore, they began to suffer heavy casualties themselves. In the event of serious trouble, the Army now had to take over internal security, with the police in support, instead of the reverse. In conjunction with the RAF Regiment, our airfield kept remarkably free from night attacks – not only were we arguably the most desirable operational target in Aden, but we lay between Crater and Sheikh Othman, which were the two focal points of terrorist activity.

11th February 1967 was the eighth anniversary of the founding of the Federation — 'The Day of the Volcano' — as it was called by both terrorist organizations. They decided to use it to mount a large scale and violent demonstration to discredit the Federal Government, and to show that the British authorities could only rule through repression and brutality. As the demonstration was well advertised, we had time to take appropriate measures, with the result that it became the first test for the new policy over the Army's security role. Aden Brigade was deployed in strength to the two focal points, a strict curfew was imposed, all passenger-carrying traffic was stopped, and people were advised to stay at home. In consequence, the day of violent demonstration turned out to be extremely quiet, but 705 curfew breakers were arrested. So furious were the nationalists that they called for a general strike on the following day and the curfew was re-imposed, resulting in the arrests of a further 150 law breakers.

After this, we slowly returned to 'normal', but our families had been confined to their homes for four days, and the Army had been attacked on sixty-six occasions with casualties of eight killed and sixty-four wounded. The whole operation was a success, but the price paid was high; two British wives were killed and eleven British civilians injured during the February incidents; the risk to British life in Aden was rapidly becoming unacceptable.

After all the formal ceremonies that 8 Sqn had instigated in the early days of 1967, it did make a pleasant change to have some new, professional play-toys. The FAA again arrived in quantity in May, with the return of HMS Eagle in company with HMS Hermes[1]. The carriers each had two Buccaneer and two Sea Vixen Sqns aboard to play with, and a show of force, to prove to the various terrorist organisations that we were not going to be a push over, was to be staged.

After acting as airborne escorts, showing them around the Federation to familiarize them with the territory during the first few days, we were then able to relinquish the air defence role to them for a while, bringing us a little relief. Photo 26 was one of those Kodak moments, when Ken Simpson, one of our 1417 recce flt pilots, managed to capture Hermes at full speed, not only as our nine-ship flew past, but also with a Buccaneer just about to land on. Contrary to the RAF News, which published this photo on their front page, it is a single Buccaneer with its shadow on the boat's wake, not a pair of Buccaneers trying to land simultaneously as originally reported!

Later on the same day, we flew a thirty-ship fly past around much of Aden and the nearer parts of the Federation; sixteen of us together with eight Sea Vixens and six Buccaneers behind. Again I was No 2 in the formation. This fun flight was a great success, which culminated in a riotous cocktail party aboard Hermes, in turn keeping many of us on the ground the following day!

However, we weren't the only ones to fly. Quite quickly after the flypast, the rumours also flew! The locals, if not their local paper, published the story that the flypast was the great Hunter Strike Wing of Khormaksar being chased around the skies by these other funny shapes that could only be the Yemeni Migs! This required some reaction on our part.

A major flag waving exercise was obviously now necessary; a real show of force this time! 208 Sqn arrived from Bahrain for a few days, so we put together a 56-ship formation (55 plus one FR10 photo aircraft). Sixty was the target, but it couldn't quite be managed, though nobody had ever seen so many fighters together over Aden before – and never since. This was going to be better than any air-show but this time, to scotch the local rumour, the FAA would lead with the Hunters aft!

We put up 28 Hunters from Khormaksar for that formation, following sixteen Sea Vixens and twelve Buccaneers. Things started well, but then the FAA got 'slightly lost', and then to cap it all, while trying to sort out their problems, our air traffic called up to say they had found rubber tread from a tyre on the runway from which the 28 Hunters had just taken off! At that point the orderly formation became a total shambles as 28 Hunters put their undercarriages down. Both tyres of each aircraft were closely inspected by a next door neighbour to find the offending wheel – fourteen pairs careering all over the sky, and the FAA's 'no-show' for some reason or other! Finally, the aircraft with a stripped tread was found and positioned last to land after twenty-seven uneventful arrivals, and no more was said about flying with the FAA!

Soon after the beginning of '67, I was posted home after two wonderful years. Unfortunately, 'their Airships' had decided I was going to the Flight Simulator Staff at RAF Chivenor, to teach budding Hunter pilots their emergency drills. This meant, horror of horrors, a ground tour: no flying. Fortunately, despite the leg-breaking incident some years earlier, my boss pulled strings and succeeded in cancelling my posting, provided I extended my present tour for another year.

Despite Sir David Lee's caustic comments about Aden, we did live in a different world from his. The Sunday Times Magazine produced a superb article on aircrew life in Aden at the time. This stated: *"They worked hard, they played hard, and blamed it all on the danger"*! On the contrary, we thought of ourselves quite differently. We were normal young men just doing a difficult military job in appalling conditions, and trying, as young men do, to enjoy to the full what little social life was to be had.

As can be imagined, Aden could have been pretty boring socially for a 20 year old, particularly as there were only 54 single servicewomen in the whole colony, and single European girls were very scarce – mainly some nurses, a few schoolteachers and one or two Aden Airways Stewardesses. For me though, I had been having the time of my life: a young fighter pilot in an operational zone, with Dakotas to go places in; the Desert Rescue Team for some up-country adventure; a General Service Medal for active service in the South Arabian campaign, and the tropical sun, sand, sea and cheap living. I'd just lost my virginity, and had never found the supply of girls short including the odd senior-officer's daughter! What more could a young man want? The prospect of a further year in the Middle East was ideal.

What I now know to be true, but didn't realise at the time, was that we were to pull out of Aden within the year and the air force didn't want to post new, unblooded pilots into the cauldron of South Arabia when there would have been no time to train them up to operational standard. After all, we faced all the problems of withdrawal from a hostile and possibly uncontrollable situation. Experienced hands were needed and 8 Sqn at that time probably had the greatest bunch of young experienced pilots you could ever wish to fly with – nine of them made Grp Capt, air rank or equivalent. By Christmas 1966, I'd received my Op 4 status to lead the standby pair, and had been in theatre longer than any of them. If you think two years in theatre was not 'experienced', that was the normal tour length, but I went on for nearly three years. In fact, Tim Smith, who arrived on the Sqn some three months after me, but was a year older, always had to bite his tongue when I was able to retort, "It's not age that counts – it's experience!" All of three extra months in theatre made the difference in the pecking order, especially later when achieving Op4 status, which was not given lightly to first tourists in those days.

But back in Aden in 1967, with the Argylls' major battles in Crater led by "Mad" Mitch, and the families commencing their repatriation leading up to our final withdrawal from Aden, even social life had its serious elements with armed guards now covering the beach club. When wives and families started to be killed, and mortars and rifle fire were directed across our airfield from the FRA barracks on the far north side, then playing hard and blaming it on the danger was no longer acceptable. Withdrawal from this vestige of the Empire, for long a distinct possibility, was now a certainty.

Notes
1. HMS Hermes is still going strong as the Indian Navy ship: *Viraat*.

Chapter Thirteen

The Final Six Months

As both the FRA and the police were being infiltrated by terrorists and were now untrustworthy, it was a welcome respite for us when rival nationalist organisations, NLF and FLOSY, suspecting an earlier pullout of Aden by Britain, turned viciously upon each other in a pre-emptive power struggle, notably in Sheikh Othman. With screaming bodies falling from the roof tops, gunfights in every street and bazooka and mortar attacks destroying buildings, it was like a scene from a "spagetti western."

The deterioration was not confined to Aden; guerrilla warfare continued unabated up-country. We were kept fully occupied in flying daily air defence patrols along the Yemen border, and supporting the FRA and British army in combating widespread dissident activity in the Radfan, Dhala and Beihan areas. On 19th February for instance, a party of forty dissidents again attacked the British and FRA camp at Dhala with rifles, machine guns, mortars and bazookas, causing three casualties, and yet again we were called in to relieve the beleaguered garrison. Eight aircraft fired rockets and guns over a two-hour period while the remnants of the dissident party as usual, streamed back across the border to safety.

Confusion reigned throughout much of 1967 as to the exact date of the final exit. Until June, HMG did not commit itself to anything more specific than 'shortly after independence at the beginning of 1968'. In June, however, we were officially told to plan on 20 November as the final day, but then on 2nd November the MOD changed it to 30 November and, later that month it was brought forward by twenty-four hours to 29 November, a date that remained unchanged. However, we had to plan for every eventuality including a fighting withdrawal in the face of terrorist opposition. This was a real possibility, particularly if the UN talks in Geneva were to break down at the last moment.

As the Suez Canal remained closed after the Six Day War in June and, as Aden port was virtually at a standstill through strikes and terrorist activity, there was no possibility of evacuating personnel by sea. Everybody, with the exception of some naval personnel, would have to leave by air. Two battalion groups were the minimum force needed for guarding the airfield perimeter on the last day, before being lifted out well before dark with air cover provided from the Naval Task Force of HMS Eagle and HMS Albion, in the Gulf of Aden. This would allow the last of our sister sqn, 43, and our recce flight, 1417, to maintain an air defence presence and to leave from a still secure airfield.

An airlift, for us second in size only to the Berlin airlift of twenty years earlier, was therefore planned. Bahrain was to act as a staging post around which the main lift from Khormaksar to the United Kingdom hinged. Besides our own Argosy and Beverley aircraft, a few civil charter aircraft also assisted Air Support Command strategic transports. Admittedly and surprisingly, Nasser had given permission for aircraft carrying evacuees to overfly Egypt on the direct route from Aden to the UK and a few such flights were made, but there was no trust that this route would remain open. One interesting operational rule introduced was that all transport aircraft flying out of Khormaksar should have the ability to take off with one engine out of action if necessary, to avoid having to leave an expensive aircraft at Khormaksar merely for an engine change. This was especially so for the Hercules, which were brand new into RAF service.

Meanwhile, those of us left behind were messed about over domestic accommodation. All those accompanied senior officers whose families had been shipped home in mid-summer were brought into the bachelor quarters behind the barbed wire on base. Hence the pecking order for the few air-conditioned bachelor rooms was, after nearly three years, changed overnight!

Up country, as well as the in-flight loss of an Aden Airways Dakota to a bomb, we lost two Beverleys: one to an engine failure on take off from Beihan, the other to a landmine on landing at Habilayn. Moreover, aviation fuel supply during the civil unrest and strikes had become a real worry; we were using a million gallons of aviation fuel per month. AVTAG and AVTUR were mixed for MT fuel, and our Shackletons and Beverleys ferried AVTUR from Djibouti in their outboard tanks to keep us flying, though with AVTAG inboard for themselves, their engineers and flight safety officer were unimpressed! During 1966–67 alone, we lost 23 aircraft to hostile action including one Beverley and one Hunter, and 17 Hunters received battle damage.

Effects of the Arab–Israeli War

Of course, to add to the equation, a marked increase in terrorism resulted because of the six-day Arab-Israeli war in June '67. The Adenese blamed the British for the Arab losses, because they had perceived that we supported Israel. They were staggered that their idol, Nasser, had lost, and so took it out on us! Indeed, the Voice of Cairo Radio pushed out unlimited quantities of propaganda and lies, including blaming British and American aircraft for their losses.

Infiltration of the Aden Police now began to have serious repercussions. The newly styled South Arabian Army (SAA – formerly the FRA) was itself not free from infiltration and tribal susceptibilities. All these factors led to a serious incident on 20th June when a riot flared up among some apprentices of the SAA in Lake Lines near Sheikh Othman (see Fig 3). Shots were fired, which subsequently led to a mutiny in the Police barracks at the nearby Champion Lines. The Police had heard the shooting and mistakenly concluded that their Arab colleagues down the road were being attacked by British troops. An entirely innocent, un-armoured three-ton truck, conveying nine-

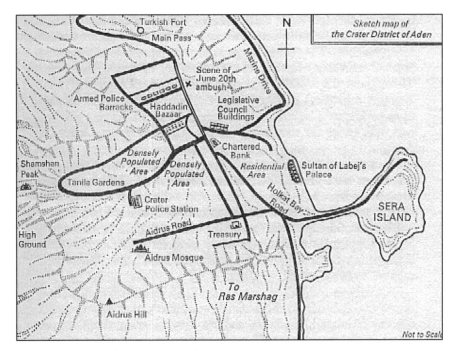

Fig 8. Sketchmap of Crater (© *Stephen Harper 1978*).

teen soldiers of the RCT past Champion Lines on our northern boundary was attacked, resulting in eight of the soldiers killed and another eight wounded. This situation was eventually brought under control by a strong force of British troops, which sustained several more casualties, but not before a number of shots had been fired across the airfield at our aircraft and ourselves.

Unfortunately, rumours had spread to Crater (see Fig 8), causing near panic in the large barracks of the Armed Police there. In the absence of their Commanding Officer, the police rushed their own armoury and obtained weapons with which to defend themselves. Meanwhile, The Northumberland Fusiliers (RNF) were in the process of handing over duties to the Argyll and Sutherland Highlanders. As was customary, the Fusiliers left a small rear party to facilitate the handover. The NLF took full advantage of the situation, creating as much disturbance as possible. An extremely dangerous situation developed which the Fusiliers responsible for Crater were quite unable to control. One of its company commanders, with another major, a warrant officer and six men were caught in the intense rifle and machinegun fire from the Armed Police barracks (usually one of the safest spots in Crater). The patrol had gone into Crater in two Ferret armoured cars, which came under heavy attack, and in defending themselves, the Fusiliers ran out of their small arms ammunition. In Aden, firing orders required single aimed shots. The patrol radioed Aden Brigade for authority to open fire with the 0.5 Browning machine guns fitted to the vehicles. Incredibly, but typically, permission was denied, resulting in all but one being killed and their vehicles set on fire. Several

109

attempts were made during the day to recover the bodies from off the road but they were all unsuccessful, so intense was the fire that met the rescuers on each occasion, even after nightfall.

This heart-rending situation produced an appalling dilemma. A full-scale military attack could be mounted and it would undoubtedly be successful, but would probably decide the fate of South Arabia for the future. The Federal Government, supported by the British, was still the official authority, even if the terrorists had gravely undermined its power. A British attack on the Armed Police and the South Arabian Army would finally undermine that tenuous authority and lead to the final collapse of the Federation, and all that had been achieved over the years would be irretrievably lost. On the other hand, nine British servicemen had been killed and their bodies still lay in the main street of Crater. Moreover, a further twelve had lost their lives in various rescue attempts and other incidents during the day, and all because of Nasser's propaganda against us in his attempt to mitigate his loss of the six-day war.

But Crater was in a state of siege, and the fury and frustration of the RNF and the Argylls reached danger point. The boys were not just angry: they were incensed. More than a week passed, but the GOC, Maj Gen Philip Tower, a man of straw, who took full responsibility for not permitting a fighting return to Crater, promised that they certainly would return in due course. This led to the most famous episode of the Aden Campaign, which was the entry into Crater by Lt Col Mitchell and his Argyll and Sutherland Highlanders. The Colonel continued to ask permission to go and recover the bodies, and was continually denied. Two weeks after the initial eruption, he decided that enough was enough. He formed up his regiment at the top of the Crater Pass, a pass covered in regimental cap badges carved into the hillside. With pipes playing and bayonets fixed, the Argylls marched into the 'no go' area of Crater. It was a terrific sight, if technically illegal, but it won the day and they brought out the bodies without a casualty. The inhabitants of Crater were awakened on the morning of 4 July by the pipes and drums of the Argyll and Sutherland Highlanders playing Reveille on the roof of the Chartered Bank. The surprise was total, not only for the locals, as even the SAS, who had patrols in Crater, did not know. This brought to an end what had undoubtedly been the most anxious and explosive situation so far experienced in Aden.

The press in England gave Col. Mitchell the title "Mad Mitch", but there was nothing mad about him, just a rational man responding as a true officer and gentleman to a terrible situation caused entirely by Nasser and the Arab misconception of our part in the Arab-Israeli war. However, this six-day war was the key event which created the modern Middle East. By achieving their goals so comprehensively, the Israelis collected problems for decades afterwards, and lost the moral high ground they had occupied since 1947. The Arabs then lost faith with the West and turned instead to their own mosques for counsel.

Not all these incidents of violence, in Sheikh Othman, Al Mansoura Lake Lines, Champion Lines and Crater, could be directly attributed to Arab chagrin at the outcome of the Arab-Israeli war. But there is no doubt that the war fanned the flames of violence in Aden and led indirectly to a crucial turning point not only in the affairs of South Arabia, but the entire Middle East. The failure of the Federal Government to show effective leadership finally revealed its basic weakness, and even its own followers began to realise that it could never control an independent country. Thus more and more turned towards the nationalists, who were encouraged to become ever bolder in their bid for power. It must also be said that the robust responses of our troops, in particular the RNF and the Argylls, did nothing to help and everything to fan further the flames of local Arab nationalism.

Withdrawal Planning

When the results of the terrorist incidents in June '67 were assessed, the total reached the terrible figure of 492, higher than the total for the whole of 1966. Sixty-one people had been killed, and 113 had been injured, of which twenty-eight and fifty-nine, respectively, were servicemen.

For the first time it had been necessary to close our airfield at Khormaksar when our RAF Regiment perimeter patrols had come under heavy attack. The Federal Government had lost what little control it had of the terrorists and, after the pitched battles between the NLF and FLOSY in Sheikh Othman, the NLF was reaching a dominant position to assume control after independence. Any prospect of handing over to a stable Federal Government had now disappeared completely, and we could only hope to withdraw as early as possible in good order and without heavy casualties.

The broad concept was to bring all remaining British forces back into Aden from up-country after handing over to the South Arabian Army, but to afford the latter our continued air support from Khormaksar for as long as we remained. We on the Hunter Wing continued air defence patrols along the whole of the border, to discourage any infiltration by Egyptian or Yemeni aircraft which might have endangered the security of Aden itself. In those last months alone, amongst other operational missions I flew eight border patrols covering the whole length of the Yemeni border, including long, boring, high-level, coastal patrols from Perim Island at the mouth of the Red Sea through Aden itself and out to Mukalla in the far east. Within Aden State, it was intended to close down all outlying units and to concentrate everyone in our base at Khormaksar for the final stages of the departure.

Our air defence radar installation, located up country in a tented camp on top of the escarpment at Mukeiras, extremely close to the Yemeni border, and upon which we on Strike Wing continued to rely daily, was becoming something of a hostage to fortune. It was the last permanent RAF unit to return from up-country into the Colony, and in so doing reduced the effectiveness of our patrols.

The phased withdrawal of all our Sqns was now planned, and:

My Squadron, No 8, moved to Muharraq to form a fighter/ground attack wing with 208 Squadron, the ex-Naval 8 Sqn, who were already there. The Sqn stayed en route at Masirah and Sharjah for some time until the air evacuation was completed.

Our sister Sqn, **No. 43(F)** (**Hunter FGA9**), remained at Khormaksar augmented by four 8 Sqn pilots, including myself, until completion of the withdrawal. 43 then disbanded, its aircraft being redistributed to 8 and 208 Squadrons.

No. 1417 Recce Flight (Hunter FR10) was re-amalgamated into 8 Sqn from which they had come in the first place, at Bahrain.

No 21 Sqn (MECS)(Andover/Twin Pioneer/Dakota) disbanded at Khormaksar, most of its aircraft being re-allocated to other squadrons, and my lovely, old lady Dakota was flown home to be sold off.

No. 37 Squadron (Shackleton) was disbanded at Khormaksar, the aircraft being returned to the UK.

All the other squadrons moved to the gulf stations.

The Struggle for Power

The NLF and FLOSY were still trying to settle their differences if one of them was to take over South Arabia. As was to be expected after the Sheikh Othman battle, it was the NLF which took up this challenge, issuing to all and sundry, including the original UN Mission which had returned to life and was deliberating in Geneva, an arrogant and unequivocal declaration of its aims. In doing so, the NLF took on three opponents, the Federal Government, Britain and FLOSY, and, as will be seen, eventually emerged triumphant from all three conflicts.

The thinning out process continued throughout August, which turned out to be a particularly active month. This month produced an all time 'high' in terrorist incidents during which seven servicemen were killed and forty-seven injured in the course of 821 attacks with small arms, rockets and grenades. The Service casualties unhappily included five of our airmen individually assassinated while off duty, each filling their car or motorcycle at local filling stations.

On our base the only mortar attack which could be described as at all successful, also occurred in August. The bombers managed to elude security patrols and fired a number of mortar bombs into the aircraft parking areas, but the revetments of oil drums proved their worth and absorbed much of the blast, although splinters and flying debris damaged two Shackletons. Remarkably, this was the only attack that damaged aircraft on the airfield throughout the whole of the troubles – one of the few missed chances of the terrorist campaign.

The first significant move by the NLF was against the Federal Rulers, a number of whom had gone to Geneva at the end of July to see the UN Mission. In their absence, the NLF moved in and took over control of some of their States. It was astonishing that the Rulers had taken no precautions against such an obvious development, and had even left their families and their wealth at the mercy of the terrorists. In mid-August, the Supreme Council of the Federation announced that no less than eight States were in the hands of the NLF. By the end of the month a further four States had succumbed and the Sultan of Lahej, who had retreated into Aden, was the only Ruler left in the country, and his State was also in the hands of the NLF. The other Rulers then turned down every entreaty from the High Commissioner to return from Geneva. Consequently, the Federal Government no longer existed as an effective authority, and the Federation lay in ruins.

With this great victory over the Federal Government securely in its pocket, the NLF turned its attention to FLOSY, after setting up a headquarters openly at Zinjibar, twenty-five miles from the Aden State frontier, and declaring that it was now the true representative of the people. In a final attempt to stem the NLF tide, FLOSY issued a belligerent statement, with the result that fierce fighting broke out between the two factions at the beginning of September. It centred again on Sheikh Othman and for five days, we watched with amazement, keeping our own heads well down.

I left Aden on September 9th, but the battle reached its climax on the 10th when 1,000 Yemenis arrived to support FLOSY. A bitter battle ensued with many casualties on either side, until the SAA decided that it must intervene to prevent the whole country disintegrating into a bloodbath. In spite of blandishments from all sides, the SAA had remained firmly independent, concerned only with the well being of their country, even after the virtual collapse of their masters, the Federal Government. Their unarmed and courageous intervention in the battle of Sheikh Othman brought the fighting to a halt, and resulted in a breathing space while negotiations were conducted.

Only six weeks later would the final outcome of the NLF/FLOSY confrontation be settled. Although it had been evident for some time that Britain would withdraw early, it was not until November 2nd that the date was bought forward to late November 1967. This prompted both nationalist parties to resume their struggle for power in a final, violent, four-day round of heavy fighting. Once again, it was most violent in Sheikh Othman where the SAA had assumed control from British forces. After three days of slaughter, the SAA decided that they must once again intervene to prevent widespread civil war. The Arab Army, siding with the NLF this time, completely ignored years of British training, tore up our rule of minimum force and, with total ruthlessness, using heavy arms and without regard to civilian casualties, wiped out the last of FLOSY. On day four, any outside help for FLOSY disappeared as the pro-Nasser regime in the Yemen was finally ousted in an army coup.

Finally, that night, the South Arabian army chiefs, rid of fears of Egyptian intervention, openly declared themselves as long standing NLF chiefs. It was a momentous decision and made the SAA the decisive factor in the situation, totally typical of the Arab mentality of those parts: absolutely corrupt, utterly duplicitous, and completely untrustworthy. They were open to the highest bidder, or willing to transfer their loyalty to the biggest gun around. The only surprise was that our chiefs were surprised by this declaration.

Two examples of this Arab duplicity are worth a mention. One of our journalists expecting a secret rendezvous with a top FLOSY leader, found himself in a room full of uniformed Arabs. There were eleven senior officers of the Aden Civil Police, twenty-four officers of the SAA including seven lieutenant colonels, and two senior CID officers: all top FLOSY leaders. Secondly, a European bank accountant was shot in Steamer Point in broad daylight. His driver, another white bank manager, threw himself into the road and drew his pistol. When he finally got up, there was no one there, as was often the case, except two Arab policemen fifty yards away making no move to help.

The SAA now held the key to the future of South Arabia and, although it was feared that the declaration for the NLF might split the SAA, only some

113

ten officers who supported FLOSY resigned. The RAF then flew them back the 150 miles to their own tribal area at Ataq. The remainder of the SAA formed a stable and authoritative element around which the people of South Arabia rallied as we completed our final plans to depart.

The Withdrawal Gains Momentum

On our Hunter Wing, 43 Sqn would remain to the bitter end, and as the Hunter FR10s of 1417 Flight might possibly be left for a South Arabian air force, 8 Sqn was the unit to move out first. The Sqn had been based at Khormaksar for forty years with hardly a break. It had operated from Iraq to Rhodesia and from Cyprus to Somaliland. Its aircraft must have been familiar to almost every tribesman in the Arabian Peninsula, and many had cause to know its rocket accuracy. There could have been hardly a day, except the occasional Christmas Day, in those forty years when the Squadron was not carrying out active operations somewhere. Hence, it was understandably an emotional moment when 'the pieces of 8', as we now irreverently called ourselves, flew out of Aden for the last time on the 3rd August.

In spite of the run-down of squadrons, we flew no fewer than 142 operational Hunter sorties in support of the SAA during the month of September, the highest number since the Radfan campaign of '64. The reason was not an upsurge in the fighting up-country, but the introduction of a new policy whereby we would fly a pair of Hunters on combat air patrol overhead whenever any RAF or AAC aircraft was on the ground at up-country strips. We would make our presence known initially by flying low over the airstrip, and then patrol in the vicinity at high altitude to conserve fuel. This was a sensible precaution against the grounded aircraft being unexpectedly attacked, as happened later at RAF Riyan, as all British troops had now been withdrawn and the reliability of the SAA could not be accepted entirely without question.

As it was vitally important to be seen to be giving full air support to the SAA until the end, Beverleys and the helicopter force were fully engaged with supply tasks to the various SAA outposts, but we remained on both ground and airborne alert to intervene if they were ambushed or fired upon. The tribesmen sensed that the British aircraft would soon withdraw as the army had already done from their up country areas. Except at Riyan, and despite losing a Beverley at Beihan due to engine failure on take off, there were no untoward incidents involving aircraft during those last difficult weeks in South Arabia.

Chapter Fourteen

The Last Days

As 8 Sqn flew out of Aden for the Gulf on 3rd August 1967, leaving behind four experienced pilots, viz: Daz James, John Loftus, Ron Pattinson and myself, to reinforce 43 Sqn, I well remember seeing them off, and nearly shedding a tear as my "support" group had gone – we'd lost our identity. We four felt a little misplaced while trying to come to terms with operating on a different Sqn and a different bunch of guys. Even though we knew them all as friends, they had always been on duty when we were socialising, and vice-versa.

Khormaksar was left with the remainder of the Hunters of 43 Squadron to maintain the air defence standby. The Wessexes of 78 Squadron also remained to meet the search and rescue commitment and carry out internal security patrols until embarking in one of the naval vessels during the last days in Aden for the move to the Gulf. Buccaneers and Sea Vixens from *HMS Eagle* were to take over the air defence role, while RN helicopters from *HMS Albion* provided the final link with Khormaksar.

The AOC, Air Vice-Marshal A H Humphrey, transferred his flag to Bahrain on 27 October, and handed over command in Aden to his Senior Air Staff Officer, Air Commodore Fred B Sowrey CBE AFC, another ex-8 Sqn Cdr and later to retire as an Air Marshal. "Bent Fred" as he was affectionately known to us, due to his hunchback appearance. I have every sympathy for him because this was the same problem that I was later to contract myself with demoralizing results. The AOC's departure signalled the end of AFME, while Bent Fred commanded the remainder of us at Khormaksar. By the end of the month, concentration of the remaining units and sections into Khormaksar and its immediate surroundings was almost complete, with Steamer Point finally evacuated.

On 6th November, the Navy arrived in strength. *HMS Eagle,* the strike carrier, again hove over the horizon with a powerful armada of twenty-five boats to cover our withdrawal. A fine sight it was giving those left on the ground some final sense of confidence and security! However, where would the navy find twenty-five operational boats today?

Back on the Hunter wing, we had been an effective deterrent. The Hunter was the first aircraft capable of breaking the sound barrier to be stationed in Aden, and tribesmen could not readily distinguish between a sonic bang and the distant sound of a 1000lb bomb exploding in a neighbouring wadi. A few well-directed sonic bangs gave the impression of a heavier scale of attack than had in fact been carried out, and this illusion was used from time to time. We flew many such flagwave sorties, where just our noise and the odd glimpse of us, was often enough to quell trouble.

A classic example of flagwaving was shown in the Hunters' final operational mission into the Eastern Aden Protectorate. A French owned Dakota from Djibouti Airways was hijacked at the now deserted airstrip of RAF Riyan, where the Captain, a French national, had just delivered the Hadramaut Bedouin Legion wages. He was ordered to fly gunrunning missions into the Hadramaut and refused, so his Pakistani co-pilot completed the job. Anxious about the fate of a foreign national, we were ordered into the air to shadow the Dakota, with Beverleys flying eight hour missions acting as airborne radio-relays. Meanwhile, an AAC Beaver on its way from Aden to Bahrain ran into trouble and force landed at Riyan, followed by a second en-route Beaver to evacuate the first crew if necessary. Tribesmen, firing their rifles into the air in triumph, refused to let the Beavers leave until our Hunters turned from their high flight shadowing to stage Riyan's lowest and fastest official beat up! That's airborne flagwaving, with its implicit threat, and the Beavers were suddenly released to go on their way!

Several bargains were made out of the market that sprung up from our -withdrawal. Aden Airways, which was a BOAC subsidiary, and also flying, inter alia, Dakotas, closed down. Djibouti Airways picked up four Dakotas from Aden Air for the amazingly cheap sum of £35,000! The hijacking at Riyan involved one of these, but at least some money was exchanged, which is more than can be said for the Aden Air Viscount airliner. The NLF summarily burnt it after its last flight to stop the aircraft being ferried home to the UK.

By now, the old native rulers, the Sultans and Sheikhs of the various states, had fled from Aden or joined the NLF. To a man, they felt themselves betrayed by our unilateral decision to withdraw, and the consequent revocation of the perpetual treaties of protection with us, which they had all signed. Chaos reigned, with many grenade and shooting incidents. Although everything quietened down towards the last few days, as the NLF began to realize that they needed to keep European technicians to run things, particularly the oil flow from the BP Refinery at Little Aden, it was still unsafe to walk the streets.

At the request of the SAA, the last Hunter ground attack sorties were flown by 43 Sqn at 8.30am on 9th November. Heavy mortar and machine gun positions around the border town of Kirch, being manned by FLOSY supporters, were attacked and destroyed with rockets and guns.

"Forty-Three" had come from Cyprus four years earlier to reinforce 8 and 208 Squadrons in the emergency and had never returned. The last Hunters to leave were the FR10s of 1417 Flight with our recce mates aboard. Three years earlier these aircraft had originally been C Flt of 8 Sqn, and now they flew to Muharraq on the last day to rejoin No.8.

Astonishing scenes took place on the last day, the 28th of November. An astounded Arab army colonel was handed the keys to 1,700 furnished flats in Maalla, and told the rents had been paid until the year's end, even though they'd been empty since June. Landrovers and 3-ton Bedford trucks were left, with the keys in them, on the aircraft aprons for the Arab army officers, who quickly quarrelled over their ownership. Millions of pounds worth of equipment was just left, including a fully working international airport: RAF Khormaksar, until recently the busiest RAF airbase in the world.

But perhaps the RAF in some ways had the last laugh. Two large ships-buoys, painted with red, white and blue RAF roundels were lifted by helicopter and chained deep in concrete, high up on the barren, black rocks of Aden's Shamsan Mountain, as a farewell memento. I often wonder whether they are still there today, or has that appalling climate eroded them, along with the rest of the Empire, to dust?

Thus did 29th November 1967 bring to an end 128 years of British rule in Aden and, for the RAF and 8 Sqn, forty-eight years of occupation of Khormaksar and Steamer Point. The final departures from most overseas stations, which became fairly frequent occurrences for British servicemen between 1950 and 1970, were usually accompanied by many regrets and a certain nostalgia. Sir David Lee wrote, "It is doubtful whether any soldier or airman regretted leaving Aden. An uncomfortable and exhausting place at the best of times, the last few years [sic] had been grim, dangerous, frustrating and almost intolerably restricted."

Accordingly, Sir David went on to say, "Having said that, however, it is impossible to ignore the sense of satisfaction which many, indeed most servicemen obtained from having carried out a tour of duty there. It was the satisfaction which comes from completing a hard and challenging task, something to be talked about, an experience to be recounted, often with much exaggeration and boring detail. There is no doubt that service in Aden gave immense experience and a certain maturity to all of us in AFME . . . The loss of Aden was, therefore, the loss to the RAF of a unique testing ground for both men and materials and, to that extent, it was a cause for regret."

I have every sympathy with this latter point of view, but many of us had a most enjoyable time; unlike Sir David and many others, I had a marvellous time, but I was very much younger. The young have a greater ability to withstand the sort of everyday problems of life in Aden. It was one hell of a challenge, and an excellent proving ground for a young man. There were far too many, especially those unaccompanied by their families, who were ready to do nothing more with their leisure time than sit in the mess bar, drinking and moaning. For them Aden was grim; for the rest of us, we learned to be men in every sense of the word. There was a ditty we often sang to wind up others in the mess Jungle Bar:

> "I'm an AFME Hunter pilot,
> and the weather's getting clear,
> What's the course to steer,
> A crate of Carlsberg beer,
> Oh it's great to be an AFME Hunter Piiiiiiiiiiiiiiilot!"

Those Mess and Sqn songs, so soon to disappear from everyday RAF life, brings me to a more serious note. Being so well cocooned inside Khormaksar, we often only knew of local incidents on delivery of the UK papers five days later, and, as usual, the media had exaggerated for sales effect. Nevertheless, final UK casualty figures prove the facts of life during 1964 to '67. The totals

117

for those last four years were 330 killed including 57 UK servicemen, and 1,714 injured including 655 UK servicemen. It was, therefore, by no means all sea, sand and beer. This period was an extremely difficult time for all British personnel based in South Arabia and, in particular, for the British Army units trying to maintain a secure environment. They were fighting on three fronts: security of the Aden colony, suppression of cross border dissident activity, and politicians both in the Federal Government and in London. Yet without the air force offensive air support up-country, the casualty figures would have been a lot more alarming: we kept many dissidents from making it through to Aden at all. A more discerning enemy could have stopped our fighter operations completely by targeting the aircrew, or the Hunters on the ground neatly lined up next to the civilian airport!

Nevertheless, the key to power in any Arab land is the army, and the SAA with most of its senior officers "under cover" as NLF leaders, were always leaning heavily towards this extreme terrorist organisation. The NLF carried overwhelming weight, as they eventually "liberated" fifteen of the Federation's twenty states, the others remaining archaic, leaving us little choice in the end over the colony's future. Equally, there was no valid reason why British soldiers' lives should be put further at risk merely to buy time for Aden's psychopathically quarrelsome people to develop a glimmer of reason. However, that does not absolve our unthinking abrogation of those solemn treaties.

Regrettable though the grim story of the last years in Aden may be, redeeming features which stand out, were the courage, efficiency and remarkable restraint of our patrolling soldiers, and that of our airmen, not only those of us protecting from the air, but our indomitable groundcrew who had to service the machines in atrocious conditions. We were all abused and provoked, ambushed and sniped at by a ruthless and often unseen enemy. We were also not above criticism from our peers elsewhere, who had no concept of the conditions under which we had to live, work and fight. With their mismanagement of the economy and lack of understanding of foreign affairs, Labour politicians were mainly to blame for the South Arabian débâcle. Nevertheless, the final withdrawal without a shot fired or a life lost, under appalling conditions, must rank as one of the best planned and executed operations in the Empire's military history.

> *"Politician. n. An eel in the fundamental mud upon which the super-structure of organised society is reared. As compared with the Statesman, he suffers the disadvantage of being alive."*
>
> (Definition from "The Devil's Dictionary" by Ambrose Bierce)

Withdrawal Comment

This Middle Eastern section would be incomplete without comment on our humiliating retreat from east of Suez.

Since the Second World War, twenty-seven years passed during which

Britain relinquished control of much of her Empire and withdrew her military forces from many parts of the world where her soldiers, sailors and airmen had gained experience to an extent that must be unrivalled among nations. During its short life the RAF has certainly partaken of its full share of this experience and nowhere more so than in the Middle East, but the opportunity to continue to acquire this experience ceased in December 1971 on our withdrawal from Bahrain. Appropriately, it was 8 Sqn that was the last to leave: first in – last out. If ever there was a desert Sqn in the RAF, 8 earned the accolade.

The story, however, cannot be abruptly terminated with the departure of 8 Sqn from Muharraq. At most a man serves for forty years and the average is less than half of that period. By 1990, therefore, there would have been but a handful of serving airmen who had ever experienced service in the Middle East, and a generation of aircraft and weapons which would have had only a transitory acquaintance with the region, if that. By the turn of the millennium, few if any would have had more than an odd few weeks' detachment in the area. It is tragic for future generations of servicemen that all the experience and lessons learned by us of desert operations would be irretrievably lost through failure to place them on record against a time when perhaps the RAF may again be required to operate in the area. The two Gulf Wars saw some experience regained, but not before some appalling tactical mistakes, due to lack of experience, were made. With the present and ever-growing problems in Iraq, Afghanistan, and the tinderbox of Palestine, what price for the desert experience gained on 8 Sqn and its sister units?

The vital need to retain control of aircraft under one authority in order to exploit their inherent flexibility to the maximum has been demonstrated time and time again, but nowhere more convincingly than in the vast area of Arabia. Middle East Command, which never possessed more than a handful of squadrons, stretched for more than 3,000 miles from Dar-Es-Salaam in the south to the Iraq/Turkish border in the north. For most of that time the Command was never without operational activity in some part of its territory, and yet its few squadrons were always to be found controlling the trouble-spots, switching with great rapidity from one danger spot to another. As a result, a remarkable economy of force was obtained by the skilful and timely switching of modest resources. It was in the Middle East that the flexibility of air power was finally proven.

This permitted us to change from garrison air forces located in static positions overseas, to a policy of world-wide reinforcement from the United Kingdom. It is this inherent flexibility of air power, demonstrated since in the Falklands and the Gulf Wars, that allowed us to withdraw from our overseas bases – but at immense cost to hard won experience, and international stability?

On a more parochial note, 'Fair wear and tear' is an expression that it never seemed possible to apply to Aden, so destructive were the elements and so short lived were some of our mechanical components. The conditions in which some engines, airframes and components including our Hunters, never mind the pilots, were returned to the United Kingdom for major servicing, was so appalling that inefficiency was often blamed. Nevertheless, today, aircraft in the condition of our Hunters would not be allowed to fly, never mind ferried half-way round the world; my last ferry trip home showed numerous stark examples of these atrocious problems.

I have made mention of the difficulties of navigation, largely due to the inadequacies of the available maps, lack of reliable communications, and the lack of long range navigational aids for ferrying. The frequency with which these inadequacies threw us back upon basic principles of airmanship was the most excellent grounding for a first tourist. For we fighter pilots, the single-handed navigation to a target in hostile, mountainous country, followed by its accurate identification and determined attack, often presented an immense challenge, particularly when the safety of nearby troops had to be considered. For transport pilots such as our Dakota crew, the greatest test was frequently that of landing and taking off from rough, stony airstrips of minimal length, situated in deep valleys, and totally devoid of any form of landing aid, unless the odd windsock and white ground strip can be classed as 'landing aids'. For all our aircrew there was the constant risk of damage, or worse, from ground fire. It was rare for an aircraft to be shot down but commonplace to return to base with one or more bullet holes, the origin of which was, more often than not, unknown to us. Modern aircraft, tightly-packed with delicate avionics, could not survive such constant damage.

Perhaps the greatest value of service in the Middle East was the maturity, self-confidence and adaptability, which it gave to servicemen and to their families. The relatively primitive conditions which they encountered, often called for great tolerance, not a little hardship at times, and the need to adapt to a new and unusual style of life. Airmen working in these conditions were frequently called upon to improvise and to display initiative well beyond that usually required. We often held positions of greater responsibility than at home: rules and regulations could not be so strictly enforced and much more scope was left to the initiative of the individual. Indeed, even when I had command of units later in my career, I don't think I ever had a greater responsibility than when I was leading the standby pair attacking enemy positions close to my army colleagues in up-country Aden. It was, indeed, a life and death responsibility foisted on one at a very early age.

Finally, British Middle Eastern policy during this period must be mentioned. Only later in life did I realise that it had been a failure – my first experience of British foreign policy. If only we had had the wisdom and foresight to look at the longer term, we should, perhaps with American help, have kept one or two main bases in the Middle East. If the 1967 Arab/Israeli Six Day War was the key event that produced today's troubled Middle East, and fanned the flames of Aden terrorism, then remaining there could have produced the stability that the whole region required. We would have remained the main stabilizing influence helping curb the upsurge in Islamic fundamentalism and not even allowing a Gulf Crisis, never mind a Gulf War, as in our timely presence in Kuwait in 1961. Perhaps it would have even provided the steadfast immutability required to solve the Palestinian/Israeli problem, if not Arab terrorism as a whole.

For want of financing two main bases at, say, Aden and Bahrain or Muscat, we would have remained a powerful stabilising influence in that part of the world which many western minds perceive as the cause of many of our problems today. There would have been no Sep 11th, and a vastly different outlook by Islam and Muslims alike on world peace and terrorism. And let's not suggest we weren't wanted in the region, as some Arab Sheikhs, such as those of the Oman, Kuwait, Bahrain and the Trucial States, would have been very happy for us to have stayed. Indeed, our withdrawal was seen by some rulers, notably those of Beihan and Bahrain, as a treacherous betrayal of all we had previously promised them. Indeed, we lost our willingness, and ability, to do what America is learning to do today: act as the world's policeman.

Despite our successes, we haven't fought in the Middle East against a **determined** enemy (the Iraqi military were certainly not determined) since the Omani Dohar campaign, but think what might have been if our previous experience had been maintained? War in the Middle East would probably have been avoided completely by keeping permanently based forces in the area. Count the cost in lives lost since by not so doing.

Late in 1966, parliament amended the Armed Forces Act to include colonies in the definition of "active service" in tardy recognition of service in Aden. After suffering 49 dead and nearly 600 wounded, the young veterans of the Empire's last rearguard action were officially on active service and were thrown a bar to their GSM. The Daily Express described the troops in Aden as *'men whose steadfast patience had been tested and found to hold firm on thousands of unrecorded, forgotten occasions'*. Hopefully, this book will go some way towards rectifying that situation – they should not be forgotten.

I have tried to portray my part in the Middle East as it seemed to a young bachelor of those times. Yet it was a sad time leaving AFME. Aden and the Middle East taught me to be a man, showed me how other people lived and thought, explained to me what the world was all about and, above all else, made me yearn for the days of the real Empire. But in the end, we never won the war in South Arabia because, despite serious attempts, we never fully won their hearts and minds. Indeed, the Aden campaign was not just a loss, it was an inglorious retreat from what was no more than a bunch of thugs, only surpassed by the American withdrawal from Vietnam.

Unlike Vietnam though, Aden and the Radfan Campaign rarely hit the UK headlines, and no one in official circles wanted it to resurface; it's not British to dwell on one's failures. Indeed, Col Mitchell summed up British policies in Aden as "old English humbug." Apart from the "Mad Mitch" episode, Aden sank under the surface of media attention, to be quietly forgotten within days of the withdrawal. Even a couple of years later when British Petroleum handed over the Little Aden refinery, nothing was mentioned in the press. It had all been a shabby chapter in our recent colonial background, fuelled by a Labour government who had no proper experience of, or interest in, the world at large, whose members most certainly couldn't think strategically and could never be called statesmen.

As we rarely learn lessons from history, is it not strange that as I write in 2006, there are similar situations, with identical tribal outlooks, in southern Iraq and Afghanistan? However, it was we, the British, who drew the original lines in the sand of many Middle Eastern states including Aden and Iraq, and we are now paying the price of that draughtsmanship. How often in the past have we ignored the tribal histories, and tried to piece them together regardless? There were eighteen sheikhdoms in what was British South Arabia, but at least with historical tribal borders! In Iraq, the Kurds, the Sunnis and the

Shi'ites are never going to rub shoulders harmoniously long enough to maintain a stable state, and another civil war can be traced back to British imperialism.

It seems that Yemen is now cooperating in part with the Americans over international terrorism, and is at the beginnings of coming in from the cold. This will take time, time we in the West haven't got. They are like children: cowardly, unremittingly treacherous and incessantly quarrelling amongst themselves. This is what frustrated Lawrence over 80 years ago. The Arab world's very nature is exquisitely shown by the exposure of Iraq's army and air force – twice, and answers the question of why they didn't fight! As the Bangladeshis said: "They haven't got the bottle!" Even so, the mountainous areas of central and south Yemen are, like those of Afghanistan, to all extents and purposes, ungovernable. Only in March 2004, an Al Qaeda chief had been caught on the Lawder Plain in the Abyan Province of Southern Yemen – it is the very Plain over which we used to fly the majority of our Hunter low level training missions until 1967: an excellent, noisy deterrent to terrorism. The vacuum caused by our untidy withdrawal is today still filled by terrorism. That part of the world remains deeply stuck in medieval times – and that's on a good day. It will take a century or two yet, if ever, before the tribes of south and central Yemen capitulate and are dragged, kicking and screaming, successfully into the modern world.

Nonetheless, it is perhaps worth quoting Commander Stafford Haines, who was the founder of the Aden Colony. He wrote in 1851 to the East India Company, *"I have visited every part of Arabia, and the tribes in the neighbourhood of Aden are more treacherous and false than any other. Justice and right thinking is unknown to them. They are a people incapable of estimating the value of good government."*

Little had changed by the time we left in 1967. Indeed, inter-tribal feuding among the seventeen, old, federation states, plus the three from the Eastern Aden Protectorate and the Aden Colony itself, and bad external influences from Egypt and the Yemen, had, if anything, increased the problem. Later in November 1967, Britain opened the gates of its prison for political detainees at Al-Mansour. Out into the sunlight came thirty-one well-groomed, well-fed Arabs, all hard-core terrorists held on positive evidence of murder. Soon after smiling handshakes with their British jailers, they began relating stories of British brutality, totally at variance with their sleek, polished appearance. This is yet another example of the Yemeni-Arab duplicity. Thirty-five years later, it has, not surprisingly, become one of the greatest hotbeds of terrorism, with major Al Qaeda influences causing severe headaches for the rest of the world.

Even so, it is no wonder that we, as the colonial power, treated the South Arabians the way we did. Only bigger weapons than their own ever stopped them. They only understood greater force and power as a stabilising influence, and little else. Modern arguments hold no sway where inter-village/tribal vendettas go back hundreds of years, and the power of the gun is the only master.

Back in 1839 and '40, after numerous attacks on the fledgling colony, Haines had become convinced that persuasive argument had no more than a temporary effect on the Arab mind. An Arab notable, discussing feuds, told him, "It is our custom." It still is today. Similarly, buying off enemies is a hallowed tradition in an area where bribery at every level of government is still an expected practice, whether you're buying a new driving licence or transacting multi-million pound defence contracts. Even after amalgamation with North Yemen, not much changed, and in the few short years after British withdrawal, the wheel had turned a full circle. Aden reverted to the state of poverty and piracy which we, the British, had found in 1839.

Piracy in its modern form of terrorist blackmail and extortion found a natural habitat in South Arabia. The People's Republic of South Yemen, outcast even in its own Arab world, had cordial relations only with the Communist countries and their third world client states. It is too late to turn back the clock but, whatever else, we must return to, remain and engage in, the Middle East. But Arabs have long memories. Their feuds and vendettas continue through generations . . . **we haven't heard the last of them yet!**

Significantly, because of Nasser and Wilson, Aden was to be one of only two former colonies which never joined the Commonwealth after independence. After all, it was the last colonial war fought by the British, and as I flew out for the last time en-route for the UK, on that epic trip home, I thought that my Empire days were over. Nothing could have been further from the truth!

Chapter Fifteen

The Ferry

Finally, the posting home came through the mail, but life is never simple, and neither was this. In short, this was to one of the only two elite fighter recce sqns of 2 TAF in Northern Germany, flying the Hunter FR10 recce version on low level tactical army reconnaissance. Agreeably, this was my first choice, and providentially to be my next home. Specifically, "Tatty Two", or No. 2 (Army Co-operation) Sqn at RAF Gutersloh had the pleasure of my company. But my withdrawal from Aden, and how I got to 2 Sqn became another saga.

Initially unplanned, I would take the scenic route home, spending five weeks en-route! The journey commenced as a result of the Arab-Israeli six-day war. During those six days in June '67, Jordan lost most of its operational air force. They only had fifteen fighter aircraft, all Hunters, at the beginning, and lost fourteen of them. Within weeks the British Government had decided to replace them, and the "new" aircraft came from our wing. Owing to our departure from Aden with several disbandments and amalgamations, surplus aircraft to our future requirements were now available.

Hence, on 9 Sep 67, 24 hours after the disbandment of 1417 Flight and its amalgamation into 8 Sqn, I finally departed from the cauldron of Aden for Amman in my own aircraft, XG255, as part of a flight of three. These three Strike Wing aircraft were all Hunter FGA9s, repainted beforehand in Royal Jordanian Air Force colours, which Wg Cdr 'Pancho' Ramirez (The Strike Wing Cdr), Wally Willman from 43Sqn and I, flew to Jordan via Jeddah on their delivery flights, and that take off from Khormaksar in a Jordanian Hunter was my last, never to return.

While planning this two-stage ferry flight, we signalled the air attaché (AA) in Jordan, to ask which airfields we could use for diversion purposes, if needed, and suggesting, tongue in cheek, that Jerusalem International would suit! The reply contained one of those, "NOT, repeat NOT . . . s" in its text – no way would we be allowed anywhere near Jerusalem! But he did give us Dawson's Field, a large 25,000 by 4,000yds strip of desert which, exactly two years later, came to fame as the rough airstrip where the PFLP, a Palestinian terrorist organisation, blew up three airliners, a Swissair DC8, a TWA Boeing 707, and a BOAC VC10. Perhaps the AA was right; as we passed over Aqaba at 40,000ft, only a few miles from the Israeli border town and airfield of Eilat, an Israeli Air Force aircraft shadowed us North all the way to abeam Amman! Nevertheless, we landed safely at the old combined Amman military/civil airport at Marqa, albeit on a heavily bomb-damaged runway, and handed the aircraft over to the RJAF.

We were lauded in Amman. After all, we had quadrupled the size of their air force! Tea at the palace, party at the embassy, five-star Intercontinental Hotel accommodation, once-in-a-lifetime trips to the Living City of Petra, the colonnaded ruins of Jerash, probably the best preserved city of the Roman Empire, and a free day's water skiing – they couldn't do enough for us!

We were there for nearly a week waiting for the repairs to the main runway, one side of which was still unusable after the Israeli bombings of the recent war. Eventually, our RJAF hosts asked about our sporting activities and we cynically suggested water skiing only because 8 Sqn had had its own boat in Aden, we all skied, and there was no water in Jordan! What we didn't tell the Jordanians was that our boat was a tinny aluminium one with only a 35hp Johnson outboard that couldn't pull two up! Imagine our surprise, then, when the next day we were ushered into an RJAF Dakota, and flown down to Aqaba just to go water skiing at the Royal Jordanian Water Skiing Club! Incredibly, the Captain of the Dakota, Hassan, had trained with me in the UK on Hunters some four years earlier, and a good reunion was had in the cockpit all the way there, especially as, having flown Daks with the MECS in Aden, I was allowed to fly it into and out of Aqaba. A great treat for me, but not without some concern and trepidation on the part of Pancho and Wally!

On the beach at Aqaba we found a water-hangar out of which they drove a twin diesel, twin screw 215hp inboard polished limousine of a speed boat! You've heard the phrase, "pride comes before a fall"? Well, it does when you are drenched in front of all those Jordanian pilots! I don't think any of us stayed up on the skis for more than a minute at a time, but we did have a lot of laughs, mainly at our own expense.

Arriving back in Amman, we found a different mood afoot. By this time the RJAF groundcrew had started pulling our Hunters apart to service them. One of the first things to attend to on a Hunter's major servicing is the dismantling of the rear fuselage for access to the engine. The whole rear comes away in one piece, exposing the jet pipe. Our wonderful squadron groundcrew in Aden who had repainted the fuselages and wings in Jordanian colours had also, it appeared, painted Stars of David on the outside of the jet-pipes, which were now exposed to the Arab ground-crew! The Jordanians were not amused!

This was bad news for us, and almost caused an international incident. We were quickly out of the hotel, into the embassy, and on to the next plane out of the country; they couldn't get rid of us fast enough! Thus, after Aden, this was the second country out of which I'd been kicked!

We flew out to Beirut where, after a good night out (Beirut was the Monte Carlo of the Middle East in those days), Pancho and Wally flew back civvyair to Aden, but I journeyed on by myself on the Lebanese airline, Middle East Airways, direct to Bahrain to rejoin 8 Squadron. That last flight out of the Lebanon was my first-hand experience of Arab cooking on primus stoves in the alleyway between the aircraft seats. The smells would make you sick on the ground, never mind while airborne!

8 Sqn had recently moved into Muharraq from Sharjah, where they had been resting after their final dramatic months in Aden while awaiting new

permanent accommodation. Eventually, this accommodation was revealed as the top floor in a hangar above our new sister squadron, No.208. Of course, from then on all our rubbish got tipped off our balcony into 208's domain as a regular occurrence. Indeed, so good was the rivalry, that one of the rolled sand airstrips near Seeb on the Omani coast north of Muscat, which as usual was delineated by white painted rocks, was visited one day by 8 Sqn personnel. The rocks were later found to have been rearranged at the beach end of the runway to read "208 go home"!

My stay on 8 at Muharraq was only three weeks before continuing my scenic journey home, and I was glad of that. The heat was so oppressive compared with Aden; not a lot different in temperature, but the humidity was massively higher. Indeed, the true tale was oft heard that in the days before air-conditioning when the temperature and humidity rose higher than body temperature, which it did regularly, it is impossible to sweat in those conditions. Hence, a bell was rung on the RAF base for everyone to down tools and to go and lie on their beds so as not to overheat. There aren't many occasions when one can lie down officially on duty, but that was one of them!

During my few weeks there, Gp Cpt "Twinkle" Storey, the station commander, who was one of the best COs one could wish for, was regularly required to issue informal reprimands for various misdemeanours. Reprimands were not allowed for commissioned officers; a court martial was required for that, so informal discipline was kept by "inviting" an officer to donate to charity, usually to the CO's charity fund[1]. As the CO, often deep in it along with the rest of us, he saw fit to "invite" himself to make a donation. Also as the CO, and therefore the most senior, the donations were always invited pro-rata, and he therefore always donated the most to his own fund!

But on 8 Sqn's arrival, he made one considerable mistake. He organised a formal dining-in night, especially to dine the Squadron in to the Mess. This was to be the best ever such night's entertainment.

Within the close knit community of the Sqn aircrew, we had a number of reprobates whose skills and ingenuity included lock-picking, explosives and detonators, the art of bartering, nicking, filching, acquiring, and ducking from under. Chief amongst them was another major eccentric, one Dai Heather-Hayes of the Masirah Thunderflash infamy, and now many years later a Civil Aviation Examiner. Dai was rather a lovable oddball for a first tourist, who easily upstaged my greatcoat arrival in Aden by coming down the trooping flight steps to join his first squadron in a Sherlock Holmes three-piece suit, wing collar, bow-tie, deer-stalker and umbrella; a sight that stunned our reception party! It was a while before we realised that this was no joke. It was his normal garb! The man had an exuberant manner and was an excellent comrade in arms, albeit always bringing trouble with him wherever he went. He was officially disciplined three times for various minor misdemeanours, once with us in Aden but, despite this, nothing would keep him down.

He somehow acquired from local army sources, two 105mm, brass Centurion-tank shell cases, wire, batteries and detonators, and filched enough flour from the kitchen to fill them. That afternoon was spent inserting the ingredients into the two enormous plant pots behind the top table in the dining room, the connecting wires running under the carpet to a battery alongside his table place.

126

Twinkle was only five-foot-nothing in his stocking feet, but compensated for this with a great personality and a grand reputation. When he rose to deliver his after dinner speech to cries of "up,up", meaning "get on the table 'cos we can't see you", which he duly did, Dai touched the wire end to the battery terminal! With an enormous crack, flour exploded everywhere, covering the top table, and expanding in clouds across the entire room. Twinkle was blanketed in it! It was I imagine, like being in a thick dry pea-souper of a fog with visibility down to a metre. What an uproar, and everything white with flour, non-self-raising variety!

When the commotion and the flour died down, and visibility was restored, everything was a ghostly hue of white. Everybody's hair, eyebrows and mess kits were a whiter shade of pale! Meanwhile, Twinkle stood silently on the table top until the uproar abated. Minutes later when silence eventually ensued, all he said was, "Gentlemen, I will see 8 Sqn outside on the patio after dinner."

Afterwards, having trooped out onto the patio, while 208 were back in the bar getting in some drinking time, we waited for Twinkle. He eventually arrived, and standing in the entrance door with hands behind him, and drawing himself up to his full 5ft, he said, "Gentlemen, ATTENTION-SHUN!" That woke us up! He then proceeded, "The first person that moves, I'll see in my office tomorrow morning at 9am". Whereupon, he pulled out from behind his back a Thunderflash, which he lit and threw amongst us!

The resulting explosion started our participation in the best night's Mess games ever. At one point before my memory failed me, there was Twinkle sitting on my shoulders with a mop in his hands, while I was riding a cycle down the length of the bar trying to knock over our opponents from 208 coming the other way!

The Route Home

We regularly ferried battered old, time-expired Hunter aircraft some 7000 miles back to the UK for major servicing. Now that's no big thing in today's environment of international communications, and accurate digital inertial and satellite navigation systems. But back in the '60s, things were not quite like that. Inertial and satellite nav systems had not been invented, and neither had mobile phones. In fact, international phones were not exactly reliable either. There was no such thing as in-flight refuelling available on 1950s aircraft, no autopilot, few landing grounds and a distinct lack of long-range communications. Moreover, in the Middle East weather forecasting was at the whim of whichever local Arab forecaster decided that morning to arise from his bed. The only saving grace was that the weather was usually pretty good but, of course, that's when complacency could set in and catch you out. Help from non-English speaking air traffic controllers was distinctly patchy, un-reliable, indiscernible or unintelligible, and often unavailable, especially over France. Finally, the cockpit only contained the standard six-instrument panel with a decent compass, stop watch, and two old fashioned nav aids called Radio Compass(radio true-bearings from ground beacons(ADF)) and DME (Distance Measuring Equipment). In that environment we ferried long distances around the world.

As I flew out of Bahrain on 28 September in my own aircraft again, ferrying an old Hunter back to St Athan in South Wales for major servicing, I realised it was the same aircraft that had nearly been shot from under me on the 16 Aug, some two months earlier – XJ689. This aircraft had not only had a number of bullet holes in it, but had been around since 1956, and in Aden for at least the whole of my tour there. In other words by definition, like me, it was distinctly knackered! The problems associated with this and my wing-man's aircraft, indeed any aircraft going UK-wards for deep servicing, would have a major bearing on the next few weeks' saga of a journey. These time-expired machines were flown back for refurbishing, which certainly they desperately needed and, after so long in the desert, so did we!

Although the ferry route from Bahrain to UK was in theory of only three days duration, due to breakdowns while trying to nurse these battered aircraft into each further stage, the voyage usually took longer. This ferry was no exception. As I flew out for the last time en-route for the UK, on what was to be an epic trip home, little did I realise that I had, in fact, completed my "Wings Over The Middle Eastern Empire" saga.

Traditionally, ferrying to and from the UK had been a simple two-day, four-flight trip using the southern Egyptian route: Aden to El Adem, the RAF base in NE Libya just south of Tobruk. A quick refuel, then overhead Benghazi and on to Malta for a night of debauchery down 'The Gut' above Valetta harbour! Great if the navy wasn't around! On to 100% oxygen to clear the head as soon as you climbed into the aircraft the following morning, and depart for Nice or Istres in southern France. Another quick refuel, and take off for RAF St Athan near Cardiff. Some quick reunion flings were usually followed by a good long sleep-it-off trooping flight back to Aden from Gatwick. That was the theory, anyway!

Nasser put paid to that! After his closing the canal, we lost our over-flying rights, and staging via Khartoum and then North up the length of Libya along its eastern border with Egypt was not a good idea for a single engined jet. There were only two rules to these trips: you never ferried on your own, ie: two aircraft minimum, and you never ferried at night due to lack of navigation aids in the Hunter. The two nav aids, a relatively poor ADF and DME together gave track and distance, but not necessarily to the same beacon! There was only one problem with this set up: if you switched both on at the same time, they more often than not locked on to each other! So either course or distance was sometimes available but not always both simultaneously. As the aircraft had no autopilot either, you couldn't spend any time winding the handle round searching for beacons on these two bits of kit: you'd be upside down by the time you finished, and with few features over the desert, dead-reckoning was also inaccurate.

Hence two aircraft: leader calling course while No 2 gave distances. Of course with no beacons in the Sahara, no nav aids, and a map showing two square feet of uninterrupted, yellow desert, all you could do was head North and hope you knew which way to turn when you hit the Libyan Mediterranean coast. It was a good measure of our optimism that it always worked, but not before some moments of trepidation, that pit-of-the-stomach feeling, until the El Adem radar controller finally replied to your bleats and said, "I've got you!" He then usually proceeded to tell you just how far you were off course, and you humbly replied that you were, as usual, very short of fuel and would he mind expediting our arrival!

An alternative route had to be found because Nasser didn't like us, and The Central Treaty Organisation (CENTO) came to our rescue. There was a time when we had three basic military treaties, NATO, CENTO and SEATO, the latter being the Far East. The bit in the middle included Turkey and Persia, so what better way to lengthen our sought-after ferry trips than to fly the long way round?

All British military, civilian and trooping aircraft going to or from the Middle and Far East now used this route, and staged from RAF Bahrain via Teheran International to RAF Akrotiri in Cyprus. We soon found The Commodore Hotel in Teheran which contained all the international airlines' slip crews (half way house Europe to the Far East). By definition that meant at least fifty new air stewardesses in one hotel with nothing better to do! Add two fighter pilots, mix, and stand back! In those days, every RAF aircraft going through Teheran found some reason to go unserviceable (u/s), and that meant a night stop or, better still, two! Ferries were never the same again!

In theory, our little four-day CENTO route ferry trips went something like this:

Khormaksar to RAF Masirah Island.
Masirah to RAF Sharjah on the Trucial Coast – night stop.
Sharjah to Teheran.
Teheran to either Diyarbakir (SE Turkey TAF base), or RAF Akrotiri in
*   Cyprus if the tail-winds were strong enough to get there in one hop)*
*   – night stop.*
RAF Akrotiri to RAF El Adem, Libya.
El Adem to RAF Luqa, Malta – night stop.
Malta to Nice or Istres (FAF base near Marseilles).
Nice/Istres to the UK.

So now the ferry was twice as long as the original Egyptian/Libyan route, which of course quadrupled (2+2 ya know!) the problems, most of which were naturally self-inflicted!

My first Ferry trip in 1966 was actually the other way round. Three of us had flown to the UK by VC10 transport to pick up and return with three newly refurbished Hunters from RAF Kemble, and all went well on the first four legs, until the take-off from Akrotiri, Cyprus en-route for Teheran. In those days, if you bought a Kebab in any of the tavernas downtown Limassol, the wine came free! And so it should, it was called Cochinelli, and could be bought in five-gallon Jerry-cans!

Indeed, I remember one beach party in which the whole squadron fell ill simply because they had filled up a Jerry-can with 99.9% Cochinelli, forgetting the 0.1% jet fuel still swilling about in the bottom! We were all sick as dogs! Even so, Cochinelli could be bought for about two shillings per five-litre flagon, and these flagons appeared to fit neatly, one under each knee, when seated in the Hunter cockpit on a Martin-Baker ejection seat! On take off from Akrotiri after a night downtown Limassol, one of these flagons nudged into the centre between my knees so, at take-off speed, when it came to pulling the stick back to leave the ground, the thing wouldn't budge.

In these circumstances the runway is never long enough, and the whole day's adrenalin supply was instantly burnt up. With both hands jabbing the stick back as hard as it could go, the flagon finally burst, and at 150 knots with the runway's end looming large, and Cochinelli flowing all over the floor of the cockpit, we all staggered into the air! Now warm Cochinelli fumes, mixed with oxygen, are guaranteed to put you on a 'high' very quickly, especially in the rarefied atmosphere at high level after the climb. It remains one of the most enjoyable flights I can remember, and I was still giggling when I landed at Teheran. Although later, whilst I didn't dare tell the story on arrival at the squadron in Bahrain, the cockpit smell was an unfortunate giveaway!

Well, it was now the end of my time in the Middle East and I was leaving from Bahrain with my No 2 wingman, a Fg Off who was out on detachment from No 1(F) Sqn in the UK, and supposedly learning what real Empire flying was all about. To complicate the issue, we were not allowed by the Iranians to fly directly from Bahrain into Iranian territory, because of a schoolboy dispute about the name of the Gulf. The Iranians wouldn't accept the term "Arabian Gulf"; they called it the "Iranian Gulf", and that had to be displayed on our flight plan, which, in turn, was refused by the Arab nations. Aren't politicians and civil servants the world over consumed with niff-naff and trivia!?

So what followed was entirely the Iranians' fault. It meant flying out of Bahrain Southeast to Sharjah on the Trucial Coast, and spending the night there, before setting off for Akrotiri via Teheran the following day. Leaving from Bahrain on a Thursday meant a whole weekend's Cochinelli drinking in Cyprus before flying on the following Monday. Sounded a good plan to me, and it could always be Teheran instead! After all, what no-one else knew was that the parents of a good friend of mine, Steve George, who was a Whirlwind Helicopter Search and Rescue pilot in Aden, lived in Teheran, and Steve had arranged for them to meet us and take us up to the Caspian Sea Coast for the weekend!

Back in '65 the Trucial States were still completely undeveloped. The only tarmac was on the two runways: one at Dubai (civilian) and one at Sharjah (RAF), and there were no metalled roads. Indeed, the Abu Dabi and Doha airfields were still rolled sand delineated by white-painted rocks, but in the intervening two years, all four towns had become major cities with large international airports. The old RAF Sharjah runway running alongside the river estuary is now subsumed into one of the major city roads, but back in the mid-'60s the small towns of Sharjah and Dubai, with their runways both in similar positions with respect to their estuaries, looked similar from the air. Many were the arrivals at the wrong airfield, mine included!

But not this time! All was well until after landing at Sharjah, when my No 2, Joe, asked me for a second opinion on his port tyre; he thought it was a bit bald and probably needed changing. Hell, this was red rag to a bull! We certainly didn't want to stop any longer at this rough desert airfield and, more to the point, Teheran, with the BOAC and BUA stewardesses, Steve's parents and the Caspian Sea, beckoning. What better excuse with which to go u/s at

130

Teheran? The decision was simple. "That'll last one more landing, won't it Joe?" How right I was, and we launched to Teheran the next morning – Friday.

We parked at Teheran International on the dispersal just outside the main international airport terminal, where in short order two things happened. Next to us was a BUA trooping VC10 going the other way, and who should come waltzing down the aircraft steps but Air Stewardess Rita B. . . . whom I had met off a trooping flight in Aden a year earlier. What a coincidence and an even greater reason to stay a night or two!

The second happening was much more momentous. We were ground handled in those days by BOAC groundcrew at Teheran, so we sauntered into the BOAC office and announced that "Joe's" aircraft needed a new tyre. Before we knew what was happening, the RAF Group Captain Air Attaché arrived in high dudgeon. His words to me went something like this: "Every RAF aircraft through here in the past three months has gone u/s, and you're not going to! Get out of here right NOW!"

With others I'd recently been kicked out of Aden, and thrown out of Jordan. Now this was the third country we'd been thrown out of, and we hadn't finished yet! Hence, with great disappointment and lots of mutterings, we lumbered off the ground en-route to Akrotiri as fast as we could go, with Steve's parents, Rita and an irate Air Attaché waving goodbye in the distance. Though I think the attaché's wave only included two fingers! All the best laid plans . . . . . etc, etc!

Nevertheless, Cyprus for the weekend wasn't a bad second bet. However, Cyprus was not to be . . . more bad luck followed. Half way there, just past the Iranian/Turkish border over Lake Van, and having been meaconed[2] by the Russians scrambling our Nav aids, the headwinds were higher than expected and we decided that we didn't have the fuel to make it in one hop. Plan B: diverting into Diyarbakir, a Turkish Air Force (TAF) base 4,500 feet above sea level in South-eastern Turkey, that wasn't expecting us, was the next grave mistake. Not only that, but there was, for once outside France, a distinct lack of the English language over the Turkish air-radios.

On descending below cloud, after a couple of hours' dead reckoning, there was a moment of total alarm as we failed to recognize anything below us. This was followed by a finger-in-the-wind, I-think-it's-north-of-us decision to fly that way more in hope than judgement. What we eventually found, after a dreadfully uneasy couple of minutes, was an airfield with a single runway that was like any major road in the UK today: full of JCBs, traffic cones and holes! It wouldn't have been surprising if they'd had a contraflow system, but it left us with a narrow, fifty foot wide parallel taxiway in a howling cross-wind for landing.

Well, I got down in one piece – just, but as you may have suspected by now, my wingman's bald tyre didn't like crosswinds on a Turkish taxiway! For once I had been right: it had lasted only one landing! On this second landing, it exploded, the brake catching fire and causing him to run off the side of the taxiway. With no standard towing arm to tow the aircraft, it blocked their only runway and we were not exactly popular. But from our viewpoint, there we were on a Friday afternoon, neither at Teheran nor Akrotiri for the weekend, but at some God-forsaken, backward outpost in the far reaches of SE Turkey, stuck with a u/s aircraft, no spares, no servicing facilities and no English language. This was hardly the "standard NATO" base it claimed to be, nor was it likely to be the joyful weekend planned. Hoisted by . . . !

Could I get them to understand I needed to send a signal/radio message to tell our people to send help? Could I hell! I even showed them a pad of signal message forms, but it meant nothing! Eventually, I found one ancient Turkish WO air traffic controller, who purported to be an ex-WW2 Spitfire pilot, and spoke a little English. He directed us to telephone RAF Akrotiri in Cyprus, and that was the longest phone call I ever made! Nearly three hours of Turkish gobbledegook and click, click, click and a dead line! I finally got through to the Cyprus HQ Exchange at Episkopi, but every time they put me through to Akrotiri Ops the line went dead. Eventually I had to relay everything through the little WRAF operator at Episkopi but the line was so bad, and we were constantly being cut off, that I had to spell every word phonetically! Well, when it came to spelling Diyarbakir phonetically, I think she lost the whole plot! Where? Diy . . . ! Where's that? Turk . . . ? Never heard of it! Well . . . . . ! And so on, and so on, and so on!

It was now getting late on Friday and the base wanted to close, so we asked about accommodation and were taken downtown to an hotel. The only hotel in town, on the noisy main street, rated at minus-five-stars and we were there for the weekend! Heart of Turkey's Kurdish community, Diyarbakir was the city of Atatürk's Palace. Its ancient, dusty streets, surrounded by forty feet thick and equally high stone walls with enormous turrets, teemed with Turks, Kurds, donkeys and horse drawn carriages.

On Saturday morning we went back to the base to check on the aircraft. As soon as we walked into ATC, they gave me two signals that had arrived for me overnight! "Where did these come from?" I asked. "Oh, Comcen", they said, "Comcen"! Our standard term for a signals centre, "Comcen", meaning Communications Centre, was so obvious, yet we never thought of that term in Turkish the night before! Still, we knew then that we were in contact with the outside world and that help was on the way, but not before Monday at the earliest. Far from Teheran or Cyprus, Diyarbakir was to be our weekend penance!

From the signals that had arrived, would you believe that the RAF's answer to our problem was that one LAC technician and a spare wheel and brake were to be flown by Hercules from Bahrain right past us and all the way on to Cyprus? There they'd be transferred to a Hastings of 70Sqn, which would then fly them half-way back along the same route to us at Diyarbakir!

The Hastings was due to arrive at approximately 2pm on Monday, so we needed to plan our departure for Cyprus soon after that. We had to give the Turkish authorities 48hrs notice of our request for new diplomatic clearance times for take-off so, allowing two hours to repair the aircraft and an hour for Mum, we signalled the Embassy to obtain diplomatic clearance for a 5pm take-off on Monday. A dip clearance time gave us plus or minus two hours on the stated time for take-off to get airborne, otherwise we were grounded for a further 48hrs awaiting a further takeoff clearance. The 5pm request left precious little time if the Hastings was late, and no time at all before it got

17a & b. The airfield information board – Kamaran Island 67. (See Chap 11 for board interpretation)

18a & b. Views of Hadibo Beach, Socotra Island – Summer 67.

19. Socotra Island and the Aden Airways Dakota wreck Reg: VR-AAA marking the end of the runway at Hadibo 67.

20. Gone Native! The author under the wing of the Dak at Al Ghuraf in the Hadrumaut Wadi while taking Lord Shackleton on a 3 day area recce – 26 May 67.

21. The Sultan's Palace at Say'un, South Arabia May 67, during a visit with Lord Shackleton. Probably the most pretentious, it is now mostly empty but for a small museum.

22a. The great walled city of Shibam in the Wadi Hadrumaut – 1967. Top taken from a FR10 Hunter.

(© Crown Copyright/MOD)

22b. *Below:* Shibam taken from our Dakota.

23. 8 Sqn diamond nine over Radfan territory. *(© Crown Copyright/MOD)*

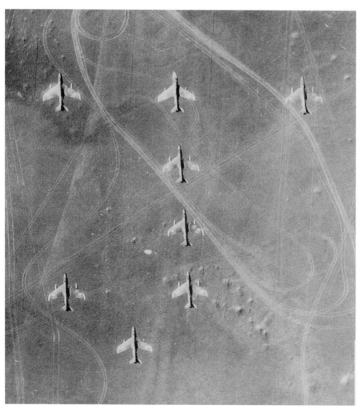

24. J-shape formation fly-past for AVM Johnny Johnson's depature from Aden, 14 Dec 65.

(© Crown Copyright/MOD)

25. 8 Sqn diamond nine flies past HMS *Hermes* at speed – May 67. The author is No 2 in this formation.
(© Crown Copyright/MOD)

26. 8 Sqn Diamond 9 fly-past HMS *Hermes* at full speed while a Buccaneer lands on – 12 May 67. Picture taken with fantastic timing by Ken Simpson of 1417 Flt in an FR10 Hunter. The author is No 2 in this formation.

(© Crown Copyright/MOD)

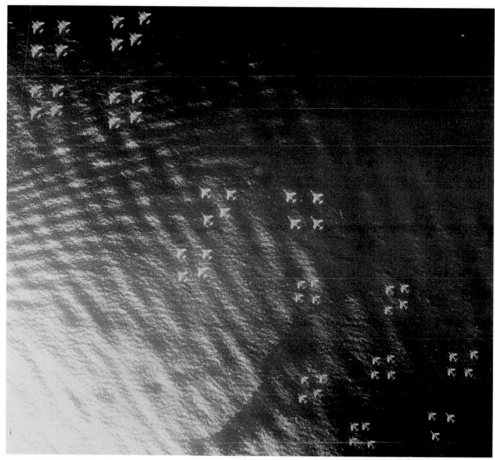

27. 55 Ship fly-past – 17 May 67. 16 Sea Vixens and 12 Buccaneers from HMSs' *Eagle* and *Hermes*, followed by 27 Hunters from 8 and 43 Sqns, RAF Khormaksar. *(© Crown Copyright/MOD)*

28. 8 Sqn aircrew outside the Sqn Ops Building – RAF Khormaksar, Aden 1967. Rear row L to R: The Author, Ron Pattinson, Dai Heather-Hayes, JB Hill, Brian Morris, Al Johnson, John Loftus, Tim Smith, John Grogan, Daz James, Al Mathie, Johnny Pym. Front row L to R: Colin Jones (Eng Off), Dai Rastall, Ron Etheridge, Peter PW Taylor, Sqn Ldr Des Melaniphy, Mike Webb, Kip Kemball, Bob Morris, GLO.

29. 8 Sqn Diamond 9 – 12 May 67 Lead – The Boss, Des Melaniphy, No2 – The Author, 3 – Mike Webb, 4 – John Loftus, 5 – Al Mathie, 6 – Daz James, 7 – John Grogan, 8 – Ken Rhodes (208 Sqn), 9 – Dai Heather-Hayes.

30. 8 Sqn departure from Aden after 40 years – 3 Aug 67.

31. The Royal Jordanian Air Force Trio who quadrupled the size of the RJAF – 9 Sep 67. L to R: Flt Lt Wally Willman, Self and Wg Cdr 'Pancho' Ramirez.

32. The Horse drawn carriages on Diyarbakir's main street from our hotel window – Sep 67.

dark about 6.30pm. Of course, we were not allowed to ferry in the dark either! But naturally, this wasn't going to be a problem when it was requested on the Saturday afternoon.

Saturday night was spent savouring the delights of downtown Diyarbakir. If you've never been to a genuine Turkish nightclub, you ain't lived! We walked into this reeking, dimly lit, square, windowless room early for Saturday – no other customers there, but the swarthy manager was almost wringing his hands with delight when he saw the colour of our skin and money: US dollars from our official imprest. Now if I failed to mention it before, I was a tall, blond, skinny guy in those days, but Joe was the opposite: dark, of medium height, and a black, Iraqi-style droopy moustache.

In the night club there was a three-piece band playing third rate Turkish music centre stage, and a row of chairs filled with dolled-up, black-haired girls down the right hand side, behind which were red curtained-off alcoves. Then we found the source of the smell: a large uncovered pit in the ground with overhanging wooden seats at the back that had been the club's communal open toilet for years! But, with nowhere else to go, we had a beer and then the manager started to barter with us. It was soon obvious that he was offering the services of the girls. It also soon became clear that they were all interested in Joe – they loved his dark looks – God knows why! Not having got the hang of Turkish currency at this stage, we were having more than a little trouble working out the price on offer, from Turkish Lira – they could have been widgets – via US dollars to £sterling. But once we did, it appeared on first calculations that he was being offered any or all of the girls for the equivalent of 4/9d (or approx 23p) FOR THE NIGHT!! Now maybe we got our sums wrong, but . . . !

You'll be disappointed to know that we declined his generous offer – I know, I would say that wouldn't I! But we then watched the best Turkish belly dance of all time. Again you wouldn't believe me. Believe me! This dusky, voluptuous Kurdish beauty danced for nearly two hours, took off forty-nine veils and, at the finale still didn't strip off the last veil, but it was the most sensual, erotic dancing one could wish for – more belly than dancing!

Sunday was spent recovering and sightseeing. On Monday morning we tried to pay our hotel bill and leave, only to find that we'd run out of Dollars and they wouldn't accept Sterling. Neither would the local bank change any! Eventually the manager called the police, who frog-marched us to the bank, which was ordered to change exactly the right amount. The police then ran us out of town at gunpoint in a taxi: a horse-drawn, handsome-carriage taxi!

That made four! Aden, Jordan, Iran and now Turkey had all thrown us out! We were certainly becoming experts at it by now, but from horse-drawn to jet-blown, we got out of there as fast as we could!

Typically, that afternoon the Hastings with our spares arrived an hour and a half late, and we were now starting to worry about our dip clearance time. So while the wheel was being repaired, we started to pre-flight check the aircraft, and that's when we found the real surprises! Everything that could have leaked out of those aircraft had leaked over the weekend, because they'd been parked in the low air pressure at 4500ft above sea level, and these old machines were full of holes and worn seals. Between us this was the inventory of problems we found:

Neither engine had any engine oil showing in the sight glass.
Neither aircraft had any emergency undercarriage, accumulator air
*   pressure.*
Neither aircraft had any emergency flap, accumulator air pressure.
Neither aircraft had any cockpit pressurisation.

And no help was available from the Turks! They didn't have the right oil for our engine, nor the right connectors for our air pressure accumulators.

"Houston, we have a problem!"[3]

At this point, I began to understand the dilemmas of the early aviation trail-blazers from Europe across the Middle East through the far-flung wastes of Empire! If we couldn't hack it in the 1960's, what must it have been like in the early flying days of the century?

Nonetheless, the wheel repair was completed about 5.30pm, and we were ready to move half an hour later. However, most of that half-hour was spent discussing our dilemma, and prioritising our alternatives. In the end there were only two:

1. Postpone for 48hrs, and get the aircraft serviceable in the meantime, IF WE COULD. But we'd just been run out of town at gun-point by the Keystone Cops, and told: DON'T COME BACK in very clear un-equivocal Turkish! Hence, unless we slept in the cockpits, this was really NOT an option!

Or 2. Try and get airborne in aircraft which, in any normal circum-stances, would never have been allowed out of any respectable hangar by any decent crew chief to see the light of day, never mind the express order that ferrying at night was forbidden!

Rock and hard place came to mind, but when it came to a decision between armed Turkish Policemen and an unserviceable Hunter, there wasn't really any choice: better the devil you know. The latter won hands down! Pragmatically, this was our ONLY option – it had been made profoundly clear that we were less than welcome here! We looked at each other, donned our flight kit and went for it!

With only fifteen minutes left before dusk, and with dip clearance time fast running out, we fired up the engines, taxied out and got airborne for Akrotiri as fast as we could. I was now about to find out the extent of my wingman's night formation technique, when he called, "Put your nav lights ON." But they were ON! In the next five minutes, by visually checking each other as it was getting darker, we found yet another problem: there was only one nav light serviceable between us – my starboard one! Joe's technique was pretty good – it had to be – because he then proceeded to close formate on me in the dark for the next two hours, using only one nav light and the jet-glow from my rear jet-pipe!

We couldn't fly too high because we had no cockpit pressurisation, so fuel was being used faster than we'd have liked, but we'd just about got enough to see us to Cyprus. Then, as we throttled back over Nicosia to let down towards Akrotiri, my jet-glow went out, and Joe, left with no perspective, disappeared. We found our own way separately those last few miles, and hit Akrotiri circuit with no nav lights while the resident Argosy transport Sqn was undertaking its night continuation training. They didn't like that, and complained!

To complete the Turkish-Cypriot leg of this saga, after landing in Cyprus, Joe said to me, "How much fuel did you land with?" I replied, "About Piccadilly[4] (650lbs a side)." He said, "I thought you'd be short. I had nearly double that." He went on, "When you taxied out in front of me at Diyarbakir, there was fuel pissing out the back of your aircraft, but I was damned if I was going to tell you!" I nearly hit him, but I certainly learnt about flying from that!

So, when we were hurled out of bed for a one-sided interview with OC Akrotiri Ops early the following morning, we really thought we were for the high jump. As it turned out, he was only unhappy about us arriving in his circuit the night before with no nav lights, and disrupting his Argosy training. But I do remember saying to him that we'd make a note in our end-of-ferry report, and thinking that a thousand, inconceivable, petty worldlinesses were weighing with me in this latter crisis, while face was being saved on both sides! He didn't know about the previous real crises, thank goodness, and we weren't about to tell him! But what report? There was no such thing as an end-of-ferry report but he didn't know that either, and we survived and lived to fight and fly another day!

Would I have done it the same way again? Yes BUT, being realistic, it wouldn't have been allowed to happen in today's environment. The world as it was in the '60s no longer exists; there was no Health and Safety Act then! It was an old, complex world of difference and danger and hard travelling, with Somerset Maughan characters who yarned about their experiences. Today we have instant communications, and credit cards. Today you wouldn't be allowed to fly aircraft in such bad states of repair, never mind that distance. Today, flight safety is *all* in the aviation world. Today, modern nations have a greater understanding of others' customs, traits, foibles and needs; we are now all much the same. Today, you can buy coke and a hamburger in Afghanistan amongst most places in the world, and use the same bit of plastic world wide to pay for it. But 40 years ago, flying 55year old designs now, it was a very different world, especially in the Middle East, with its unreliable communications and little supporting infrastructure. Initiative and making do with what little was available were the order of the day, particularly as each country had different standards, customs and currency, and the definition of "standard NATO" was not necessarily understood by your average Johnny Foreigner.

They put over a gallon of engine oil into each of our engines! It took four days of intensive repairs, including changing the windscreens to restore the cockpit pressurisation, before the aircraft were declared serviceable again in Cyprus. Hence, we got our 'weekend' in Cyprus in the end, for all our troubles and escapades, and four days socializing was more than enough to get engaged to an RAF nursing sister!

By contrast, the following two days ferrying from Akrotiri were quite banal. We weren't thrown out of anywhere else! We hadn't been exactly welcome in

Cyprus either, but at least we weren't kicked out. Via a refuelling stop at El Adem, near Tobruk, for a night stop at Malta, we had a raucous night down the Valletta 'Gut' with the Navy. The next day followed with a flagstop at Nice, and a final leg into RAF St Athan in South Wales, which were comparatively non-events. Yet we did win one small, final battle in the end. With no customs at St Athan, Glamorgan/Rhoose civvy airfield had to provide the VAT-men to meet us on our arrival. Typically, we were a week late on our original itinerary, but an hour early on our last flight plan. By the time customs arrived from Rhoose, there was nothing left to declare!

After five weeks en-route, I finally returned to Blighty on 7th October. That "simple" ferry had given us an astonishing, incident-filled month, but surely the Empire really had dwindled; it would be many years before I was to step back into any of those countries again.

On arrival in St Athan, I reflected with sadness upon that magnificent introduction to the Empire and its place in the world. You make good friends temporarily in a squadron situation, but just as things seem settled you'd be posted in different directions, so acquaintances would be a more appropriate description. There were many with a similar fund of names, incidents and places as yourself but whom you never saw again. It's often thought the reason so many in my profession clamber all over the others to get to the top – very few long term friends!

During my time on 8 Sqn, I had been unleashed to fly long distances across the world on my own, in my own jet fighter, a boys' dream. I was only twenty when I arrived in Aden, and within the first year I was already leading four aircrafts' worth of airborne weapons, raining down destruction on the terrorist elements up-country, thus making regular life and death decisions. I have never had so much importance attached to my decisions and actions; at least half, if not most of the indigenous population of the country must have hated me! I doubt any one gets that sort of start in life these days, but it is such responsibility, given so early, that produces men with wiser heads. Today's tame human rights regime (all rights and no responsibilities) can only work if some sense of duty is inculcated early in life. If laws are broken, no rights should be expected. Rights should be taken away until behaviour becomes responsible.

But in accepting heavy responsibility, never let it be said that at the same time we did not know how to enjoy ourselves. The fighter flying, the Dakota resupply work, and the Desert Rescue Team missions into the cauldron of the South Arabian Desert and high mountains, bestowed a deeply satisfying "Lawrence of Arabia" feeling. It was a sentiment partially of contentment in that environment, and partially being alive to the practical problems and realities of survival, particularly against the elements; so wanting to investigate the next wadi, the next sand dune, the next turn in the track, that the fulfilment wasn't realised until it was left permanently behind. Probably because survival had to be worked at just to stay alive, there is something about the desert, the mystery of frontier beyond which few humans had been, which is both forbidding and inviting. It contains a respectful fascination and an enthralment to this day.

These were experiences not available today to modern youth; we have lost the art of giving our youth, whether through the forces or otherwise, the worldwide, empire-building experiences necessary to produce a good start in life; instead of conscription, we now have "The Gap Year". It's just not the same. It's inadequate and unfulfilling, and it doesn't effectively prepare one for adult life.

Aden gave a taste of the freedom of the Empire, but now back in the UK, it was already too late – culture was changing fast, and bureaucrats had got UK society stitched-up a treat. Life in the Middle East in the early '60s was open and fun; life in the UK in the new millenium was an absolutely officious throbbing of nothing working, Gestapo-like police, and call centres: *"I'm Mandy, how can I help yuuu?"*. The last forty years have witnessed a burgeoning 'Nanny State' legislating for a hazard-free society, baulking at the very thought of risk and, in so doing, reducing to banality the lives of naturally adventurous youngsters. A shallow society lacking in morals, principles or reliability! Perhaps we do have something in common with the devious and treacherous tribes of South Arabia. Certainly by the end of the '60s decade, flying was becoming over-regulated and initiative was no longer endorsed. You could not "do your own thing" in a modern, regulated society, and that ferry flight had been the end of an exhilarating era.

Notes
1. The CO's fund on any station was his pile for charitable use when public funds were not allowed.
2. Meaconing = deliberately bending a beacon's radio wave to force us to fly off course across the Russian border.
3. From Apollo 13, 17 April 1970.
4. Cockney slang – Piccadilly Circle and lights! The circle on a map beyond which you haven't got the fuel to get home when the fuel lights come on. There are two bright yellow lights on the cockpit coaming that come on to show a low fuel state of 650lbs/side.

Part 3

Europe and the Cold War

"He knew what's what, and that's as high
As metaphysic wit can fly."

(Samuel Butler – Hudibras 1612 –1680)

Chapter Sixteen

The Eyes in the Sky – Part I

No. 79 SQUADRON, RAF CHIVENOR

From hot climate to cold climate, hot wings to Cold War, the atmosphere was becoming decidedly chilly. What a change, but it's what I had requested. From inter-tribal disputes with 18th century muskets, to mutually assured nuclear destruction. No wonder life became more serious. Following a long, recuperative leave after being 'kicked out' of the Middle East, I moved to No. 79 Hunter Sqn of the 229 Operational Conversion Unit at RAF Chivenor in North Devon for a short period. Keeping in flying practice and running their operations took a few weeks while I waited for my Fighter Recce course to start. For me, the Empire was on hold; the Cold War was about to start.

As written in Ray Hannah's obituary, fighter reconnaissance was the most demanding role for a single-seat fighter pilot. The pilots selected for this demanding role had to show an ability to operate alone over long distances with only their basic pilot-nav techniques to help them achieve incredible accuracies at high speed and ultra low level. Mainly, we were nearly all second or third tour ground attack pilots, and I was lucky to be one amongst them. This task allowed constant, authorized low flying, rather like licensing hooliganism! However, the job's prerequisite necessitated a detailed knowledge of most industries, all NATO and Soviet ground, air and sea equipment and dispositions, all missile systems, and many militarily significant constructions such as bridges, electronics and radar systems, harbours and ports, missile sites, factories and storage sites and, of course, airfields. What really mattered was the knack of recognizing the present and future capability of each site. For example, was that Nike Hercules site conventional or nuclear capable, and if the latter, at what readiness state was it? Upon your report the local army commander would base his next action. Add that to the ability to fly low, fast and extremely accurately with the need to recognise any target in a split second's fly-past, and you have a fighter-recce pilot – he is the one with the brains, though some of us managed to fool the system!

Acquiring this intelligence was only part of the battle. The aim now was to convert to the FR10 version of the Hunter, only thirty-three of which were ever produced, and to learn the art of European low-level tactical photo and visual air-reconnaissance. The aircraft was similar, apart from a redesigned cockpit, and three cameras which replaced the nose radar of the FGA9, making the aircraft 600lbs lighter. The aircraft's centre of gravity was at the rear end of the range, making it more subject to dutch-roll if the hydraulics failed in manual control at slow speed on final approach. You could turn the hydraulic controls off in the cockpit, so in practising manual approaches, you could actually set the aircraft up on long finals and hands-off, it would quite happily dutch-roll itself down the approach like a falling leaf, rotating about 10 to 15degrees either side of the horizontal until you dampened it down just before touch-down.

Undeniably, the aircraft could be trimmed extremely accurately. A Danish FR10 flamed out at three miles on the final approach one day and the pilot ejected. The aircraft subsequently executed a perfect, pilotless, wheels-up landing on its belly, and was flying again within the month.

The newly designed cockpit was also very welcome. It seemed the only one, in those unenlightened days, designed by pilots rather than aeronautical engineers, and had some innovative features for the early '60s. Our problem in selecting radio frequencies manually at low level shaped the major change. The radio, positioned on the starboard console, was impossible to see safely while operating four separate control knobs to change, say, 243.0m/cs – one knob for each digit while flying left-handed. So, with the FR10, we obtained our first ever head-up radio. No, not just the display, but the whole radio! It was now positioned on top of the coaming on the left side where the ergonomics allowed left hand usage, while still flying with the right hand and looking over the coaming through the radio at the outside world in order to stay clear of the ground – a real winner! It was disappointing to find, a few years later, that no such lesson had been learned on the early Harriers. Its radio was initially behind the control column at the bottom of the centre console, thus requiring the left hand to change the hundreds and tens, and the right hand (while flying left-handed) to change the units and decimals of a mega-cycle: an accident waiting to happen!

Meanwhile, on the FR10, in order to make room for the radio, the gun-sight was moved off centre. Whatever next? In order to fire the guns now, one had to lean to one's right to peer forward through the sight – a bit tricky when pulling "g" during air-to-air firing! Although sounding tricky, gunnery was not the recce squadron's primary role, so it didn't matter much to our operations: that infinitely adaptable machine – the fighter pilot – coped again with this unique anomaly.

The main instrument panel was the other area where pilot input had achieved some simple but remarkable ergonomics. In a move which may now seem obvious, the instruments were rearranged from the standard RAF six-instrument system to one that accorded more with the recce role. Hence for long distance, accurate, low-level flying, the compass was positioned top dead centre, immediately above the top of the control column; no parallax error there. The ASI (Air Speed Indicator), which was mostly used at slow speed on the normal left hand final turn to land, was positioned in the top left hand corner of the panel, allowing minimum eye and head movement between looking outside and reading the instrument. Further, the Artificial Horizon remained dead centre below the compass to minimize 'the leans' during instrument flying.

All in all, the FR10 was a real pilot's aircraft, and a wonderfully stable plat-form for accurate low-level navigation and photography. With four underwing tanks it could stay airborne for 1hr30mins to 1hr45mins at low level and 420 knots, providing excellent range and endurance for operations in and around the North German Plain. Indeed we sorely missed the FR10's capability when converting to the same role on shorter range Harriers some years later.

Meanwhile, through the demise of Fighter Command, I met Frankie. Frankie was a WRAF Flying Officer at RAF Coltishall ATC talkdown radar. When she was guiding me down the Coltishall glidepath, I entered her dark area . . . her radar dark area[1] . . . for the first time, and all because of the Fighter Command disbandment fly past. It was 26th Feb '68, and Coltishall and Frankie had been waiting for me for two days, while the FR10 I was to fly in the fly-past was unserviceable! The object of the exercise was to fly a formation of one of every single mark of aircraft being flown by the command at the time to celebrate the disbandment of Fighter Command, and all had assembled on the 24th at Coltishall except me. At last, just before lunch on the 26th, the jet became serviceable and I flew a mad, cross-country dash – the first of a few weekend aircraft – to Coltishall for my first Frankie talk-down! The demise of Fighter Command was my gain!

With no training facilities in the Middle East, once a year we each had to return to Chivenor for an HSE course. This was a Hunter Simulator and Emergencies Course, in which we spent seven hours flying the simulator during a week going through emergency drills, which culminated in a full sea dinghy drill. This latter entailed being thrown, in full flying gear with an un-inflated dinghy, into the Bristol Channel off the Appledore lifeboat. After inflation, you clambered into the rubber dinghy, blew up all the floors and walls, got out your emergency radio, and sat there waiting for the SAR helicopter to come and winch you up. The chopper then deposited you back on the aft deck of the lifeboat, where a large tot of navy rum was awaiting you! You can imagine how cold it felt, coming directly from Aden and being thrown into the Atlantic in the middle of our UK winter!

My various promotion exams were never meant to be easy either; looking back everything seemed a saga of one sort or another. In those days there were promotion exams, the "B" exams, from Fg Off to Flt Lt, followed by the "C" promotion exams from Flt Lt to Sqn Ldr. On top of that, there were "Q" exams for qualification to enter Staff College. On one of my winter return trips to the UK for a Hunter HSE course I made my first attempt at passing my "B" promotion exams. They were preceded by the worst possible studying time. One week beforehand, I'd travelled from Aden, a tropical thirty-five degrees in the shade, to minus five in a UK winter, had no books available from which to do any final cramming while living out of a single suitcase, and was suffering from jet lag. I took the exams in an old, black-painted, wartime wooden hut with nothing but an old coke boiler to keep the frost-bite at bay, and wondered whether there was the remotest possibility of passing anything! I'll swear to my dying day that my hands were shaking so much with the cold that the examiner couldn't read my writing! Well, I did get a partial pass, meaning I only had to retake the two exams I'd failed rather than all five.

Anyway, that was 1967, and I took my re-sit some time the following year

143

in a warm environment! I was promoted to Flt Lt some three months later, (a second ring!) soon after joining 2 Sqn at Gütersloh. One was entitled to time promotion to Flt Lt after three and a half years in the rank of Fg Off as long as one had passed the five exams. I had missed my time promotion by a couple of months, and the extra cash by then was very welcome.

One year later, the "B" promotion exams were suspended for good: the rank was given away on time only: typical of my luck!

My failure to pass fully the first time was by no means an isolated case. We had a Flying Officer at Chivenor at the time, a well liked staff flying instructor, but elderly for the rank. He was over thirty years old and had an unheard of eleven years seniority in the rank, having failed the exams, and had then refused to bother any longer. When the exams were suspended, to my knowledge, he made the fastest promotion from Flying Officer through Flight Lieutenant to Squadron Leader, and spent the shortest time ever in the rank of Flt Lt, as he leapt up the ladder in subsequent promotion boards!

None of these exams exists today!

*"**Epaulet. n.** An ornamental badge, serving to distinguish a military officer from the enemy – that is to say, from the officer of lower rank to whom his death would give promotion."*
(Definition from "The Devil's Dictionary"
by Ambrose Bierce)

After two months holding at Chivenor, I eventually started my conversion to the fighter reconnaissance role. There were only two recce instructors, George Cole and Bill Armstrong. It was a small, elite role in the air force, with only two and a half Sqns worth: a flight on 8 Sqn, and two Germany Sqns, Nos 2(AC) and 4(AC), forming the Gütersloh wing.

So I was joining this set of brainy fighter pilots, but, of course, I didn't believe them – I'd done a tour of proper ops on active service in the Middle East, and had even flown their FR10s on 1417 Flt in Aden! Despite the mysticism surrounding the tactical recce role in the air force, of course I knew it all! Bill and George soon brought me down to size, when on my first recce trip North into Wales, I was lost within ten minutes! Actually it was not difficult to become unsure of one's position over the mid-Welsh hills which could be rather featureless from an air-navigation perspective. Two skills were honed on this course: the ability to navigate to within twenty-five metres at 250feet altitude, while doing 420kts, and to recognize, from the air with but a short glance, the detailed composition and construction of all militarily significant targets.

Aerial Reconnaissance – "to see over the hill" – and the oldest military aircraft role, designed originally to check fall of shot for the artillery, and find out what dastardly plans the other side was developing, was seen as the most rewarding roll in the fighter business. The reward came from the three F95 cameras, with three to six-inch lenses, carried in the nose of the FR10. Every mission brought back black-and-white, cine-celluloid of your targets, which showed not only if you had found the right one, but if you had produced an accurate visual report. No wonder the rest of the Hunter force looked at the Gütersloh Wing as the elite. I was going to join them.

144

In mid-April I was posted to No. 2 (AC) Sqn at RAF Gütersloh in Germany. I drove from Chivenor via Dover-Ostende ferry. Having paid sixteen guineas to UK customs for my new hi-fi from Aden, when I got to Dover I presented the bill and my hi-fi for export and asked for my entitlement: the return of the sixteen guineas. The customs officer was offhand and reluctant, but eventually he went off and came back with my money. After handing it over he then said, "You know you can only take £15 sterling out of the country?" The little swine made me put £1-16s-0d (£1.80p new money) into an envelope and address it to my bank. I even had to pay the 2½d (1p) to him for a postage stamp!

Notes
1. A radar dark area is that part of the radarscope close in to the radar-head where the radar can't see. In the case of talkdown radar, it's just before touchdown!

Chapter Seventeen

The Eyes in the Sky – Part II

No. 2 (AC) Squadron, RAF GÜTERSLOH

(FIGHTER RECONNAISSANCE:
THE WORLD IS YOUR OYSTER . . . IF YOU DON'T GET LOST!)

If my first exposure to the Empire had had more of a tropical flying club atmosphere, then NATO, the Warsaw Pact, and the Inner German Border (IGB) now wrapped their earnest, chilly tentacles around us. Aden, despite its problems, had been warm and fun; Germany was cold, dull, and the role deadly serious. Paradoxically, my introduction to The Cold War was a hot one with a lot to learn about low-level, European, anti-Warsaw Pact operations.

A wholly different outlook preoccupied us, sometimes twenty-four hours a day. Here was something to win: I was now at the forefront of the RAF's contribution to the Cold War – a far more disturbing and disconcerting problem than any we had faced out East! Having shed youthful immaturity in the dusty heat of Aden, now came the cloudy gloom of adulthood on NATO's European front-line. And although this low level recce flying was outstandingly rewarding, the consequences of failure, in NATO training competitions, Tactical Evaluations (TACEVAL), and the Cold War, were unsettling in the extreme.

At least by 1968, NATO had just changed its policy from the instant trigger nuclear response scenario, to the "new" system of flexible response – a graduated answer to anything the Warsaw Pact could throw at us. Yet we were flying a conventional role in a nuclear age. It was readily admitted that if the Soviets had crossed the IGB, we would very soon have had to go nuclear to stop ourselves from being pressed back to Dunkirk again. This was, with the benefit of hindsight, a false premise, but there'd be very few "little ships" this time to take us off the beach. Yet another incongruity of pre-planned war missions: flying eastwards into East Germany, against the pertaining conformist wisdom of being pushed back west to Calais within a couple of weeks, and thus being hell bent on going nuclear to stop the retreating debacle! Those of us who had spent a few years in the forces, were constantly brainwashed by the assertations that the Warsaw Pact forces were so superior to us in quantity, without due consideration of their considerable lack of quality, that we couldn't win any European battle without the first use of nuclear weapons. So what were we doing planning to fly recce missions eastwards with such large conventional forces? We simply needed to know the positions and directions of the apparent "vast hordes" of Soviet tanks and, our low-level recce capability should provide the initial intelligence of their dispositions.

However, from reconnaissance of the profusion of military sites in Germany, there's no doubt we were in a missile age. It was the age of the Sputnik, H-bombs, Mutually Assured Destruction (MAD) and the recent Cuban Missile Crisis. Duncan Sandy's 'age of the missile' 1957 Defence Review had belatedly come quite close to reality. Along with their attendant Hawk SAM missile sites, nuclear tipped Nike Hercules missile bases were to be seen everywhere in Germany, as were M109 and M110 nuclear capable guns, together with the Honest John, Sergeant and Pershing army missiles, with Thor nukes in the UK. Nuclear-capable aircraft, F100s, F101s, F104s, F111s, F4s, Buccaneers, Canberras, Jaguars, F15s, F16s and later F18s were parked on most NATO airbases, and nuclear storage sites were seen in vast number. In central Europe here was the largest collection of nuclear capable artillery ever assembled. Their signature – the 'give-away' to the recce pilot – was the extra security attached to them: double fencing and guard towers were always to be seen. In any wartime situation these sites would have easily doubled as good POW camps but, thankfully, our station at Gütersloh with recce Hunters and air-defence Lightnings was one of the very few non-nuclear air bases.

All the same, it was a frightening scenario, which came home to me during my German induction phase. Soon after arrival in Germany, a coach took a few "new" pilots to see the IGB on the ground. The fences, barbed wire, mine-fields and watchtowers were an ominously intimidating sight. As it was, on strolling up to the border, I inadvertently strolled across it! And then I saw the tower guards swing their machine guns towards me. Our instructor was screaming at me to get back, but I hadn't realised where I was. What was not well known, and I certainly didn't know at the time, was that the first line of barbed wire fencing was not the actual border. The fencing was some ten metres back on the East German side, with the actual border marked by single wooden posts painted in yellow, red and black, and cemented about fifteen to twenty metres apart into an entirely normal rough grassy area in front of the first fence. By strolling round the post, one had passed into East German territory. I am positive that from that day on, they had my photo in their Stasi archives, if it wasn't already there!

The emphasis had just started to revert to conventional forces with gradu-ated response war roles, and although on the conventional side (non-nuclear forces), RAF Gütersloh was THE most forward base of the British air forces. Only three other bases, all nuclear capable, supported us: Wildenrath, Bruggen and Laarbruch. They were all positioned along the Dutch/German border, whilst we had the only fighters up front at Gütersloh.

There were two allied army groups in Germany: the Northern and the Central Group (South being Italy). Central was American and German only, based in the American Zone of South Germany, ranged along the Southern part of the IGB, and was covered by 4 ATAF. The Northern Group defending the British Zone was a real mixture. It consisted of German, Dutch, Belgian

Fig 9. Germany in the 1960s still divided into the allied zones.

and British forces, and we, of 2 ATAF could be tasked by any of these national force commanders. In the British Sector, we had three divisions, with a 4th from UK in reserve, and again we could be tasked by any of these divisional commanders. On the positive side, there was ample free skiing to be enjoyed, cheap German lager to be consumed, and most of Europe to be toured when off-duty.

We had regular practice alerts and war-style exercises, backed up by volumes and volumes of convoluted multi-national NATO procedures. Each pilot had his pre-planned war sorties that he had to know blindfold and by heart, and we were relentlessly tested on all aspects of our individual war missions.

There were four front line fighter squadrons based at Gütersloh: two Hunter Recce Sqns, 2(AC) and 4(AC), and two Lightning all-weather, air-defence Sqns, 19 and 92. I remember arriving at Gütersloh with a posting notice to 4 Sqn in my pocket, being met in the mess bar by Flt Lt John Thomson (Later to be ACM Sir John Thomson, CinC Strike Command) who greeted me with the words, "Welcome to 2!" They had changed my posting while I was driving from UK en-route to Gütersloh. I still don't know whether they were both fighting to have me, or more probably, the reverse!

Gütersloh, some twenty miles Southwest of Bielefeld, is a large town famous for its Miele washing machines. The air base, to the west of the town, used to be a Luftwaffe night fighter base during WW2, and much of the airfield and particularly the buildings were all Luftwaffe design with massive rooms, cellars and underground central heating systems.

In particular, the Officers Mess was an old German Schloss with a baroque clock tower in the front right hand corner. The top room of the tower, above the clock, was Goering's Room. This reputedly was where Reichsmarschall Herman Goering entertained his fighter pilots whenever he came to inspect them. The room is quite small with eight scrubbed wooden tables and benches, a large wooden beam dividing the ceiling, and his portrait hanging on one wall, together with other of his medals and memorabilia. The RAF kept it throughout their tenure in exactly the same fashion as it was found in 1945[1].

The Goering-Gütersloh story is a lovely military anecdote about one's enemy, and worth repeating here. It is said that he was a very good story-teller, keeping his pilots in fits of laughter over numerous steins of beer in this, his favourite drinking room. When he was telling a tall story, his favourite expression was to point at the roof beam in the ceiling and say, "So help me if the beam doesn't split . . . . . 'the story' is true!"

After numerous tall stories, the pilots decided to play a real jape on him, so together with local carpenters one day, they sawed through the centre of the beam, connected the two centre ends with a large hinge which in turn was connected above to a heavy wire. The wire was routed over a suitable system of sprung pulleys along/above the beam, down the inside of one wall, coming up attached to a handle in a small hatch cut in the floor under one of the tables; pulling the handle allowed the beam to sag about a foot in the middle, thus looking as though the beam had split!

The next time Goering started his stories, well let's say the pilots got the last laugh as the beam split. It is still there, and splits the same way today!

Nonetheless, Gütersloh was considered by the Luftwaffe to be a punishment posting. Cold and dreary, it was built on low-lying swampland that bred mosquitoes almost as bad as in Belize. So different from the lively joy of the warm middle-eastern atmosphere, one also had to re-learn the art of bad weather flying here. So often, the North German Plain area was covered in low cloud. If forced from VFR low-level flight up into cloud, the continental upper airspace was totally controlled, and difficult for fighter ops after an emergency pull-up. Besides the usual civvy traffic, we were also sharing the airspace with Dutch, Belgian, German, Canadian, American and other British military aircraft, so it was quite crowded up there.

Unfortunately, the RAF had added a long tarmac East/West runway across the old, grass, Luftwaffe airfield, and its Eastern end was quite close to the Officers Mess and its bachelor accommodation. On the opposite side of the runway from the Mess, a "Battle Flight" hangar had been built to house the two QRA Lightning Fighters. These two maintained a fifteen minute quick reaction alert to police the airspace of Northern Germany, and, in particular, the Inner German Border for intruders from the Russian and East German Air Forces. 1968 after all, was still very much Cold War era, and only one year after NATO's major change of policy from Instant Nuclear Response (INR) to a Flexible Response (FR).

Whenever the Lightnings were scrambled at night, which averaged once every two nights, the whole Mess accommodation, and your bed with it, reverberated to the sound of four x 300series Avon engines, in full reheat, taking-off nearby. A good excuse for the bachelors yawning and looking tired on duty first thing the following morning!

I served for only fifteen months on "Tatty2", but they will remain the most rewarding undertaken during my time in the air force. The recce role, and the manner in which the Sqn was organised on a daily basis for that role, was probably what gave tactical recce sqns the edge over others. One should say that with two budding C's-in-C as my Flt Cdrs, the place should have run like clockwork. Even more galling then to find our sister Sqn, No 4, not only beating us in both Royal Flushes during my time there, but actually winning the competition in 1969! Exercise Royal Flush was the premier NATO Air Forces Central Europe, Annual Reconnaissance Competition. All recce sqns throughout Europe were required to take part and their prime raison d'être was to win.

Any Sqn Cdr who won this competition was destined for the top. Guess what? Tony Hopkins was the Boss of 4 when they won it in 1969. Tony was the personnel guy who had covertly extracted Al Pollock out of Valley onto my Chivenor Hunter course in a hurry after Al's unauthorised BofB solo aeros, literally at five minutes notice!

Together with the annual NATO TACEVAL, Royal Flush governed our lives. So much so that, generally, the training year was equally divided between the two.

TACEVAL was the annual NATO no-notice evaluation of the squadron's ability to conduct its war role. NATO assessors would arrive at your base's front gate, and press the war alarm button. Then, over a three to four day period, they would assess each Sqn in everything to do with its wartime role. The intensity would gradually increase from initial peacetime, high-alert status through full preparations for war, the pre-planned war missions that you were to fly for real, role play in NBC[2] conditions, qualifying strafe scores on the air firing range, to evaluation of your photos and reports from simulated recce war missions. You had to know the details of your two war missions backwards, without looking at your planning documents or maps. For TACEVAL you had to be able to talk your way through the mission by headings and times and fuel levels, together with known landmarks, waypoints, IPs[3] and targets, and basically "fly" the mission blindfold. The evaluation usually culminated in operating with NBC suits and masks as we eventually 'lost' the simulated conventional war, and everyone waited for the first simulated nuclear weapon to land while attempting to continue fighting!

Umpires, co-opted onto the team from any other nationality within NATO, usually arrived without notice, unannounced, and always in the early hours. They then followed you about unremittingly while they injected many absurd and false scenarios while you played war games and flew the simulated war missions. You were then graded on your presumed abilities and reactions.

After the more devil-may-care, active service, attitude of the Middle East, the annual NATO TACEVAL was certainly a strain on one's sense of well being!

While TACEVAL was a pain in the backside, Royal Flush, while serious, was one in which we could really show our expertise: it was professionally exhilarating fun. Exercise Royal Flush was designed to test your knowledge of target systems, and your ability to fly fast, accurate, recce missions to within twenty-five metres ground accuracy, with a TOT[4] of plus or minus thirty seconds for each of three targets. You then had to send an accurate radio report of your targets, return to base as fast as possible, write a visual report on each target, and have those reports and your printed target photos off base to HQ within thirty minutes of landing. It was so intense that one suspected everyone cheated! Each Sqn, for example, was allowed one "weather check" aircraft each day, and for the first Royal Flush, the week after I arrived, that was my duty. My "task" was to fly round all the known army targets and covertly check what was there before the exercise aircraft took-off, while overtly checking the weather in the general target area. If that was cheating, then the Canadian wing out of Baden-Baden, who had two Sqns of RF104 Recce Starfighters, covertly used their whole squadron of T33 training aircraft for so-called 'weather checks'! On one occasion, thirteen Canadian T33 "weather check" missions over the target area were counted during one competition day!

Royal Flush was, given our training, not that difficult, and with targets anywhere within Germany, Belgium or Holland, it was played in a far better spirit than TACEVAL. One of the three targets on each mission was a mobile army target, which could be provided by any of the allied armies, and they were rated on how well they camouflaged themselves in the field. This target was the only difficult aspect and, more points were scored from these than the other two. The other two static targets were usually fairly simple, but only because we had all flown against them at some time during training in the recent past. Nobody ever flew a RF mission without knowing exactly what the static targets were beforehand from our comprehensive target library of photos. All that was needed was to note on the recce report the actual moving/mobile/movable activity within the target as you flew past!

The recce targets were divided into categories such as: Bridging, Electronics Sites, Storage Facilities, SAM sites, army and navy targets, airfields, HQs and barracks, and many more besides. But recce sqns each needed expertise in the knowledge of the intricate details and capabilities of each type of target – this was the 'brains' bit! Hence on 2 Sqn, each pilot was designated as the Sqn specialist on one or two of these categories. I had SSVs (soft-skinned vehicles [military]), as different from AFVs(Armoured Fighting Vehicles). One could often tell the type of army unit one was looking at by the type and designation of their lorries, jeeps and cars, especially if the AFVs were, as usual, well camouflaged. We practised daily our ability to identify all and any NATO or Soviet AFVs and SSVs, and I could tell instantly a Canadian lorry from an American one just by looking at its mudguards!

We studied Warsaw Pact equipment interminably, mainly using intelligence-gathered photos. Publications such as the monthly Recognition Magazine were also studied avidly. I made up a loose leaf album of my specialist equipment with photo copies of all WP vehicles deployed in East

Germany. But the main spur to learning the different styles, markings and vehicle shapes from all angles was yet another daily recce competition. A selection of photos in 35mm slide form was individually and rapidly shone onto a slide screen for no more than a couple of seconds, and we each had to write down our best guess. Papers were exchanged, marked, and the results and order of merit were published with the recognition lessons. Good sport, if a dubious skill, but considered mandatory in the context of Central European NATO/Soviet Cold War scenarios of the 1960s. Indeed, it is a skill that one never loses. Even now, some forty years later, I can, and do, instantly recognize a particular type of tank, say, on a TV screen.

The best part of the Sqn flying organisation was the "Trip-of-the-day". For all competition work, we individually flew the same targets as each other every day. So after weather checking first thing, three target coordinates were written on the main Ops board and we each planned, briefed, and flew those three targets throughout that day. On landing, photos were developed and reports written, and at the end of the day, they were all pinned up on a large briefing board in front of which we all sat for a public debrief by the Sqn Photographic Interpreter (PI). You certainly knew where you stood in the pecking order, as no punches were pulled, and a better peer-group pressure system of competition I've yet to see. You strived for the PI's praise every day in front of your Boss and all your peers. It became your whole life, except for the bottle of wine!

The unofficial bottle of wine competition was a typical sequel to the trip-of-the-day flying that became our way of life. On the Sqn Ops Desk was kept an up-to-date version of the book, "Wines of the World". On every Monday morning, an empty bottle of wine from a German, Belgian, Dutch or Luxembourg vineyard was placed next to the book. The 'rools' of the game were simple: the first pilot to return from a mission with the WHOLE vineyard in one frame of the cine-film from any one of the three cameras, received a bottle of wine for the following weekend paid from the Sqn funds. He bought a bottle of his choosing, drank it over the weekend, and then on the Monday, placed it on the ops desk for the next week's competition. It all sounds good sport until you appreciate that the cameras had three-inch lenses and were angled down from the horizontal by some fifteen degrees. With the large size of many vineyards, a 75degree bank turn at about 8000feet may generate a full vertical shot of it, if there were no clouds about at the time – a set of circumstances that happened rarely in central Europe! Timing was of the essence, but at least it was less dangerous than the previous competition, which was to bring back film with the least number of bricks/tiles showing on a single frame of any church spire! With few bricks showing on some film, there were some very close calls, believe me!

On one training phase during Sep '68, in order to gain a break from the unremitting low level recce requirements, all the underwing tanks were taken off and we climbed to really high level in these now lightweight aircraft to practise some high level combat tactics. Clean, uncluttered aircraft have quite a performance difference compared with the normally heavily laden ones that we flew daily on our bread and butter, low-level, recce missions. Just for once you are able to appreciate the pure performance that the manufacturers had striven for all those years ago. We started at 46,000feet in wide battle formation, initially combating our own Lightnings, but on one memorable flight, some twenty-six aircraft pitched in from all over NATO.

Commencing with four Hunters and four Lightnings, some German F104 Starfighters joined in, followed by a couple of USAF F15 Eagles, four Canadian CF101 Voodoos, some Dutch Starfighters, and a couple of Belgium F86 Sabres. There were aircraft everywhere you looked, but not dangerously close – the lack of turning performance at those high levels meant the battle area was spread widely across the sky. Then four USAF F102s from Soesterberg arrived. Their big delta wings gave them the edge at high level because they could turn tighter than the rest at slow speed and keep it up all day long. They were the last in the fight with us after everyone else had run for home short of fuel – the Lightnings and Starfighters particularly having no endurance. It was a momentous fight and certainly the largest with which I'd been involved. I always felt we should have done more "liaison flying" against these dissimilar types, as unofficially, it's the only way to learn aircraft handling to the limits and be totally confident in your aircraft's capabilities.

A measure of the FR10's stability as a firing platform came during our one and only air-to-ground phase conducted on Nordhorn range close to Hopsten airfield. Over twelve firing missions I averaged 43% in strafing with a top score of 64% . . . not bad for an out of practice recce pilot! More so when compared with the lesser average gained over three years constant practice on my first tour.

We kept the four guns in each aircraft full of high explosive rounds in readiness for any war eventuality except that, for safety's sake, the first five rounds in the gun were practice ball ammunition, and the guns were left electrically disconnected. This made the change to a wartime role in a hurry much easier without compromising peacetime safety. During servicing inside our small hangar, the aircraft were parked in pairs, nose-to-tail, pointing at the side wall of the hangar behind which was our squadron flying ops room, the GLO's[5] office, the outside hangar wall and then two or three large, mobile photographic vans, beyond which was the wood line. On this particular day in Sep '68 the ground crew were checking the electrical circuits of the guns, and had mistakenly made them live. On putting the circuit switch over, the guns all fired some twenty rounds across the hangar and up the jet pipe of the next aircraft. They then came out through its engine intakes, through the inner hangar wall, across the ops desk in which Stu Penny was leaning, demolished a second dividing wall into the GLO's office, blew a large hole through the main hangar wall, and destroyed two photo vans. In a split second one aircraft, two vans, three walls and two offices were destroyed, and Stu's hair turned white for life! Finally, as I was the only pilot from the Sqn airborne and some 200 miles away at the time, I was the only one on the Squadron who could not have the finger pointed at him!

The remarkable "safety" feature of the incident was that each gun had fired exactly the five rounds of ball ammunition before ceasing; the very next round in each of the four chambers was the first high explosive round for each gun; God alone knows what damage would have ensued with the high explosive rounds. Conversely, this was a striking example of the firepower of the Aden cannon, while using only simple 30mm metallic non-explosive ball projectiles! For the first time I'd been able to see close up exactly what destruction these guns could produce; it was impressive, and I could now better understand what the tribesmen in Aden had felt like when we were around.

At last I was considered mature enough to take an aircraft away for a weekend on my own; this after what I'd been doing for three years in the Middle East, but with the Inner German Border (IGB) so close, no-one was trusted! Here, the most heinous crime was to violate, not a WAAF, but the IGB! It was a different air force in Germany, and no allowance was made for Middle Eastern operational active service.

There was a NATO requirement for air-base engineering personnel to be familiar with the technical servicing requirements of all other types of NATO aircraft. As part of this, I was sent off to two German Air Force bases in Bavaria for the weekend of 9th to 11th May '69. The first was GAF Erding, some twenty miles Northeast of Munich, where, on a Friday morning the German Air Force personnel were to complete a NATO cross-servicing of my aircraft for the first time. After this I was to fly on that afternoon to GAF Memmingen, sixty miles West of Munich, to place my aircraft in the static display in readiness for the air base's 10th anniversary air display open day on Saturday, the following day. The plan was that if I could extract my plane from the static park, I was then to fly it back home on the Sunday morning. Our base was open 24hrs a day every day for the Battle Flight commitment, so no restrictions on arrival times.

The critical factor about this sort of three-day trip was not my capability, as one may think, but the AVPIN fluid necessary to start the aircraft's engine. The AVPIN tank held approximately three starts worth before it needed topping up. So, one start at Gütersloh to get going; one at Erding to fly to Memmingen, and one at Memmingen to fly home. It only needed one start failure, which was a not infrequent occurrence, and I would be stuck. Notwithstanding I only required a maximum of three *PINTS* of AVPIN, the solution was to send an airman driver in a little J2 'eight people-carrier' the whole length of Germany by road all the way to Memmingen with a 25 *GALLON* drum of this highly volatile fluid to top me up before departure on the Sunday morning. More of this later!

Well, Erding went OK, but you are aware by now how trouble seemed to follow me everywhere? On my arrival at Erding Ops before departure, they said that the base commander of local German military radar, known as Shandy Radar, was trying to get hold of me, so naturally I returned his call. He only wanted me to produce a simple display for their radar open day on the way past from Erding to Memmingen, and as it wasn't far off my route, how could I refuse?

When I arrived over the radar station 45mins later, I found a gathering of aircraft in semi-loose close-formation, including a USAF F4 Phantom, a GAF F104 Starfighter, the FAF Mirage III also on its way to the display at Memmingen, a GAF Fiat G91, and a Canadian Air Force F101 Voodoo; I was invited to join in! So why not, I thought, and without any radio comms between us, I latched on to their starboard wing, and started taking photos. After all, you don't see that combination of aircraft together very often – if at all. As a recce jet, it seemed a good idea at the time to take some photos of all those aircraft with the radar station in the background, which I did, then high-tailed it to Memmingen for a fast, noisy but uneventful arrival. By 3pm on Friday, I was safely tucked up at Memmingen with the aircraft parked for the static display the following day, an interesting and easy weekend in the offing, and not a care in the world. Then it really started to happen!

After my arrival, the host officer mentioned that there was an RAF Harrier featured in the flying display for the following afternoon. That certainly surprised me as the RAF Harrier force hadn't even started up at Wittering by then. In fact I believe the Harrier conversion unit had just received their first aircraft. Anyway, they said if I wanted to, I could go along to the briefing for the air display crews, and as I had nothing better to do until the bar opened, I duly did. The briefing showed that with the exception of an FAF Mirage III, an RAF Canberra, and the Harrier, there was nothing but a succession of GAF Memmingen F104 Starfighters flying straight and level, tediously the same way-same day all afternoon! Typical GAF, they were a strictly non-aerobatic air-force at the time, having written off their whole aerobatic display team in one huge accident a few years earlier! Boring, boring! Sitting at the back of the briefing room, minding my own business, I was nodding off when the Harrier slot came up for discussion. The GAF briefer said that the Harrier had cancelled, and was the Hunter driver in the room? That woke me up with a start! I put my hand up, and was promptly asked whether I could fill a fifteen minute flying slot doing an aerobatic display for them! Could I! The honour of our service had to be served and seen to be served!

Compared with today's bureaucracy it was rather like an unregulated flying club in those days, but there was still a code – like flight authorization – and I *had* learnt something in the past four years! Still, there's nothing like a chal-lenge, and I had come second in my flying training aerobatics' competition six years earlier! So I phoned my Boss, Tim Barrett, at Gütersloh, and eventually found him at home on the Saturday morning. I seem to remember that he finally authorised me to fly only three fast passes straight and level, with no aerobatics, and that was the best I could wheedle out of him. Looking back, I would probably have done something similar in his shoes. After all, it took a whole season to work up a low level aerobatics display to the standards of safety required.

But how do you fill fifteen minutes with only three fast passes! Even the Red Arrows don't fill that length of slot with a full-blooded display! Then Al Pollock came to mind, and I knew what I had to do. There was no way I could let the RAF, my Sqn or myself down by doing a weeny little display. I had to make sure we provided a show to which the RAF would have been proud!

My slot was the final one of the afternoon – the grande-finale – and the rest had been boring. The Mirage III had done little, and most of it out of sight because it had such a large turning circle. The Canberra gave an excellent slow speed show, flying upwind into a 25kt wind allowing it to slow to below 100Kts groundspeed. So here came my third start-up without Avpin, and which worked, thank God! I took off and then proceeded to fill fifteen minutes at full power getting ever faster, noisier, and pulling maximum g forces. The Hunter is excellent for showing off as it has the power and good, low-aspect wings for a low-radius, turning circle even at high speed.

They watched the best unrehearsed aeros show I could manage, and that evening at the party, I was the local hero! I could do no wrong, even when the FAF brought in suitcases of red wine for free, and proceeded to perform the handstands-against-the-wall-while-drinking-it-upside-down routine! So that's my excuse for what happened next! Sunday morning came round far too soon, and my hangover wasn't playing ball! I don't do Sunday mornings, especially after an air-show party with free French vino, but my first task was to manhandle the 25gallon drum of Avpin on to the top surface of the wing, and try and pour it into the three-inch diameter neck of the aircraft's Avpin tank without a funnel! Despite the high wind, the driver and I did manage it eventually, but not without spilling most of this volatile fuel all over the place and ourselves. So, by the time the next unplanned number came into the equation, I was feeling pretty rough –Avpin fumes on top of a hangover – and pretty fed up.

Under the port wing of the Hunter is the Master Air Safety Break (MASB). By disconnecting the MASB on the ground, it ensured that all weapons were disconnected electrically, and it also deactivated the undercarriage buttons, thus ensuring that the wheels could not be raised inadvertently on the ground. This is a very reasonable ground safety device, which was the first thing the groundcrew disconnected after engine shut down in dispersal at the end of every mission. It was also the last thing they connected after engine start before taxiing for the next mission. When the MASB was disconnected, it hung down below the wing with a large red flag on it to catch attention, but it had become common practice, if leaving the aircraft for sometime outside, to bundle it all up inside, and close the panel. Gotcha! When you had no groundcrew, you had to do it yourself! Yes, you've guessed it . . . nothing hanging below the wing as a reminder on the pre-flight walk-round, so I forgot to reconnect it!

Later that morning I got airborne for Gütersloh, and surprise, surprise, couldn't raise the undercarriage! That meant I had to keep the speed below 250Kts, and fly the length of Germany at medium level where no-one could see me at slow speed with my undercarriage down! A very ignominious end to a good weekend away! Knowing that my Boss was meeting me on arrival at Gütersloh, I elected to do a straight in radar approach instead of the usual fighter fast run-in and break, so no-one actually saw the undercarriage down in the wrong place: the Boss was pleased, maybe relieved, to see me and his aircraft in one piece.

And I got away with it, till now! No one else ever knew! But just to end the story, Monday came round, and all was sunny on the horizon until late morning, when I was called into the Boss's office. "Tell me about Shandy Radar," he said! The unthinking American Colonel from the radar station had rung up to thank my Boss for allowing me to display, and wanting to know when he could get copies of my photos! Ruined my whole week!

The only thing my Father helped to teach me was the game of Cricket. I played for my school, and for most of my air force career at station and RAF Command levels, and was often officer i/c Cricket or even team captain. Everyone had to have a secondary duty or two, and cricket was immeasurably preferable to "Officer i/c Bogs and Drains"!

I recall that before one particular away cricket match, I had left my Cortina engine running outside the Mess whilst I went off to arrange a late dinner. Into the dining room walked Puddy Catt, the jovial, rotund and handlebar moustached resident Sqn joker. "Hey Chris! Is that your car on fire outside?" he asked. My two-fingered response evoked an emphatic reiteration, and I realising he was deadly serious, I rushed out into billows of smoke. The ignition key only just retrieved before the fire really took off, the air cleared, and I could see the dashboard was nought but a pool of plastic goo with all the instruments and, indeed, the total electrical system, completely burnt out. The fault was eventually traced to the coil leads having been replaced the wrong way round by the local Ford Taunus agent during a recent servicing. When the engine apparently stalled, the electrics reversed direction! I missed that cricket match!

There's hardly a skill you can name that doesn't exist somewhere on every station! Ch Tech Smith (Smiffy) was the Sqn electrician par excellence who, at a cost of one crate of beer, rewired the vehicle sufficiently to get me back to UK. With no instruments, and bare wires sparking from where the dashboard had been, I eventually arrived at a Ford agency in Orpington, owned by the brother-in-law of another of our pilots. Just my luck, Ford were on strike, and it took ten days to assemble all the spares. Meanwhile I manned the petrol pumps for him and slept in the back of his garage for ten days. His garage electrician was magic. They only charged me at cost, and the car was as good as new. You certainly need some luck and friends in this world!

Meanwhile, back to the Cricket. I played, managed, and captained the team at RAF Wittering and Wildenrath, in both local and RAF matches. I enjoyed more Cricket on the continent while in Germany at both Gütersloh and Wildenrath, as much for playing Command Cricket as for the places we went. These included Geneva, playing the International Red Cross team, Brussels, playing NATO HQ teams, Amsterdam, playing anyone, and Berlin where we played the army garrison and RAF Gatow.

The Berlin trips were usually the most momentous, and my second visit travelling on the military train produced an unlikely baggage-van full of Champagne! In those days, the French Berlin Garrison at Tegel used to obtain their Champagne from France for roughly sixpence a bottle. They sold it on to RAF Gatow for one shilling a bottle, who sold it on to us for two shillings a bottle. So with thirteen players travelling in my Cricket team, and my marriage due shortly afterwards, thirteen crates of Champagne were bought on my behalf from Gatow for £15.12s.0p (£1.60p) for 156 bottles! These crates were duly humped into the baggage wagon of the train at Charlottenburg for the journey home, and off we set. Now German trains had bench seats in individual compartments with three a side and a central aisle. But you could pull the benches out into the middle and the backs slid down to provide a completely flat and comfortable divan bed, covering the whole compartment, with room for at least four to sleep on. I've never seen this method anywhere else in the world before or since, but what a super way to travel by train.

So there we all were, the whole team, sprawled across these divans in four or five compartments travelling through East Germany, when about ten minutes out from the Helmstedt border with West Germany, the train warrant officer (Guard) came along. On enquiring as to whether these crates of

Champers in his guard van belonged to us, and hearing an affirmative answer, he said, "You know there's customs at the Helmstedt border!"

Panic!

"Customs between West Berlin and West Germany?" we queried.

"How come?", we asked.

Receiving no appropriate answer, we were galvanized into action. The whole team spread down the corridors and swung these crates one to another along the length of the train, from the baggage van at the rear, to our compartments, where they were hidden under the seats, which we had by then pulled out into divan beds. Just in time, we managed to sprawl across the compartments, feigning sleep, as we drew into Helmstedt. On clumped half a dozen German customs officers. Passports and papers were minutely scrutinized, but after a few apprehensive minutes they went on their officious way never having sniffed a whiff of the Champers! Ten minutes further down the line, where we changed trains at Brunswick, they would have been very surprised to see thirteen Brits humping thirteen crates of best French Champagne across the platforms and onto our Gütersloh bound train!

Three months later three of us were asked to volunteer for the Harrier force that was just forming up at RAF Wittering, near Stamford. Apparently, they were forming four squadrons, three of which were coming out to Germany, and the nucleus of the pilots was coming from the ground attack background of the Hunter Wing at RAF West Raynham: Nos. 1(F) and 54 Sqns. It transpired that they needed a recce instructor with experience of Germany for each of these new Harrier Sqns. Pad Williams and Ken Jones from our sister recce sqn, No4(AC), and I, were posted to West Raynham to join 54 Sqn whose pilots were going to form the second Sqn to convert to Harriers after No 1(F). 1(F) were staying to be the UK Harrier Sqn, and 54 was going to divide to form the first two Germany Harrier Sqns.

And so, after such a rewarding role under my belt, and a superb place to live, it was a real wrench to leave Germany, but it wouldn't be long before I was back in Deutschland fighting the Cold War yet again.

Notes

1. The RAF pulled out of Gütersloh in the 1990s as part of the reduction in UK forces in Germany, and handed it over to the British Army who used it for a Helicopter base, and a large, road-transport, logistics unit. I revisited the place in 1995 for a few hours, and found that the army had still maintained this tradition.
2. NBC – Nuclear, Biological and Chemical conditions.
3. IP – Initial Point – the final check point on a map prior to any target.
4. TOT – Time On Target.
5. GLO – Ground Liaison Officer – usually an army artillery officer who's job was to liaise with the army units we were supporting, to organise targets etc.

Chapter Eighteen

The Conversion

The Transition from Hunters to VSTOL Harriers

"1940s to 1970s technology:
the error-prone airborne analogue computer . . .
you were never where it said you were!"

This next period in my air force career was characterized by the force's reorganisational requirements to accommodate new types of aircraft coming into service. It spans the period from June 1969 until October 1970, during which time the use of the new F4 Phantoms in the strike/attack role, the phasing out of the Hunter force, the replacement of the Lightnings with F4 Phantoms in the air defence role, and in particular, the introduction of the Jaguar and Harrier forces took place. For some of us, it meant changing squadrons, aircraft and bases on numerous occasions.

At the start of this process, I was 'short toured' from 2 Sqn in Germany as a volunteer for the new Harrier force, but bases and sqn numbers changed so rapidly that it certainly became extremely difficult to maintain any semblance of loyalty and esprit de corps, even if you did learn more. One day your aircraft, flying suit etc, had navy blue and yellow markings, the next the same aircraft had red and black; within weeks it had become light blue and white! This chapter gives an idea of the problems involved, and because of the many changes, I have included a table on page 160 to allow easier following of my movements.

The table shows that between Apr '68 and Oct '70, a period of only two and a half years, confusingly there had been six unit changes and four station changes, not including the residence change to a satellite base at Bircham Newton while on the posted strength at West Raynham. All had been caused by the necessity to prepare for Harrier conversion, the delays in introduction of the new aircraft into service, and problems which regularly grounded it during its first couple of years in service.

If *you* find it confusing, at the time we found it even more so. At one point we even had two No. 4 Squadrons in full service at the same time: an aberration if there was ever one. 4 Sqn recce Hunters at Gütersloh had not disbanded before 4 Sqn DFGA Hunters at West Raynham was formed from the old 54

Author's movements and units leading up to, during and immediately after Harrier conversion

DATE	No. of Months	RAF STATION	SQUADRON	AIRCRAFT
27 Apr 68 – 17 Jun 69	15	Gütersloh	2 (AC) Sqn	Hunter FR10
18 Jun – 31 Aug 69	3	West Raynham	54 Sqn	Hunter FGA9
1 Sep 69 – 15 Mar 70	6.5	West Raynham	4 Sqn (UK Echelon)	Hunter FGA9
16 Mar – 30 Jun 70	2.5	Wittering	4 Sqn	Hunter FGA9
1 Jul – 19 Oct 70	4	Wittering	Harrier Conversion Unit (No 4 Course)	Whirlwind 10, Hunter and HarrierGR1
20 Oct 70 – 29 Feb 72	16	Wildenrath	20 Sqn	Harrier GR1
1 Mar 72 – 22 Nov 73	20	Wildenrath	3 Sqn	Harrier GR1A
23 Nov 73 for 2.5 years	29	Wittering	233 OCU	Harrier GR3

Sqn, an unprecedented situation. The UK Squadron was therefore parochially called 4 Sqn (UK Echelon)! With numbers and bases changing every few months, just where did one's loyalty lie?

For me, this reorganisation all started with a 'short period' at West Raynham in Norfolk, but the original 'short period' became longer and longer with continuing delays into service of the Harrier. West Raynham was the first, and now only, Hunter base in the UK. It had also been home to the Harrier's predecessor, the Kestrel with its tripartite[1] sqn, which had only recently disbanded from its experimental existence.

So the three of us arrived back in UK at RAF West Raynham to join No. 54 Squadron for a short ground attack warm up prior to converting to our newest aircraft – the Harrier. Within days we were off to El Adem, just south of Tobruk in Libya, for an APC (Armament Practice Camp). The whole squadron flew out for five weeks, during which we spent all our working time on some consolidated air-to-ground weaponry training. On every sortie one's accuracy was measured and checked from gunsight film and range scores, and competition ladders were produced for all three weapons. Minimum standards had to be attained to become a NATO qualified pilot, and 70% of the squadron pilots had to qualify to allow the Squadron to retain its NATO certification.

A measure of our proficiency was that on the penultimate day, Ken Jones, Pad Williams and myself, the three recce pilots from Germany, were top of the strafe and bombing. Furthermore, Ken and Pad were also top of the rocketing ladder, while I was lying about sixth or seventh out of fifteen, and needed a good final sortie score to move into the top three. You've already heard how good the middle-eastern squadrons were at rocketry, and as I was the only one with an 8 Sqn background, I really had to pull out the stops to prove it. Although inexperienced with this new, French SNEB rocket, it was inherently far more accurate than the WW2 ones we'd been throwing around the South Arabian peninsular. A consequence of this accuracy was that the minimum firing range had been increased for safety purposes without compromising accuracy. Our WW2 rockets were fired at 800yards, with a minimum of 750yards, whereas the new SNEB was being fired at 1000yards with a 900yard minimum. If your gunsight film showed you firing inside the minimum, your score didn't count.

So on the final mission I flew off to the range with ten rockets, tipped in and fired the first, and managed a score of 5feet at 12 o-clock. After that sighter, I went on and fired the other nine, one at a time, with increasing incredulity until by the time I received my 10th score, I had fired nine direct hits. This was unheard of at the time, and has never been beaten to my knowledge since, but it put me at the top of the rocketing ladder at the end of five weeks firing!

However, when Bert Loveday, our ex-43Sqn QWI, checked through my film later that morning, he measured my firing range for all ten rockets at 800yards, and scrubbed the lot: none of them were allowed to count! On the other hand, no-one has ever fired nine or more direct hit rockets before or since on consecutive attacks, and I maintain my claim to fame!

The beauty of ferrying Hunters to and from the West Raynham wing at that time was that this fighter wing was part of Transport Command (TC), the mobile defensive part of any deployed transport operation. One of TC's rules laid down that only TC Captains were allowed a single room in Messes and hotels when staging overseas; the other crew members had to share. As West Raynham Hunter Captains we were, by definition, also TC Captains!

Twelve of us – all 'TC Captains' – staging home to Raynham at the end of the APC produced a requirement for twelve single rooms at Malta. Not having enough accommodation in the Mess meant duty-paid rooms in a five-star hotel instead, before staging at Nice for the final leg home. This happened soon after the new VC10 transport was introduced into RAF service and, in typical fashion, it was decided that only Sqn Ldrs or above could Captain this new aircraft. Of course, to the rest of us, this policy gave rise to the cry, "Are you a real Sqn Ldr, or just a VC10 Captain!?"

Leaving Nice on the final leg, I was in the two-seater Mk T7, with Barry Adcock, our Sqn QFI. At Nice we had precious little Met. information about the UK, but had an earlier indication before leaving Malta that West Raynham was Yellow and forecasting Yellow.[2] So, we launched with a Mk 9 in formation, expecting to receive an update en-route. Now anyone who has ferried fighters across France will know how difficult French ATC could be. For a start it was almost impossible to get them to speak the international language of the air, English, but, if that was attained, not much more would be, least of all any control!

Just over an hour and a quarter North of Nice, having been in or above thick cloud all the way, with not a single lock-on to any French beacon by any of our navigation aids, and with not a pip-squeak out of French ATC as usual, we were becoming *'unsure of our position'!* While discussing our next move, we heard UK's Eastern Radar calling us on 'guard': the emergency frequency. Relief – a familiar voice on the ball. Relief not for long though, because on replying, we heard the bad news. Not only were we somewhere over Belgium, but also West Raynham was Red in low cloud and teeming rain. They wanted to divert us to Chivenor in North Devon, the only other Hunter unit in the UK, and the only base with decent weather, but by this time we were so short of fuel and, with headwinds all the way from Belgium to Chivenor, we definitely couldn't make North Devon. Eastern Radar eventually guided us down through the London Air Traffic Zone to Thorney Island near Portsmouth, which was also Yellow. It was rather a relief when we broke cloud at 200feet and saw Thorney's runway lights, but that's what comes of flying with a QFI . . . they're supposed to know it all!

After landing at Thorney, we phoned ops at West Raynham, where the Wg Cdr Flying said they were Amber forecasting Red or Amber in pouring rain for the rest of the day, *but we could make it, couldn't we?!* So we launched from Thorney, and the radar approach at Raynham was one of the most difficult approaches I've ever attempted. The approach was conducted through thick cloud, high winds, driving rain and heavy turbulence. Barry flew it on instruments, while I watched through the useless rain-shrouded windscreen for any appearance of the runway lights. At 100 feet, way below our break-off height but with nowhere else to go, I glimpsed the lights high and off to the right, which meant we were left and very low. I took over and, at fifty feet in appalling visibility, hurled it hard right then left and literally threw it at the flooded runway, landing late, firm and fast a third of the way down. We then aquaplaned out of control right to the end! How that aircraft stopped I shall never know, but we skidded sideways off the end onto the taxiway and again got away with it! Mind you, I'm glad I wasn't in the Mk 9 trying to formate on us throughout, but that was the classic accident-prone "get-home-itis" flight! Explained in Chapter 3's psychology section, these flights were trouble with a capital 'T'! It's human nature, but we should have known better!

When I arrived on 54 Sqn at West Raynham, I joined not just the only UK based Hunter Wing alongside 1(F) Squadron, but also the home of the Piano Smashing Competition (PSC)[3]. Indeed, the UK Hunter Wing had refined the operation to a fine art form! The wing already had permanent advertisements in the Eastern Daily Press looking for old pianos, and stating, "going to a good home"! It was amazing how many pianos were donated in this way!

Every dining-in night became a competition between 1 and 54 Sqns for the highest throw and fastest piano smashing. It occurred outside the front of the Mess sometime around midnight, and conformed to only two rules: to win, every piece of the piano had to be smashed small enough to be passed through a toilet seat, and the two pianos had to be burnt after the competition in order that the local fire brigade could earn their crust.

The local, Massingham, civilian Fire Brigade loved turning out because after midnight they were on double time (some collusion here?) and the fire was easy to extinguish. Secondly, they could drink with us afterwards whilst on double time on the excuse that we had, as usual, pinched their ignition keys.

Laying into pianos with axes and sledge-hammers is hard work and a more modern, refined method was always being sought. We invented the simple insertion of a box of twelve Thunderflashes and running like hell method! Believe me, twelve Thunder-flashes exploding inside a piano makes an indescribable harmonious, multi-toned, cascading reverberation! Subsequently, all that is required is to pick up the pieces, feed them through the toilet seat, pour petrol over them, and call for the fire brigade! The added bonus being that it takes a much shorter time than the conventional method, thus not only winning the competition but leading to more drinking time!

No. 4 SQUADRON (UK ECHELON)

Three months later we gave up our 54 Sqn number to a newly formed FGR2 Phantom Sqn, and overnight on 1st Sep '69 became No. 4 Squadron (UK Echelon). Immediately after changing numbers we were off again, this time to the Danish Air Force Base at Skrydstrup in South Jutland, just North of the German border. This exercise was remarkable if only because of the Danish women and their hospitality to all. Three or four RAF pilots of our Sqn would be sitting in the Mess bar in the evening, having a drink with the two Danish QRA pilots who were on an hour's standby duty overnight. The phone would ring, and the barman would pass it to the nearest RAF pilot, who found he was talking to the wife of one of the Danish standby pilots with whom we were drinking. There was the usual invitation on the phone to go round as her husband was away for the night! It happened to quite a few of us: it's true what they say about Scandinavian hospitality!

A couple of months later, still alive and kicking, I celebrated my 1,000 hours on the Hunter in true fashion when the boys met my aircraft with a bottle of Champagne. But the psychological word of caution: 1,000hours, "get-home-itis", and you know it all, don't you!

The final episode in the demise[5] of the West Raynham wing before we moved to Wittering

Fig 10. 4 Sqn name patch for the flying suit[4].

163

for the Harrier conversion was the selection criteria. Everyone supposedly moving to the new aircraft, in those days before Harrier simulators and two-seat trainers, had to be re-assessed on a flight check in the Hunter from one of the Central Flying Schools 'Trappers', or senior instructors who set the flying standards for the whole air force. Anyone less than above average was posted elsewhere. and there were a few guys who didn't make it. But I scrambled through and was picked with the initial tranche of pilots to fly the Harrier, and later was lucky to be awarded "exceptional" ratings as a pilot and an instructor on the most difficult aircraft to fly in the RAF. Good annual ratings recorded in your logbooks by the Sqn Cdr were probably the most treasured symbols of affection, albeit psychologically. Though even your peers rarely saw them, these ratings were the ultimate measure of your capability in relation to them.

RAF WITTERING 1970

RAF Wittering, an amalgamation of two pre-war airfields, and built on the sight of the ancient Wittering race course which dates back to at least the beginning of the nineteenth century, was also the base from which Operation Grapple, Britain's first live megaton thermo-nuclear weapon's test, was mounted in 1957. But in 1969, Wittering lost its V-force Bomber Command tag and became "The Home of the Harrier" when the aircraft first arrived in service; it still is today. At the same time, it was to become my home for the next couple of years, but two incidents there were nothing of which to be proud.

Aerial combat is perhaps one of the more dangerous manoeuvres in fighter flying. Every combat mission lands after some incident or other that was probably unbriefed, or at least unforeseen. The one combat that I remember well was, perhaps surprisingly, only a 'one-v-one' against Colin Coombes, another experienced pilot, and it took place on a beautiful, cloudless day. I had won the early manoeuvres on this particular fight and, while chasing him throughout, had inched into Colin's rear quadrant as I closed in slowly for a kill. Then he suddenly pulled up into the sun in a last ditch attempt to blind me. It did just that. At this point we were both climbing vertically up the sky into sun with me totally unsighted, and both decelerating very quickly. Colin must then have stalled out and flipped over to nose vertically downwards, because the next thing I heard and felt, rather than saw, was an enormous slipstream air-shock as he dived past cockpit to cockpit so close I could see his frightened eyes! The shockwave was so hard that for a second I thought we'd hit each other. Time seemed to stand still for a second or two before realisation that everything was still intact. Extremely shaken, we recovered, called it off and limped back to base, suitably subdued. I should never have followed him into sun – we'd been warned many times, but luckily we had missed becoming another mid-air accident statistic by inches.

Having separated while at West Raynham, the termination of my marriage precipitated the second incident that was the closest ever call to a full-blown aircraft accident. The day before I was due in court for the divorce case, my first time in any court for any reason whatsoever, I was flying a Hunter round

164

33. Hunter F6 & T7 overfly RAF Chivenor – Jan 68. Photo taken by the author from a Hunter FR10.   (© Crown Copyright/MOD)

34a & b. The Fighter Command disbandment flypast flown from RAF Coltishall – 26 Feb 68. Photos taken by the author from an FR10 while participating in the flypast, show:

Left: Canberra T33 and 2 Meteors, with nose of Hunter FGA9 and rear of T7 Hunter XL586.

Right: Hurricane and two Spitfires at the rear of the flypast, with the drop tanks of the FGA9 above.

(© Crown Copyright/MOD)

35. 2 (AC) Sqn Officers – RAF Gütersloh 1968. Rear row L to R: Photo Off Felix Leiter, Eng Off Al Jones, "Puddy" Catt, JnrGLO, Dave Bridge, SnrGLO Maj Fitzgerald, the Author, Pete Atkins, PI: Dave Oxlee, Dave Bagshaw. Front row L to R: Stu Penny, "Sandy" Wilson, Roy Holmes, CO-Sqn Ldr Tim Barratt, John Thomson, Geoff Hall, Roger Norton.

36. Typical recce target – a German Barracks 1972.
(Note top right the dummy inflatable rubber APCs with sagging barrels!)

(© Crown Copyright/MOD)

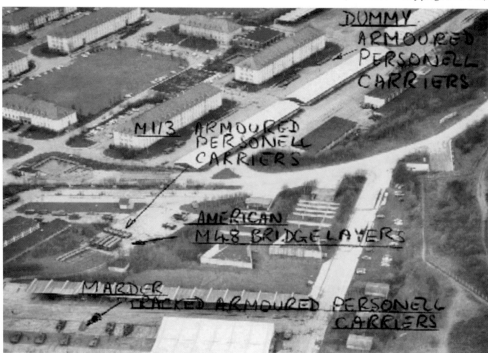

37. 2(AC) Sqn Hunter FR10 XF422 flown by author.

(© Crown Copyright/MOD)

38. Exercise Green Express – four-ship Hunter scramble – RDAF Skrydstrup – Sep 69. L to R: Barry Adcock, Stu Penny, Dave Lott and Self scrambling.

(© Crown Copyright/MOD)

39. The Mk GR1 Harrier – note its non-laser aerodynamic nose.

40. Jun 1970 – No 4 Harrier Conversion Course, the nine of us who formed the nucleus of No 20 Sqn. L to R: Dave Lott, Colin Coombes, The Author, Witney Griffiths, Qu Oswell, Pad Williams, Sandy Aitken, Brian Pegnall and Pete Tait. *(© Crown Copyright/MOD)*

Nº 4 HARRIER CONVERSION COURSE   JUNE 1970.

41. Receiving the 20 Sqn Standard at RAFC Cranwell with OC 20 Sqn Wg Cdr Cannon and the boys looking on – 6 Oct 70, before flying it out to RAF Wildenrath on a B737 of Britannia Airways.

(© Crown Copyright/MOD)

42. Harrier GR1 XV757 of 20 Sqn RAF Wildenrath. The author's first 20 Sqn sortie 10 Nov 70, with Pad Williams and Dave Lott looking on.

43a. The VTOL Landing Pads, with the runway off to the right, at GESEKE, an ex-Luftwaffe WWII grass base – Jun 71 after three days usage. If anything proved the rough landing capability of the Harrier, it was this wet, muddy field site – 20 Sqn's first!

43b & c. Wheels-up landing on the MEXE PAD at GESEKE – 2nd field deployment – 23 Mar 72.

(© Crown Copyright/MOD)

44. 3 Sqn Grass Landing at RAF Wildenrath 1972.

45. 4 Sqn ten-ship Harrier grass take-off line abreast from Bad Lippspringe – 18 Oct 73. Photo taken by the author while hovering alongside in a 3 Sqn aircraft from Moosdorf site.

(© Crown Copyright/MOD)

46. Surviving The Course No 2/69 – Winter survival, Bad Kohlgrub, Bavaria – 1969.

47. 1(F) Sqn aircraft ready for deployment. (Ferry tanks and in-flight refuelling probes fitted.)   *(© Crown Copyright/MOD)*

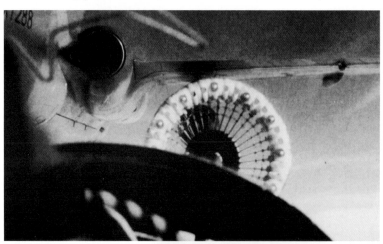

48a. *Above:* The basket as seen from the cockpit.

48b. *Right:* Harrier GR1 refuelling behind a Victor Tanker.

(© Crown Copyright/MOD)

the circuit at Wittering, doing practice touch-and-goes. On this particular approach, I had actually started to round out and cut the throttle over the runway threshold in readiness for touch down, priding myself on another immaculate approach and anticipating a perfect landing, when I heard another pilot scream over the radio "Overshoot, overshoot!" Without thinking, I just slammed the throttle fully open as it hit me like a bolt of lightning that my wheels were still up, and waited . . . and waited . . . and waited! A jet engine can take nearly ten seconds to spool up from idle RPM and develop enough power to accelerate out of a near stall situation. The aircraft and my stomach were sinking ever lower, and those were the longest sinking-sensation ten seconds of my life as I came within inches of the ground!

In shock, a very chastened pilot, I flew round the circuit for a second time, and put the aircraft down very gently on its wheels prior to a very one-sided interview with the Station Commander.

To this day I know not why the runway controller in a caravan at the end of the runway didn't see me. That's exactly what he was there for: to check the aircraft on the approach to ensure it was in the correct configuration for landing. Afterwards, Joe Sim, the pilot who had made the "overshoot" call while waiting for takeoff as I came in to land, told me that my DME aerial, a radio aerial on the underside of the fuselage which was the lowest part of the aircraft, had come within six inches of hitting the runway! Needless to say, Joe[6] received more than a beer or two out of me that night!

But I couldn't tell anybody, least of all the Station Commander, why it happened, so had to take my punishment. But I knew that I had missed my pre-landing downwind checks for the only time in my life, and simply because I had spent the whole circuit worrying myself silly about what the judge was going to say to me next day in court! It just goes to show how an unsettling, distracting and frenetic home life can spread to become a matter of life and death. Yet another classic example of the failing aviator from Chapter 3's psychology section: clever blokes those psychologists – they should have made them fighter pilots!

It was oft said that, as far as wheels-up landings were concerned, there were only two types of pilot: those that had done it, and those that were going to! I must be the only lucky guy in a third category: tried and failed!

THE HARRIER CONVERSION UNIT

Having recovered from these problems, and now back on an even keel, I just had to be patient waiting for the impending commencement of the Harrier conversion. There were no training aids, and the only answer to learning hovering and slow speed flight for ex-Hunter pilots was, 'teach them to fly helicopters.'

The pre-Harrier Helicopter course on the Whirlwind must rate as the most enjoyable flying course going. You weren't expected to know anything about the aircraft, its technicalities, its idiosyncrasies or its cockpit and emergency drills. All they wanted you to do was to get in it and fly the beast, especially at slow speed: five days of trying to hover and put the thing into and out of small clearings in the woods. The instructor did all the drills while you had some real thrill throwing it around: he even made the coffee for you afterwards! Low level helicopter work must be the second best type of flying. Indeed, by the end of the fifth day we were all able to fly it solo (but for the background knowledge), so much so that we were instrumental in changing the method of helicopter training for regular chopper pilots.

Previously, as with all aircrew training, a course usually commenced with a few week's ground school, learning all about the theory of the aeroplane and its technical bits and limitations. Initial flying training then followed. In teaching us to fly the machine without ground school, the instructors found that by running the ground instruction second to the basic flying, they could cut the ground school in half, simply because everything said in the classroom could be better and quicker understood by the students in assimilating it with their flying experience.

But it wasn't to be as easy as that. Is it ever? Returning from the helicopter course only to find that the Harrier was grounded and all the courses put back, we had to carry on flying Hunters again, and eventually, three months later, went back for a second helicopter refamiliarization course to learn hovering all over again.

"Learning, that cobweb of the brain,
Profane, erroneous, and vain."
(Samuel Butler – Hudibras 1612–1680)

And so on to the Harrier at long last.

The Harrier aircraft is unique. By the "simple" process of vectoring the engine thrust, it can take-off vertically, hover in the air, fly backwards or sideways, and land vertically. So can helicopters; but the Harrier can also make a running take-off, burdened with a much heavier, useful load, accelerate forwards over a sloping ramp that catapults it high into the air, fly at transonic speeds, and make previously impossible flight manoeuvres using viffing (vectoring in forward flight) so that the engine thrust pushes it 'round the corner'. No helicopter can do this, and neither can any other of man's flying machines.

I doubt if there is anyone remotely interested in aviation who is not broadly familiar with what a Harrier can do. Millions have watched enraptured as these aircraft have performed at air shows, but new ideas take a long time to be accepted. For at least the first ten years it was

Happiness
is

VECTORED
THRUST

Fig 11. The unofficial Harrier Motto!

166

fashionable to deride the VSTOL, revolving around the belief that it must suffer severe penalties, or have an oversized engine, or be unable to fly far, or carry a useful load. Only very gradually did the truth become accepted by military minds that were all but closed. If we were only playing at it, it was certainly a good toy to play with! The truth is that in military aviation, vectored thrust is as fundamentally important today as the wing. The Harrier was the pioneer of operational VSTOL, the starting-point for a future generation of aircraft, which has so far produced not only a pretty useless Russian copy, a naval aircraft code-named 'Forger' by NATO, but nine marks of UK Harrier also in service with the Indians, Spanish and the US Marine Corps.

Its success was in the beautiful marriage of engine and airframe. Hence from the cockpit at slow speed you had no knowledge of how much control was aerodynamic or reaction, the join was seamless. With hot air coming from twelve outlets – four nozzles and eight reaction controls – you may have thought it complex, but its very simplicity in pushing 21,500lbs of hot air out of multi-orifices on a 12,300lb airframe was its triumph. Yet, at the time, it was the most unstable aircraft to fly in the RAF, particularly the T2 two-seater. The Mk 1s to 4s were nothing like the present day Harrier. There was no auto-stabilization, no autopilot, no modern computers and no navigation aids. In the Mk 1, known as the Mod 9, certainly initially it was 1950s standard six-instrument panel of steam driven instruments together with raw, low speed instability, and little experience anywhere to tap for inside information. We were driving back the frontiers of aerodynamics, and in some cases doing it by trial and error using the three or four company test pilots to help. Even so, one day you were flying Hunters, the next on your own in a single seat Harrier.

The apprehension during these first sorties was palpable. Though no-one would admit it, it was etched into our faces (mine included) so clearly as to be obvious to all around. Then suddenly, holding my breath, and as if by magic, I found myself airborne in this trembling, shaky, noisy machine, though going nowhere but straight up into a roller-coaster of something resembling a hover, if hovering can be described as such: gyrating around the airfield is a much better description of our first hovering attempts. Indeed some, to their chagrin, even made it outside the airfield boundary! The concrete take-off and landing pad was maybe 40yds x 20yds, and all of one's skills were needed to keep within its limits, never mind the changes in height due to the rapid adrenalin-driven throttle movements. Stick and throttle were a blur of motion, arms and legs as tense as they could be, oxygen rasping in your throat, adrenalin used so fast it was in short supply, a grip so tight you'd have throttled a giant, though all this not having much effect on the aeroplane. From outside all appeared quite calm, despite the steam bubble rising above the cockpit. For the first time ever, a throttle movement produced a vertical rather than a horizontal motion – a major and very fast learning curve, in order to keep away from the only thing that causes crashes: the ground!

Rivers of sweat ran down foreheads and backs of necks, but instinctively limbs reacted like the well-regulated levers of a robot. The long, tedious months of training and preparation had produced the right, if not rather rough, reactions: many incidents but no bad crashes. How light she was on the controls compared with the Hunter; the slightest pressure with hand or foot, and she leapt all over the sky!

I was only up there for perhaps two minutes at most, but as I tried to tame this bucking bronco, they were the longest hardest worked of my life. The instructor on the ground was talking sweet-nothings into my ears through the radio, trying to keep me calm, but having got up there, and unsteadily at that, now I had to land this outrageous machine! More pit-of-the-stomach apprehension and panic! How I ever got this thoroughbred, with no auto stabilization, back on the concrete pad in one piece that first time, I shall never know. But it happened safely after an extremely unsteady decent – there's a natural reluctance to come anywhere near the ground, but touchdown came with enormous feelings of both relief and ecstasy. It was a better high than any drugs. I'd got away with it again, and what a delight to have managed it in one piece that first time after waiting for so long! But then, with little time to recover, I had to do it twice more before they'd let me out! My US Marine Corps instructor was happy, "Nothing to worry about!" he said. All the same, I'm sure he knew how proud I felt, especially as the others were all watching, and some, not unnaturally, had made a real mess of it on the first attempt.

Some of my peers had had terrible trouble handling this aspect of the new aircraft. After all, it was combining the high quality skills of a fighter pilot with that of a helicopter driver. Some spent many minutes "manoeuvring" in only partial control, up, down, around, and over the whole airfield, pretending they were hovering, trying to calm the brute. One future senior officer even managed to rotate the aircraft round the nose wheel on takeoff to such an extent that, as the rear lifted off, the pitot-head sticking out in front of the nose touched the ground and was bent upwards at a 45degree angle! Put another way, the fuselage was tilted downwards at a 45degree angle while the nose-wheel remained firmly on the ground! He then carried on upwards into an unsteady hover and took a long time to come back down again! But we all managed it in the end.

Because of the lack of training aids, a Harrier photo unit was established to film every single landing and take-off during the first couple of years of Harrier operations. The film was then used to debrief each sortie. Of course, this meant that every landing or take-off problem, and every incident, was captured on film. Later, once the two-seaters came into service, the photo unit was disbanded, and the OCU instructors kept all the film. Eventually, they spliced all the incidents together as a "Harrier Horror Movie", and showed it to every subsequent course of students – but only after they had completed their VSTOL training successfully themselves! I still have a copy of this film, and thirty-five years on, it still produces some great laughs any time we have guests. Besides the unsteady VSTOL incidents, it shows the undercarriage strengths as landings are seen where the aircraft is travelling literally sideways down the runway at ninety knots, totally uncontrollably, but the undercarriage, particularly the outriggers, don't even bend!

VSTOL – PARTLY EXPLAINED!

In my archives are coveted copies of both the P1127 and Kestrel FGA Mk1 Pilot's Notes and also the Operating Data Manuals for the Bristol Siddeley Pegasus Mks 5 and 6 engines. These early manuals describe these Harrier predecessors as 'inherently unstable', and truly it is a good place to start with this machine, as it is at the opposite end of the stability spectrum in contrast to the beautifully stable Hunter. So, look no further for some of the idiosyncrasies or 'gotchas' of this aircraft. The early marks of Harrier were little more stable than the Kestrel, especially in the slow speed range. An aircraft that looks right always flies right, but gone were the sleek streamlined, stunning lines of the Hunter. In its place was a groundhog rearing up from the back into a couple of large, earlike intakes with flapping side-door appendages that together dominated the nose area, with its little wings drooping downwards to allow the outriggers to touch the ground. It didn't look right, and it sure was a real handful to fly!

Unlike the Hunter whose handling notes are overstated, this new VSTOL concept fighter was grossly understated. It would bite back, given the slightest opportunity, especially in the slow speed VSTOL range, but amazingly, it wouldn't spin. I've seen one in full reverse thrust with full crossed-controls going backwards at fifty knots, and all it does is flutter downwards like a wounded bird.

Sideslip and turning at low speed between 30 and 90 knots was absolutely forbidden. The aircraft did not have the available reaction control to overcome the side forces that could be generated by intake momentum drag, which occurred below 90knots when in a crosswind situation. Hence, in all transitionary flight from the hover to above 90 knots or the reverse, no bank could be applied in these early models of the aircraft. The golden rule was to keep the wind-vane in the middle! Of all the modern technology that had gone into this machine, this little, mechanical, free-spinning wind-vane mounted on top of the nose just in front of the cockpit, was by far the best indication of any sideslip or crosswind developing.

But the remarkable truth behind the early Harrier problems lay in its engine failures. For a jet engine to work well at low level, the main operating area for army support aircraft, the engine must be able to sustain bird ingestion damage and continue working. The Pegasus was no exception. In order to prove this concept, Bristol Siddeley, so the story goes, went downtown to the local Tesco, and bought their whole stock of 1lb frozen chickens. They then started up an engine on a test-bed, and threw these (by now unfrozen) chickens at the front end. To their great surprise and, no doubt, delight, the engine swallowed up these chickens, spat the bits out the back end, and continued motoring as though nothing untoward had happened!

So they sold the concept to the MOD who put the aircraft into service. We then proceeded to lose somewhere around six to eight aircraft when, after hitting birds, the engine went out and the pilot had to eject. Indeed, the most famous of these accidents happened on the 4 May '72 to Wg Cdr Peter P. Wallington Taylor, who was flying low level (250ft) at 420Kts in Schleswig-Holstein fairly close to the IGB, when he suffered a bird strike which put the engine out. Peter pulled up and tried to relight the engine, which he failed to do. Now with a dead engine descending back through 200ft at approximately 250Kts, he finally ejected.

Swinging in his parachute on recovering from the ejection, he was surprised to hear a roar, and he then watched his aircraft climbing upwards and disappearing into the sky at full throttle. The air traffic/air defence authorities, seeing this happen on radar, scrambled a couple of Kriegsmarine F104 Starfighters from the nearest GAF base to try and shoot it down before it crossed the IGB into the Russians' hands. The F104s found this Harrier doing lazy barrel rolls at 25,000ft, and failed to come close enough to shoot it down. They can't turn as quickly as Harriers! The Harrier eventually crashed on our side of the border, some 44 minutes after the ejection, but only after it ran out of fuel!

Subsequent investigations revealed that it was not the body of our little sparrow causing the problem. It was the feathers that were blocking the air pressure detectors that regulate the fuel injected into the combustion chamber. The morale of the story is: little sparrows are far more dangerous than 1lb frozen chickens!

As a sequel to PPWT's ejection, the RAF fitted a further fuel system – a manual one which could, if required, easily override the automatics. We then found out that the US Marine Corps had bought the manual system as a standard fit for their jets, while the penny-pinching RAF had declined it as unnecessary!

Interestingly, as an aside to the F104s v Harrier story, we always laughed at the way the F104 with its afterburner, and Mach 2.2 performance, couldn't out-turn a Harrier. But in 1974, No 1(F) Sqn had an exchange visit with 311 Sqn of the German Air Force, and arranged a race from a standing start to 10,000feet. The two-seater trainers were used, giving the Harrier a real handicap being some 1500lbs heavier. Yet, on the day, the Harrier beat the F104 by seven seconds! Subsequently we found out that while the Harrier had a full fuel load, the Germans had pared theirs down to absolute minimum. The F104 scurried straight home from 10,000ft, while the Harrier continued to complete an hour-long combat mission. Vertical take-off was the secret – the Harrier was through 1,000ft before the F104 even got airborne, and although it was always catching the Harrier up, it couldn't make it in time!

The other major change for us in converting from Hunter to Harrier was in the instrumentation system. The Hunter had the typical WW2 standard "steam-driven" instrument panel, whereas soon after conversion, the GR1A mark of Harrier was fitted with the first analogue Inertial Navigation and Attack System (INAS), which was prone to gross errors and frequent breakdowns.

Fig 12. The Harrier Pilot's badge of office – worn on the left arm by all.

Now it must be remembered that this system was originally designed for the TSR2, which itself was produced to put a nuclear bomb down the left drainpipe of the Kremlin. This required little accuracy – roughly half-a-mile – and it wasn't capable of achieving that! So they put it into a Harrier that was going to fire rockets, drop cluster bombs, and strafe, all of which needed an aiming accuracy of around ten to fifteen feet. Then they spent ten years trying to make it work!

In the early days after take-off from Wildenrath on the Dutch/German border, by the time you were out of sight of the airfield, the INAS was usually racing across East Germany looking for Russia and that Kremlin drain-pipe! Hence it was often turned off because we could navigate manually much more accurately, though of course, it was not beneficial to its long term serviceability.

Here for example, is a typical Harrier Pilot's approach to the INAS:

A SIMPLIFIED APPROACH TO INERTIAL NAVIGATION

The following explanation is typical of all inertial navigation systems:

First, the aircraft knows where it is at all times. It knows this because it knows where it isn't. By subtracting where it isn't from where it is, or where it is from where it isn't, (whichever is the greater), it obtains the difference called deviation.

The inertial system uses deviation to generate corrective commands to drive the system from a position where it is, to a position where it isn't, arriving at a position where it-isn't-it-is-now.

In the event the position where it is now, is not the position where it wasn't, the system has acquired a variation (variations are caused by external factors, and the discussion of these factors is not considered to be within the scope of this explanation). However, the variation is the difference between where the aircraft is and where the aircraft wasn't. If the variation is considered to be a significant factor, it may also be corrected by use of the doppler system; however, the aircraft must know where it was also.

The "thought process" of the system, therefore, is as follows: because a variation has modified some of the information which the aircraft has obtained, it is not sure where it is. However, it is sure where it isn't (within reason), and it knows where it was.

It now subtracts where it should be from where it wasn't (or vice versa), and by differentiating this from the algebraic difference between its deviation and its variation, which is called error, it computes the correct information to compensate for all factors supplying accurate navigation information.

(Who said this stuff was so complicated ?)
Contributed from a source too devious to mention!

Flying these new, clean, very short range Harriers, the average sortie length during that first month was only twenty minutes, and the whole months flying only came to four hours despite filling half a log-book page! It was hard work for everyone, particularly due to the lack of flying hours and continuity, even though it was mid-summer. Indeed, the twenty-seven hours total flying on the course took three months to achieve at nine hours per month. Too few aircraft and constant groundings didn't help, so much so that we hadn't even tried flying it at night by the end of the course. There was little continuity, and indeed, I saw less than 100 flying hours in the whole of my first year on the aircraft[7]. It was a struggle for us all to progress, as the only learning curve came from trial and error. Finally, to end the course and, as a sop to actually using the aircraft for operations, we flew three combined rocketing and dive bombing sorties on Holbeach range: guns had yet to be fitted!

As the final deed before forming No. 20 Squadron at Wildenrath, on the 6th Oct '70 we all went to the RAF College at Cranwell to receive the Squadron Standard, which had been laid up there ever since the Sqn had disbanded in Singapore a few years earlier. It was one of the few occasions since the Aden days for some pomp and ceremony, except once again muggins was lumbered (he'd done it before!) as the Standard Bearer. (See photo). At least it got me some duty frees, as I had to escort it via a Britannia Airways trooping flight from Luton to Wildenrath, where I had all of half an hour on the ground handing it over to the station SWO[8], before climbing back on the same Boeing 737 for return to UK.

Aviation-minded readers will now have to forgive me as I have to lapse back into my personal life just a little, simply because it had a major bearing on the future of my professional flying career. Suffice to say that late on a Sunday morning, my having embarrassed him earlier, my old retainer of a batman gave me a real rollicking. "If you need two cups of tea in bed in the morning, Sir," he said, "kindly put two pairs of shoes outside the door for cleaning!"

As we had resolved to go to Germany together and set up house, my new partner and I decided to leave for the Continent the day the course ended in order to find somewhere to live. Not being married, we weren't entitled to air force married quarters; consequently, while the others took their embarkation leave, we packed up quickly and drove in convoy to Germany.

Notes
1. Tripartite: Combined US, German and RAF Sqn.
2. Yellow. Weather info in the military world was summed up in a colour code system, the best being Blue then White, Green, Yellow 1, Yellow 2, Amber and Red. In general, Amber and Red were below flying limits, Yellow was on the limit, and the rest were OK.
3. PSC stands for Piano Smashing Competition, and not Passed Staff College! We got there first!

4. The X of Xris is not a misspelling! With three Chris's on the Sqn, we each became XRIS, YRIS and ZRIS to differentiate our names on the daily flying programme, and it stuck ever since!
5. After the departure of our Hunter Wing for Wittering and Harrier conversion, West Raynham as an active airfield closed down, although the RAF Regiment, and Bloodhound missiles used the site for some years before it closed for good. The pianos of East Anglia were now much safer, and the life of Massingham Fire Brigade Firemen was much the poorer, both in body, and spirit of both kinds!
6. Tragically, Joe was killed in a car crash 34 years later in 2003, but is, obviously, included in my dedication.
7. The normal in those days was 250 flying hours per year.
8. SWO - Station Warrant Officer.

Chapter Nineteen

Vertical over Europe

Nos. 20 and 3(AC) SQUADRONS
RAF WILDENRATH

It was late autumn 1970, and my new partner and I were driving in convoy through the Netherlands to the Roermond – Wassenberg border crossing for the first time. I was going to RAF Wildenrath to help form No. 20 Squadron, the second Harrier Sqn in Germany, and I was going to be the first one there. Imagine my utter horror when, on walking into the Mess bar, I found my soon-to-be-ex-wife sitting on a barstool and drinking with another girl, and both were in identical uniforms! "Now what?" I thought. "How the hell do I get out of this one?" A live-in girlfriend in an hotel downtown and the wife in the Mess, and I'd got to live there with no-one to turn to . . . HELP!

I was flabbergasted. She knew I had been posted to Wildenrath before we had separated, so what in hell was she doing here? Luckily, she hadn't seen me, and I silently backed out on tiptoe.

My arrival at Wildenrath was about to take a very unexpected turn, because we had been hoping to find temporary accommodation in the female block for my partner. When overseas, your whole daily and social life revolves around the Mess, and with our final decree still pending, it would have been untenable living in the same Mess alongside a previous partner even without a live-in girl friend in an hotel downtown!

However, when I mentioned the problem to OC Ops, whom I had known at Wittering, he had the "ex" off-base and posted to Laarbruch within 48hours! What a relief! You can imagine my partner's reaction when I told her what a fix we had been in! Even today, I still don't know why the "ex" put herself in that position. There was no question on either side of a reunion, yet she knew I had been posted there and had clearly expected my imminent arrival.

The sequel to this story is quite comical. As I was not married in the eyes of the air force I was forced to maintain and pay for a bachelor room in the Mess despite the fact it wasn't used. Even though I was actually living downtown with a partner, (the air force couldn't stop me putting my head down wherever I liked) officially I had to be seen to be living-in. I then spent nearly two years worrying that my "ex" would find out that I was living with another woman, and cite this in our divorce case. Meanwhile, unbeknown to me, she was going out with a helicopter pilot who lived in the room next-door to mine in the Mess, and it appears that they also spent the next two years avoiding me like the plague to ensure that I never found out about them!

They actually succeeded because it was three years later on a return visit to Wildenrath that the girls – the single schoolteachers living in the Mess – told me what had been going on throughout that time! We'd both been running scared of each other for the same reasons, and it badly tainted our whole time at Wildenrath. Where personal relationships are concerned, what a very silly world we live in!

One incident illustrates the official thinking in those days. I soon became the Mess Entertainments Officer. On one occasion I was standing in the Mess Office discussing the forthcoming ball when the President of the Mess Committee (PMC), a Wing Commander Educator, came in looking worried. Glancing at the room allocation board, it became obvious that he had run out of accommodation for some visiting crews and didn't have a ready solution: no beds available anywhere. Being helpful, I volunteered my room in the Mess because it was never used, and was utterly astounded by his reply. He said that if I were notifying him officially that I was not actually living in the mess, he would have to take official action against me! "Sod you!" I thought, "Sort your own accommodation problem out then!" Even so, it came home to me then that the powers-that-be had turned a Nelson's eye to my unofficial living out. I learnt that, apparently, in those days, you had to obtain official permission to live off base overseas!

Hence, by the end of the first week I had seen off the "ex", been given a room to store things in the Mess, found a grim, semi-furnished house to live in only one and a half miles from the base, and, looked round the Sqn hangar accommodation. Our Sqn accommodation, an ex-Canberra hangar, large enough for twelve Harriers, was totally lacking in furniture or paraphernalia to run a flying unit. There had been a fire in the barrack stores two weeks earlier and all our new equipment had been destroyed. Hence, the rest of my available time was spent finding desks and chairs, a toolbox and a couple of phones that worked – in time for the arrival of the others on Monday. What a start, both! A titubant beginning, personally and professionally, which would remain frustrating on both fronts as we stumbled through the next couple of years.

Aiming to produce any form of continuity in its initial flying training was to prove an habitual struggle. Few aircraft, little engineering knowledge of its systems, a bare minimum of flying hours, and constant groundings for little technical quirks made for an exasperating time. It didn't help that 4 Sqn, who had started up in the next hangar a few months before us, was always given priority in order to gain a new combat-ready squadron for the NATO tote-board as fast as possible. Three weeks passed before we managed our first flight. As seen from photo 42, mine finally took place on 10th November, some thirty-three days after my last Harrier training flight at Wittering. It was almost like starting over again in a barely familiar cockpit, but unlike most of the others on the new squadron, at least I had the advantage of a previous tour in Germany and knew the local countryside reasonably well. Every little helped in those circumstances because the lack of flying was really beginning to show: only five flights throughout the month, and only six in December. It had been six months of Harrier flying with less than forty hours airborne, compared with the common average in those days of a hundred and twenty-five to stay current.

Those three years at Wildenrath, particularly at the beginning, proved strange and trying. With the advent of VSTOL aircraft, pushing back the frontiers of fighter aviation, it seemed every obstacle was put in our way. Air staffs, neither understanding nor wanting to understand, initially insisted that we conformed to the same rules as conventional aircraft. The simplest example was the necessity to maintain the same weather and crash diversions, and minimum fuel states, with no regard to our ability to land and take-off from the smallest piece of ground. We would have been better off under the command of helicopter commanders! There was little support or equipment available and few serviceable aircraft, or if serviceable then not for long: progress inevitably was slow. Often we planned, briefed and authorised a four-ship mission, walked out as a three-ship, and got airborne as a pair. Adding in a number of bizarre accidents and constant groundings, our frustration was palpable.

This was, of course, a time of experimentation, almost as if the Air Force knew not what to do with us. Over the next three years, as the first VSTOL wing, whilst being based on a full-sized 'standard-NATO' airfield, we operated from old narrow roads, clearings in the woods, temporary metal-planking runways, old Luftwaffe grass airfields and new autobahn strips especially designed for aircraft. Given our Achilles heel – the enormous logistic support required – none of our options seemed viable in a European wartime scenario. On the other hand, I take my hat off to German government projects that allowed their highways agency to build autobahns to MOD specifications successfully. Can you imagine it happening here? The chaos and overspend!

Yet these years were, at the same time, oddly exotic and exciting: an elite bunch of guys struggling against enormous ignorance and lacking in leadership, flying hours and experience, but determined to see the task through while yearning for the next of their few and far between flights. It seemed a continuing, classic case of one step forward and two back.

Everything had to be obtained piecemeal. Given the job of Squadron Adjutant, I had to start up a complete administrative system from scratch, including a new registry and a new filing system. At least the one perk of this role was an office with one's own desk, chair and telephone: gold dust at the time! No wonder the RAF's aircrew branch was officially called 'the General Duties branch': more like Jack-of-all-trades and master of heck all! But the beauty of it was the pervasive 'can-do' attitude in the aircrew branch.

As for the lack of leadership, we started 20 Sqn without a Wg Cdr boss, and only a single Sqn Ldr temporarily in charge. When the new Wg Cdr boss finally arrived together with a second Flt Cdr, he lost his health very quickly and had to give up his post within two months. I thought the two Flt Cdrs were ineffectual and had little in the way of leadership qualities to lift morale in those wearisome but demanding times. Admittedly it wasn't easy for them, but we desperately needed a good leader. To replace the Boss in a hurry, along came the man who had been an instructor of the Harrier Conversion Team at Wittering, then Sqn Ldr, now Wg Cdr (it's a small world). He obviously was a QFI, and didn't last long either.

In the meantime, 3 Sqn was formed as our wing's third squadron but again without any proper accommodation, so they parked the aircraft on the old Canberra QRA dispersal whilst using a four-roomed wooden hut as their total Sqn aircrew and operational accommodation. The new boss of 3 Sqn was none other than that super guy who, as a Sqn Ldr, had commanded our sister Sqn in Aden, Wg Cdr Phil Champniss (it's a smaller world). You may remember that he was also the guy who rang me the day Al Pollock flew under Tower Bridge. Phil soon got to grips with the problems, provided the leadership required, and found he needed theatre qualified instructors for his new Sqn. Accordingly, Tim Smith as the QWI from 4 Sqn, another ex-8 Sqn Aden mate (it's a *very small* world), and myself from 20 Sqn as the FRI, were posted across the hangar to join the new outfit.

For three months we were in heaven working for Phil Champniss, the best boss I've ever had. He was a real leader who knew how to motivate and get the finest out of his guys; leadership seemed to come naturally to him, and we'd have done anything for him anyway: he had savoir faire! Our four-roomed wooden hut, for instance, contained only his office, an ops room, a crew room and our nav/briefing/planning room, all divided by very thin, single-chipboard walls: we could hear anything that was said in his office, and the rollockings were something to behold! He soon realized this, and subsequently when he was about to give you a rollocking, he replaced his "my office" phrase with, "Let's go for a walk on the grass!" He'd take you by the elbow and you'd both stroll round the grassy surrounds of the two QRA hangars while receiving your admonishment out of sight and sound of the others.

Later, when we moved into our new permanent accommodation in the main hangar, his new office always had a metal in-tray with a piece of turf filling it, just large enough for a pair of size 10s. If you were summoned to the presence for a dressing down, you dutifully had to climb onto this turfed in-tray for your "walk on the grass!"

The answer to the 20 Sqn problem was to move Phil Champniss down the hangar to take over and sort it out. We on 3 Sqn were devastated at losing him, but soldiered on without a Boss yet again for another few months. Once more a Sqn Ldr, this time Jack Rust, took over the outfit for three months whilst Tim and I became the Flight Commanders until the next Wing Commander arrived: this time it was Graham Williams. Graham had been a Flt Cdr of mine on 8 Sqn in Aden (it's an extremely small world) during my first few months out there and was known as a hard man. With him came my new Flt Cdr, Al Cleaver, who had been with me on the Gütersloh recce wing two years previously (can the world get any smaller?).

Finally, to further shrink the world, Des Melaniphy, my cadet Flt Cdr and my boss on 8 Sqn in Aden, also arrived to take over 4 Sqn. From Nov '70 until Aug '72, we had worked on the two Sqns for seven different bosses: three Sqn Ldrs and four Wg Cdrs during a period of only twenty-one months. A new boss every three months, albeit the first one was most unfortunate, and he at least had had the balls to own up to his own problems. We wished him well. But is it any wonder that we were discouraged by the lack of leadership and continuity?

The continual firing of Sqn Cdrs appeared to be an air force wide policy during this period, and wasn't just confined to the Harrier force. For example, at the far end of our airfield was the Germany Communications Sqn, No. 60 Sqn, which was flying twin Pembrokes on, inter alia, recce missions up the corridors to and from West Berlin. OC 60 Sqn also left early during this period. So we lost three Sqn Cdrs on one airfield in approximately a year. I have often wondered whether it had anything to do with having two Group Captains: a station commander and a Harrier Force commander? But then the two jobs were amalgamated.

Nevertheless, the GD Branch has never been famed for its man-manage-ment expertise – no experience while young, no training in mid-career,and an uninterested hierarchy above.

There is a big difference between management and leadership. When Noah heard the flood forecast, he ordered the ark for all the animals – that's leader-ship! Once afloat, he said, "Make sure the elephants don't see what the rabbits are up to." – that's management!

There was an amusing sequel amongst all this hiring and firing. 3 Sqn dined me in on the same night as they dined Phil out. We all wore Sqn cummerbunds on formal occasions and, on this one, we both stood up during the speeches and swapped cummerbunds: a simple, cheap, easy transaction that kept every-thing very tidy, and was roundly approved by the members. The only trouble was that his went round my waist nearly twice; he was a big man in every sense!

In these frustrating times, it is hardly surprising that numerous and bizarre accidents happened. In Chapter 18 the problem of bird strikes was mentioned and the almost unbelievable bird-strike incident of Pete Taylor's when his aircraft nearly flew over the East German border on its own whilst staying airborne for forty-four minutes after his ejection. That and several other bird strike/engine failures all occurred during this period with the loss of eight aircraft before retrofitting a manual fuel system to overcome the problem.

Chris Humphreys of 4 Sqn died tragically on 12 Jan 72 during a demonstration when he and his aircraft went into low cloud immediately after take off on the easterly runway. Seconds later it was glimpsed coming out of the cloud bottom almost vertically. Unable to recover in time, Chris ejected but struck a farmhouse and was killed.

Another 4 Sqn pilot died in one of the most unfortunate of accidents at medium level on 23 Jan 74 when his aircraft had a flap failure on one side, putting the machine into an uncontrollable spiral from which he was forced to eject. The seat worked correctly but on release from his seat his main para-chute was severely damaged. Inspection revealed that the Koch fastener of the pilot's left parachute riser was undone, all the port parachute shroud lines and one of the starboard was severed, the parachute canopy was damaged, and the seat shoulder harness showed signs of entanglement with the parachute canopy and shroud lines. On this occasion, it appeared that the left seat buckle overrode the parachute Koch fastener undoing it during the early stages of ejection. After many testings and many actual ejections, it was not an accident that could have been previously foreseen, and a simple modification ensured no further instances.

Jim Downey and Steve Beckley were also extremely unlucky and ill-fated Harrier pilots whose details are already well categorized and are too long to linger on here. Suffice it to say that Steve was forced to eject on two separate occasions and Jim on three: five major accidents with both men failing to make it. One major accident is bad enough, so it seems quite unfair to them when some of us came through unscathed . . . lady luck continued to be with me!

During our second off-base field site detachment at Geseke in March 1972, Al Holman performed an inadvertent wheels-up vertical landing on a MEXE pad in the field. This wheels-up vertical landing, outside the helicopter world, must have been unique.

Equally bizarre was Pad Williams's accident on 25 November 1970. He had always been a short, paunchy guy, but we never realized he had been having trouble with high "g" forces due to his girth and weight. In those days we still wore our anti-g suits 'hidden' underneath our flying suits. It appears that one day while flying at low level somewhere near Hameln, the north German town from where the Pied Piper came, with little or no anti-g protection, he just blacked out in a turn and flew straight into the ground. Bizarre – yes, but again, you couldn't legislate for that. The accident summary states that he was not wearing an anti-G-suit at the time.

Finally in this series of strange accidents is the incredible one that happened on 23 April 1971 to a very popular pilot of our 20 Sqn. He was manoeuvring in the hover around the dispersals to the SW of the airfield where we had turned some short taxiways into short landing strips and had built two concrete, vertical landing-pads onto two teardrop aprons. The whole dispersal area, in typical continental fashion, had been hewn out of a young pine forest. The trees (about forty feet high with trunks one foot thick) had been left in place to grow around the dispersals as good camouflage. The pilot lost control of the aircraft which, on hitting the ground near a tree line, dug its nose in and reared up tail first. It continued upwards until he thought it was going to flip right over on its back, and at about 85 degrees with the nose embedded in the ground, he finally ejected. As he had ejected almost horizontally, his seat fired straight into the trees, ricocheted off three tree trunks and came to rest on hitting the fourth. There hadn't been time for the full ejection sequence and he landed still sitting in his seat with a broken neck. The aircraft subsequently settled back to the horizontal the right way up but, of course, he was not to know that at the time of ejection. Astonishingly few survive such an ordeal un-paralysed, and we spent many a week feeding him beer through a straw while he was immobilized in traction in Wegberg RAF Hospital. I'm glad to say that he eventually made a full recovery, though never flew ejection seats again.

All these accidents, including many more that have not made these pages, came rather as a series of greater and greater shocks. The practice of war is cruel – you can only put up with it if you stop yourself getting depressed by making jokes and laughing. To the uninitiated it may seem extremely irreverent, but believe me, this was not so. Quite the opposite: it was our way of bottling things up, coping with death, and getting on with life. I hadn't had any fatal or major accidents on my units, and certainly no military funerals to attend during my time flying Hunters. Then suddenly this new untried VSTOL aircraft was hitting back at us all too frequently. During these first few years of Harrier operations, there was not the same feeling of security and confidence prevalent in the Hunter years. This new aircraft kept you on your toes!

As an example of the dangerous times we encountered during these early years when introducing the Harrier into service, of the seventy-eight GR1s/1As and fourteen T2s/T2As delivered to the RAF, thirty-one (29 GR1s and two T2s) were involved in major accidents and ten pilots were killed in less than three years. Thirty-one out of a fleet of seventy-eight is horrendous: a near 40% accident rate. By comparison, of the thirty-six new-build GR3s delivered later, only 2 were written off, with one of them fatal, while four were shot down in the Falklands.

In the early days we were led to believe that the US Marine Corp had incurred a worse accident rate with their AV8B variation, but statistics now show that they had thirty-two crashes, ten fatal, out of 102 delivered aircraft over five years. We also ruefully looked at the German Air Force's "Widowmaker", the F104 Starfighter, which had a high accident rate. But they had an excuse: they had no middle management, being without an air force from 1945 to the mid-'50s. They lost over 200 aircraft, but they bought over 800 of them! Ten times the size of our fleet. So maybe our accident rates were worse, or is it just statistics?

In fact it didn't help that the new (and first into RAF service) analogue Inertial Navigation and Attack System (INAS) had now been retro-fitted to the Harrier. Unfortunately, it proved so unreliable initially that we often switched it off, as most of us could navigate far more accurately using the usual technique of stop watch, dead reckoning and map reading. But it came into its own if one was forced to pull up from low level into cloud when the weather closed in suddenly: a frequent occurrence in German winters. With no other nav. aids and no sight of the ground, the inertial system at least gave you a rough idea of where you were. Constant vigilance and exertion were required. Vertical over Europe . . . not just the Harrier but tempers too!

In March 1971 I became a Harrier air tester for the first time and by May had also experienced the first of many engine failures. These happened regularly at high level during engine slam tests and are fully described in Chapter 22.

By June that year, nine months after reforming, we had finally accepted our full complement of aircraft, and were considered experienced enough to try our first off-base field site practice. This was to be at a little, ex-Luftwaffe, grass site called Geseke-Störmede, some twenty-five miles due South of Gütersloh. A local baron, who kept his own Cessna there in a little hangar, now owned Geseke, and our first Harrier detachment there became notable for four reasons.

Firstly, the Baron had advertised in his local paper our arrival as his own flying show, so crowds of tourists watching the Harrier perform for the first time continually hampered us. Secondly was the wonderful formal dinner given by the Baron in his hangar in our honour, in which he had had a stag killed and slowly spit roasted. Thirdly, his hospitality ran to the use of his heated outdoor swimming pool a few miles away in the grounds of his magnificent schloss. Unfortunately, he hadn't appreciated that, after a week in the field, we were somewhat scruffy and smelly, and the pool with soap and shampoo gave us our first bath since leaving home! However, on arrival in the dark at his poolside, we found that he'd been called away, but he had left for us an enormous pile of beautiful towels and a couple of cases of the local Pilsner. A good scrub-up in a heated pool in beautiful surroundings and free beer: it was a memorable evening after the muddy, military tents, NAAFI rations, and Elsan bogs of Geseke airstrip!

Fourthly, we quickly learnt the enormous limitations of operating the Harrier on soft, muddy ground, but not before we experienced the, still only, wheels-up vertical landing. With much use in rainy weather, the short grass runway strip was soon turned into a potholed, badly repaired, muddy, rutted track, which became difficult enough for a Landrover and impossible for a Harrier. But we found that if you could drive a Landrover over grass at 45 mph without your backside leaving the seat, it was safe for Harrier take-offs and landings! This was used to great effect in choosing sites. The experience of Geseke started a process that took Harrier field sites away from the original concept of grass fields towards hardened off-base runways such as roads, autobahns, or even specially laid metal planking strips.

One month later, we deployed for our first "Deci" detachment. Since we'd pulled out of Libya with the demise of King Idris II and the rise to power of Gaddafi, Deci replaced the old RAF El Adem armament practice camps. Decimomannu is an Italian Air Force base on Sardinia just North of Cagliari. Decci had been set up as a NATO weapons training base with both air-to-ground and air-to-air instrumented firing facilities shared by four nations: Italy, W.Germany, UK and USA. Five weeks of concentrated weapons firing practice of rockets, bombs and gunnery, not only set the aircraft weapons' systems into perfect harmonisation, but put the pilots back into the Wyatt Earp, sharp-shooting category: well some of us anyway!

My "C" promotion exams, necessary for promotion to squadron leader, were sat here at Deci during my visit with 3 Sqn in Mar '73. Two of us sat the exams, invigilated by one of our own squadron pilots. I have to say, the invigilator who shall remain nameless, was very good to us, supplying coffee and biscuits throughout both of the three-hour exams. One year later they suspended "C" promotion exams for good, and gave the rank on annual report competition only. Again, as with the previous "B" exams, it was typical of my luck, but I was finally promoted to Sqn Ldr in 1981.

Meanwhile, the "Q" exams were also suspended just before I was due to take them, but this time, less fortunately, they were replaced by an eighteen-month, twelve-module, correspondence course for entry into staff college. So I also had to slog through that system and then went to staff college also in 1981.

In Nov '71, I went back to Wittering to complete a month's flying course to qualify as a Fighter Reconnaissance Instructor. This was the first of these courses, and was really an occasion for all the Harrier guys with previous recce experience to devise a syllabus of recce instruction for the future Harrier Force. This great month's flying gave us all an immense amount of satisfaction while flying rewarding, pure-recce missions for the first time since 2 Sqn Hunter days. Subsequently, the RAF never did use the Harrier's recce capability to the same profound extent of the old Gütersloh Hunter recce wing. Instead, the recce tasks went mainly to 2 (AC) Sqn now flying F4 Phantoms for a short period before reconverting to Jaguars at Laarbruch.

Back on the FRI course at Wittering, I was missing my partner, so thought

181

I'd surprise her. In the middle of the course, I set off to drive back to Germany on the Friday night to spend the weekend with her, and managed to catch the 9pm Dover-Ostende boat. I drove like a mad thing across Belgium, round Antwerp, into the bottom of Holland, through Roermond, and then made a fatal decision. The shortest route from Roermond to home was through the Wassenberg border crossing, but it was closed from midnight until 6am. However, there was nothing to stop you driving through – only a red light showing, but no physical barriers or guards, and it was nearly 2am! It was also a further 20 mile detour to the next crossing, and we had previously been across the Wassenberg border at night. I was in a hurry to see my love, so why not again?

Why not indeed!? Yet another case of accidents occurring on a get-home-itis mission!

I stopped at the border . . . had a good look round . . . the straight road ahead lined on both sides by high fir trees was empty and beckoning . . . and so I drove on. Some two hundred yards beyond the border in Germany I ran straight into an armed, frontier-police trap that suddenly erupted out of the woods on both sides of the road! Searchlights lit up the area and machine guns bristled at me. My heart hit the floor, with my stomach in hot pursuit! With many 'donner und blitzens' they ejected me from the car at gunpoint and went through all my papers, licences, ID card and passport while searching the car with a fine tooth comb. A shout from the rear said they'd found the Jerry Cans in the boot. In British Forces Germany, you had special petrol coupons to obtain duty free petrol; it was incredibly cheap. So when doing a run to the UK, you'd fill up every can you could find to save having to buy at exorbitant UK prices. This was illegal, but we all did it! Fortunately, I had used all mine on the round trip and the cans were now empty. You should have seen their disappointed faces! Having empty petrol cans isn't a crime. It was the petrol that was illegal. As their primary purpose was to catch smugglers they reluctantly let me on my way but not without a few more explicit words about 'der Grossbritannischen' adhering to border controls!

No. 3(F) SQUADRON

In Mar '72 as I moved down the hangar to join No. 3(F) Squadron, the wing had received its first two-seat trainer versions, the Harrier T2. An ungainly looking machine with its rear second cockpit perched high on top, and its extra length with a long, pointed tail, the T2 had less hover performance than the single seater and was even more unstable. Nobody except QFIs enjoyed flying it. However, in May that year, some eighteen months after Harrier conversion, I finally flew my first night VSTOL sortie, and this was with Phil Champniss, my new Boss, in the back seat. This sortie is forever stuck in my memory as the first ever night hover, something we had dreaded for months. We came down the glidepath off a GCA approach to hover over the runway threshold and all was going well, I thought. A steady hover followed by a final rolling-vertical landing, though the turbine temperatures were a bit high. In fact, it appeared much easier to hover at night because of the languid weather conditions and darkness, than with the many external distractions encountered

182

during day flying. Everything seems so much slower and calmer at night amidst the cosy, soft-red glow of the cockpit lighting.

However, after landing during the debrief, Phil said to put my thumbs and index fingers together in a six-inch circle, which I did. He then went on to say that in the hover, the aircraft was totally steady – very nice, but within the circle of his thumbs and index fingers the stick was going round so fast that it was a blur! Apparently I had been so tensed up that I was stirring that stick like you whisk crêpe suzette ingredients; this increased the turbine temperatures due to the extra air bleed from the combustion chamber, but had no effect whatsoever on the aircraft! Indeed, my forearm muscles had been so tight they ached for days afterwards.

Air Forces Northern Europe (AFNORTH) had a similar competition, known as Ex Big Click, to the AFCENT Royal Flush exercise described in Chapter 17. In August 1972 during my time on 3 Sqn, Big Click was held at RNoAF Base Stavanger-Sola. I was delegated to umpire the USAF No 38 Tac Recce Sqn flying RF4C Phantoms out of Zweibrucken, in southern Germany, but based at Sola with all the other competitors.

The 38TRS were very sophisticated rule-benders, as with most competitors, who took some catching. Inside their RF4Cs, unlike the other competitors, they had a SSB-HF radio. So they were taking off for a competition mission in Norway, and then transmitting the target co-ordinates back to their base in southern Germany on a discreet HF frequency. There, their photo interpreters were looking up the target information in their vast European-wide, target library and radioing it back to the aircraft prior to target over-flight! As a sop to try and put me off, their Sqn Cdr, Lt Col McCann, got me airborne in one of his RF4Cs flying low level round the Norwegian mastiff: a wonderful sight and also a very impressive aircraft. Like a limousine compared to the Harrier, it was large and comfortable, with little noise and no vibration.

In February 1973, the Squadron departed again to Deci in Sardinia for the annual concentrated weapons range practice. Wanting to make an impressive start whilst on my first range mission on Capa Frasca Range, arrowing down the first straffing run in the dive at 450kts . . . slight left bank on to counter the cross wind . . . sight steady on the top left of the target . . . coming into range . . . gently squeezing the trigger . . . a short half second burst, then pulling hard to 6g to clear the ground . . . a split second later the aircraft flicked uncontrollably and I found myself descending upside-down and out of control at 100feet over the target – scary in the extreme!

Now it's amazing what adrenalin will do for you in tight situations. It's a pity you can't pull a pint of the stuff before every mission! Rolling rapidly upright again, I stopped the descent into the ground, but it was an awfully close call and, I skulked, very chastened, gingerly back to base. There's no complete explanation for this sort of incident. It's usually accepted to be due to over-controlling – too much "g" pulled too quickly in a slight asymmetric condition which "g" stalls the wings dissimilarly: result – instant flick!

Famous as the major 617 Sqn Bomber Command target during WW2, the rebuilt Mohne Dam still has its uses in the aviation world. Every Harrier Sqn had its United States exchange pilot either from the USAF, the USN or the USMC. Just thirty miles south of Gütersloh, the Möhne Dam was the best landmark in the area. Even Bud Isles, one of many USAF exchange pilots who had never flown low level before, could find it! US military pilots trained procedurally and rarely were given the opportunity to fly our way: low level without air traffic control. The USAF also didn't need to because of all their support aircraft which allowed them to survive at medium level: to them low level was unnecessary. Anyway, Bud couldn't read a half-million map to save his life, and this made it impossible for him to find any targets. We caught him one day with reams of 50-thou. targeting maps (like ordnance survey maps) all stuck together in a long line, and starting at the Möhne Dam. No matter where his target was he always set off on his target run from the Möhne Dam, even if his target was a hundred miles away! He was always grateful to the Germans for rebuilding that dam after WW2! In fact today you can still see the slightly newer stonework in the dam's centre.

While on 3 Sqn, I was given the post of Wing Fighter Recce Instructor. Wing jobs were established to provide standardisation and training across the Wing's three squadrons. Initially at Wildenrath, having taken over part of the FR10 recce commitment from the previous Gütersloh wing but with only three trained recce pilots, wing standardization was seen as a necessity. The replacement of the old MFPUs (see Chapter 17), by the new concept Recce Intelligence Centres (RICs), full of photographers and photo interpreters, gave standards even more importance. However, this was the era of diminishing wing staff and wing responsibilities. The undoubted greater capability of individual aircraft over its predecessors, together with higher ranking squadron commanders – wing commanders now instead of squadron leaders – made wing authority almost redundant as the sqns became more autonomous. Writing, for example, to OC 4 Sqn demanding some standardization was like farting into wind!

That year we as a Sqn participated in the tactical demonstration for the Farnborough air show, and had a wonderful time amongst the various company chalets. It made for a pleasant relaxing few days from the hard work of the Cold War in Germany.

Our last visit to Berlin in 1973 was, unlike the previous occasion, nothing to do with cricket. Berlin is a fabulous city for almost any activity. With great shops, buildings, people and night-life, it also has a rich history, plus the front line of the east/west Cold War situation with its intelligence intrigue. On this occasion we went to Berlin because we particularly wanted to explore the Russian sector and see their Memorial to the Unknown Soldier, the Opera, the Babylonian Museum, the Reichstag, the Brandenburg Gate, and The Berlin Philharmonia on the western side.

After receiving special military travel papers, (my wife was an American citizen) we drove via the East German autobahn from Helmstedt to Berlin and back through East Germany. When we arrived at Helmstedt, our papers were easily cleared at the Russian Check Point, so we tootled along this pot-holed autobahn towards Berlin for a couple of hours (you weren't allowed to stop), until we came to the Russian check point at the West Berlin end. I left my wife in the car and went into the reception area. This was a completely bare, five-metre square, lino ed room, painted lime-green, with cheap, hard, tubular-metal chairs round three sides. On the fourth side was a door alongside which was a painted out window, also in yucky lime-green. The window had a small slot at the bottom through which to push your papers, which I duly did and sat down to wait.

Five minutes later, another man came in, and did the same thing. A further five minutes went by and his papers were returned stamped, and off he went. This happened a second time and then I started to worry. By the third time, I was now really concerned when, with no warning at all, the internal door swung open with a crash and there stood an enormous Russian Officer dressed in full parade uniform, peaked hat, Sam-Brown, medals, the works. Now I'm 6ft 3inches but he was taller and he also had the biggest looking revolver you've ever seen in his polished-leather holster! In one hand he held our papers, and the other was jabbing at them as though they were my arrest warrant! For a full five minutes I was given the biggest dressing down in Russian I'd ever had . . . the *ONLY* dressing down in Russian I've ever had! Not understanding a word, I instantly realized that I was in trouble here with a capital *T!* Then, just as I feared the worst, he flung the papers at me in dismissal, turned around, and stalked back into his inner-sanctum, slamming the door behind him.

Taking some time to calm down, I tottered back to the car where we examined the papers I'd retrieved from the floor. It soon became obvious that it was not us he was angry at, but his own side. Unnoticed by us, his opposite number back at Helmstedt had not stamped our papers properly, and he had been on the phone taking it out of his counterpart at Helmstedt while checking that we had actually come through there as shown. That was as close a call as I ever want to have with Russian bureaucracy!

Just to rub it in, a few days later we were in a British Military guardroom in West Berlin being briefed on our visit to East Berlin by the military police, and there was a poster on their wall showing Russian rank badges. On checking the insignia that my border guard had been wearing, I found that he was one rank lower then me! But as the old adage stated, "What do you call a Russian Corporal?" In those days, the answer was always, "Sir!"

Walking around East Berlin was perturbing. It was easy to drive through Check Point "Charlie", because we were entitled to pass through unmolested while on duty in uniform. But, as I had to be in full No.1 dress uniform, I felt that not only was everyone staring at me, but also that someone with a big gun was always following me. It was the only experience I've had of the hairs raised on the back of my neck, and we were only window shopping in the Unter den Linden at the time!

Much better was the chase around the Russian May Day Parade at the point where they were forming up their army columns prior to the official march past. The parade column was forming along a winding canal, which had small bridges over it. Together with our Brixmis intelligence boys in their Landrovers, we were trying to cross over these bridges for closer photography of the various military vehicles, tanks and weapons, while the Ost-Deutsch Volkspolitzei were determined we shouldn't. The resulting exhilarating chase between our three Landrovers, and as many of theirs, along and around the back streets near the canal, from blocked bridge to blocked bridge, would have put Michael Caine and his "The Italian Job" to shame! It could only have happened in the Cold War!

Notwithstanding all the Cold War hassle from the Russians and East German guards, the visit was also remarkable for the city's sights. The sound of the Berlin Philharmonic Orchestra under von Karajan's baton, playing Beethoven and Tchaikovsky, was divine in its own surroundings. The East Berlin Opera House was well worth a visit, as was the changing of the Russian guard at their Tomb for the Unknown Warrior. However, the greatest delight had to be the Babylonian Museum. A complete set of thick walls, part of the palace of King Nebuchadnezzar II from the banks of the Euphrates, which were many metres high with their hanging (terraced) gardens, had been transported from Iraq and rebuilt in East Berlin. This was a greater feat than moving London Bridge to Texas. Its magic was greater then anything seen in ancient Egypt, probably because it was so out of the context of immediate surroundings. The real surprise is in the initial confrontation with this set of three to four storey high, thick, sand-coloured walls, built in traditional fashion with their high terraced gardens, and it took me right back to the visit, some six years earlier, to the walled city of Shibam in the Hadrumaut area of the Eastern Aden Protectorate.

Our return through the Eastern Sector was uneventful; we met no Russian Corporals!

During the summer of '73 a new length of 'aircraft capable' autobahn was opened along the **west** bank of the Rhine, south of Cologne – parking spaces for fighters, lay-bys for taxying/refuelling, dispersals . . . the lot! In peacetime these reverted to ordinary autobahn and lay-bys, and there were many throughout both Eastern and Western continental Europe.

This new autobahn runway strip at Gelsdorf was used by the German Air Force for some training flying during the week before opening the road to the public. In typical German fashion, they had flown only one pair of G91s each morning and each afternoon, but they gave the Wednesday afternoon for use by the Harrier force, which in turn had become a 3 Sqn task. We put eight Harriers in there at twelve o'clock lunchtime, flew thirty-two sorties, four each, and were back in the bar at Wildenrath by 6pm! The Germans were astounded – they'd never seen such a surge of sortie capability, but this was typical of the way *we* always trained: many short sorties and fast turn-rounds with telebrief tasking without leaving the cockpit. Indeed, throughout my whole time in Germany on both Hunters and Harriers, we over-trained so much that when it came to a real no-notice TACEVAL run by NATO officers, it was a slow, boring, non-event. Without any doubt, by this time we were in an excellent state of readiness if the Russian hordes had crossed the IGB, though it had taken three long, frustrating years to achieve it.

The final highlight of this tour of duty happened in mid-October that same year. The wing deployed to off-base sites around the Bad Lippspringe army training area to the Southeast of Gütersloh. 4 Sqn went to the old Luftwaffe grass airfield of Bad Lippspringe itself, while we went to a new site at Moosdorf. On October 18th, 4 Sqn decided to fly off all ten of their aircraft in line abreast across Bad Lippspringe grass field simultaneously. Accordingly the Sqn wanted the event recorded using aerial photography, and who better to expose celluloid than the Wing Recce Instructor: yours truly!

The task initially looked simple because we knew where the target was, until we started the planning. It became evident that there was only an extremely small gap in my aircraft's capability – only about 2 minutes of flight time – when the aircraft was capable of doing the job. Simply, in order to use my port oblique camera, I had to be able to hover alongside the right-hand end of the ten aircraft, while they were lined up on the field prior to take-off. I would then conduct an accelerating transition from the hover to wing-borne flight in unison with their take-off while taking cine-film simultaneously. But the tricky bit was going to be the timing, which had to be most carefully planned because of my fuel requirements. In order to hover the aircraft I had to have on board less than 1600lbs of fuel, which would be used at 200lbs/min. Two minutes of hovering, the probable minimum time, would leave me only 1200lbs, which was below minimum to return and land at Moosdorf with enough diversion fuel for Gütersloh. Needless to say, despite 4 Sqn being late, we got the job done and, sucking out the last few pounds of fuel, I landed back at Moosdorf, but not before another close call. The tenth 4 Sqn aircraft in their take-off line – the one nearest to me – had lined up offset from the rest towards me, and during the final take-off run he actually got airborne right underneath me, and I was only at approximately 100 feet. I was unable to turn away because I was photographing the show, and also I was in the slow speed range – 30 to 90 knots – where no bank was allowed because of side-slip problems. Let's just say, he came rather close, but the resulting photo made it all worthwhile (see photo). The take-off is typical of the sort of fighter take-offs you may have seen in WW2, but certainly not since because of the advent of narrow, hard runways and jet aircraft.

Posted home in early 1974, I was delighted to be going back to the Harrier Operational Conversion Unit (OCU) at Wittering as a recce instructor to run the Fighter Recce Instructor's Course, the new course which earlier I'd helped design specifically for the Harrier Force's future recce capability. As the surviving ex-Germany recce pilot from my 2 Sqn days, and one of the few who had qualified back in 1971 as an FRI, I was probably the only one left in the Harrier force with previous recce experience. Of the three recce guys who had come across to the new Harrier force from the Gütersloh Recce Wing back in 1969, Ken Jones had been promoted as a QFI, and subsequently left the service for British Aerospace and Saudi Arabian duties, while Pad Williams had been killed in the aforementioned Harrier accident in Germany eighteen months earlier.

Now came the big crunch: even the best laid plans come to nought. Throughout this whole episode at Wildenrath my back trouble had continued and worsened. It had now become so severe that flying a mission strapped immobile into the aircraft for an hour or more would cause my sacroiliac and hip joints to seize up completely. After landing and unstrapping I couldn't move, and the groundcrew, bless their socks, used to lift me out of the cockpit, whence I would stagger around, hopefully unseen, for a few minutes to re-mobilize the joints before joining the others, but this was always a painful process.

This problem had occurred regularly over many months when, one day at the end of a mission, the Boss saw me being lifted out of a Harrier cockpit by the groundcrew. Before I knew it, I was in his Landrover on the way to sick quarters where he barged into the SMO's office and almost ordered him to sort me out! They made an instant appointment at the RAF Hospital Wegberg, where I saw yet another orthopaedic specialist, but all he did was refer me to the physiotherapy dept. Finally, after many years of pain and popping anti-inflammatories, it was the Flt Lt Physio who diagnosed me, apparently, correctly. After reporting back-trouble for many years, along with my original feet problems, and going through the slipped discs, lumbago, ordinary-strains diagnoses ad infinitum, it was this young Physio who eventually got it right! I had Ankylosing Spondylitis, an arthritic condition of the spine. The condition, in its worst state, produces a humped-back appearance. Indeed, as you may recall I had met earlier in Aden, Air Marshal Sir Freddie Sowrey, who, as an Air Commodore, had been in charge of the later RAF days in Aden in Nov '67. He had a similar condition, but had still managed to continue flying, which was good for my own morale.

Nonetheless, I was grounded because of my medical condition. My world collapsed, and I left Germany for good on posting for a six-week, medical rehabilitation course at the RAF Rehabilitation Centre at Headley Court alongside Epsom Downs. Once again my life was in a real mess with my flying career hanging in the balance due to this bloody arthritis in my back. I'm also convinced to this day that this was the final nail in the coffin of my marriage. She didn't like being on her own, or being around a cripple.

Within a few months of my return to the UK, 20 Sqn's trying times ended when it disbanded and was subsumed into the other two Germany Harrier Sqns, which then moved in Toto from Wildenrath to Gütersloh. For me, both personally and professionally, Wildenrath can be summed up very simply: it was both exhilarating and frustrating in equal measures.

Chapter Twenty

Survival and the Grounding

WINTER SURVIVAL 1

Military aircrews, by virtue of the long reach of modern aircraft, over possibly hostile territory, had to be conversant not only with ejection procedures but also with survival techniques for sea, desert, jungle and winter conditions. Additonally aircrew would need to widen their experience of combat survival and learn the best escape and evasion techniques for use if downed in hostile territory.

Having already survived the desert, this was where I was taught to ski, simply because I was sent on a winter survival course. The best winter survival course was the one run by the Norwegian air force, in which item number one on the joining instructions stated, "Bring a dinner jacket"! No such luck for the RAF course! For the second two weeks of January 1969, I was sent on the RAF's course in Bavaria with forty other aircrew. For three months from January to March each year, the RAF took over a lovely old Gasthaus. Das Gasthaus zur Post, in the village of Bad Kohlgrub, five kilometres North of Oberammergau with its famous Passion Play close to the Austrian border, and nestling in the foothills of the Bavarian Alps, had been used for years.

In order to ensure your fitness for the survival exercise, (of course, aircrew are always notoriously fit as a matter of course!) the course commenced with ten days skiing instruction using local Bavarian ski instructors. Sounds great, but there was always a catch: this wasn't normal ski instruction – no ski lifts were allowed! Three-quarters of your time was spent tramping up the slopes on your skis in order to ski down again, and after ten days of skiing *UP* Alps, one could say that you were reasonably fit! This was followed by a five day winter survival exercise, which was designed to simulate a pilot baling out over enemy territory during wartime, who then tries to evade enemy troops and escape to friendly territory. Hence, you were flung out in the snow in only your flying gear and parachute.

Just to make it a bit interesting, not only were the crack German Army Mountain Ski Troops acting as enemy but, if you were caught, our very own "Ashford Boys" were acting the enemy interrogator role. It was reasonably fair in that one only had a small chance of making the run, no skis this time, of 25kms through deep snow in one night without being caught! This was unlike the Combat Survival and Rescue Instructor's Course (CSRI) run on Dartmoor with 42 Commando against you, and a set of known sadists running the Combat Survival Centre at Mountbatten, Plymouth. The CSRI course continued from rendezvous to rendezvous (RV) regardless, until everyone was finally caught. They then spent anything up to 24hrs in the interrogation centre. This latter course I completed later, but in the meantime I managed the Bad Kholgrub course twice! After all, they fitted you up in all-black, ski gear, and gave you twenty days of free equipment and skiing for only ten days survival purgatory!

Before this course I had never skied. So Horst, the very-patient Bavarian chief ski instructor, taught me from scratch well enough to win the 3rd prize "Bronze Ski" award on the final day after the giant-slalom ski competition, which was always held on the main slope at Oberammergau. There you will see a bunch of absolute fools, dressed all in black, hurtling down the main slalom course totally out of control. Known locally as the Black Bombers, their sole objective is simple: the one that stays on his feet longest wins!

Having won the Bronze Skis, I then had to learn to survive. For three days we survived off the snow-laden land in flying kit with only our parachutes. Wrapped in one's parachute as a makeshift sleeping bag, in one homemade parachute tepee, with a very smoky fire inside, afforded two feet of smoke-free air at ground level but sufficed for the four of us. One live chicken was allowed between us, and unlike today's environment, there was no squeamishness – its neck was instantly wrung and into the pot it went! Chicken bones boiled for the umpteenth time on day five, after being carried in one's pockets between meals, tasted exquisite!

Then came the *pièce-de-résistance*: the escape and evasion phase against the German ski troops and our Ashford boys. We set off in pairs at 7pm in the dark aiming for a 'friendly' RV, 25kms away through deep-snow, hilly, coniferous forest. Six hours later and halfway there we stumbled into a German Ski Troop trap. They'd deployed in force and used an anti-personnel radar system, which could pick out anything that moved against the snow miles away. We didn't think this was playing the game – not British, old boy – but they didn't understand that, so we lost!

We didn't have a chance and soon finished up at the interrogation centre, where we spent roughly twelve hours overnight being cross-examined, in between bouts of being hooded and spread-eagled against a wall, while subjected to white noise for sensory deprivation. Any movement immediately produced a sergeant-major voice bellowing close to your ear, and you got the message loud and clear!

Every half hour or so you'd be given the third degree in an interrogation room. "Name, rank and number?", then "I cannot answer that question" for what seemed like an eternity. So much so, that when they said the exercise was over and we could get dressed, you didn't believe them, thinking this was yet another catch!

The diploma we were each given at the end of the course, stated, ". . . *who successfully survived No 2 Course which was the Coldest, Most Arduous, and by Far the Most Excruciatingly Agonising Course in the History of the School*". But then, weren't they all!

Overall the course was most enjoyable if you didn't weaken over the twelve hours of interrogation. The rest of the course taught you a lot about how to survive and evade in the wild, and one hell of a lot about yourself, while giving

190

some valuable lessons in the art of avoiding answering interrogator's questions. No politicians need be sent on it! Nevertheless, after watching various survival programmes recently, particularly one showing the RAF's present survival course, I cannot believe how soft is today's youth. The lack of realism in the interrogation phase is nothing short of criminally astonishing. In a real survival situation, their *'I'd rather go hungry than kill a poor little fluffy bunny'* attitude will get themselves killed instead!

RAF REHABILITATION CENTRE – HEADLEY COURT

RAF Headley Court is a unique centre, unequalled for anyone needing both physical and/or mental help to return to full fitness. It is a 25-room, old, Tudor, country house in large grounds with added, modern, fitness facilities built around the gardens. Perched on the Epsom Downs near Leatherhead, it was bequeathed to the RAF by Lord Booth during WW2 as a place to re-habilitate wartime aircrew after injury in the air war. Nowadays, it has amalgamated not just with the other two services, but also the other ranks' centre originally at Chessington. The facility acts as a sort of halfway house between hospital and a full, normal life, fulfilling these aims using a combination of medical/physiotherapy skills and military physical fitness training.

A standard day at the Court for the 'inmates' would consist of:

AM	15mins	Warm up exercises to music
	30mins	Specialist exercises for your particular problem
	30mins	Exercises in the hydrotherapy pool (water at blood temperature!)
	Coffee Break	
	30mins	Croquet on the front lawn
	30mins	Occupational therapy
	30mins	Run to the pub for lunch
PM	15mins	Warm-up exercises
	30mins	Badminton/Volleyball in the gym
	30mins	Walk round the grounds
	Tea break	
	30mins	On the Squash Court
	30mins	Physiotherapy
	30mins	Team games in the gym
	Assessment appointment with the Rheumatoid and Rehabilitation Specialist	

Exercises like that, all day every day for six weeks, together with a properly balanced diet, would most certainly cure most problems, especially as all patients, even those with broken limbs, willingly partook of all exercises at all times within the bounds of their abilities. With everyone there for similar reasons, healthy competition between patients and teams was rife. Punishments for small misdemeanours during warm-ups and exercises usually meant more press-ups, and the atmosphere engendered by the staff produced a wonderful lightening of the spirit. Any depression from injuries was soon dissipated. I was so privileged to have such a bunch of experts (probably in those days they were the world's foremost authority for rehabilitation) available to me, and I used them on three occasions to keep my flying category valid. I had a thirty-three year, flying career blighted by this bloody Ankylosing Spondylitis, frequently in pain and relentlessly popping anti-inflammatories. Without Headley Court, I would have had no flying career at all.

Indeed, Headley Court saved my life more than once over the next few years, but particularly so during my first visit in 1974 and my last visit in 1993. Although I arrived there in a bent, abject state. I left ramrod straight, fitter than I'd ever been with no pain or stiffness in my back. I was raring to start flying again and feeling I could take on the world. Life had *not* ended with the loss of one's flying category, and a new life was soon to begin. Unfortunately, reality soon hit: there was little opportunity. I remained downgraded medically to A3G4Z5, which still meant no ejection seats! I WAS GROUNDED, and had to face up to a complete life style and career change. The prospect of continuing my career in aviation looked pretty bleak, but there proved to be more than one way of skinning a cat!

233 OPERATIONAL CONVERSION UNIT – FLIGHT SIMULATOR, UNIT TEST PILOT et al.

My Boss back at RAF Wittering – we were not the best of buddies since West Raynham days – would not countenance a posting to a non-ejection seat aircraft, but instead chucked me into the Harrier flight simulator (HFS) as an instructor. Horror of horrors, the OCU had never had any Harrier experienced instructors on the simulator staff, so they saw me as a prize worth keeping for this role.

Thus did I become immersed in the simulator with all its many idio-syncrasies – it never flew anything like the real thing – while I tried to find some way of partaking in flying, but things are never quite as bad as I had originally dreaded. The HFS was the very first 'full mission' simulator to enter service. Fully computerised, for those days, it had a unique visual system. Two enormous hangars, some 150 feet by 90 feet, were built solely to house two large papier-mâché scale models of the ground.[1] The smallest scale, main model was of a large area of central Poland, whilst the larger scale one was of RAF Kemble airfield and this was electronically superimposed on a Polish airfield position in the main model. The models each had an enormous moving gantry above and across them, each holding a TV camera pointing vertically downwards at the model, while the whole roof-space was filled with banks of massive floodlights.

The idea behind this enormous construction was that the view from the simulator cockpit should be so real that one could fly full missions looking out, just like the real thing, and even simulate full weapons attacks. Unfortunately, the reality was that this was never to be so. HFS was not really up to the job, being at the cutting edge of technology available at that time when most computers were still using analogue techniques: the Harrier itself certainly was, so why should we expect the Harrier simulator to do better . . . ?

192

Yet we tried, and, despite a limited view-field, with experience it was even possible to vertically land it on one of the models, but we were not using proper Harrier landing techniques to achieve this dubious skill! HFS became a rather expensive toy, and whilst useful for cockpit and emergency procedures training, was little more than great fun but heck all use in its marketed role!

Nevertheless, soon after commencing on this contraption, I was seconded to the Ministry of Defence Operational Requirements Branch, and sent to the manufacturer, Link-Miles, at Lancing, Sussex, to conduct some future-simulator trials. The original installation at Wittering had been an early version without any Inertial Navigation or Attack Systems. It also had the software for an older aircraft engine than the Harrier Mk GR3 in operational service. My new role was to prove these modifications at the factory, and then to take them on-site both at Wittering and Wildenrath, install, trial and test them, and approve them for RAF usage.

I believe I now hold some sort of rare but pretty secure record: 375 flying hours in the Harrier flight simulator![2] So much of testing consists of long, boring, waiting periods between short bouts of 'flying' while the engineers tweak one thing or another. They then say, "Try that", and two minutes later you're waiting again while they try another tweak! To relieve the boredom something always comes round the next corner. At the Link-Miles factory, the test simulator had a set of old models, in ten foot squares, casually pushed together. Each square comprised some 240 x 240 miles of actual ground cover, and the squares were not always properly abutted against each other. This left, at the magnitude in the cockpit, a dead straight 'canyon', some 240 miles long, into which, with some experience, you could 'fly' the TV eye without catching the edge of the model. The limitations of the TV eye view made the model edges look just like dark canyon sides. You could 'fly' this machine at full throttle below 'ground' level down the narrowest of 'valleys', lower and faster than anything in the real world! It was a huge laugh until, during one coffee break, one of the engineers put a dead spider in the canyon gap! Blown up some 200% by the TV and the computer and filling the cockpit view-screen, it looked like a positively malevolent, horror-movie style, alien being, and produced an instant, head-on crash – I was doing 640 knots at the time!

Finally, after many weeks of testing and despite the 'crashes', the new concept was 'proven'. HFS was never going to come close to the real thing, but we'd tested it as far as their expertise, equipment, and our purse would allow. We then took the modifications to Wildenrath and Wittering, where they were reinstalled, proved, and tested for training use. By this stage I could fly that machine better than anyone, for what that was worth! One could even fly fully automatic attacks in it – something that couldn't be done in the real aircraft, but this bore little relation to flying the Harrier and was only useful as a procedures trainer. Digital technology was still in its infancy at the time, and a realistic full-mission simulator, while broadly the correct path to follow, was still a few years from fruition. But, like the real Harrier, we were blazing a trail with a new concept while waiting for technology to catch up.

But there was no future in this job: no flying and no regular adrenalin flow meant I had to search for some other activities, not just to fill my time but also for a new career. Firstly, I joined the Air Experience Flight at Cambridge Airport, flying cadets around in Chipmunks. That palled after a while, so I joined the local Sibson Parachute Club as one of their relief pilots – an extremely interesting period of civil flying in which I obtained my twin engine rating and flew many different types of aircraft. Of especial significance were the Britten-Norman Islander and the Pilatus Turbo Porter.

Now, it has to go on record that I have never, ever parachuted, nor have had any wish to. In my trade, one doesn't bale out of a serviceable aircraft! Moreover, if necessary, then the only decent way out is via a Martin-Baker ejection seat! Hence, it was interesting watching the parachutists attempting to willingly commit suicide by throwing themselves out of my aircraft! I had the most sublime moments from the beginners. You'd climb these first-timers up to 2,500 feet with a parachute instructor (PaI) aboard, and put the aircraft into wind over the drop zone, flying very slowly at some ten knots above the stall. You'd watch the first frightened face shuffle towards the door and get ready, when, as the PaI shouted "cut", you'd throttle right back and watch as the white-faced, terrified student, holding on to the door frame for dear life, was given the 'go' . . . and given another 'go' . . . and given yet another 'go', at which point we were nearly stalled, and I would imperceptibly lower the nose to hold the speed. With each 'go' you could watch the student's grip tighten on the aeroplane, until after the third one, the PaI literally booted the student out from behind. This procedure was then repeated for each student before returning to land.

Thirty minutes later, you'd watch as you recognized these same, terrified students clambering back on board with inane grins, ready to try the death dive all over again . . . and in the name of sport . . . and they were paying for it!

The club soon sold its little Cessna tail-draggers, and bought a BandN Islander which gave me my civilian twin-engine rating. Red Devils, the army's parachute display team, also used an Islander, and occasionally, when their aircraft was in servicing, they'd use ours. But then came a Swiss Pilatus Turbo Porter (TP), by far the nearest civilian equivalent to the Harrier. The TP was the aircraft used by the Swiss mountain rescue teams, and was a really fascinating aircraft to fly. It had an unbelievably low stalling-speed, could out-climb anything else, take off and land in its own length, and dive vertically using reverse prop without increasing speed. As a civilian aircraft it was so versatile that it was, for once, a real thrill and a challenge; it also gave me my first taste of turboprop engine systems. Once the parachutists had dived over-board, you could, for once, land the aircraft before them – diving at 30 degrees and only 45 knots directly at the end of the runway. On round out into any wind the TP would alight in its own length, almost like a bird, with no landing run.

WINTER SURVIVAL II

During this same period, I volunteered for a second winter survival course! Oh, what a fool I was! Flying out to Munich on BEA for the last two weeks of Feb '74, I caught the train to Bad Kohlgrub, and went through the same ski training and survival phase again. As ever, no one complains about ten days' free ski training even though we had to walk UP the hills first, but valuable survival training was only ever partially realistic. Gratuitous advice was often the name of the game: "If you're going to parachute into forestry, keep your legs closed!" Skills learnt were often useless in a real situation, as shown later on this course, usually because one never had the right implements available. The most useful tool on any of these courses was a machete; it could be used for almost any survival task. Indeed, being issued with one on a survival course under the guise that you would need one to survive was all very well, but you'd never find one included in your real survival pack in your real operational aeroplane! There just wasn't room in the small fighter ejection seat packs.

The final escape and evasion exercise was conducted in a similar fashion to my first course two years earlier, only this time we were caught by the German Alpine Troops much, much earlier. So early in fact that within half an hour of the start we were the first to be caught. I lay the blame on Frank Hoare for this! Frank, at the time, was a Sqn Ldr and had been an acquaintance of mine from Gütersloh days and also my Flt Cdr for a short time during 3 Sqn Harrier days!

Frank and I paired up, and his cunning plan was deceptively simple: we knew we had half an hour from the start until the German Ski Troops were deployed. The front line of their deployment was some four kilometres from our starting point along a road that ran at right angles to and perpendicularly across our track. Frank's premise was that if we ran for the first half an hour in the dark of the early evening, we would cross the road unseen and be alright before the troops were deployed!

Great plan . . . . . .more like a typical military débacle!

Yes, you guessed it! We ran slap bang into the first troops at almost exactly the thirty minute point! In fact I wasn't sure who was most amazed, them or us! Of course we remonstrated that they'd deployed early, but that got us nowhere! Neither did smiling at them and offering English cigarettes – all those war films were wrong! They obviously weren't ready for us either, so we had to wait some time for their transport to take us on to the interrogation centre. Imagine, it was barely even moonlit, and we were standing under a large pine in deep snow on the verge of a minor road lined with a single line of pine trees – two German guards with rifles, and two of us. The ten feet wide, snow verge was cut off from the adjacent field by a low, three-stranded, barbed-wire fence, and there was nothing but an unbroken, white blanket of deep snow to be seen wherever one looked.

As time went by, to our amusement, more were caught and herded into our group until, by the time their coach arrived, there was at least a dozen of us, but still only two guards! Hence, I had positioned myself near to the fence and, as the coach arrived and everyone's attention was diverted that way, I threw myself head first over it, landing in a four foot snow-drift in the field. Totally covered by snow, I stayed as immobile as my panting would allow, dreading that they'd see my steaming breath wafting upwards, for what seemed like hours while waiting for the coach to move off, which it eventually did. The Colditz chaps would have been proud of me!

Unbelievably, in the ensuing mêlée while boarding the coach, the guards didn't count their prisoners. No one missed me! I'd love to have seen Frank's face as it dawned on him that I was absent! The coach, of course, sped off to the interrogation centre while yours truely thrashed around in the dark trying to get out of this snowdrift. Unfortunately, in the scuffle I had lost my survival pack and, more importantly, my map. On the other hand, the strict, exercise rules stated that, if you escaped and stayed free for more than thirty minutes, you could then give yourself up and would not have to go through the interrogation.

Bain knew better! 'Twas ever thus and normally spelled trouble. Why change the habits of a lifetime? I was sure I knew the map in my head anyway, so on I ploughed across this half mile field of thick snow to the opposite side where I passed an old, wooden barn, beyond which was a horseshoe-shaped, steep incline full of closely grown, ten-feet tall, snow-covered, Christmas Trees. I started up this hillside through the trees, still sinking deep into snow. Every pace seemed to rise only one foot upwards and then slide and stumble two feet downwards, while every tree brushed against shed its load of snow straight down my neck. By the time I'd made the halfway point, floundering around surrounded by these densely-packed, fir trees making the hill impassable, I was wet, exhausted and, by now, totally unsure of which way I was supposed to be going. There was no way forward in these conditions. I'd been struggling for nearly two hours since my escape and had only made just over half a mile. Right then it started snowing again heavily. I had no energy left at that point to do anything, never mind re-cross the half-mile stretch of field back to the road. Without my survival pack, this was fast becoming a *real*, winter-survival situation.

Common sense finally kicked in: downwards was the only option. I turned back for the barn to find some shelter, and eventually, by retracing my tracks, found my way back to the barn. Holed up there trying to get my breath and energy back in the comparative warmth, I set to wondering what to do next. With my sweat drying on my soaked clothing, I was now starting to get really cold. There was no chance of lighting a fire with little energy left for movement to keep me warm. I had just decided that the only way was back across this field of snow to give myself up to the German troops, when I heard voices and the sounds of people crunching through the snow. Sound, as the German troops well knew, carries a long way over snow, so, hurrying to the barn door, and knowing by exercise rules that I was now quite OK, I started shouting for help.

There was instant and utter silence outside but I was sure the voices had been English. This meant they were probably other members of the course passing through, having taken more slowly and sensibly than Frank and I had. But the evaders, thinking this was a German trap, threw themselves into the deep snow and remained still and silent.

Impasse!

It took much persuasion, including my leaving the barn to be seen, and swearing loudly in English, to convince them that I was English and no threat. Dim figures slowly and unsurely showed themselves. How relieved we all were when we finally got together! These guys who had themselves been thrashing around in the snow all these hours, had been taking it slowly and hadn't been caught, but had also decided that conditions now were too severe for further progress. They had intended to hole up in the barn until daybreak.

Accordingly, we repaired to the barn for discussion where, after much argument, we finally decided to turn back towards the road and the German troops. Suffice it to say, after getting our breath back, we stumbled across this uphill, snow-covered field, which eventually resulted in capture again. Later at the interrogation centre, having been the first to escape, I became the first and fortunate one to successfully finish the exercise, while the others went off for their interrogation! From real survival to instant success in one rather difficult move! Yet, if any exercise had been designed to teach survival lessons, this one produced the real thing, though no one else knew how close I had come to a desperate situation! Lesson one had always been the earlier you try, the better chance any prisoner has of escaping. Lesson two: never ever underestimate winter conditions – protection is everything! There was certainly a major learning curve that night, but the training finally kicked in ... and after a successful escape I avoided the interrogation!

Back at the 'ranch', having been the first to be caught, Frank had gone through the night's interrogation and had been given the real third degree! Now one of the other inviolate rules of this serious "game" was that you knew the genuine end of the exercise, rather than an interrogator's bluff to get you to talk, was when the CO of the survival school told you so – he was the final arbiter of good taste and judgement, supposedly entirely neutral!

So picture Frank in a single-storey, long, low building, with a central entrance on one side, while inside there was a long corridor with rooms on either side. Frank came out of what was to be his last interrogation, and was shown into a room next to the main entrance where his clothes lay. He was told that the exercise was all over and, once he'd dressed, there'd be a hot bowl of soup waiting for him down the corridor. Not seeing the CO, he thought this was a clever bluff! Seeing an escape opportunity, he dressed as fast as he could. Then, on opening the curtains, he found a microphone on the window shelf, which confirmed the bluff. He then ripped the microphone out of its leads, opened the window and climbed onto the sill ready to jump out. Outside he noticed there was a tall, wire fence round the building, and a pathway leading from the front door, through the fence and out to the road on the other side of which was a wood line. As he knelt on the sill, two guards walked past, looked at him queerly, greeted him with a "Gute Nacht" and walked on! Astounded, he waited for them to disappear, then jumped down, ran across the road through the opening in the fence and holed up in the woods for the necessary thirty minutes.

Thirty minutes or so later, cold but happy, he retraced his steps out of the woods and, looking all pleased with himself because of his escape, strolled across the road back into the interrogation centre. On seeing him, the CO said, "Where the hell have you been? The exercise's been over for half an hour!" Frank was furious! He was absolutely livid! I'm told they had to physically restrain him from hitting the CO!

Frank Hoare had also been the staff officer who wrote to me with an air force board letter of thanks for my service when I finally left the RAF. Retiring with Group Captain rank, he sadly died a few years ago and was sorely missed.

On the way back to Wittering from the survival course, via Munich and Frankfurt, by a curious coincidence I made a name for myself. The BA flight out of Munich to London had been cancelled due to fog and ice: hardly surprising after the conditions we had recently experienced! The only way home was by using Lufthansa with a change of aircraft at Frankfurt where the transit timings were extremely short. Six of us were making the trip back together and we had to run through the terminal at Frankfurt to make the second flight onward to Heathrow. Running out of the terminal to the aircraft, whose engines were already started, we saw the most gorgeous blond air-stewardess standing at the top of the steps, urging us to hurry.

As I climbed the steps I realised she was shouting my Christian name, and then I recognised Kiki, the Officers Mess receptionist at RAF Wildenrath, after whom every single bachelor in the Mess lusted! She was a gorgeous lady, a tall, slim, leggy blond with film star looks. In the short time I'd been away from Wildenrath, Kiki had also left and qualified as a Lufthansa stewardess . . . and now there she was, waiting especially for me! She gave me the biggest public hug and kiss imaginable, and was dying to catch up on the Wildenrath gossip. Of course, she hadn't heard of my problems, so we had a lot to chat about in a very short time. Well, the six of us had VIP treatment all the way home, being plied with free drinks by Kiki on the basis of our friendship: the boys couldn't believe their luck! Neither could they believe that such a beautiful girl could possibly know me! I could do no wrong for that short period, and she finally decanted six rather drunken survivors off at Heathrow! What a pity this was such a short flight, and I never saw her again.

If you are now thinking these winter survival courses were hard work, my next one was far worse. To qualify as a Combat Survival Instructor, one had to commit professional suicide and endure the Combat Survival Officers Course at RAF Mountbatten, situated upon the eastern promontory of Plymouth Hoe. This lovely white, neo-Georgian house, overlooking the Sound, used to be 18 Group Maritime HQ, and was now used as the Officers Mess for the Survival School. Underneath, buried in the cliffs, was an old prison dungeon hewn out of the rocks. This was the centre used to interrogate those un-successful in their attempts to evade 'capture' on that forbidding of all moors: Dartmoor.

Unlike the Bavarian course, this one was designed to catch everyone. Hence, everyone was forced to endure the interrogation system. Having watched on TV recently a programme showing what air force survival course students go through today, it confirms my suspicions that today's society is soft. Political correctness and the Health and Safety Act have ensured that today's aircrews will have less hope of surviving compared with their predecessors. The degree of harshness employed in the 1960s and '70s obviously isn't allowed today. Killing chickens and rabbits for instance – commandos putting the boot in when they captured you – being thrown into thorn bushes with hands tied behind your back to rough you up ready for interrogation – twelve hours of standing still, spread up against the dungeon wall while blind-folded and subjected to white noise – stripped naked and intimately inspected – none of that today! This typically modern soft approach acts to the detriment of our crews in wartime.

Many self-respecting aircrew had an Air Force dog, probably the most famous of which was Nigger of 617Sqn fame. But Nigger was a bomber dog

– my Scruffy was a fighter, not afraid to get stuck in, and get stuck in he did
. . . to the AOC's sandwiches! During this period I was in the habit of taking
Scruffy with me to work where he would lie down to be patted, stroked and
fed by all and sundry in the office or a corner of the crew room. Meanwhile
our AOC, AVM Donaldson, used to join us once a month for a day to keep
his hand in at flying the Harrier. Between sorties, in order to fly twice, he
would have a quick sandwich lunch provided on a silver platter by the
Officers Mess in the crewroom. Unfortunately, on this occasion Scruff got to
the sandwiches first! When the AOC walked in, all that was left was some
chewed cucumber with a few splinters of cold chicken bone! The culprit was
obvious –Scruff wouldn't come near the crew room afterwards, but the AOC
thought it a huge joke and ate some of our ordinary fare instead! However,
the station commander was really upset and banned Scruffy from the station:
a little OTT, I thought!

The sequel was equally amusing. The following month, while the AOC was
flying his morning mission, the OCU instructors replaced the silver sandwich
salver with a plate of dog biscuits! Again the AOC had a huge laugh, but the
station commander never forgave us and Scruffy never went to work with me
again!

REHABILITATION COMPLETE

Throughout this period, before and during the grounding, with fighter flying
now denied me, I had been studying hard for my Commercial Pilot's Licence,
still wishing to join the airlines. Unfortunately, because of my medical circumstances, no airline was about to offer me a job, except Safari Air Services of
Nairobi who, inter alia, offered me an extra shilling per flying mile every time
I carried a body! I never found out whether they were referring to animal or
human! Therefore, as the Air Force had said they'd continue to employ me, I
was left with no other immediate option. Having been told by numerous
medical specialists during this time that I'd never fly ejection seat aircraft
again, I had also started to apply for any flying job on aircraft without ejection seats! I'd always fancied the big stuff so I applied for, and made a fuss
about, a tour flying VC10s – at the time the RAF's only "modern" long-range,
four-engined, jet-transport aircraft. This never came to fruition and I certainly
never got anywhere near 10 Sqn but, for many years afterwards, when I
occasionally met old acquaintances, they often asked whether I'd enjoyed my
VC10 tour! My rumours certainly did the rounds but no one acted on them!
For all that, eighteen months later, I eventually did regain my medical flying
category by a big fiddle and judicious use of aspirins!

One day in the office I read the usual routine orders notice asking for
volunteers to fly the Twin Otter for the British Antarctic Survey (BAS).
Sniffing the spirit of adventure, I really fancied the idea of Antarctic flying.
It was worth a try, especially as I had also flown similar aircraft such as the
Islander, the Dakota, and the Pilatus Turbo Porter. As a result, I put in an
application for secondment to the BAS, had an interview, was offered the job
and started collecting the necessary cold-weather kit. Some weeks later I
received a phone call from one of their administrators. He had been looking

through my personal file, checking everything was OK for the trip South, and had noticed my RAF medical category: A3-G2-Z5. He, as we all did, understood the A for Air and the G for ground, but wanted to know what the Z5 meant. Now, as aircrew, all one ever worries about is the A category, but the Z cat, which we tended to ignore, is a geographic 'fitness-for-role' category. I was off to the Antarctic and Z5 actually meant "no cold climates"!

This was a typical doctor's indication that I had some form of arthritis. Stalemate, but there *had* to be a solution! My first port of call was our local SMO, a doctor whom I'd known for some time and subsequently became the Senior Flight Surgeon for Cathay Pacific. He made an instant appointment for me to see the rheumatoid specialist at our Central Medical Establishment near the Middlesex Hospital in North London. I knew exactly who would be waiting for me when I walked into the consulting rooms: Gp Capt Wynn-Parry, the man whose original downgrading had scotched my flying career. I also knew he had a liking for those of us with AS who could still flex their spines enough to bend down and touch their toes. In an attempt to pre-empt his diagnosis, I took three aspirins before seeing him. Sure enough, after greetings – I'd seen him professionally a few times in the last couple of years – his first words were, "Bend down and touch your toes." For the first time in many years I duly did as I was bidden, not just surprising myself, but astounding him!

Once he'd recovered, he asked me to sit down in front of his desk, and I watched him pull out a pad of medical forms and write on the top sheet (which I still have), "This officer is incredibly fit: A1-G1-Z1"!

My medical category amazingly restored, two days later I became the Unit Test Pilot flying Harriers again!

For my work on the Harrier Flight Simulator at the Link-Miles Factory in Lancing while grounded and unsure of my future, I was awarded a CinC's Commendation. This is one below a Queen's Commendation, but, in typical air force fashion, he was unavailable to present it himself. The AOC did the honours – really goes to show what it's worth! I had spent twenty-one months grounded from the Harrier, gained two survival course qualifications, lost a wife, flew fifty-three hours cadet flying on Chipmunks, eighty-two hours in various civvy aircraft, mainly parachute flying, and twelve Harrier flights in the two-seater! Needless to say, I never went to the Antarctic!

Besides the test flying I still had to maintain my simulator instructor's role. Also I was able to use my recce instructor's category to help the OCU staff on some of their advanced training courses. Furthermore, I managed my first Belize, Central America, detachment with No 1(F) Sqn when they were sent there for the very first time in Nov '75[3]. Apparently, I had just become a spare body on base, available for anything and everything from boards of inquiry to Central American Operations Officer. This was yet another frustrating episode – neither one thing nor another, but at least I was back in the fold, fully qualified to fly fighters once more . . . and with a resolve *never* to see a service doctor professionally ever again!

A year later I was posted back to another operational fighter unit: No. 1(F) Squadron.

Notes
1. Today the models would be produced digitally in a computer no larger than your own PC.
2. Compared with approx. forty hours total during the rest of my 33 year career!
3. Belize is the subject of Chapters 27 and 28.

Chapter Twenty-One

The First Squadron

No. 1 (Fighter) Squadron (Motto: In Omnibus Princeps – "First in all things" or "Never do it on a bus!") can trace its ancestry back to No. 1 Balloon Squadron, Royal Engineers at the Woolwich Arsenal in 1878. The Sqn was the first in the RFC and the RAF. Hence, during my tour on No 1(F), no further excuse was deemed necessary for the first aviation unit world-wide to celebrate its centenary in 1978. Their colours were red and white, and we wore them both as cummerbunds in formal kit, and as the ribbon round boater hats in informal kit!

When I joined them in '76, I believe that I became the first pilot to have served operationally on the first four RAF front line squadrons, having previously been operational on 2(AC), 3(F) and 4(AC) Sqns: perhaps some sort of a record.

1(F) Sqn's main role in life differed from the other Harrier units, being part of the air element of the ACE[1] Mobile Force. This required the Sqn to be on permanent, seventy-two hours stand-by to move anywhere in the NATO region in times of trouble. Our main operational areas were notionally on the Cold War flanks of NATO – no sneaky attacks from the sides! In the North, we operated in northern Norway, whilst in the South, it could have been Greece, Turkey, or more probably the Italian/Yugoslavian border.

Our daily lives on this Sqn were probably more varied than on any other. The diverse nature of our war role gave us carte blanche to deploy almost anywhere within reason. Our deployment area was geographically so variable that our peacetime training encompassed a wider variety of environments than most Sqns. During my time we operated from the North Cape of Norway in deep winter, in minus thirties temperatures, to Belize with 120 degrees in the shade. Such scope made one extremely versatile and flexible in one's outlook on fighter flying.

In the '70s the only major aspect of Harrier flying not undertaken by other Harrier units, and therefore new to those arriving on 1(F) Sqn, was the air-to-air refuelling (AAR) role required for the ACE deployments, yet another skill to be learned and maintained. Initially this made a frightening prospect because one spends one's aeronautical life avoiding all other flying machines like the plague. Now we were deliberately learning how to poke our noses into one, and a bigger one at that! Today of course, AAR is conducted by dedicated tankers such as the VC10 and Tristar but, back in the '70s and '80s we were still using the lumbering, 1950s converted bomber, the Victor, which didn't carry enough fuel for some of our longer range deployments, so we needed a lot of them. For example, when we deployed in 1975 for the first time across the Atlantic (known in the trade as The Pond), six little Harriers required twelve Victor Tankers to do the job.

There is an art to tanking using the British method; it's maxim is 'don't get stressed up'! The tanker waves at you a large shuttle-cock style of basket on the end of a long rubber pipe that reels out of a pod underneath the outer part of each wing. It also has another larger basket that deploys out of the rear of the fuselage for refuelling larger aircraft. Using the wing stations, two fighters can be refuelled simultaneously. However, being on the end of the wing, any slight aircraft movement is intensified down the length of the pipe so that this shuttle cock is waving about handsomely in the breeze. Your job is to chase this basket around and stick your probe inside it – an art that should be highly familiar to any macho fighter pilot! But even for the best, this can take a protracted courtship at 0.8 Mach!

Hence, once cleared behind the tanker, you line up with this wandering, oversized, Badminton accessory. Just as you think you're in the right place, and shove the throttle forward to jam your pipe inside, it waves the other way and you go flying over the top of it. There's only one thing worse, and that's pushing the probe in at an angle so it sticks out through the sides. It can jam solid and, in the worst case, pull the whole pipe off the tanker. Believe me this has happened and doesn't do anyone's reputation any good at all if seen landing back at base trailing behind a length of in-flight re-fuelling hose!

In Aug '76 within a month of arriving on the Sqn, my first AAR mission took place on a real deployment: no time for a practice! We flew a three-ship southern ranger to the Italian Air Force base at Rivolto, near Udine, north-east of Venice close to the Yugoslav border. Dave Lott and I went in a two seater T4, with Paddy Roberts and Bill Green flying single seaters in formation with us. It was always necessary to reconnoitre a possible future, whole squadron, deployment base before times of trouble. In particular, we had to plan our logistics move to any future deployment base, as so much relied on available host base facilities. At some places, it was "bring your own tent", but at others, there was full domestic and engineering support. On the Monday morning when we came to leave, we found that our two-seater had leaked all its liquid oxygen (LOX), and there was no replenishment capability at Rivolto. The only place locally that had any LOX was the US base at Taranto, some twenty minutes flight time away, but this base was not keen to accept us. Here we go again – it's always the same when away from home base – lack of NATO standardization producing problems. We had to fly home over the Alps, and at those heights pure oxygen is a basic necessity. The solution was in fact quite simple – do it without oxygen at the lowest possible level and, once clear of the Alps, divert into Dijon French Air Force base where LOX was available. This meant flying across the Alps at the lowest available flight level to give us a cabin altitude of roughly 10–12,000 feet. While being on the wrong side of our limits (maximum cabin altitude 10,000 feet in daylight without oxygen), it was, with a seaman's eye, barely acceptable. Having no alternative, we launched to Dijon, but typically, there was no flight level free below 24,000 feet, giving us a 14,000 feet cabin altitude.

Nonetheless, flying VFR with an 'unserviceable' IFF, allowed us just enough oxygenated air to remain in control.

Now one of the early signs of anoxia[2] is merriment and not having a care in the world. On the way to Dijon, Dave and I, in an hour's duet, must have sung every hymn in the book, and many a dirty version besides, until in the descent into Dijon on the other side of the Alps, we found ourselves in perfect working order. Naughty – yes, but the job was done and we returned home without further event! Tell the climbing fraternity that the Alps can be conquered without oxygen!

A further two-week, Squadron exchange visit to the French Mirage III Wing at Dijon passed off without further controversy until the final day. Come the time to depart, our two-seater was missing. While scratching our heads and wondering where she was, the hangar doors opened, and the French ground-crew wheeled her out – resplendently painted, all in pink, with a girl's eyes and large eyelashes and a bright red mouth across the nose, together with red nipples on the front of each inboard drop tank!

We all thought this was a huge French joke, and were still laughing when we arrived at home base later that day, only to find that our Station Commander, realizing that it was oil based pink paint and wouldn't wash off, was livid!

While Dijon shall be forever pink, our Northern deployments were perhaps more a whiter shade of pale. Bardufoss, of Rock Hangar fame, or Tromsø of Norwegian University girls' fame, were our two regular deployment bases. Bardufoss, some fifty miles south of Tromso inside the Arctic Circle at minus 30 degrees at lunchtime, was a combined Norwegian Air Force base and civilian airport with a single runway that started or ended, depending on which way you were facing, at the western end in a sheer cliff. The runway literally disappears straight into the sheer rock-face, within which was an enormous, semicircular hangar hewn out of the solid rock. Inside the rock doors is a complete suite of accommodation for all our aircraft and including squadron maintenance offices and workshops. Landing eastwards over the top of the rock onto the pack-ice topped runway required a steep approach, and the ability to stop before running off the far end necessitated some tricky flying!

On the other hand, 186 miles North of the Arctic Circle with only three hours of daylight at this time of year, the tiny university city of Tromsø had a well-used, modern civilian airport, though quite small alongside the fjord with only the one runway. The town's young and lively population welcomed us warmly each winter, providing every comfort for the troops – every possible comfort, including some eighty-five bars and its own brewery!

Flying north of Tromsø low level up into the North Cape area is like flying over a white version of the Arabian empty quarter. Instead of uninterrupted sand-dunes, it is continuous, undulating snow-dunes in unrelenting, unbroken white as far as the eye can see in every direction. While flying in these conditions snow-blindness could creep upon you. It was dangerously easy to get lost over the inland, featureless landscape and, especially if your old, analogue, inertial nav system had given up, as often happened, you had to revert to dead reckoning. Despite its obvious strategic importance, it was impossible to imagine any conflict taking place in that forbidding, frozen territory, but together with the British Commandos, we defended it every January!

In Sep '76 we deployed our twelve aircraft to Oerland on the coast of Central Norway. Here we operated with a US Marine Air Wing who had their own Harriers (AV8As), some 80 aircraft strong, from the USS *John F Kennedy*. After flying from the carrier, they eventually joined us ashore to try operating from a tented encampment, I believe, for the first time. They appeared to have little idea of how to operate away from their cosy carrier. With no track discipline they were operating heavy lorries in the field camp around the tents and in the same areas as the aircraft. The whole area became a quagmire with lorries and aircraft bogged down in the thickest mud every-where you looked. Within 24 hours we had christened it "Mud City" – no one could move anywhere, on foot or otherwise, for two foot thick mud tracks. To cap it all, once their Admiral found out that we had flown more missions that week with our twelve aircraft than his marines had with a whole eighty strong air wing, he went Harpic. This US Marine Corps camp was the worst I had seen with little clear thought or planning.

Early in '77, I finally received my postgraduate rating by completing a Qualified Weapons Instructor's (QWI) course at the Harrier OCU. This four-month, intensive flying course took me back to school: the use of mathematics, algebra and geometry, up to and including calculus, which we used for calcu-lating weapons' ballistics as the foundation phase. But while the others had done all this before, I found calculus completely new and an extremely hard learning curve ensued. The course then continued into learning to teach the art of firing all the weapons correctly and accurately in the two-seater training aircraft. Finally, one also learnt how to calculate mentally, in front of your peers, the fall of shot from measuring gunsight film. Every aspect of air-to-ground weaponry, and how best to teach it, was covered.

On completion of the course, I became the No 1 (F) Squadron QWI, a position of some power on any front line fighter squadron. The QWI was in charge of all weapons safety and training, the conduct of all weapons training missions, aircraft weapons systems such as the gunsights, and aircraft harmonization of sights to guns. He checked all squadron pilots during two-seater training sorties on the range for each type of weapon. He briefed all weaponeering aspects, debriefed all weapons' gunsight film from every mission, and ran the squadron's annual five-week, armament-practice camp (APC) conducted at that time on Capo Frasca firing range while based at Decimomannu in southern Sardinia. In other words, anything to do with weapons and their firing, accuracy and quality, was the QWI's domain.

Within a month of becoming the Sqn QWI, I was bowled a fast, swerving ball. As a ground attack QWI, there was one aspect of weaponry we did not cover: air-to-air (AtoA) gunnery. This wasn't in our syllabus, we didn't practise it, we weren't expected to hit a barn door in AtoA, and, in wartime, would only ever have to fire at airborne targets in self-defence. Then the words 'Belize' and 'the Guatemalan Air Force' arrived to plague us.

By the time of the second Harrier deployment to save Belize from the Guatemalans in 1977, command had finally realized that our role would be essentially an air defence one, and that we could be in theatre for a longer time than the few months of the earlier 1975 detachment. Accordingly, it followed that, being a 'mud-moving' outfit, we did not have the AtoA background or training to counter the Guatemalan air force if it ever decided to attack Belize. Jeremy Saye, our new Squadron Commander, who was very operationally minded, I believe had a lot to do with this realization. Of course, in those days, we had no AtoA missiles either. This was in the days before Sidewinder (DBS), and our only AtoA weapons were our two 30mm cannons. It was guns or nothing!

Hence, my first major task as a brand-new, wet-behind-the-ears, sqn QWI, was to train the whole squadron in the AtoA role before our deployment within a week from scratch! Yet no Harriers had ever fired AtoA before, none of the aircraft had ever been harmonized, and 80% of the pilots had never fired AtoA, EVER! Even as the QWI 'expert', I had fired live AtoA against the banner on my Hunter conversion course in Dec '64, some eleven years earlier, in a well oiled and regulated system only on nine occasions and never in a Harrier with its peculiar hybrid AtoA sighting system. Neither was there any RAF AtoA standard gunnery 'Bible' from which to learn.

In accuracy terms, AtoA gunnery is probably the most difficult of any air-weapons delivery profiles. Consequently, the basic, essential element is that the guns and gunsights must be perfectly harmonised. On the Harrier, not only had the AtoA sight never been used, never mind harmonised, but it was known that it didn't deflect correctly. The full harmonization process is also a time consuming process, which takes an otherwise serviceable aircraft out of commission. To fully harmonize a whole Sqn in one week is an impossibility. Even if we'd had the wherewithal, it would have been a very tall order! I'd never known the background theory to QWI level . . . I know now!

We were only given three days of AtoA range practice firing with four towed banners per day to train the whole squadron, allowing sixteen missions per day – four aircraft per banner, a maximum of four missions per pilot, at less than a week's notice. This was limiting enough, but we had no coloured bullets[3], no tracer ammo. and twelve un-harmonized aircraft. On contacting the weapons system manufacturers, Ferranti, even they admitted that the sight didn't work in the AtoA mode, had never worked and, in fact, couldn't be made to work! No one had believed we'd ever use the AtoA role, so there had

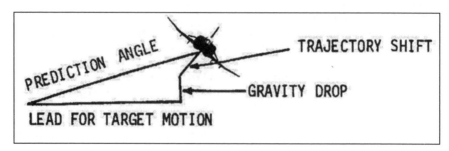

Fig 13. Diagram showing the three basic components of AtoA sighting predictions[4].

never been any political or military will to set up the gunsight correctly in this mode. Talk about firing at nothing with nothing – an unmitigated disaster loomed!

There are three basic components that require continuous calculation to provide an accurate AtoA sighting system: trajectory shift, gravity drop, and lead for target motion, and that is the easy bit. As the guns are some six feet below the gunsight, a fourth small additional calculation for Dip or Parallax is included to account for the different sight line of the gun from the gunsight. Making the actual sight software follow these predictions, and/or changing it to fit the circumstances, is not an easy task. Moreover, an extra sighting allowance had to be made for a turning target because banner targets were towed by Canberra aircraft in a 30degree banked, circular towline.

The nylon banner itself, on a 600foot towline, was six feet high and twenty-five feet long with a large steel spreader-bar at the front to make it fly vertically. Our aim was to fire between 425 and 375yards, and even at that close range, looking through a gunsight, it looked smaller than a tick's testicle!

The Hunter era's AtoA sqn average was about 20% with harmonized aircraft and well-trained crews in constant practice. Some personal averages could double that figure: if so, you were an ace! With no sight handling experience, our pilots didn't even know how to set up the pattern to arrive at the correct firing range, at the right speed, and most importantly, at the right angle-off[5] simultaneously: too shallow and you fired up the backside of the towing aircraft; too steep and the banner passed you by so fast there was no chance of getting any lead for target motion, and less chance of hitting, even if it had been a B52! On the first day, for example, one pilot, who shall remain nameless, came back with film showing the banner crossing his path in *THREE* film-frames! At a film speed of sixteen frames per second, and comparing it with the 15 degrees we were attempting to achieve, this equated to a three-sixteenth of a second attack at an 86 degree angle-off! More simply put: a "right-angle" attack! The chance of ever seeing a single bullet hole in any banner using these parameters was zero! At this point I would have been extremely happy to see just a single hit all day: at least we could have cross-referred it to the film and roughly calculated the sighting problems! Like Radfan rocketry, this was going to be another, cobbled together, fudged operation.

Using Ferranti system experts, and pleading with the air defence OCU at Coningsby, I obtained not only the theory, but the services of a superbly gifted AtoA IWI[6], Steve Nicholl[7], an F4 Phantom pilot. Between us we briefed the squadron into thinking they were only going on a pattern proving exercise while we, Steve and I, worked hard to come up with a sight firing solution. Even so, all the boys really wanted to hit these banners! The solution – the theory – was easy, but applying it to the Harrier sighting system proved frustratingly difficult. There had been time to harmonize only one aircraft, and no one was sure where the AtoA sight was pointing anyway!

Day one: sixteen missions and 960 bullets[8] later, four virgin banners had arrived back from Staxton Wold range, off Flamborough Head, dropped by the Canberra towing aircraft on the airfield for all to see. It was heartbreaking, but at least Steve and I now had sixteen gun-sight films to evaluate, and these would give us some idea of how the sights were working in relation to each other together with a mean, and how the pilots were coping with the pattern. The pattern is everything: start in the right place, right height and right speed, and a good approach and attack ensues, but, if any starting parameter is wrong it is hopeless continuing. To be an AtoA gunnery ace requires more skill than any other type of attack. The Battle of Britain showed that, and the AtoA arena has now been taken over by the guided missile. Fourteen of the films were useless as the pilots hadn't really coped with the pattern on their first attempts. We needed film showing good, steady tracking in the region of 400kts, 400 yards range and 15 degrees angle-off, so after a thorough debrief for each pilot, whose learning curve was stratospheric, we left it to try again the following day.

Day two: sixteen missions and another 960 bullets later, four virgin banners had arrived back, again for all to see. Yet another heartbreaking day, but now we had some good tracking film to evaluate, including one that Steve and I had ourselves taken in the two-seater Harrier first thing that morning. Steve and I worked throughout that night evaluating every frame of every film, then working the theory against our findings, until we came to a not unreasonable, and very tired, conclusion in the early hours. Those sights that were working tolerably were consistently under-deflecting by some 10 to 15%, putting all the bullets behind the target – no bad thing if you're going to miss – at least it was safe but what a waste of all that effort! On the other hand, at least we had something to work upon. Calculations suggested that to obtain a greater and correct sight deflection for a 400 yard firing range meant selecting a false setting, some 550 yards on the range drum. That setting gave a greater deflection, and hopefully was the correct one for the 400 yard firing range. I'd like to have fired at a much closer range – better chance of hitting – but we had to set 350 yards as a minimum in order that we didn't hit the banner ourselves on the breakaway afterwards!

We also found that for the parameters we were attempting, the correct deflection in the fixed sight was just off and below the fixed lower horizon bar in the head-up display (HUD), which in turn would give a good fixed indication of the sight's correct deflection. So on day three, now with four harmonized aircraft, we decided to attempt two things. Firstly we would use 550 yards ranging and a fixed sight solution for those pilots who were managing reasonably steady tracking at low angles-off. Secondly, for Steve and I, and one or two others in harmonized jets, would put the aiming pipper on and slightly above the tow line ahead of the banner, and while firing, allow the pipper to "slide" down the tow line onto the spreader bar at the front of the banner.

Day three: sixteen missions and another 960 bullets later, three virgin banners had arrived back, but the fourth. . . . . . had one bullet hole in it! Yes! Joy, success and relief in equal amounts. Though minimal, we now had something concrete to evaluate. Of the four aircraft firing on that banner, two had film that wouldn't have hit a Jumbo Jet! Of the other two, one was Steve's and mine, from our two-seater, and we discounted the other because it showed an unserviceable gunsight. Mainly due to Steve's herculean efforts, we had produced the one and only hit. Justice was done and seen to be done. After all, we were the final arbiters of good taste and judgement in this matter!

As it turned out, this episode was nothing new. It was a typical air force hotchpotch arrangement: we will muddle through; it will be alright on the night! Air Chief Marshal Sir Christopher Foxley-Norris, an exceptional low-level, ship buster, and Battle of Britain pilot of WW2, is reported as saying, *"My failure to distinguish myself in the Battle was by no means as uncommon as many people would imagine. Particularly, one's shooting was haphazard and untutored, most of us having been thrown in quite without adequate training in that highly scientific art. We did not often get into an attacking position, and when we did we missed, firing at too long range and without enough deflection. Those who survived learned by experience, and success went to the few old hands, the naturally gifted and the lucky."*

Thirty-five years later nothing had changed. What a way to go to war: I'm only glad the Guatemalans never found out!

We eventually confirmed the over-deflecting sights, settled on the fixed sighting solution for shooting down Guatemalan A37s, and went off to Belize to have at them![9] Subsequently, with help from the INAS[10] bay chief, Ferranti, Dave Fisher, the chief QWI on the OCU, and especially the theory provided by Steve Nicholl, I wrote the definitive paper developing the full theory, equations and practice of AtoA gunnery in the Harrier. Our combined report was sent up the chain of command, recommending further trials and possible modification to Harrier gunsights. I was also of the opinion that Harrier and all ground attack sqns should practise more cine-weave as taught on the old Hunter OCU. This is an AtoA sight handling exercise, and is an excellent one that teaches you how to properly track a manoeuvring aircraft. Unfortunately, in the order of priority for training in these days of multi-roll Jack-of-all-trades, AtoA cine weave gunnery exercises come close to the bottom, and are rarely taught. In my opinion, this is short-sighted; even if this is mainly required for self-defence, we are denying one of the basic skills of fighter flying. Disconcertingly, and also myopically, our latest fighter, the Typhoon, has no usable gun at all! Yet against terrorist targets, air-gunnery should always be an option.

When I left the Harrier force five years later, no trials or action had been undertaken. Having had no preparation time, and using unharmonized aircraft and novice pilots, producing just the one bullet hole was exceptionally lucky. A further trial prepared in slow time, preceded by a cine-weave phase, would have been of considerable benefit, but was not to be. I am now even more convinced that we are denying our pilots a basic tool of their trade. Sqn Ldr John Hall, a Mosquito Ace of WW2, was yet another who, after having trouble with line and deflection, likened the problem to shooting game birds where an estimate of 'range, line and deflection' held the key to success. He became a gunnery instructor and an ardent believer in the need for fighter pilots to understand fully the basics of AtoA shooting, something he felt that most of them lacked. Nothing has changed today.

For this affair I received an exceptional annual rating as a Harrier pilot and instructor, but I have to thank Steve Nicholl – thankyou Steve – for his encyclopaedic knowledge of AtoA technology, its applications, and his willingness to impart it. This rating on the most difficult aircraft to fly in the air force, for me, was the ultimate accolade of my career, but remember . . . it only took one bullet!

After that, running a five-week armament practice camp at Decimomannu in Sardinia, and working up the whole Sqn in air-to-ground (AtoG) weapons was a piece of cake. Decci detachments consisted of five waves of four aircraft each day, dedicated to weapons practice on Capa Frasca range. The time was divided into rocketing, lay-down bombing, freefall bombing, and strafing, with a full operational phase at the end completing three disciplines at high speed in one mission. Finally, there was always a competition between the pilots. Throughout the deployment, a ladder was kept showing the cumulative scores, or errors, chalked up for each weapon by each pilot. Of course, it was a real feather in anyone's cap to be top of the various ladders, though the gunnery one was the most sought after. As the Sqn QWI, it was a matter of professional credibility to be at, or at least near, the top of them all!

At times one difficulty was keeping the Italian range controllers awake: any excuse and they were siesta-ing. On one famous occasion we were flying the last slot of the day and had finished our allotted time but still had weapons left on board. On asking the range controller's permission to continue, we received over the radio in pidgin English the following transmission: "No . . . ya go away . . . I wanna go to sleep!"

The whole five week detachment went according to plan, with few if any incidents until we came to leave. After take-off on the way home in a fully loaded two-seater, the aircraft had a control restriction resulting in a quick return to land back at Decci. When the groundcrew started their investigation, they initially pulled a packet of 200 cigarettes out from under one of the wing panels. As the investigation continued, 20,000 cigarettes were found stashed away in different parts of the aircraft! This was the only time I saw a 'major' smuggling operation, rather incredible considering how many opportunities we all had. Eventually one of our sergeants was found guilty of smuggling tobacco.

It was during this period that I started to feel old. Daz James, our sqn QFI, who had also been with me on 8 Sqn in Aden, (recently retired as Deputy Chief Test Pilot for Marshalls of Cambridge), and I were sitting at the sqn coffee bar one morning reminiscing about our times at Khormaksar when a young pilot called Nick overhearing us, asked, "Where's Khormaksar?" Only the largest RAF base ever, and yet, 10 years after leaving Aden the youngsters had never heard of it! Daz and I were astounded and gave Nick a thorough history lesson!

Yet the Air Force was, in those days, extremely insular. Living off-base in your own house, especially as a bachelor, was certainly frowned upon. Bachelors had to live in the Mess, married couples in official married quarters. Living away from the base meant you weren't seen to be supporting the Mess – a heinous crime despite drink/driving laws. Nor was account ever given for the good work that ensued amongst the local community. For example, I bought and lived in a little thatched cottage in a village called Helpston, famous for its poet, John Clare, exactly five miles on the centre of the main runway and was, therefore, extremely noisy from all our jet over-flights and traffic avoiding the MATZ[11]. Complaints were numerous. Then one evening in the local pub I was accosted by the village fete committee who, having had a few beers, enquired as to why I shouldn't obtain the services of the Red Arrows for the next Fete some three weeks away.

Nearly three weeks later on the Friday prior to the Saturday Fete, I was standing in our Sqn ops room putting the finishing touches to Monday's flying programme at around 5pm when the station PRO came in and asked whether I was coming in to work on the Saturday to watch the Red Arrows. As luck would have it, apparently the Arrows were staging through for a refuel that afternoon, and the PRO was most surprised when I thrust a phone at him with instructions to ring the Arrows with the geographical position of the fête.

That Saturday afternoon the Red Arrows overflew the village fête on their way in to land. We had no further low flying complaints for the rest of the year from the village, and I could do no wrong in their eyes! But I carefully avoided the fête committee the following year in case they wanted a repeat show!

In my opinion, towards the end of 1978 everything changed for the worse: we lost our operational zeal and were treated just like an aerobatic team. In Sep '78, we deployed as a diamond-nine to Kirkwall airfield in the Orkney Islands. The northern NATO exercise that year was based not in northern Norway, but on the Shetlands, and we camped out on Kirkwall's airfield, flying North into the Shetlands every day.

This detachment is remembered for the 'horror hover'. On this occasion I was number four in a four ship mission to the Shetlands and back at dusk. The weather was on the limits with low cloud, heavy rain, very high gusting winds – our diversions couldn't have been much good either – and it was now extremely dark: not nice at all. Arriving back at Kirkwall the crosswind was out of limits for the only runway, so we were forced to land vertically on the one and only MEXE metal landing pad. In winds gusting over forty knots and higher, we were forced to follow each other in line astern in the most unstable speed range (ninety to thirty knots) while waiting for the one in front not only to land but clear the pad. It was like riding a roller coaster, not knowing whether the aircraft was able to sustain controlled flight in these gusty conditions, and seeing very little in the heavy rain and darkness. As No.4, I had to wait the longest while the other three landed. Indeed, this recovery took so long that I was way beyond the engine limits of 2½minutes at high RPM with the nozzles down, so was forced to put the aircraft unserviceable. Once it came to my turn to land, I couldn't see the markers for the landing pad, and felt my way down not knowing exactly where the ground was! Never again – I certainly found my limit that night, if not the aircraft's!

Kirkwall's Harrier camp was different from most in that we were parked right by the side of the runway. It wasn't a busy runway then, as only the Loganair Islanders puttered in and out on their round-the-islands scheduled services. Their early morning schedule was used as our alarm clock. Many were the mornings we'd be woken by two little Lycoming O.540 two-bladed piston engines puttering away at 2700 rpm on take-off. Peeping out of the tent flap, many times we'd find the fog was so thick we couldn't see the next tent. Knowing then that we wouldn't be flying, we'd turn over and go back to sleep, only to be awoken an hour later by the same noise, this time arriving back from his 'routine' flight. That meant breakfast for us, but those Islander pilots were remarkable: the Orkney Islanders relied on their Islander schedule for everything, and the pilots, who knew every geographical detail of the Orkneys, would ensure a reliable service come hail, rain or shine. When we had been grounded for hours, you could still hear, if not see, the Islanders going about their usual business.

Having flown the Islander myself on parachute work, it didn't take long to make myself known to the local Loganair pilots, and of course, when the Harriers were grounded, wean a few flights in the right hand seat round the islands. This included what is renowned as the shortest scheduled service in the world: the short hop across a narrow strait from the beach of Westray Island to the beach of Papa Westray Island, which takes approximately 45 seconds. However, I am assured that when the winds are right, the flight record stands at fourteen seconds from take-off to touchdown!

One of our Sqn airmen had been detached to the civilian Fire Station at St Andrews in Fife for cover during the firemen's strike, and it was his birthday coming up soon. So the Mess baked a birthday cake, and four Harriers flew to RAF Leuchars, near to St Andrews, on this airman's birthday. A staff car, with the cake, was then sent off to St Andrews Fire Station, for the presentation. On arrival, the fire-crews looked amazed, and said, "Your guy's gone on holiday for his birthday – he's at home in Scunthorpe!"

Later, a near fatal mid-air collision ensued during combat training over Wisbech. The two pilots both ejected successfully, but one of the aircraft hit a house in the town and people on the ground were killed – a dreadful period for the squadron.

The final, and most tremendous event that occurred during this tour of duty was the birth of my only offspring, Andrew. I watched his arrival, and his first action in this world was to pee on my shoes! Nonetheless, his very existence over the next twenty-odd years had a marked effect on my professional life.

All good things come to an end, and after two superb and one variable year on the First Squadron, it was posting time. Although I expected with my QWI and FRI qualifications to move to the OCU staff, I was, surprisingly at the time, given a very different role instead: Unit Test Pilot.

Notes
1. NATO's Allied Command Europe.
2. Oxygen sickness due to lack of oxygen.
3. Bullets were painted different colours and each aircraft had its own colour. In this way we could tell whose bullets had hit the banner as they left a coloured trace round the edges of the hole.
4. The terms shown should be self-explanatory, except that Trajectory Shift is the change in bullet motion after it leaves the muzzle and becomes influenced by the exterior air flow.

5. Angle-off: the angle between the target's longitudinal axis and the fighter's trajectory. Ten to fifteen degrees is a normal range for accurate firing.
6. IWI: Interceptor Weapons Instructor.
7. To retire as AVM S. M. Nicholl CB CBE AFC BA FRAeS RAF(Ret'd)
8. 60 rounds in one gun per aircraft - enough for 6 good firing passes.
9. We never did "have at them", so it all remained just theory. The Belize story is one in its own right, and is the subject of Chapters 27 and 28.
10. Inertial Navigation and Attack System - the computers that, inter alia, ran the gunnery sighting.
11. MATZ - Military Air Traffic Zone of 5 miles radius around each military airfield.

Chapter Twenty-Two

The Testing

RAF HARRIER FORCE UNIT TEST PILOT et al

Support for the front line comes in many guises, but none so rewarding as flight-testing. Working from the Operations and Engineering Wings' HQ, this new role had two Bosses and three hats. I was under the command of the Wing Commander Operations, an ex-Harrier pilot himself, but was responsible to the Wing Commander Engineering, whose remit it was to service the aircraft and return them to the front line in a fully fit-for-operations condition. It was working with his engineering staff that afforded the most pleasurable and rewarding aspects of the role. I was also the Harrier Wing Weapons Officer, and the Station Flight Safety Officer, but it was the flight-testing that took up the majority of my time. All three hats allowed a great measure of independence, which I valued.

Aircraft required flight-testing after an engine change, or any deeper form of servicing which occurred every 480 flying hours. Not only did we have the task of major servicing for the whole Harrier force, but also there was a permanent British Aerospace working party conducting retrofits of various modifications, the finale of which was a flight test. Part of the role, therefore, entailed collection and delivery of aircraft, both to and from Germany and to and from the manufacturers, British Aerospace at Dunsfold. Indeed, I delivered XZ128, the first aircraft to be built as a GR3, to Wittering on 15th March 1976, and XZ129 a month later.

This latter aspect was always good fun, particularly collecting a brand new aircraft from the factory because it meant flying a clean aircraft – no underwing stores, tanks or even pylons – in its most pristine condition, one that was unusual within the services. As soon as the service gets its hands on a new aircraft, it adds all sorts of extras, which mean more weight and drag and diminished performance. Hence, each of these new aircraft was capable of flying faster and higher than any others. This turned the delivery flights into exhilarating, record-breaking attempts: I climbed one to over 48,500 feet at the highest[1], whilst 650kts straight and level at sea level was the fastest.

During one of these delivery flights I had my only experience of that little understood phenomenon: St Elmo's Fire. I was on my way back to Wittering from Dunsfold in a brand new aircraft. In order to avoid traffic on the airways, I had been routed straight through a line of storm clouds at around 20,000 feet near Daventry. The adrenalin was already pumping as I was being

214

buffeted around in semi-darkness inside this storm cloud, when without warning there was an almighty bang, more a vicious crack, almost as if I'd hit something solid. A lightning bolt had hit me, instantly failing most of my instruments, including my main radio. On looking out through the canopy backwards and sideways, I was surprised to see that the whole aircraft appeared to be on fire: a phantasmagoria of little, yellow-tipped, bluish, efflorescent flames was dancing and writhing all round the airframe, lending a coruscating iridescence to the whole machine. It was a quite extraordinarily beautiful sight but, an emergency situation had now presented itself, and there was little time for wonderment at this impalpable, transitory experience. It lasted no more than what seemed like a couple of minutes, but it was probably only a few seconds before the training kicked in. The emergency compass and radio were selected, and out of cloud we popped to prelude an uneventful landing some twenty minutes later.

However, back on the ground, it was immediately apparent that the lightning had sought every possible way into the machine. Every single rivet hole was blackened around its circumference, along the top surfaces of the wings and fuselage, luckily without any real damage to the skin. The electrical systems were a different matter: they had been grossly overloaded. It took some weeks to put this spanking new aircraft back in the air again, but I'll never forget those prancing flames of St Elmo's Fire!

As you can appreciate from the above incident, flight-testing, contrary to popular opinion, is far from glamorous. Some of it is what is commonly called in the trade, "shake-down" flying: after major changes to the aircraft, get it airborne, shake it about, and see what falls out! Sometimes, the odd tool was found, and, on one occasion, two pints of hydraulic fluid!

During the following three years I learnt more about the aircraft and its systems, the intricacy of the engine and it's complicated fuel system, and the engineering aspects of this amazing aircraft than in the rest of my career put together. In order to test something, an intimate knowledge of all its parts and their inter-relationship really is a basic necessity. Working out of an engineering hangar greatly enhances ones knowledge of the aircraft, and shows how ignorant are most pilots of such details.

The main approach to the testing was simply that after the aircraft had been signed off fit-for-flight at the end of the testing, it could be an OCU student on his first solo who flew it next; the jet therefore had to fly exactly within its parameters and limits. The cockpit was your office, but it had to work perfectly with no secretarial help. Testing a Mk GR3 or T4 Harrier after deep maintenance to the point of signing it off fit for operations often took two or three flights over a three to four day period or more, and were some of the hardest working flights of all. Every detailed aspect of the aircraft had to be checked and tested, and so was always approached with some circumspection. The longest took sixteen flights over twenty-five days, and included three engine changes, whereas the shortest, which happened only once in all of my three years, was a single flight taking just over an hour. This shortest could only happen if there were no air traffic or weather delays and every single check and test point on the schedule were correct the first time of checking. These timescales don't include the numerous attempts to pre-flight inspect the aircraft before finding some aspect of the ground inspection amiss, and having to cancel the flight. The grounding problems came in all guises, from large hatches missing (such as the equipment bay hatch) to systems working the opposite way from the true.

An example of the latter was a laughable occurrence I had with the oxygen system. In one instance, after strapping into the aircraft and turning on the system, a red, oxygen warning-light came on with its attendant klaxon and flashing, emergency lights. This should only come on when the system is depleted or at low pressure. But then I noticed that the light flashed on and off in time with my breathing, which was getting quicker and quicker with the noise of the bells and red lights flashing in my eyes. When I turned the system off, the black/white breathing doll's eye that *should* blink with one's breathing, went permanently black. It took me some time to realize that the technicians had cross-wired the red light and the doll's eye – the red light was showing my breathing rate, and the doll's eye was giving me the warning that the LOX was turned off instead of the other way round. Every breath produced the klaxon and red emergency lights!

A further premise from which to approach testing is that, "All aircraft are bent!" Every single model flies differently from its partner. Often years of mishandling, overstressing, heavy landings, and groundcrew boots (never aircrew boots!) can be partially blamed, but even new ones have subtle differences in weight and balance. There could be some 300lbs weight difference across the Harrier fleet for example, but it is in the trim positions in straight and level flight that one mostly notices the differences. Commonly offset rudder and aileron trims are a good sign of something bent . . . besides the pilot!

Of course, there had to be many checks on the ground before any thought of take off. The Harrier was really an airframe built round a very complex Bristol-Siddeley (latterly Hawker-Siddeley) Pegasus engine arrangement – a streamlined flying bedstead. It was an engine that, to obtain hover performance, operated closer to its maximum limits than any other jet, and 70% of any test flight was usually taken up with checking some part of the Pegasus fuel system for correct operation.

After checking all instrumentation including engine start up times and idling parameters, the main area of consideration was the acceleration times of the engine from idle to full power, and the full power reading itself. Now, just for once, a little technical detail (not a lot) is required to ensure that non-aircrew and non-aeronautical engineers can understand the logic behind the test schedule. The engine acceleration is a compromise between obtaining the fastest rate without surging the engine through over fuelling, but not too slow a rate that would lead to top end stagnation, ie: the engine would not reach full power. In other words, it is checking the set up of the high-pressure fuel acceleration unit. This was measured by the time it took to accelerate from idle to 55% RPM, and then a further timing check from 55 to 100% RPM. The first could be achieved at a standstill against the brakes, but they couldn't hold the incredible power above 55%, so the second was done on a run down the runway. Only three attempts at the latter were allowed before the brakes became too hot. Three hands and two feet were required for this check: simultaneously you released the toe-breaks, put the throttle to full power with the left hand and pressed the stopwatch on the top right coaming with the right-

216

hand. Immediately, the right hand had to grab the control column to engage nose-wheel steering, then return to the stopwatch as the RPM hit 100%, all in two seconds. You mentally note the top RPM, if correct of around 102.5%, as you re-engaged the steering, retarded the throttle and commenced toe braking. The aircraft could easily have achieved forty knots and moved a hundred yards down the runway while your arms and legs worked in a blur. Then this would have to be done at least twice to obtain some consistency. Note that the in-limits time for this 55 to 100% acceleration, and therefore, for all the above actions, was from two to three seconds[2]! Anything faster and the engine might surge; anything slower and it might stagnate to the point of never reaching full power. What was necessary was the engine ability to accelerate from idle to full power at between 4.5 and 6.5 seconds: quite an achievement for something so large.

And that was just one of the main ground checks!

If all looked good, then once airborne, after a careful, highish-speed take off, the main aspects to check first were the engine limits, though of course, you were constantly mentally checking that everything looked, felt, sounded and flew right. The airborne engine checks required what is known as a "creep climb" to 40,000feet at a set 98% RPM to check that the engine fuel system could maintain a steady RPM throughout the differing air pressures and densities of the full height range. During this period, there is time to check out the various on board systems: radio, IFF, navigation aids, head-up display in all modes including weapons sights, and all instruments, pressures and warning systems.

Next comes one of the most critical tests: that of the Pressure Ratio Limiter (PRL). This part of the Fuel Control Unit (FCU) governs the maximum RPM, which varies with air pressure, which, in turn changes with height. Hence, the maximum RPM will also vary with height. Readings are taken at 30,000feet and 40,000feet, and plotted against a graph that you carry on your kneepad, together with the test schedule which is being gradually completed throughout the flight. Of course, there's no autopilot, so right hand writing while flying left-handed is the order of the day – it pays to be ambidextrous, which I hear is not only dangerous but also illegal in some non-Christian countries!

It's not possible to set up the PRL on the ground beforehand, so rarely is it within limits on the first attempt, but having obtained accurate readings, the rest of flight is aborted, and a quick return to base effected. Once on the ground, the servicing crew can adjust it while you stay in the cockpit. Then a further creep climb to 30,000 and 40,000 feet is commenced, followed by a further check of the PRL at both heights. This could sometimes take three or four climbs and adjustments before the limiter was correctly set up, and not until then could the most vital of checks be performed: the engine slam checks. The slam checks are designed to ensure the engine will continue to operate at the extremes of the flight envelope, and in this case it is conducted at maximum height, maximum angle of attack (i.e. worst possible airflow through the intakes), and maximum engine acceleration. At 40,000 feet and 200 knots with the throttle closed, maximum "g" is pulled to the buffet or twelve degrees angle-of-attack, whichever comes sooner, and the throttle is then slammed fully open. Yes, it's rough, but proves the engine will withstand any mis-handling in the worst possible conditions.

Unfortunately, the slam check often put the engine into a surge situation. More often than not, if you pulled the throttle back quickly enough while releasing the angle-of-attack, you might get away with a simple pop-surge. This is a transient surge in which the engine stagnates as jet pipe temperatures rapidly increase, but the ram airflow through the compressor is just laminar enough to keep the engine alight, and it instantly recovers. In some cases though, the Pegasus would lock in a full surge with RPM winding down as turbine temperatures sped off the clock. There was no alternative but to shut it down snappily before the turbine was roasted and the whole engine calamitously ruined.

At this point she became a very heavy, badly designed glider, with you aboard, which starts sliding earthwards at a rate of one to 1½ miles per 1000 feet of height: only fifty odd miles range and less than ten minutes to the ground! At the same time, besides the 'dropped-brick' trajectory, the cockpit mists over completely as it depressurises and the oxygen system then reacts to this lack of pressure by converting to full pressure breathing. So while getting over the shock of losing your only engine, you can't see out and you can hardly speak! It is difficult enough to breath, never mind talk on the radio! A Mayday call in those conditions comes out as a little squeak! What little could be seen through the mist only confirms a lot of red flashing emergency lights, and a load of bells (yes, bells!) ringing in your ears. 'Twas a little disconcerting to say the least, but by the time this had happened to you a dozen times you became anaesthetized with a tendency to become blasé about it!

But patience is a virtue. Believe me, the engine always relit . . . always, but not necessarily the first time! There was rarely enough airflow through the compressor above 20,000feet (lack of air density at height) to rotate the engine again, and if you tried too often, a flat battery could result. You had to sit there and take it on the nose while the aircraft slipped steeply down to 20,000 feet before you could do anything about it: that was half your height and distance gone before you could even start to resurrect a normal situation. The Harrier has the forced landing characteristics of a space shuttle, but without the length of Edwards Air Force Base[3] to land on. As the minimum ejection height was 10,000 feet, that left precious little time to relight; perhaps enough for two, or at best three attempts. But she always relit! The worst scare came after two unsuccessful relight attempts, but luckily the third was successful. Nevertheless, as I was passing 12,000 feet on the way down by then, I had already tightened my seat straps ready for a possible ejection!

It is in these situations that you really earn your flying pay, but after being in the job for a few months, these engine surges became so regular that a Mayday was not used, only the lower safety call of "Pan". The bonus was that the fire and crash crews not only got to know you well, but even brought a beer out to meet you on landing! Indeed, I'm sure that when they heard it was my call-sign in trouble yet again (these things rarely happened on normal training flights), they enjoyed the chase down the runway. They knew that all would be well, and the worst they'd have to contend with was pulling my sixteen stone out of the cockpit, which *they* found hilarious even if I didn't!

So the aircraft would be ground tested, sometimes the engine changed yet again, and we'd restart the whole procedure! I did say that flight testing could be boring!

Once the slam checks had proved successful, there were many system checks to perform on the way down, including pressurization, control trim checks, and the one I disliked most: the negative "g" checks to ensure the engine fuel system would continue working with the aircraft upside-down. At full power, the aircraft is inverted for 15 seconds to ensure the fuel tanks' negative g traps are working correctly. This check produced the "shake-down" items mentioned earlier from the floor of the cockpit. On one occasion as I turned the aircraft over I was drenched with two or three pints of hydraulic fluid left lying in the rear corners of the cockpit floor underneath the ejection seat. Apparently, the five hydraulic gauges in the cockpit had been purged earlier in the servicing. The smell was awful, but 100% oxygen soon cured that problem. However, on rolling the right way up, some of the fluid collected on the canvas cover at the bottom of the control column and gradually seeped through into the cavity below the cockpit floor.

In the Harrier, immediately below the control column under the floor is the main reaction control pipe from the engine combustion chamber through to the front reaction nozzle. This pipe carries hot air at anything up to 750degrees centigrade, and hydraulic fluid takes exception to such high temperatures and turns into a toxic, misty smoke. When this filters back up into the cockpit, it eventually becomes thick enough to make the eyes smart, blur the vision and cause loss of sight of the instruments, which gradually disappear into the mist. Though there is a ram-fresh-air capability, the canopy cannot be opened in flight, so it turned into a race to land before the smoke became too thick. The weather wasn't good at Base requiring a radar approach, which didn't help, but the controller gave me what was known in the trade as a 'fighter command quickie'! This is not a fighter pilot's perversion; it is a short pattern radar approach designed to put you on the deck as quickly as possible, which, thank goodness, was managed – just! And on this occasion, the crash-crews, seeing the smoke, had me lifted out of the cockpit in record time, and for once it was my buying them the beers!

The expensive finale to this incident was the wholesale destruction of all my flying equipment and clothing, right down to my underwear and socks. The hydraulic oil had seeped into every nook and cranny, and not only does it not wash off but also corrodes everything it touches! £10,000 pounds worth of oxygen equipment, parachute harness, Mae-West, bone-dome, flying suit, anti-g suit, and flying boots etc. were completely written off. The worst problem, though, was that all attempts to wash the fluid off your skin and out of your hair proved ineffective – carbolic and even my best after-shave couldn't rid me of the hydraulic reek for days afterwards – BO had nothing on this!

The final and major aspect of the test profile was one unique to the Harrier, called Performance Hovers. As the only aircraft able to stay airborne without any wing lift, relying totally on engine performance, that exact performance had to be known in detail. Obviously there are manufacturing tolerances in any batch of engines but, as the Pegasus operated closer to its maximum surge boundary than any other in order to obtain the vertical take off and hovering capability, hovering performance had to be calculated for every engine and ambient conditions for every take-off and landing. Prior to any mission, using a special VSTOL computer which we all carried, aircraft weight, fuel, outside air temperature and pressure, and underwing stores' weight were calculated to generate the proper take-off nozzle angle, take-off speed, and the maximum hover weight. Hover weight was calculated for a 98% RPM situation, where max RPM was 102.5% without water injection augmentation. This allowed a few percentage revs available for hover manoeuvring without the turbine temperatures reaching their limit because, if they did, the fuel control system automatically cut back the RPM, you ran out of steam, had a very heavy landing, and a one-sided interview!

It was, therefore, vital that the airframe/engine combination you were testing was shown to sustain a 98% RPM and an average turbine-temperature, hover capability. The object now was to complete three very smooth hovers in known atmospheric temperatures and pressures, and read fuel weight against hover RPM and turbine temperature. Any wind effects or too much stick movement increased these RPM and turbine temperatures, producing false readings. The readings were then compared with a graph to show what your combination's results were in terms of + or – RPM and + or – degs centigrade against a standard engine. So a minus 1% engine meant it was operating 1% less efficiently than a standard one, and a +20 degree engine was one in which the turbine temperatures were operating 20 degrees higher than standard. Once these were established, every pilot considered them when calculating his pre take-off performances. In this way, a hover/VSTOL safety margin was always maintained, regardless of any engine performance variations.

Having sorted out any engine surge problems at high altitude, then the same problem could occur during VTOL. Climbing vertically off the pad for the performance hovers for the first time is yet another high-risk area of Harrier operations. If, as sometimes happens, the rear leaves the ground first, requiring a rearward stick movement to counter, the front puffer duct, which is connected directly to the stick, then opens, pouring hot air onto the concrete just in front of the intakes. Re-ingesting this hot air not only loses engine performance but often produces a pop-surge, and the aircraft, therefore, stagnates.

The only time I knowingly damaged one of HM's aircraft was during this manoeuvre. I was testing a new engine on a concrete pad at Wittering for a VTO into the hover. I'd climbed very slowly to about ten feet off the pad when there was an enormous bang, and the engine locked in surge so fast that there was no time for thought. The aircraft, now with about five degrees of right bank on, dropped instantly back onto the ground with a very heavy thud. The right outrigger hit first and bent, and I slightly hurt my back from the impact. The rest of the aircraft was OK but, an engine change was necessary as the turbine temperatures had rocketed off the clock. If an engine was lost at fifty feet in the hover then there was enough time to eject safely, but at any height below that, the aircraft would hit the ground so fast that there was no time to think about it, never mind any physical reaction.

But this particular incident wasn't a patch on that of my successor's. An experienced pilot, whom I'd known in Aden on 1417 Flight, was manoeuvring at 50feet altitude in a slightly banked turn at 33kts when he should have been below 30kts, when the aircraft suddenly flicked violently. I watched the whole incident from the crewroom window. It was quite alarming the speed at which that aircraft flicked both ways before pancaking hard into the ground, slightly nose down, cockpit hitting first! The bottom of the cockpit partially sheered off along the underside, pulling the control cables with it, thus moving the nozzles from the vertical to the horizontal position. With the nose-wheel written off, the aircraft, still at full power, slid firstly across the grass at a high rate of knots, then right across the runway, back on to the grass on the opposite side, and only stopped after enough dirt and turf had been ingested to completely block up the intakes and stop the engine! That last manoeuvre across the ground must have been quite frightening! I should mention here that he was found not guilty of any negligence as the ASI was found to be under-reading. I know: despite having watched the accident, I was a member of the ensuing Board of Inquiry!

As Station Flight Safety Officer, my only memory was how important we considered this aspect of our flying, when compared with earlier post-war years. In the 1970s and '80s, it was a bad year if the whole air force lost twenty aircraft in peacetime accidents. But found in the bottom of my flight safety filing cabinet were the statistics for the 1950s.

In 1952, for example, the Air Force lost in peacetime accidents 515 aircraft! Yes, *Five hundred and Fifteen aircraft*! I remember reading through the list, and finding number eighteen – a Harvard – which had flown into a railway tunnel during a cross-country exercise! It was still the 14th January 1952 and this was already the 18th accident of the year and the 8th fatal one! I know that to find their way around they used to read railway station name-boards in those days, but that was one of numerous, unnecessary tragedies! Between 1950 and 1953, over 1800 RAF aircraft were written off in peacetime accidents[4]!

We've come a long way in flight safety since those days and it was heartening for once to have some efforts rewarded. After the annual flight safety inspection, the Command HQ Flight Safety Inspector, a Group Captain, wrote to my Station Commander, and I quote: *"The formal flight safety system we saw was probably the best we have seen on any station; Chris Bain deserves great credit for his efforts."* Rather nice for once to see it in writing, but I think they hadn't seen many organisations and, more to the point, I don't think we actually stopped any accidents: trouble is, you never can tell!

At the end of this 'testing' tour, my dining out from Wittering on departure for Belize was also memorable. My station navigator, Bill, who had introduced me to my present wife only a few months earlier, was also the Mess Entertainments Officer. Only a couple of weeks earlier, Twickenham had had their first streaker, which gave Bill the idea to interrupt Pat King, the Station Commander, as he rose to make his after dinner speech. This was unheard of in an Officers Mess at that time. After the meal, as Pat rose from the top table to speak, the main dining room doors flashed open, and this gorgeous, young, totally-naked, blonde girl ran all round the room, plonked a kiss on Pat's forehead, and fled amidst a massive uproar and applause!

After dinner, Bill went to pay the girl, who was changing in one of the Mess bedrooms. On entering her room, he was confronted by the still totally naked girl, and had great trouble counting out the fivers into her hand! However, in classic British 'stiff-upper-lip' fashion, he did manage to persuade her to come back into the Mess bar and complete a full scale striptease for all and sundry, and what a raunchy nothing-hidden strip it was too! So much so, that one of the WRAF officers later complained. Well there's always one, isn't there!?

Because of the complaint, Bill and I were subjected to another un-comfortably one-sided interview in front of the Stn Cdr in his office the following morning. Fortunately, Pat had a great sense of humour and had himself enjoyed every minute of it but had to be seen to be doing something because of this one WRAF! So ended my long association with Wittering.

Notes
1. Not as high as a Hunter which I'd had over 49,500 feet.
2. The lower end acceleration times: idle to 55% were 2.5 to 3.5 seconds.
3. The Californian desert airstrip used for Space Shuttle landings.
4. See bibliography No. 24.

Chapter Twenty-Three

The Spy in the Sky

After the excitement and exhilaration of flying and testing Harriers in a tightly knit professional community, maybe this chapter should be entitled, "The Clash of Cultures". It's a pilot versus navigator clash. It is fighter versus bomber culture. Marry a Formula 1 car to a 40ton pantechnicon, and you've got the idea. It's my own fault for thinking I could marry the two successfully. As a single-seater fighter man all my life, I had heard rumours about bomber procedures and the "Navigators' Union", but as I'd never flown with a nav in my life, I had taken it with a pinch of salt. Didn't all aviators think the same way? Was I about to be disillusioned? Yes, in a big way, but the nav has rightly been phased out by the Air Force.

A second aspect of changing from fighters to what, in effect, were the last remnants of Bomber Command, was a greater appreciation of the extremely high standard of aircrews we had in the fighter world. Many crews on the Canberra were long-in-the-tooth specialist-aircrews with little motivation, especially on the ground. If it wasn't laid down in the book, it couldn't be done, and in any case they'd always take the easy way out. It was always procedures, procedures, . . . with no original thought. Well, I suppose that's why they always posted the best to the fighter world.

For example, while I was still on the Canberra OCU learning the role, I had this conversation with one of "their" well-respected QFIs. We were talking about a procedure that stated that all asymmetric overshoots had to be commenced by 600feet altitude because, if you lost an engine, you would need that height to recover into a climb-away situation. (And they practised that ad-infinitum as though it were the only way.) So I asked, if, for real, you were below 600ft when a bus drove onto the runway, did this mean I could not overshoot, but had to land regardless? I thought this was a fair enough question, because it seemed to me that they had turned a peacetime training instruction into a be-all-and-end-all for any real life situation. After much toing and froing, and a number of discussions involving other students and instructors, I had still not been given any adequate constructive answer. Eventually on repeating my question for the umpteenth time, as to what they would do for real when below 600ft, I was ordered, yes actually ordered, to abide by the rules!! That was their official answer!

These particular navigators not only would never ever make a decision, they appeared incapable of doing so. They used to get promoted by not making decisions, because THIS WAS A CAPTAIN'S RESPONSIBILITY, and nothing to do with them, to the extent that they weren't going to help you in coming to any final airmanship decision, unless you specifically asked. A pusillanimous bunch who looked at piloting and captaincy as matters utterly divorced from their navigational duties, thus producing a totally divided crew. So much for crew cooperation! It always reminded me of a transport command co-pilot briefing: "In the event of an accident, the Captain is to be the last one off the aircraft. If you see me exiting stage left, you – nav – are to assume the rank of Captain!"

That was what I found in joining the Canberra force at Wyton in the mid-'80s. What I hadn't realized at the time, certainly not until I found copies of the letters in the PRU's files, was that before my arrival the previous CO and the present Station Commander, both navigators, had written protracted arguments up to Group and Command HQs, demanding that I be removed from this posting because I wasn't a navigator and nor was I Canberra experienced. More than anything else, that illustrated their attitude. Anybody would think the Canberra was a difficult aircraft to fly, or that the role, recce, was totally different from my previous experience in tactical recce. Nothing could be further from the truth. After Harriers, the Canberra was just so simple, and only complicated by the talking mouth in the back: the nav. I managed it without any refresher flying after three years on the ground, though not without some difficulty. The role itself was very little different from my previous recce experience, with only simple high level work to learn. It is a fact of life that everybody thinks his own little world is so expert that no-one else can learn it adequately; they hadn't the gumption to understand that no-one is indispensable.

Nevertheless, it must be said that accurate, high-level reconnaissance is an extremely difficult and often complicated role, both for the navigator and his pilot/captain. The most accurate of flying, especially for survey work, is required. No use of ailerons – the aircraft must remain level. Minute heading changes, one or two degrees only, can be achieved with rudder alone, and speed must remain stable. In other words, as my original flying instructors told me – often – straight and level flying is a tricky fine art in itself, and none more so than manual flying on long-line, photo-recce, surveys in a very low aspect-ratio, PR9 Canberra. Add to that the numerous different cameras carried: from F95-3 and 6 inch lenses through 24 and 48 inch lens cameras and survey lenses, to System III, a horizon-to-horizon panning camera, and infrared linescan in four different bays, some vertical and some oblique, and some idea of the necessary skills can be ascertained.

The easiest way to find out what's really going on in a new unit is to read the unit's files on arrival, and that's how I found out that they didn't want me around. What a hostile atmosphere I had walked into! Not only that, but they hadn't the foresight before I arrived to remove all this correspondence they'd written in trying to replace me; it was lying in the personnel files and was open for me to read . . . or was that by design? From the start they were looking for any excuse to get me out, any mistake, any problem – they made it as difficult as they possibly could. As it was, it's amazing that I made it through to my new unit at all.

For four years I had volunteered and requested to join No. 1 Photographic

Reconnaissance Unit as its Flight Commander for a number of reasons, the main one being to obtain another independent command. I had already had full command of my own unit in Belize[1], and certainly didn't want to go back to being one of three Sqn Ldrs running a sqn for a Wing Commander Boss after having already done his job myself. I was originally offered a Flight Commander's post on the Harrier Wing at Gutersloh, but after three tours already in Germany I didn't fancy that, especially as they were now working out of hardened shelter accommodation[2]. I'd already been there and done that with Hunters and Harriers, and although it was the next step in my career progression, it didn't give me the much more rewarding independent command that I had been used to with 1417 Flt. Wing Commanders now command most of the front line units, but what I needed was an operational flying unit with a Sqn Ldr Boss. The second reason was that my arthritic back had been playing up again, and another tour on high "g" aircraft would not be helpful. Thirdly, this independent command was the only one within commuting distance of where my son, Andrew, was schooling/living. I desperately needed to maintain regular contact with him, one of the few things in this world of which I was proud: my son.

Not only was No. 1 PRU the only unit that met the three goals of mine, but it was also a unique outfit as the only long range, high level, strategic recce unit in the RAF. Indeed, it was the only front line operational flying unit with a Sqn Ldr Boss in the UK. As I had had such a professionally rewarding time flying recce with 2(AC)Sqn, and to a lesser extent, on Harriers, No. 1 PRU fitted my aims admirably. Of course, aerial reconnaissance in all its various guises was an enormously fulfilling role, if not *the* most fulfilling role.

We were tasked on world-wide recce, photographing everything and anything of interest from low level tactical to ultra high level strategic, cross-border and mapping survey work. We flew covert intelligence missions, played cat-and-mouse with the Russian Navy at low level in the Baltic at night, surveyed, inter alia, Kenya, Belize, Denmark and Northern Ireland, flew for the police, customs and drug squads, and generally only flew in good weather when photography was possible. High resolution prints from each mission were instant proof of a job well done; what a fascinating and very rewarding role it was!

We also flew the only aircraft that could climb and maintain well above 60,000ft and we were consequently the only crews in the RAF required to don full pressure suits and helmets. The PR9 was queen of the stratosphere and, still today, is unique. The PR9 was the GT version, and unlike any other. It was even comfortable, comparatively vice-less and a joy to fly, attributes that most definitely couldn't be applied to any other version. We could carry more load than the American U2s or TR1s if not quite as high as they, so often took heavyweight work that they couldn't manage to over 65,000ft, above Concorde flight levels.

Also, when photography wasn't possible, we were often used as high level targets for our air defence fighters. We enjoyed this immensely for two reasons. The first was that this usually meant deploying on a Friday afternoon to Norway for the weekend. The second was that we then flew back into UK airspace at 60,000ft at 6am on the following Monday without a flight plan, and watched the rudely awakened fighter crews failing to climb to our height to intercept us, it was amusing to see those modern fighters, F4 Phantoms and F3 Tornados falling out of the sky below us.

The highlights of this tour included photographing East Germany from high level along the Inner German Border (IGB). Our cameras allowed us to see a good 200 miles across the border, and we could maintain early intelligence of their troop movements and activity.

Furthermore, my crew and I produced the quickest ever photography of the whole of Cyprus from high level. Ten days were allocated to this regular task but never before had it been completed on the first day. We did have one moment of panic though, when Syrian SAM radars lit up our missile radar warning.

The same year, on 19 Sep '86, I took a PR9 to participate in the Finningley Battle of Britain display. Unlike the Farnborough shows, participants received free tickets for their families. My, then, 7 year old son was thrilled to be going to watch Daddy's flypast but, typically of my luck, they got stuck in the inevitable traffic jam five miles from the show, I was seen as a black dot on the horizon, and they ended up diverting to the York Railway Museum for the day instead!

My first survey flight was to continue the task of mapping Northern Ireland. Survey standard photography required extremely accurate flying in height, heading and positioning, but the PR9 was such a stable aircraft after the Harrier, that flying it accurately was pretty easy.

Much recce work was conducted on behalf of various civilian authorities and, in particular, the customs and the police, e.g. covert recce looking for drugs, and infra-red photography for a murder inquiry looking for a recently buried body in forestry of North Wales. But our major success was in producing main and infrared photography of Saddleworth Moor for the Greater Manchester Police in their Moors Murder Investigation.

With the death of Myra Hindley recently, one chapter in the horrible events of 1965 was brought to an end. But in 1987, for the second inquiry, we were asked to photograph the moor again in much the same manner as our predecessors had done back in 1965 for the first investigation, and one of my crews flew low-level photographic missions across the moors, taking both normal and infra-red photos. I then had a free hand to organize the photography and deliver it. In typical fashion, the Air Force had decreed that we must NOT be seen to be helping overtly. Hence, every time I drove up to the moors with photography, I had to be in civilian clothes and use my own car: service transport was not allowed.

One of my best Navs, Phil Collins, and I, spent some time on the moors with Detective Superintendent Topping and his men, looking for changes in the landscape since the first inquiry. By comparing the two sets of photography we were able to make some sensible guesses as to the likely areas for investigation. But what I hadn't foreseen was the forbidding nature of that moor. I had spent many a short holiday and weekends tramping across the Yorkshire Moors, the Lake District, and the Galloway Hills amongst others, but nothing had prepared me for the first sight of these ugly, black, bare peat outcrops down both sides of the road and standing some twenty feet high, oozing brown water. Dull, cold winter weather didn't help, but it was never going to figure on my hill-walking holidays. It was the most chilling place I had come across in the UK, and I find it surprising that people actually go for walks over that part of the moor at all! Yet, I like to think that we were instrumental, together with Professor Hunter's work, in identifying the changes in the moor over that twenty-one year period, and in turn, helped to find the body of Pauline Reed during that second 1987–88 investigation.

As is well known, one body, that of Keith Bennett, remains undiscovered, but I do not believe the theory that his body was buried too deeply. Subsequently, from my knowledge of tramping that awful moor, I have come to a different conclusion. Brady and Hindley would never have bothered, nor probably had the time, to bury deeply, and it is more likely that a shallow grave in a watery gully had been exposed by the elements, and long been disturbed. Much as I desire to bring the longed-for closure to the bereaved, I am afraid there may be nothing left to find.

But as a revealing sequel to this criminal investigation, Greater Manchester Chief Constable Anderton invited us (Phil and I) to an "end of investigation" social gathering. One of his Assistant Chief Constables, Ralph Lees, wrote to me a couple of months after I had left the PRU, "to thank" ... us ... "who provided tremendous support in a highly complex criminal enquiry ... " and inviting us to an end-of-investigation gathering.

It took place at their Training School at Sedgley Park, Prestwich, on Thursday 28th July at 5pm, and we were given overnight accommodation, but what surprised me most was the formal side of the proceedings. Anderton took the opportunity to present members of his investigating team with various commendations and presented team members with certificates. However, when it came to thanking us, we both found ourselves being presented with a rather nice looking tie on which was a date in roman numerals, and both a red and a white rose depicting the fact that the moors area under investigation ran right through the Lancashire-Yorkshire border. It became immediately apparent that this tie had been manufactured as a special "Moors Murder Investigation" tie, which I found in extraordinarily bad taste.

Despite a lack of confidence and medical problems throughout my career, I certainly believe I was one of the fortunate ones. There aren't many pilots, even in military aviation, who had flown above 50,000feet, never mind over 65,000feet, and seen the heavens above. Most jet fighters fall out of the sky at 45,000 feet or so, and none can fly straight and level at 65,000feet, except Concorde, Blackbird, the TR2, one or two special test aircraft, and my Canberra PR9. At that height, the world really does fall away so far below that there is no horizon – you are flying in a total void – as close to being in space as one can get – and very lonely! You certainly can't use any horizon to judge level flight, as one is taught to do at lower levels during training. It feels as if you're sitting on top of the world in space with nothing around but a cobalt blue-black sky, and you're completely divorced from the planet. As the craft takes you higher and higher, the circle of scenery beneath contracts until it disappears, and there is nothing but utter blackness above. If one depends on the world around us for our spiritual and emotional needs, then our limited human imagination utterly fails us in this limitless alien environment.

"And that inverted bowl we call The Sky,
Whereunder crawling coop't we live and die,
Lift not thy hands to it for help – for it
Rolls impotently on as Thou and I."

(Rubaiyat of Omar Khayyam No. LII
from Fitzgerald's first translation 1859)

The wonder of the void, the edge of the universe, was so perfectly uniform. You felt like an intruder – that it shouldn't be despoiled by humans. You felt the need to descend, to leave this place alone in peace. It was somewhere we didn't belong – a glimpse of the world through God's eyes – a privilege to view this very edge of the cosmos.

In flying terms, it is a well-known phenomenon that you reach the maximum ceiling when the maximum indicated airspeed attainable becomes synonymous with the stalling speed. Rarely does any normal aircraft reach this position. However, flying above 50,000 feet, this speed region is often encountered and, an interesting though unusual piloting problem presents itself. Your maximum height is governed by your indicated airspeed in relation to the stalling speed. The higher you fly the closer the maximum indicated speed –reliant on air density – gets to the stalling speed which remains the same at any height. Flying straight and level at full throttle maximum airspeed, which happens to be, say, 0.85 Mach but is only two knots above the stall, you have only that two knots in which to manoeuvre – your total flight envelope is encompassed within a two knot band! Any more than a couple of degrees of bank in order to change heading and the instant increase in drag will produce the two knot decrease that stalls the aircraft. One falls a long way south before any form of aircraft control is recovered. Ergo: flight at that height is extremely limited, and any manoeuvre whatsoever usually requires descent.

The last three RAF PR9 Canberras flew their last flight recently (31 July 06) from Marham to Kemble for storage, but they are totally irreplaceable in the future. They were the longest serving operational "spy-planes" ever flown, a fitting testament to a 1940's design, though it must be said that the high-flying PR9 version really isn't anything like the others. It is a GT version with bigger wings, larger engines, a fighter-style cockpit, and was more in line with the old American version, the B57. Whereas the ordinary Canberra cockpit was grossly uncomfortable for a tall pilot, the PR9 fighter cockpit was luxurious by comparison. However, it suffered markedly from problems in asymmetric flight because of the immense extra power of its 300-series Avon engines, but then all other Canberras had a much worse asymmetric problem due to the lack of powered controls to help counter the frequent engine surging so prevalent in their original 100-series engines. This, in turn, accounted for many Canberra fatalities over a 50 year life-span and still counting! You would have expected the PR9's differences to be reflected in the flying regulations. Not so!

Some of the regulations were not just pathetic but utterly insulting to any professional pilot. For example, all Canberras were forbidden to roll from a practise-asymmetric approach, with one hot and one cold engine, due to the

228

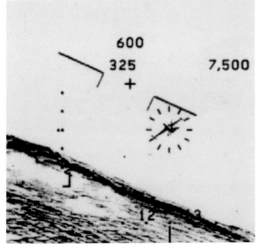

49. Harrier GR3 Air-to-Air Gun Sight through the HUD.

(© Crown Copyright/MOD)

50a & b. 1(F) Sqn tented encampment – Kirkwall air-field, Orkney, and a GR3 flies past the Old Man O'Hoy – Sep 78.

(©Crown Copyright/MOD)

51. Vertical landing accident – Wittering, Jun 79.

(© Crown Copyright/MOD)

52. Canberra PR9 of No 1 PRU – 1986

53. Infra-red vertical of March railway marshalling yards – 1986, (White is hot/black-cold) looking for underground fires.   (*©Crown Copyright/MOD*)

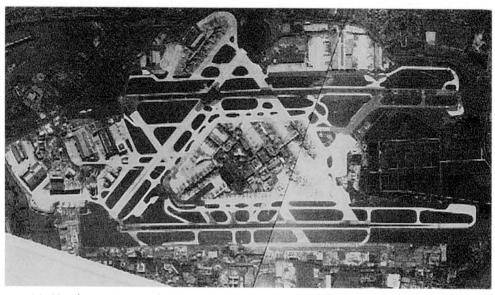

54. Heathrow Airport from 25,000ft – 1986   (*©Crown Copyright/MOD*)

55. The Briefing Team with Egyptian staff and students – Egyptian Air Force HQ, Cairo – 1988. L to R: Tony Stephens, EAF Colonel, Jack Stone, EAF Col, Peter Ruthen, another EAF Col, The Author.

56. With Air Marshal Bennett on the Omani/Yemeni Doha border. The Wadi bed is the border with South Yemen on the left. Note the holstered pistol provided by the Omanis…. just in case! Note the broken forearm – the result of an ice hockey accident.

57a & b. Bangladesh children sitting in the central sewer in Mouna's Dhaka slum – 1990.

58a &b. *Right:* The before: Mouna outside her mother's house in the slum 'street' where she lived.

Below: The after: Mouna in her posh frock – a borrowed wedding dress – with the team in the Sheraton Hotel, Dhaka.

59a. Val Taylor OBE – Founder of the CFRP and the unsung British Maria Theresa of Bangladesh – 1990.

59b. The Centre for the Rehabilitation of the Paralysed (CFRP) rickshaw – Savar, Bangladesh.

60. Chilean Tactical Presentation – 1991. Pete and I are in traditional Chilean cowboy uniforms.

61. The team hard at work – Dhaka Airport, Bangladesh 1990. I was delighted when Peter Ruthen, our guided weapons expert, on the left of the photo, was awarded the MBE for his obvious hard work in the department and with the team.

62. A shallow under-
ground burst – early testing Nevada desert.
   (© Glasstone and Dolan)

63. The Iowi Bridge. The T-shaped bridge which was at ground zero at
Hiroshima, still standing after the attack – Aug 45.

64. An Iraqi T62 tank exploding on the point of impact – Jan 91.

65. Kuwait North Road to Iraqi Border – Apr 91.

surge-prone 100-series engines. No exception was made for the PR9 with 300 series engines with no surge history . . . *because pilots may confuse it with one of the others!* It was so different; it should never have been called a Canberra! So PR9 continuation training was totally curtailed for no good reason, and I lost my flight because of it.

The time on 1 PRU was both fascinating and frustrating. A superb task ruined by shallow, opprobrious attitudes! Hence, I was more than happy to depart from there to the Air Warfare Centre as a Weapons Instructor. Nevertheless, the PR9's capability will now be surely missed: from missile sites to manhole covers, the PR9 could capture all.

Notes
1. See Chapter 18.
2. Hardened Aircraft Shelters (HAS) and similarly hardened aircrew accommodation meant one's working life was spent cut off from the outside world - no windows.

Chapter Twenty-Four

The Briefings

As one gets old with numerous years,
It is no good just shedding tears.
It's time to pass on all your teachings,
Nay, . . . profit them with many bleatings.

(The author – 1987)

THE WEAPON EMPLOYMENT COURSE (WEC)

For some years, towards the end of my time in the Air Force as a Weapons Instructor, I ran the RAF's Weapons Employment Course (WEC), commonly known as the Whitbread Enjoyment Course, ran the overseas Weapons Briefing Team, and became the Department of Air Warfare's nuclear weapons specialist. The department was the RAF's major academic institution for the post-graduate study of all aspects of air power, from the military aspects of space to the present doubtful pursuit of a fully developed and defined air power doctrine – a strict doctrine inhibiting imagination, and encouraging preparedness for the last war, not the next one.

The WEC lecture room was small, badly ventilated and crowded with examples of weapons, including the only WE177 nuke outside a barbed wire compound. Indeed, it was placed immediately under the only opening window. Every day, in order to reach the window, I had to climb on top of this nuclear bomb – presumably inert!

However, the WEC was a fun three week course with many visiting lecturers, the most explosive of which was our bomb disposal expert, Flt Lt Alan Swan MBE QGM, gongs well deserved from his bomb disposal bravery during the Falklands war. Al would always arrive early for his lecture and wire up the least popular student's briefcase or desk with various little detonators and IEDs (Incendiary Explosive Devices). After all, the odd bang kept the class awake, until one day he was wiring up an IED just after we had installed a new TV/video system. I switched this on and the IED blew up in his face! No damage, no injury, but a very shocked Al! The TV's electronic emissions were more than enough to set off a sensitive explosive device, and a salutary lesson for all of us. "That will teach him to wire up my briefcase on his last visit," went through my mind! I was so glad when he retired because after many years of bomb disposal work, he had the shakes . . . badly! He's fine now and continues to be a good friend.

During the second week of each course, I took the students to visit defence

230

industry, specifically: British Aerospace (BAe), the Royal Armament Research & Development Establishment (RARDE), and Hunting Engineering Ltd (HEL). The 3-day tour included two nights in London. In the early days we dressed in uniform and stayed at the RAF Club, even though we couldn't get breakfast unless we wore our No 1 best uniform. We had to be seen supporting the club, but on any one course there were always a number of non-members. These were accommodated as guests of the members in full compliance with club rules. As for breakfast, I had an arrangement with Betty who ran a Greasy Spoon just outside RARDE, and at 24 hours notice she would have 25 full-fry-ups ready as we came through the door for £1/head! But the truck drivers were extremely bemused by this invasion of uniformed officers!

Then the club banned non-member officers even though their introduction induced some to become members. This ludicrous ruling meant, in effect, that we could bring in a whore from round the corner in Shepherd's Market (and some did!), but not a non-member, fellow officer! We stayed at the Regents Palace Hotel instead: cheaper, more money in the boys pockets, and closer to the evening action! I resigned from the club in disgust!

At the same time, we were forced to change our dress code from uniform to civilian as the forces ran scared of the IRA et al, and any pride we had left in wearing pullovers under flasher's macs soon dissipated.

HEL manufactured a number of weapons for the RAF including BL755 our cluster bomb, and JP233 our runway denial weapon, the RAF's most expensive weapons system at the time. These were the days when the air force concentrated on trying to crater Soviet concrete as preferred but faulty reasoning over the prevention of their air operations. It didn't even stop the Iraqis! Nevertheless, a new concrete-busting, sub-munition was invented. After landing and lying on the surface, it used springs to erect to the vertical. It then fired a hollow, steel spike through the runway surface and injected a liquid explosive under the concrete, which detonated from the end of the spike to produce a crater. It was christened: ORGASM! Why? Because it lay down, had an erection, penetrated, ejaculated, and, boy, . . . the earth really moved!

After my last course, The Air Force couldn't dine me out before I left, but after 33 years service, both HEL and BAe each presented me with magnificent leaving gifts. That was really good of them.

THE BRIEFING TEAM

Despite the lack of real flying on this ground tour, I travelled further and more widely when running the overseas Weapons Briefing Team than during the rest of my time in the Air Force. The team carved a reputation for open and honest lecturing around the world, mainly to other air forces staff but sometimes to army, navy and civil servants. In so doing the word spread, and the team, or elements of the team, were invited to Bangladesh, Canada, Chile, Egypt, Germany, Holland, Jordan, Malaysia, Muscat and Oman, the NATO Staff College, Saudi Arabia, Singapore, Sweden, Switzerland, the Trucial States, and the United States. More to the point, many invitations to return followed these visits.

A nucleus of three members, sometimes up to five, we couldn't always rely on satisfactory host nation technical support so we took with us three weighty crates crammed with essentials – slide projectors, videos, reams of lecture notes and handouts etc., enough for ten to fifteen working days' worth of lectures. These boxes caused many amusing incidents, but our excess baggage bill was enormous!

Our first regular overseas customer was Egypt, fascinating not only for its culture but for the coincidence of being where our subject had originated. Modern air-delivered weaponeering was born out of the fracas of our serious bombing failures at Suez in 1956. Then our Valients and Canberras bombed nine Egyptian airfields using over one thousand, 1000lb bombs. Not only were none of the airfields put out of action, but Cairo International was bombed in error, when trying to hit Cairo West some seven miles away. Now here we were teaching the Egyptians about weaponeering!

The leader of the Cairo West raid, later as an Air Commodore, amazingly, had no idea they'd bombed the wrong airfield until after 29 years when I lectured to our Staff College in 1985! Luckily, after a public rebuttal in front of the whole staff college, I was able to produce the official Bomber Command report of the raid from which my information was sourced. He then blamed the target markers of 139 Sqn! I still have his apologetic memo, but from fiascos such as that came modern weapons planning.

On our second Egyptian trip, two of us took our wives along. We flew BA Club Class. The wives went bucket-shop, Balkan Air, cattle class at gun-point in Sofia! As we were each arriving at Cairo airport at similar times but different terminals, the air attaché, through whom the visit had been arranged, met the girls, leaving his Egyptian driver to meet us. Somehow something was lost in the translation as the driver attempted to smooth our passage through customs. In so doing they were led to believe that our boxes contained aircraft spares! Imagine three cubic metres of lecture material spread out across the tiled customs hall at Cairo International, and the ensuing chaos! Half an hour of arguments later the air attaché arrived, whereupon the chief customs officer was summoned, and oil was poured on troubled waters! Surprisingly, the Egyptian Air Force (EAF), unlike most other Air Forces, hadn't met us and guided us through their own bureaucracy, and they very nearly didn't get their fortnight's lecture course.

If Egypt was bad, then Saudi was much worse. Everything had to go in the diplomatic bag to avoid confiscation by their thought police/customs on arrival. Many were the tales of losing all lecture materials for ten days or more, some never to be returned. How hypocritical can nations become – a major government organisation invites you to lecture, then confiscates your lecture materials! Joined-up thinking is something all governments need!

Even worse was to come! On our third trip to Egypt the following year, all went well through customs on the Wednesday. We had previously arranged with the air attaché to meet the following morning at the Egyptian Air Force HQ to set up our lecture rooms, after which we had the weekend free (Friday-Saturday). On arrival at the HQ on Thursday morning, I well remember walking down the same corridor of the Weapons Department as we had done the previous year, knocking on the Colonel's office door and walking in. He looked up from behind his desk and said, *"Hello, Chris. Good to see you, but what an earth are you doing here?"* On telling him we'd come to give them the same course as last year, he was astounded, making it quite clear that he'd no idea we were coming, and no course of any sort had been arranged! At this, we all looked questioningly at the air attaché who went red in the face.

While they sorted out the problems, the girls and the team went back to our hotel where we spent a worrying weekend wondering what was going to happen. We were in a real quandary! With no course we would have to return to UK, but the girls were on a bucket-shop, non-transferable, flight ticket for a fortnight later. Not only that, they were sharing our hotel rooms, paid for by the government, and only paying for their food! Without an enormous bill, we could not return home and leave them there!

After three days of inaction and worry, all was finally solved. Apparently, the air attaché had arranged the course through the EAF's Navigation Division, under which was, inter alia, their Weapons Department. No one in the Navigation Division had bothered to tell the Weapons Dept of this arrangement! As some might say, typical of navigators – they could never organise a booze-up in a brewery! Even so, I must give the Weapons Dept their due – over the weekend they'd organised a full course for us, and we only lost one day's worth of lectures. It was a close call but, in typical Arab fashion, face was saved all round, and the girls had their cheap Egyptian holiday!

After three visits, most countries picked up enough to organise their own courses. Nevertheless, as a perk of the trade, we were always able to take advantage of tours around the sights. In Egypt these included the Pyramids and Sphinx, Luxor, Karnak and the Valley of the Kings and Queens, Philae, Abu Simbel, Aswan, and Sharm El Sheik. Pimms on the Nile in an Arab Felucca boat was a real treat, but Gin and tonics at sunset overlooking the first cataract of the Nile on the veranda of the Old Cataract Hotel at Aswan, proved moments to treasure.

Here at Aswan we learnt another cultural lesson. Abu Simbel that day sweltered in fifty-one degrees in the shade. Arriving at the hotel after a long day's flight direct from Cairo to Abu Simbel, then on to Aswan, and a boat trip to Philae, my wife fell over with sodium deficiency, and became very ill. The Arab girls thought she had stomach problems and forced raw lemon juice, a known antiseptic, down her throat but to no avail. Putting her to bed in the Old Cataract Hotel, the receptionist called a doctor. It was a Friday, their holy day, and everything was closed. Yet the doctor was there within thirty minutes. Summing up the situation, he sent out for an intravenous drip, some saline solution and three or four drugs, which again arrived within thirty minutes. He fixed the whole lot over her hotel bed, and sat with her for four hours until the whole solution had been used up and she was just about fully recovered. It was an impressive medical display. Then he presented his bill – the Egyptian equivalent of only twenty pounds sterling! I was astounded, especially when he said this included the drugs, the taxi fare and a big tip for the receptionist who'd done all the telephoning!

Three days later, when we met him by coincidence on the plane back from Luxor to Cairo, the doctor explained that the Egyptian health service was extremely well funded by the government, including provision of high quality staff. Their premise was that all were entitled to the same health benefits, and the vast majority of their population, being extremely poor, were unable to afford the full price. Does that sound like the NHS? Yes, but the Egyptians do it efficiently! I shall never ever complain about overseas medical facilities again – the five-star service made our NHS appear a disorganised shambles.

In 1989, my weapons team was invited to Muscat to lecture to the Sultan of Oman's Air Force (SOAF) at Thumrait, or Midway as we had known it back in the '60s because it was midway between Khormaksar and Masirah Island. I hadn't been there since Aden days and for a long time it had only been a rolled sand strip. Despite that, Midway had been our only diversion in that 1,000miles along the southern coastline, especially if Salalah was out in fog. Even then, we would put our Hunter T7 down on the oiled sand at Salalah simply because carrying only 100gallon drop tanks instead of the 230gallon tanks of the Mk9, the two-seater version didn't have the same range. And, boy, on rolled sand was it ever bumpy in aircraft with high-pressure tyres, though probably a good experience before trying to fly Harriers off the grass!

Renowned for both operational capability and lack of rules, the SOAF fly lower and faster than anyone. Originally stocked with pilots seconded from the RAF, it now uses mercenaries (mainly ex-RAF) alongside its own nationals. They had only one rule: "Don't F . . . Up!" If you did, you were on your bike back home with no ceremony. There was no Rule 2! Then the Omanis bought Jaguars and, within days, the Midway station commander was forced to write his first flying order. It was a simple one sentence order: *"Thou shall not fly supersonic underneath the water tower!"* This was not an attempt to reduce low flying over the base, more the conservation of water in a desert land – their only source of water was an old, rickety, wooden tower which swayed in the sonic booms!

On arriving at Midway, up on the top of the Jebel just north of Salalah, I purposely looked for their flying order book. It was refreshing to find one thin order book, in contrast to own own voluminous, encyclopaedic tomes. I purposely again turned to their order regulating low flying, simply because ours was the longest order in the book, to find but a single page on which was printed one single sentence: *"1. Low flying is operationally necessary."* Pilots were left to make their own judgement about the height to fly – how refreshing!

What a stimulating and inspirational way of writing orders! However, one low flying incident did occur. One of their pilots became the luckiest man alive when, while driving on top of the Jebel, on looking in his rear-view mirror, he ducked as a Jaguar's lower tailfins took the whole top off his car leaving him amazingly untouched.

To my surprise, six of the Hunters at Thumrait had been the same RAF ones that I had flown in Aden back in the '60s, including my own aircraft XG255, now No. 825 of the SOAF. Indeed XG255 was the plane I flew to Amman in Sep '67, when we gave it to the RJAF. It had first flown as a Mk6 in Dec '55, after being built by Hawker Siddeley at Kingston, and had seen thirty-four years service with three different Air Forces, nearly all in the appallingly corrosive environment of the Middle East, and it was still going strong! They don't build them like that any more! Now, some thirty-four years after manufacture and sixteen years after I last flew a Hunter, the Omanis were going to celebrate my return to these aircraft by letting me once again fly one. But there's always a catch! I was still wearing a plaster cast on my left arm, having broken my wrist while refereeing a premier division ice hockey match at Nottingham Ice Stadium some weeks earlier. The RAF wouldn't have allowed it, but that wasn't going to stop me: the Omanis didn't care – there was no namby-pamby Health and Safety Act here!

The fascinating part of this Hunter flight was the beginning. I walked out to the aircraft, completed the walk-round checks, sorted out the ejection seat, and strapped in without any forethought, as though I had been doing it every day of my life. I acted almost robotically as all the procedures flooded back with absolute precision. My familiarity with this beautiful aircraft had not faded after all that time.

We had been for a low level run through the wadis and over the coast, where turtles, sharks and rays abounded and, despite our speed (450kts), could be seen easily from the Hunter. We then tried some remarkably accurate, sixty degree dive bombing, which was frighteningly steep and thrilling. It reminded me of film seen of Stuka dive-bombers during WW2. In RAF Hunters, we had only used a 30 degree dive angle, and that was steep enough. Sixty degrees is very steep indeed but, of course, much more accurate in weapons delivery. We then returned to beat up the airfield! The photo on the front cover is of this flypast, approximately ten feet off the deck at 500kts, while screaming across the aircraft dispersal at Thumrait on 30 Oct 89.

Air Vice Marshal Bennett RAF, who retired as Sir Eric – Commander of the SOAF, had also started up and ran the RJAF. He then built the SOAF from scratch and turned it into the well respected outfit it is today. In 1989, he took me specially by Huey chopper from Thumrait via Salalah to the Doha border. Once there, we sat in a sanger on top of the Jebel overlooking the border wadi with Southern Yemen. We discussed at length the various targets visible on the other side of the border and how to attack them, which tactics to use, which weapons and the different effects they would have, and indeed, which would be the best way to safely deliver those weapons against the Yemeni defences. Here was a well respected and most operationally minded Commander, listening to advice – and this made a pleasant change!

Having delivered RJAF Hunters to Amman in 1967 (see Chapter 15), and received their excellent hospitality first hand, I was delighted to be invited back on three separate occasions during the late '80s and early '90s to give their Air Force operational courses on each visit. On the last two visits we were sent to their airfield at Azraq, an oasis air force base half-way between Amman and the Iraqi border on the main road to Baghdad. Having already seen the Jerash Roman ruins, The Dead Sea, Aquaba, and the Living City of Petra during that 1967 visit, I was even more delighted to be taken to see the old fort at Azraq Oasis. Here we were mentally transmogrified back into the 13th century, but for me the sense of history was nothing like that old. This ancient Fort had also been Captain Lawrence's HQ during his time leading the Arab army against the Turks in WW1. It was from here that he subsequently set out on his march to liberate Damascus and provide the Arabs, so he originally thought, with the freedom and independence promised by the British. The consequent combined British/French deception in carving up the Arab lands between them, and making provision for a Zionist state in their midst, was probably the first of many deceitful decisions which lost the British the hearts and minds of the Arabs. The issues of 1917 were little different from those of today in the Middle East. Our redrawing of the Middle Eastern map, our constant duplicity in 1947 as in Aden and the Gulf in the '60s, lost us the title of the 'honest Englishman' in their eyes. Therefore, it was a rare treat to stand in the very rooms in Azraq Fort where Lawrence had previously stood to plan the downfall of a city one hundred miles North across the desert, Damascus.

On the second visit we were accommodated at the same Amra hotel on the 6th circle in Amman and flown out to Azraq daily. On the third visit, just after the Gulf War, we were given an old married quarter on the Azraq airbase, and were fed in their Air Force canteen – they were, unsurprisingly, more than a little short of funds![1] The food was just about acceptable if you had the scrambled egg three times daily, but the MQ was something else! A three bedroomed, single-storey, white painted, flat roofed building backing on to the main Aqaba-Baghdad desert road, it hadn't been opened for over a year. The road was busier than the M25, with supply lorries for Iraq continuing both ways in constant convoys twenty-four hours a day. When we arrived and finally unlocked the door, late the first day, we were met by awfully stale-air and a putrid stink. Emanating from the kitchen was this fetid, rancid smell. On investigation we found mouldy, congealed food in every drawer and cupboard, and on every plate, cup and saucer. The toilets were unmentionable, and then we found that the beds, mattresses, sheets and blankets were stained with every possible human excretion, including blood. The place was uninhabitable, but at that late hour of the night we had no alternative but to sleep in these awful surroundings. Hey-ho – take the rough with the smooth and get on with life!

After a most uncomfortable night, a visit to the Base Commander's office became inevitable. What a great way to introduce oneself – complaining about the standard of their accommodation! After the unavoidable green tea and with diplomacy to the fore, we explained the problem and left quickly to set up our lecture room. Returning to the quarter at lunch-time we found every stick of furniture and this included the soft furnishings, out on the sand surrounds or on the road and being hosed down by some dozen airmen with a high pressure hose! Inside was more of the same – the place was awash and dripping from the ceilings. The whole building was being washed down from roof to tiled floors with a hosepipe. Beating a hasty retreat, we decided to leave and let them get on with it! Then, when we returned at the end of the working day, not only was everything spotless, but also dry; 35 degrees in the shade helped! Clean sheets and blankets had been arranged, and as a face-saving way of apologizing, they'd filled the large fridge with Fantas and Cokes and various other soft drinks – no alcohol, mind you!

In return, a few nights later, we cooked a nine-course dinner for six of them, but a dinner the like of which you've never seen before. Among other items on the menu was a tin of condensed Campbell's vegetable soup to start, some local sausages, and a tin of cubed fruit salad garnished with some local chopped-up apples for sweet, all washed down with orange juice and instant coffee with condensed milk in little, Arabic, handleless cups bought locally. The evening ended with a box of marshmallows and one of Turkish Delight, which they loved – the Arabs do like their sweet cookies – but this was Michelin stars above the airforce mess food and a real banquet out in the desert. Still without alcohol, we flew on Alia, the Royal Jordanian airline, and as a classic example of Arabic hypocrisy, Alia is alcoholically dry when flying towards Jordan, but wet on its outbound flights!

The RJAF were normally extremely hospitable, taking us to see the sights of their land, but on this last visit immediately after the Gulf War, all was different. It didn't help that on that visit I was stung by the Delhi-belly so badly that they took me into the RJAF hospital in Amman for observation for a couple of days, and a clean, well-run hospital it was too. Yet another country whose health service far surpassed our NHS! On my second day there I was astounded to receive a bunch of flowers with a handwritten card from none other than Air Vice Marshal Ihsan 'Sammy' H.Shurdom, the Chief of Air Staff of the RJAF, or, as he simply wrote it: CO RJAF! I reckon I'm the only RAF officer to have ever received pink carnations from a Chief of any Air Staff, never mind a Major General in any army[2]! Can you imagine that happening in this country? What a lovely gesture, and it brought home the close relationship between the two Air Forces engendered by King Hussein who had his RAF wings and was an honorary member of No.6 Sqn RAF.

After leaving hospital, the air attaché prevailed upon me to give my new lecture on 'Lessons of the Gulf War'[3] not only to their complete Air Force HQ staff, but also to the Jordanian Army HQ staff. Many of them were Sunni Arabs, and Hashemites of the same tribe as Saddam Hussein. While the Air Force officers would happily discuss matters amicably, the army was definitely on the Iraqi side and most unsympathetic to the western cause. Never in thirty-three years of lecturing have I spoken to a more hostile audience. You could hear a pin drop in that lecture theatre, and at the end, without ceremony or thanks, they equally silently rose and departed. Air Marshal Shurdom met us afterwards on the steps of his HQ, where among other things we discussed the war. He was a fine man, and his final parting words suggested that we should now really look to the future. It was June 1991.

In June 1990 Switzerland as a neutral country surprised us by inviting the team to lecture to their own weapons instructors at the Swiss Air Force base of Payenne, just north of Geneva. Here I achieved yet another dream – flying a Hunter, low level, around the Swiss Alps. Having spent many years flying around Germany at low level, only seeing the Alps at a distance from the German/Swiss border, my ambition had always been to get among them in a fast-jet. Major Walter Shafroth of the Swiss Air Force kindly obliged in a thrilling flight over the Alps.

I also learnt something new that day about flying: how to make an approach to land in the mountains! Until then it had never occurred to me, as we always conducted either a three or two and a half degree, gentle, glide-slope for straight-in radar or instrument approaches. What happens when there's a mountain in the way? At Payenne, the approach path was a massive, twelve degree glide-slope, and there are steeper ones. Twelve degrees required a six-thousand foot approach level in or above cloud. Descent was then commenced by lowering both undercarriage and full flap, throttling right back to idle. This configuration at approach speed generates a 12-degree glide path through cloud, descending at 1200 feet per mile or 3600 feet per minute, not unlike our 1in1 gliding approach, which in turn puts you at 1200 feet above the runway with one mile to go to touchdown. I didn't ask what his legal break off height was, but there's one hell of a round out before touchdown with an almost useless idling engine, very early use of the brake chute – and it works! Hence, an exhilarating flight round the Alps ended with quite a frightening approach in thick cloud to land! Nevertheless, I wouldn't have missed that sortie for any other flight!

Though Chile was exceptional, the Omani and Swiss Air Forces visits rated at the top simply because both air forces flew me in their Hunters. On each occasion I learnt something new about the machine that had been my favourite overcoat for many years. In Muscat I learnt about low flying and fired some weapons I hadn't used before, and in Switzerland I experienced mountain flying in the Alps. The excellent visit to the Swiss ended with a presentation, not only of an official Swiss Air Force photographic-book suitably inscribed, but also – surprise, surprise – a Swiss Army (well, Air Force actually) penknife!

Bangladesh was one of our regular annual visits. Invited to lecture at length to their combined services staff college, I was not surprised that under the Bangla Commandant, Maj Gen Nassim, their college was run by three deputy commandants: a British Brigadier, Christopher Wolverson, a British Naval Captain, Tony Peters, and a British Group Captain RAF, Tony Stephens. Consequently, the college had an excellent international reputation and catered for forty-four different nationalities including the USA. Hence, we ourselves learnt much about the thoughts and ideals of many other nations, mainly Asian and African.

The three British officers, together with the air attaché from the embassy, ensured we had a non-stop whirlwind of visits, parties and social occasions. One of them was always the Dhaka equivalent of 'Pimms on the Nile!' A long, shallow-draft, inboard motorboat, with the rear deck covered with a canvas awning, allowed a pleasant afternoon cruising round Dhaka with a picnic and Pimms. Dhaka, of course, is built close to the confluence of two of the great Asian rivers: the Ganges and the Brahmaputra, just before they spread out into the Ganges delta. These two rivers between them drain the whole of the long, southern line of the Himalayas. The continual flooding is not helped by the addition of the Rivers Jamma, Padma, Meghna, Turag and the Buriganga, each of which is pretty large in its own right but the latter of which flows right through Dhaka. So vast and changeable are the watercourses of these great rivers joining here that we reckoned it was possible to cruise right round the city at any time, yet never the same way twice!

Bangladesh should rate a full chapter on its own. A fascinating, seething cauldron of humanity all learning to live on, over, in and around water. It must be the wettest place on earth, and together with the low lying flatlands of the coastal plain and the Ganges delta, there is more area underwater than above it. Unpainted, thatched, wooden and corrugated iron hovels on spindly stilts sway over shallow brackish water, and vie with each other for the right to collapse in the next typhoon. Every colour, smell and noise is on display in a brightly coloured, cacophony of bodies, rickshaws and tricycles. Bare feet proved the order of the day; any form of footwear would collapse and rot in this sodden land with its 100% humidity and 35 degrees in the shade.

The Bangla currency is called the taka. In the late '80s, it exchanged at four taka to the sterling **PENNY**. One taka was equal to an old farthing! The smallest note is a one taka note, and there are 100 cents to a taka, one cent being **ONE FOUR HUNDREDTH OF A PENNY** sterling! There are families there that never see a one taka note; they live on the coinage below the farthing level. This sounds poor; it is poor, but consider that ten taka, or two and a half pence, would keep the family in rice for a month!

There was a bunch of lovely, friendly, but ragged and bare-footed children from the local slum, selling little flower garlands outside the Sheraton Hotel, one of only two hotels in town of western standard, where we stayed. The eldest, Mouna, was, she said, twelve years old and getting married next year! For one taka you could have every garland in her bag! But the children were not allowed into the hotel grounds. Indeed, despite living outside this grand hotel for twelve years, none of them had ever seen inside it. My wife gave Mouna something every day, and eventually she took us to see her mother and family in the little corrugated-iron and raffia fleapit where she lived. It was one of the dirtiest, smelliest slums you could ever imagine with four foot wide, muddy, watery alleyways full of detritus and sewage. There were one-room hovels on either side, hers being a ten-foot square box of corrugated iron in which five of them lived, with no father and no income except what the three eldest girls could beg.

Sitting us down, the Mother sent Mouna off with some coins from a little tin she found tucked away in a corner under some fabric. On returning five minutes later, Mouna gave us each a bottle of orange Fanta to slake our thirst. I have never felt so humble in my life.

The next day we took three of them, Mouna, her little sister and one of the boys shopping, where we found a "smart" Bata shoe shop amongst the filthy market stalls, and bought them each a pair of flip-flops. The following morning, on leaving the hotel, the boy was missing and we asked after him. After a lot of persuasion Mouna finally spoke up to say that the boy wouldn't come because he'd sold the flip-flops and couldn't face us. She went on to say that for the money he got for the flip-flops, his family could buy food for the next two months. We learnt some very hard lessons about life in Bangladesh, not least from the little children.

As a treat for Mouna before we left, we told her that if she got dressed up in a posh frock and put shoes on her feet (an hotel rule), we would take her for a tour round the hotel. We've never seen children so excited! The next day, Mouna arrived looking so lovely we almost didn't recognise her. She had borrowed a friend's wedding dress and shoes, got scrubbed up, her mother had done her hair immaculately with purple bows, and I'd have been proud to have presented her to the Queen.

Initially, the faces of the army guards at the front of the hotel were pictures of indecision and awe as we all took Mouna across the driveway and through the front entrance. They did not know what to do – the children were not allowed in, but the big white Sahibs were taking her in by the hand – should they obey orders, stop the street urchins at gunpoint and incur our wrath, or tactically withdraw and ignore the situation. Help!! In the end they ignored their orders, and all was smiles and big grins. But Mouna's face was a real picture – she'd never seen anywhere with such opulence as was on show in the foyer and lounges of a Sheraton Hotel – fitted carpets, soft sofas, wallpaper and chandeliers were all totally alien to her. As she was shown round her eyes grew wider in wonder. By the time we had shown her our bedroom and those 'normal' en suite facilities, some of which she couldn't understand – the bidet for example which is difficult to translate – she couldn't believe her eyes, no matter how wide they'd become! She'd been selling garlands outside this hotel ever since she could crawl, and had no idea what was inside – indeed, no idea that five star sumptuousness even existed. To end the visit, we all had tea and Fantas in the lounge, and Mouna went off to her friends, no doubt to retell the story of that visit for the rest of her life.

We saw Mouna for three years running, and kept in touch for a couple of years afterwards through team members visiting Dhaka, but then sadly lost touch. We believe she was married off and moved away. Pity, we'd love to know how she is doing – she had intended to become a nurse but probably has five kids by now. If she ever emigrates to the UK, tell her to look me up – we'd love to see her again[4].

Originally through Christine, an ex-PMRAFNS nursing sister and the wife of Peter Ruthen, our guided weapons specialist, the team sponsored a Bangladeshi charity. It was then a small, poor charity catering for the paralysed in the back streets of Dhaka, run by an English physiotherapist called Val Taylor (now Val Taylor OBE, for a lifetime of charitable work in the country). The charity is called The Centre for the Rehabilitation of the Paralysed (CFRP), and Christine used to help out there during the team's first few visits. Gradually, the charity did well enough to move North out of town to Savar and build a much better facility which we visited every year with well-received supplies from the UK. Before each visit, Peter and Co, and his successors, would raid all the local UK hospitals and military doctors' surgeries, begging, borrowing and filching any date-expired, medical supplies. At least five enormous cartons, each of two cubic metres, were usually filled for the CFRP, and conveyed to Bangladesh. As we flew British Airways Club Class each time, the airline was persuaded to fly these supplies for free – a real bonus as we were looking at over 100kgs of excess baggage each time. It helped, of course, that BA supported its own orphanage in the country. Dhaka airport customs were a bigger problem, however! On most occasions we had to plead with their Staff College Commandant, Major-General Nasim, and therefore a big noise in the country, to intercede on our behalf. It sometimes took days but, like the Pony Express, the supplies always got through!

On one memorable visit to the CFRP, driving in a convoy of Landrovers with the British Brigadier, Christopher Wolverson, we were stopped by an enormous traffic jam on the main road on the outskirts of a small, local village some twenty miles North of Dhaka. Being sent up the avenue on foot to investigate, it became apparent that the jam was caused by a single coach driver who had had an argument with the village elder, and then stomped off in a huff, leaving his coach across the road. This '30-seater' coach still had sixty-nine passengers in it, and some on top, but on looking more closely, I noticed the fool of a driver had left his keys in the ignition! Never having been accused of looking a gift-horse in the mouth, I immediately jumped into the driver's seat, started it up, and am now qualified to drive Bangladeshi public transport coaches! However, no-one would ever insure me! A short drive off the road followed with some improvised traffic-policing sign, verbal and blasphemous language, the like of which was well understood by the locals, and I had the traffic moving again in no time. Bring back the Raj, that's what I say – they never had it so good!

If driving Bangla coaches in a traffic jam is hilarious, try driving a Bangla rickshaw through the centre of Dhaka! In the 1980s there were conservatively estimated to be 88,000 rickshaws in Dhaka alone, and over 750,000 in Bangladesh employing over one million people – just a touch crowded, and that's without the passengers! On one of the many social occasions we were invited to the Brigadier's villa on the outskirts of town for an evening cocktail party. On departing at 2am, our transport had disappeared and there was no way back to the hotel – some five miles away – other than by rickshaw. Five rickshaws were duly hired, and a race developed back to the hotel with each of us urging/bribing our individual drivers. Somehow the whole shenanigan deteriorated into a five-abreast charge down the main street with our drivers in the back and us doing the pedalling. Then one of our group, Potty Chambers, fell out and I ran over him. The race being paramount, he was frantically gathered up and dumped in the back with the driver. Then on came a flashing blue light, and we were arrested for being drunk in charge of rickshaws! Eventually, a few taka changed hands, good humour came to the fore, and the race resumed – this time with a police escort all the way back to the hotel! Who won remains a matter of controversy as a dispute arose as to the exact position of the finishing point, but we have a cast iron case if it ever goes to court – I have two perfectly impartial witnesses: my wife who was in the back of the rickshaw and the Dhaka Copper who nicked us!

On arriving home from the 1991 Gulf War, awaiting me was an invitation to lecture in Chile.

Peter Ruthen and I flew out for the best fortnight's hospitality we could have wished for, commencing with first-class travel on their airline, Lanchile: a never to be forgotten, unique experience. When we were first invited to lecture there, Chile had just come through a shoddy little civil war, CIA backed, to return it into the western world from the deeply worrying, communist times of Allende. After putting his country on the soundest economic footing in South America, General and President Pinochet was the only dictator in the world to voluntarily give up his power in order to hold fully fair general elections allowing democracy to evolve.

What is little known was that the Russians had spent twice as much on Allende as the CIA did on Pinochet. He not only saved the country from the horrors of Allende's brutal communist regime but also created a model economy that was the envy of most of Latin America. I would not call that repressive. In his book on geopolitics, written when he was a Colonel on the Chilean General Staff back in 1968, Pinochet wrote, "*Geopolitics . . . shows . . . the objectives of the State and how they could be met in the future, so as to ensure peace, happiness, and the general well-being of his people.*" This is not the writing of a tyrannical oppressor, more that of a benign President doing his best for his country and people in difficult circumstances, which is more than can be said for our present government or any left-wing dictator in history.

241

Probably the crassest political act of the millenium was that of the British Government's incarceration of Pinochet, a well-respected ex-head of state, during a medical visit to this country. Jack Straw's inane blundering action in imprisoning Pinochet in London was nothing less than schoolboy spite; he should be ashamed of himself. It showed the narrow-mindedness of our collective cabinet and, at government level, beggared belief! How can we justify that, whilst letting the likes of Mugabe run free?

One little known aspect of the Chilean palace coup is that it was orchestrated by the Chilean Air Force (Fuerza Aerea De Chile (FADC)). Two Hunter pilots of the No 8 Groupe at Antofagusta rocketed the palace and, it appears, killed Allende, though there is some doubt as to the exact cause of his death. The finale to the story, from the FADC viewpoint, is that these two pilots are still in the air force, and well-respected senior officers. Everyone in the Hunter Wing knows who they are, yet no one will tell; it is one of their best-guarded secrets!

Despite its narrow 75 mile width, Chile's three thousand mile length encompasses almost every type of weather and geographical feature, from the driest desert in the world – the Atacama – through the rainiest area south of Porte Monte including volcanoes and glaciers, to wild Cape Horn and the frozen white wilderness of the Antarctic. Of all the countries the team visited, Chile was to be the most pleasant, welcoming and embarrassingly generous. The people were the friendliest I came across in thirty-three years of globetrotting. Of course it helped that we were looked after so well, in such fine spirit, and with such good manners and politeness. On the first visit, Major Jorge Abello, and on the second, Commandante Pato, were designated as our guides. Jorge, the quintessential, Latin fighter pilot, on being asked whether he was married, replied, *"Si, é no fanatico!"* summing up his playboy image.

In the Spring of 1982 Pato had piloted the Chilean aircraft sent to a southern up-country airstrip to pick up a British Army Patrol. After landing in the dark and on alighting with his co-pilot from the aircraft, he realized that there was no-one there, when suddenly eight of them stood up only four yards in front of him! He remarked, "They're funny people, aren't they?"

Both Jorge and Pato overwhelmed us with both FADC and personal generosity. Such was their hospitality that one weekend our hosts flew us South to Porte Monte, motto: *'It always rains in Porte Monte!'* – where we were housed in a little wooden airforce hospitality chalet overlooking the harbour and the Pacific Ocean. Walking into the chalet we found a bottle of Black Label, Johnny Walker in the lounge. As usual after RAF stinginess we thought it had been left there by mistake! It had not – it was for us!

The final weekend of our second visit was the most remarkable. Having nearly made the Antarctic with the British Antarctic Survey many years earlier, it had been one of my ambitions to see that continent. At some time during the visit to Chile I must have mentioned this in conversation. On the last working day with a free weekend before our flight home, with the usual formal presentations and luncheon at their Country Club, their General-of-Operations arrived from their Defence Ministry to present the certificates and exchange of gifts. Afterwards – mid-Friday afternoon – he collared me, saying that, if we got a move on, there was an Air Force Boeing 707 waiting for us at Santiago airport to fly us down to Cape Horn and Punta Arenas on the Southern tip of South America. He couldn't promise, but if we got there in time, there was a Hercules from Punta Arenus on a resupply mission to Antarctica and a seat for me if I wanted to go! Did I? I couldn't get to the aircraft fast enough! How can one ever repay such amazing hospitality? I came home absolutely dazed and, indeed, another member of the team even married a Chilean girl, one of our interpreters, whom he had met on this visit.

As well as all the attributes already mentioned, I should make note of a couple more, especially as some Brits seem to have the wrong impression of that country, garnered from our gutter press. Santiago was the one capital city in the world that in the early hours I was happy to walk around in complete safety. Even the girls walking home from bars and cafes and night clubs could do so without fear. Every street corner had a policeman on it and, yes, they were armed, but you'd not find hooligans, graffiti, rubbish dropped, or any unsavoury characters lurking in the shadows. Everyone, in typical Latin style, went out to enjoy themselves in the evening: no one went out just for dinner, always for a dinner-dance. Every restaurant had its own little three-piece band in the corner and a dance floor. Everyone danced with everyone else in the place, and the men escorted the girls back to their tables after each dance with almost old-fashioned but welcome politeness.

In the slight hope of paying back some hospitality, Peter and I invited our two escort officers, together with the two senior students from our course, to an evening out on our penultimate night in Chile. We went to a typical Santiago restaurant that also had a floorshow. That evening we had an excellent seven-course meal, uncountable bottles of wine and drinks, a two-hour floorshow, and danced until four o'clock in the morning. For the six of us the total bill was £90 – £15 per head – and that included a big tip! Chile is by Western standards exceptionally inexpensive.

Awaiting my return from Chile was an invitation to be the reviewing officer when "my" Standard from Aden days was finally laid up. Twenty-five years after my Standard presentation in Aden in 1967, my first Sqn, No 8, now at RAF Waddington as the RAF's AWACs[5] Sqn, was to be the first ever to receive a third Standard. I was to review the parade when "my" old Standard was paraded off and laid up for the last time on 28th May 1992. The Duke of Gloucester was hurriedly asked to present the new Standard when Princess Margaret cancelled at the last minute. She may have cried off, but I bit back a few tears as I saluted from the dais while "my" Standard was marched off for the last time. It felt like the end of an era, and symbolized finally for me the end of Empire over which my wings had flown, as we put that Squadron Standard to bed for the last time.

However, there was the little matter of the Gulf War to face before one could look towards the future with any confidence.

Notes
1. The usual funding was for all in-country expenses to be paid by the host nation, and all out-of-country expenses such as the flights paid by the UK.

2. Shurdom's title was variously Major General or Air Vice Marshal, depending on which force one was addressing. The RJAF was actually a branch of the army, hence the Maj Gen title.
3. See Chapter 27. Having spent the Gulf War with the US Defence Intelligence Agency in Washington, I was given a profound understanding of the war. With my classified lecture materials available, I was able to produce such a lecture.
4. Her full name was MOUNA NAZMA SAUNWORA at Poriabag PG Hospital, E staff quarters, Dakha 1000.
5. AWACs = Airborne Warning And Control.

Chapter Twenty-Five

Nuclear Weapons

"There's nothing so cold as an icy heart,
nor the threat of a nuke to drown your fart.
But Warsaw Pact central heating's
One hell of a way to give them a beating."

(The author – 1975)

Of course, the Cold War could never have happened without the advent and wide distribution of nuclear weapons – that's what the superpower strategies were all about. As a nuclear weapon specialist I dealt not only in our own air force capability, but also had a brief to keep in touch with both Allied and Soviet nuclear potentials. Nevertheless, I must stress that all of us in the military approached the nuclear role like any other – from a professional military viewpoint – and rarely, if ever, discussed the morality of their use. It was taken as read that if ordered to drop a nuke we'd do so, believing this would only happen in dire and proper circumstances.

The arguments over the use of nuclear weapons are well beyond the scope of this book, but since I lectured on the subject later in my career throughout the western military world, some opinion remains valid. I have to nail some colours to the mast at this point; I am a convert from an extreme hawk to a semi-dove though not without some serious reservations. Through the 1960s to the '80s, at the time of our flexible response strategy, I and most of my peers advocated, (even in the nuclear sphere) aggressive, warlike policies. We thought that in order to maintain the western "free" way of life, we were quite willing to see nuclear use if militarily necessary; this is what the forces were all about in those days. Indeed, I would go so far as to say that the world had never been so secure – constant wars before the advent of nuke, constant nationalism and terrorism ever since, with comparative stability in the middle! Modern terrorism, eg: 9/11, I would suggest, has affected the average citizen's everyday life far more than anything before. In the nuclear age, say, between Suez (1956) and when the Berlin Wall came down (1989) as the precursor to the end of the Cold War, besides Vietnam can anyone remember any significant war? Only the localised Arab/Israeli events and a few minor colonial battles such as Mau-Mau, Borneo, Oman, Radfan, Kuwait, and the Falklands.

What have we seen since? The collapse of the USSR, East Timor, Yugoslavia, Iran/Iraq 8year war, the first Gulf War, Chechnya, Sudan, Sierra Leone, Pakistan/India, Indonesia, Fiji, Afghanistan, the Iraqi War, 9/11, and, more to the point, the global rise of extreme nationalism and daily terrorism.

I truly believe our nuclear policy and the resolute stance of JFK and Ronald Reagan won the Cold War. More aware now of the brainwashing about the capability of the Warsaw Pact, I have become more of a dove. After the fall of the Berlin Wall and the IGB, I then saw the state of the Russian troops and their bases in East Germany, the shape of their nuclear forces, and the condition of their air forces and pilots. Hence, I cannot for a minute believe we would have lost any form of war in central Europe to what constituted a Ragbag agglomeration of rudimentary, untrained and unpractised rabble. Even Khrushchev wasn't mad enough to go for all-out nuclear war; it was one big bluff, but maybe not one we were about to call!

In military terms, we had to consider two aspects of Warsaw Pact strategy: intentions and capability. Intentions of the hierarchy are difficult to ascertain. Were the Soviets just defending their western borders owing to their paranoia after Stalingrad? Or were they really seeking domination of Europe as a whole, before going on to the rest of the world? Does it actually matter, when turning to the second consideration, because they never really had the capability except in certain western minds, minds bent on maintaining the hawkish level of defence expenditure to justify the size and quality of our forces? Of course, right wing governments, egged on by arms manufacturers, had a vested interest in keeping the NATO forces as large and forbidding as possible, but with massive nuclear overkill on both sides, MAD was certainly on the cards.

Another consideration was a more sinister, hidden policy underlying the Cold War, which was the determination of both Russia and America to blow away colonial rule world wide, and particularly that of the British Empire. Regrettably, in so doing, they replaced it with a vacuum within which civil wars proliferated. Remember their mutual support for Nasser in his Yemeni campaign against us in Aden and South Arabia!

The RAF approach was slightly different from that of the RN. At sea, a submarine Captain is often on his own making decisions in isolation, while in the air force one at least had the opportunity to discuss matters among the crews on one's sqn. However, as I learnt more and more about the politics of 'first use', while my professional approach never changed, I became much more questioning about their very necessity – and here I'm talking about the Air Force's role with tactical nukes – the WE177 series of weapons, not the big strategic nukes (Polaris and Trident) of the Navy. Subsequently, of course, these tactical nukes were phased out of service, though some of our aircraft – Tornado, Jaguar, Sea Harrier, RN Helicopters – still have the nuclear weapons systems capabilities inherent in them. They were phased out, not on cost or obsolescence grounds, but simply because we didn't have the capacity to produce warheads for them while providing them for Trident. But perhaps a little history may help to explain the capability, and reasons for, our last tactical nuke: the WE177.

At 5.30am on 16th July 1945, at the Alamagordo bombing range in New Mexico, J. Robert Oppenheimer, the father of the atomic bomb, watched the expanding fireball of 'Trinity', the first nuclear test. "I am become Death, the shatterer of worlds," he said, quoting the Lord Shiva's words in the ancient sacred Hindu text – the Bhagavad-Gita. On that date at Alamagordo, what little innocence humankind had left was sacrificed on the altar of 20th century physics. The world was not to know for another three weeks. The US government covered up the omnipotent big bang in the desert. They said it was an exploding ammunitions dump, but on 6th August that year, Little Boy was dropped on Hiroshima and, three days later, Fat Man vaporised much of Nagasaki. Then everybody knew, except, of course, the 300,000 or so Japanese who died. Fat Man, happily, remains the last nuclear weapon used in anger, but, unhappily, the madness did not end there.

1st November 1952 saw "Mike", the very first hydrogen bomb test. It took place on the isle of Elugelab in the Eniwetok Atoll, 3000 miles west of Hawaii. It had a yield of 10 megatons. Its fireball was three miles across and created every element in the universe as well as some artificial ones. But it weighed over 65 tons and took a further two years to be packaged into a deliverable weapon. This was tested in the 'Bravo' test at Nam Island, in March 1954, and was the biggest ever American test at fifteen Megatons, but the Russians eclipsed that by a long way. In 1958[1] at Novaya Semlia, they air burst at 12,000feet a weapon that reportedly produced *sixty-five megatons* – an obscene size, damaging the environment and proving little!

A detonating atomic bomb is like an exploding star, a supernova, and a hydrogen bomb even more so. In each case radiation has to find its way out. If it escapes too easily, the bomb (or star) will burn up too quickly; if it is too constrained, the explosion will be premature. The design aim therefore, is to hold in the radiation just long enough so that nearly all the nuclear fuel is cooked, then to let it escape as rapidly as possible. Thus smooth, stable radiation flow and the resistance of the medium through which it flows, is critical to both bomb and stars. Similarly the behaviour of shock waves and their use for compression is equally essential. Once a neutron has smashed its way into a uranium or plutonium atom nucleus, it splits, or fissions, and divides into two other elements, barium and krypton. The total mass of the new particles is slightly less than the original. The miniscule 'missing mass' is converted into energy but, under Einstein's $E=mc^2$, that mass when multiplied by the enormous square of 'c' (the speed of light), results in a colossal amount of energy. Two further loose neutrons are released to smash into further nuclei, leading eventually to an uncontrolled chain reaction but, only if there is about 10 kilograms of uranium, or slightly less plutonium, packed tightly enough to provide a sufficiently large number of targets for the neutrons.

The maximum yield from an atomic bomb is something under one megaton. The two new elements, Krypton and Barium, release massive radioactivity. This radioactivity is used to cook the hydrogen(deuterium) core to produce the greater yields of the hydrogen bombs. During the first hundred-millionth of a second, the temperature at the core of a nuclear explosion rises to several hundred million degrees – that is air hotter than the centre of the sun. Pressures reach 100million atmospheres, driving exploding gases outwards at five million miles an hour. Invisibly, matter is warped by the detonation, while X-rays, gamma rays and neutrons irradiate the millions of tons of material thrown upwards by the blast. Unstable radioactive isotopes return to ground level as "fallout", penetrating, distorting and destroying living cells.

By 1988 the US had over 23,000 weapons and the Soviet Union had over 37,000. Meanwhile, Britain, France and China had also become nuclear powers. They have since been joined by India, Pakistan and Israel, while Iran and North Korea are on the brink. These vast programmes required tests and so, between 1945 and 1992 almost 2,000 atom and hydrogen bombs were exploded. Over four hundred of these were atmospheric, above ground, until the Limited Test Ban Treaty of 1963, after which tests were conducted underground. The mushroom clouds became a memory — or possibly a vision of the future?

Accordingly, we plodded on, continuing to teach about the effects of nuclear weapons. We taught how to calculate weapons effects for military nuclear planning purposes. It was a fatuous exercise. We only taught the planning for 50% of the bomb's effects. We taught how to calculate the blast effects of either an air burst or the cratering effects of a ground burst, blast only accounting for 50% of the total effects. We did *not* calculate the 35% of heat or light because we couldn't calculate them accurately enough for military use! Neither did we calculate the 15% of radiation effects. Why not? This may come as a surprise to some, but we never targeted people! They are the one and only target for radiation, and that's the Army's job – killing people! The Air Force only targets structures such as airfields, dams, bridges, ships, tanks, military HQs and so on. The fact that there are people – military personnel – on those targets is irrelevant. Peculiarly, we then go out of our way to avoid civilian casualties – collateral damage. Yet the latest Iraq war has shown that absolutely anyone in any guise can take up arms; a Burqa can hide anybody. Hence, the difference in appearance between civilian and military in most non-western cultures is extremely blurred.

From a military damage viewpoint one needs to reiterate that nukes are not necessarily the panacea most believe. The T-shaped bridge at Hiroshima (see photo) was the designated ground zero for Little Boy. The photo shows the bridge still in use after the event. Indeed, there were nine bridges across the rivers within half a mile of Hiroshima's ground zero, and seven of them were left standing. Bridges remain one of the most difficult targets to damage from the air, and nukes are not the easy option.

Never let it be said that there was no amusement within the ranks of those entrusted with these mammoth weapons tests. Christmas Island is a 25 mile long tropical island of white sand and coconut palms, with the UK nuclear weapons test site at the southern tip. The groundcrew, in their normal Khaki Drill (KD) rig, were taken by lorry to the northern end of the island before each test, some of which were only twenty miles away. They were told to sit on the beach facing north, looking out to sea and away from the bomb, put their hands over their eyes and wait. The first realization that the bomb had detonated was in seeing their hand-bones imprinted on their retinas. You knew then the old sweats who had been there for a test or two, because they got up and ran down the beach into the sea to keep clear of the coconuts about to come whistling horizontally past them!

Nuclear weapons are also about the projection of power, and after WW2 Britain was desperate to remain a dominant power in the world. We needed two things: the bomb and a delivery system. The earliest bombs were US weapons until our first Blue Danube, a low-yield, fission-weapon, arrived: 25 feet long and five feet in diameter – hence, the size of the V-force aircraft: the Valiants, Vulcans and Victors.

No.49 Sqn, a Sqn my father had served with during WW2, was given the task, Operation Grapple, of dropping Britain's first live megaton thermo-nuclear weapon set to explode at 8,000feet above Malden Island in the South Pacific in May 1957. To achieve this they flew from RAF Wittering via Canada and the USA to Christmas Island, some 400 miles north of Malden, where they bombed up for the tests. This they did 'successfully' on May 15th from a Valiant flying at 45,000feet. The Sqn dropped two more during the next three weeks, but only because the first two were actually failures well covered up to fool the world into thinking that we had joined the megaton club. In fact the first weapon only produced 300 Kilotons. The second was actually an extremely large atomic fission weapon designed to fool everybody into thinking it was a megaton fusion weapon because Britain was desperate for the prestige of the UN's top table. Even this second test only produced 700 Kilotons, and the third was similar. A fourth test in September finally produced a 1.2 Megaton explosion.

This gave Britain the Yellow Sun Mk 1 weapon, its first ever home-made, megaton, fusion device. Yellow Sun then replaced the early British fission weapons, Blue Danube and then Red Beard. In order to produce the megaton yield, unlike any other weapon, the ball-shaped, fission warhead was manu-factured as a hollow sphere. This allowed a greater amount of fission material to be held together than in a solid ball without producing a critical mass, the extra surface area allowing more neutrons to escape. Even so, as one might imagine, elements such as uranium and plutonium are so heavy that the slightest knock could have caused an implosion producing an instant critical mass. Hence, the warhead was filled with 136,000 ball bearings to hold the hollow sphere in place, and it was the co-pilot's job to count them out during the four-minute scramble . . . ! Yellow Sun Mk 1 was replaced by a differently engineered version after only nine months . . . !

Humanity has always looked to nature to see the sublime, but here, mankind had made its *own* sublime. The truth of these explosions is that, though they were only tests, they were phenomenally destructive. Some Pacific islands were simply wiped off the map. One of the hydrogen bomb detona-tions left a crater a mile wide and 200feet deep. Furthermore, leukaemias, cancers and early deaths occurred amongst the various 'guinea pigs' out there to 'record' the weapons' effects, and the cost in human lives is known only to be vast, because exact figures do not exist, though estimates have been made up to several hundred thousand people killed or as premature deaths. It was worst in the Soviet Union and China, because communism cared nothing – slightly less than the west – for individual lives. Even we sent aircraft – Canberras – into the nuclear clouds to obtain data, but the Americans were also incredibly irresponsible. Soldiers were sent into ground zero immediately after detonations and, consequently, received catastrophically high doses of radiation. One utterly chilling picture is of their 'Simon' blast in Nevada in 1953, where soldiers crouched in open trenches while glowing particles rained down upon them.

From the beginning, these tests entailed appalling risks. At the time of the very first 'Trinity' test, there was serious concern that the atmosphere might be ignited and all life destroyed! They went ahead anyway! Hydrogen bombs were detonated without any clear idea of how big the explosion would be. 'Bravo's' fifteen megatons, for example, was two and a half times more than the scientists had predicted. As a result, fallout plumes were also unpredictable, and frequently came to earth in populated areas of Nevada or the Pacific. Even today, the effects of fallout can still be detected all around the world, as the immediate plumes from the tests travelled further than anybody anticipated. We shall never know the full cost in cancers, birth defects and lives. Yet no heads rolled, the usual excuse being that nothing could be 'scientifically' proven!

To my knowledge, only the military requirements, the weapons' effects and the damage caused were ever discussed on the WEC, or any other military nuclear weapons course. The morals of using, and the results of testing, nuclear weapons were completely avoided. We had a job to do – we had to deliver them, and morals were the politicians' province. Yet it is impossible to lecture world wide on these subjects over ten years without coming to some conclusions. After all, there is a fundamental distinction between the use of all military means to defeat a genocidal aggressor such as Imperial Japan, and the prosecution of war for its own sake. These are not just big bombs: they are world shatterers. The tests were conducted on the basis of the extraordinary idea, embraced by people, government and the military, that a nuclear war could be fought and won. The reason soldiers were sent into ground zero was that the US seriously expected these bombs would be deployed as battlefield weapons. "First use" was always built into western policy if the Soviets had invaded West Germany, if for no other reason than to avoid another Dunkirk. The policy of first-use brought WE177.

We needed the flexibility of lots of little bangs for our vast array of targets in Europe, rather than a 'militarily-meaningless' whopper. Hence, between the three marks of WE177, we had the ability to detonate in the air, on the ground or underwater using different high and low level delivery methods and platforms. Aircraft from the V-force to naval helicopters were capable of using one or more marks. These were after all, smaller/lighter than the 1000lb bomb.

WE177 also gave us flexibility of yield. From sub-kiloton up to approximately a quarter of a megaton, using fission, reinforced fission, and fission-fusion mechanisms, WE177 could deliver them all. Unlike previous weapons, the WE177 series gave our nuclear forces enormous planning -adaptability and flexibility. Nevertheless, the larger version was never deployed into Europe, as it was too large for the agreed NATO limit for tactical nuclear usage in the Central Region. Hence, it was only in use for national requirements.

Modern day terrorism, nationalism and fundamental extremism has brought war much closer to every living room than during the nuclear age. With the two exceptions of Cuba and Berlin, I sincerely believe that there was never going to be a deliberate all out nuclear war between the two major powers: it was just a lot of posturing – that is not to say that war could not have started accidentally. For example, there were enough hawks in the 1950s American military. To quote but two: General Curtis LeMay, whose recipe for success in Vietnam was to *"bomb them back to the Stone Age"* and of the same breed was General Thomas S. Power. After listening to an advisor suggesting restraint in any nuclear exchange with the Soviet Union, he exploded, *"The whole idea is to kill the bastards! Look, at the end of the war if there are two Americans and one Russian, we win!"* It was exactly this extreme attitude, particularly amongst very senior American politicians and generals that caused me to rethink the whole process. If this was the way of thinking of our closest ally, how could we ever trust them, never mind the Soviet hierarchy?

All the same, there are many myths believed widely by the public, particularly on the subject of radiation and the widespread distrust of nuclear power. One that I always found amusing was that of Grand Central Station, New York. Grand Central was built using granite from a local quarry in New Jersey. The quarry is now the site of a nuclear power station. Today one will absorb more radiation from the granite in Grand Central Station than from the nuclear power station in the quarry!

Today, the only way you can be certain that the proliferation of terrorist nuclear weapons has actually happened is when you see or hear the mushroom cloud overhead. Today you don't need big stockpiles of weapons, just a vial or two of this or that will do. You can try and stop it at the airport gates, but even if you succeed you'll bankrupt the airlines. The Left-wing is remarkably nonchalant about the new nuclear terrors. Considering how far the loony Left went in the latter part of the last century in their attitude towards nuclear weapons, it is surprising where their attitudes sit today. When nuclear weapons were an elite club of five relatively sane powers, the Left was convinced that they had proof that the planet was about to explode at any minute, and the few who survived would be walking around in a nuclear winter wonderland. Remember the loony Left's 'nuclear-free zones?' Now anyone with a few thousand dollars and an unlisted number in Islamabad in his mobile can get a nuke, *and apparently, the Left couldn't care less!*

The nuclear age really began with that first test in New Mexico in July 1945, but it's difficult to see where it will end, and, more to the point, how this will come about. Complete disarmament, in which all nuclear powers agreed to abolish their weapons, would take far too long to implement. There would always be that nagging suspicion that someone, somewhere, had cheated and kept the odd one for special occasions! If, therefore, we cannot end the nuclear age with a whimper, then it must surely end with a bang! North Korea and Iran spring to mind. Is it a testament to our success so far that, in managing the nuclear age, people are not more bothered? Nevertheless, the nuclear dilemma is a terrible legacy which each generation must pass on to the next.

Two generations have now grown up since atmospheric atomic testing was stopped, two generations which have not seen these mushroom clouds as live events. Maybe that has made them feel secure. Maybe they think we know better now. Maybe it was all a bad dream. Maybe . . . !

"Peace. *n.* In international affairs, a period of cheating between two periods of fighting."
Definition from *"The Devil's Dictionary"* by Ambrose Bierce)

Notes
1. Bibliography No:19, "Empire of the Stars" gives the date as 30 Oct 1961.

Chapter Twenty-Six

The First Gulf War

DEFENCE INTELLIGENCE AGENCY
WASHINGTON DC

In August 1990, I was in Bangladesh, on a five-man lecture tour, teaching various aspects of air warfare to the students of the Bangladeshi Combined Services Staff College. The Gulf crisis started with the Iraqi invasion of Kuwait while we were in Dhaka. One evening, we were sitting at their Mess bar talking to a couple of Bangladeshi Air Force flying instructors, when one of them said, "You know, we train some of the Iraqi pilots here." Having picked ourselves up after falling off our bar stools at the thought of Bangladeshis training Iraqis, the second Banga instructor commented, "They'll never fight, you know. They haven't got the bottle!" That was Bangladeshi Moslem opinion, six months before the war started!

On returning from Dhaka, I had just seen the doctor about of what I thought was stomach ulcers, and she wanted to send me to Ely Military Hospital for a full investigation. The following day, I was given my war posting to Washington DC to help out the Defence Intelligence Agency at their HQ Centre (The DIAC) at Bolling Air Force Base. The doctor, however, wouldn't allow it! After acrimonious conversations it became apparent that she thought I'd had stomach cancer! In typical Air Force fashion, a compromise was eventually reached – I went to war in an ambulance! Oh, the ignominy of it!

Actually I was sent to Ely Hospital by ambulance for tests under anaesthetic the day before I was due to fly out to Washington. Subsequently, in a drowsy condition, I was put back in an ambulance and driven through the evening to RAF Brize Norton, where I was kept under observation in sick quarters overnight. In the early hours I proceeded by ambulance directly to the RAF VC10, and was loaded on board as a casualty to be flown out to Washington! Well, somebody obviously wanted me badly, or rid of me badly!

It transpired that I had neither cancer or ulcers. Yet another blunder by RAF doctors, one of many encountered during my time in the service. A number of years later I went privately to see a consultant who proved conclusively my problem was, and still is, a simple hiatus hernia, easily controlled by pills.

Thus did one Sqn Ldr arrive in a drugged state at Washington Dulles, to be

252

met by an embassy intelligence guy! Luckily on the plane I had met Roger Blackburn from MOD, also going out to do the same job, and we shared a room together for our time in Washington.

Most of our working time was spent on Air Force targeting, weaponeering and Battle Damage Assessment (BDA), working in teams but with special responsibility for assessing UK weapons. There was a considerable ignorance of UK capability in the DIA, CIA, NSA (National Security Agency) and, particularly NPIC, their National Photographic Interpretation Centre. The DIA decided to run a three-shift system which went something like this: four nights on, two days off, four days on, two days off, four nights on, etc.. This was fine for the Americans, but there were only two of us to do the weapons assessments for them. So Roger and I, on opposite shifts, had to work a constant 12hrs on/12hrs off for four days or nights at a time, followed by a day off and back at it again. This schedule left us absolutely shattered to the extent that we were falling asleep during our shifts. We only just became used to the shift we were on after four days – then they changed it! The body just can't take that for any length of time. That's the DIA for you! After two or three weeks we looked and acted like zombies, so were not surprised that mistakes were made.

Some two miles West of Arlington Cemetery, "The Comfort Inn" was the totally unsuitable hotel that the embassy had pre-booked for us: it was inadequate for a long-term stay and too far out of town. On the other hand, National Airport in Washington is right in the middle of town which meant there was nowhere quiet to sleep close by during the day when on night shift. Roger and I were forced to move hotels five times in a month to try and solve the lack of sleep problem as the war progressed. The permanent staff went on with their normal business and sleep patterns at home. We found one cannot work night shift if in hotels not geared up for daytime quiet sleeping periods. Moreover, because we were the only foreign temporary staff, no-one understood our problem until one night, after two weeks, the two-star Deputy CinC of the DIA, General Carr, stopped by for a chat. He instantly organised excellent, spacious senior officer quarters in BOQs on the base. But, in typical British forces' bureaucratic fashion, if we had stayed in government accommodation we'd have lost all our allowances and would have had to pay for the privilege! Moreover, after a few days we had to go back to the General and apologise for having to move out once more because of the National Airport noise.

Three other hotels were either beneath the flight path of, or close to, National Airport, and "The Embassy Suites" hotel, otherwise ideal, suffered constant banging from ongoing renovation work. Eventually we finished up on North Courthouse Road, far enough from National to allow some daytime sleep, in "The Quality Inn Arlington Hotel", replete with a two bed-roomed suite, kitchen and lounge on the top floor – and an excellent "Club Royale" all-day breakfast bar. A great way to conduct a war!

Roger and I were only allowed one hire car between us. The off-duty guy got the car – drove it to work, and handed it over to the other going off shift. We had to look for new accommodation individually while we should have been sleeping, so one could leave work for a new hotel not knowing where one was going because the other had moved all our luggage while one was on shift! However, we always remembered the boys out in the Gulf. Were our problems worse than theirs? Actually, some had extremely plush accommodation in the Gulf and were much better off.

The security process took three days to "Badge us up", i.e. authorized to enter the DIAC building, even though we both had one of the highest security clearances from the UK especially for this job. After all the rush to get there, we weren't allowed anywhere for those first three days. As soon as we received the correct security badges, doors opened. Everything we ever imagined must have existed somewhere in the intelligence services, plus one hell of a lot more, was laid out before us. Even so, there was still an inner sanctum into which foreign officers were not allowed: a 'them and us' situation if ever there was one.

"There was a door to which I found no key:
There was a veil past which I could not see:"
(with apologies to Rubaiyat of Omar Khayyam No. XXXII
from Fitzgerald's first translation 1859)

Our main tasks were Battle Damage Assessment, and tasking and targeting for the front line air forces with particular attention to the RAF's capabilities. Every attack or recce target in the previous 12 hours of any asset – satellite or air-breather – had to be assessed. Target folders, ever more voluminous as the war progressed, arrived on one's desk. Each had full target details, many photographs, and previous post-attack assessments plus the recent attack/recce details. Not only was the damage assessed but, of prime importance, its present and future operational capability, including how long it may take to repair. A decision could then be made on the magnitude and timing of any re-attack. If a re-attack was found necessary, arrangements were made for that target, and its vulnerable points for aiming positions, to be put back on the frag for subsequent missions.

However, due to American ignorance of UK military abilities, some time was spent formally briefing other parts of the US defence community on RAF weapons and capabilities. Luckily, I had anticipated this and brought my lecture slides on British Weapons. That started a lecture circuit around Washington. To cater for their various shift systems, I sometimes had to lecture to some bleary 'red-eyes' on the night shift at 2, 3 and 4 o'clock in the morning! NPIC lectures I can remember well: a tiny blackened room, no windows and piping hot, packed with PI's, many of whom were fast asleep within seconds! In particular I had to lecture on JP233, the RAF's unique runway denial weapon, because of unbelievable BDA miscalls in the first few days of the war. When I saw my first battle damage photo of an 8-ship, RAF Tornado JP233 strike on Shaibah AFB, an American PI had annotated the cratering damage as 'strafing'! Not only did I berate their unawareness, but this meant that he'd advised that this airfield target needed an immediate restrike, sending the boys back into danger to a target already unserviceable because their first JP233 strike had well and truly closed the runways, albeit temporarily. Looking at the photos of the stream of cratering holes across the runways, my initial reaction was "Bloody big gun then!"

The DIA was one of many agencies producing a steady stream of data of which no one, it seemed, took much notice. While these US intelligence guys were extremely clever in their own narrow areas of expertise, the stereotype of American ignorance of the wider world is absolutely valid; many appeared ignorant of their next door department. Remember that we were working with some extremely intelligent agents from DIA, CIA, NSA , FBI, NPIC and the Pentagon. Yet I was asked the following questions in the corridors of the DIAC:

"Is it safe to fly to your country on holiday this year?"

"How far is it from London to Baghdad, about five hours drive?"!

Moreover, it was here that I came up against the height of political correctness – central Washington DC. Now this was 1991, and PC hadn't really taken hold yet in the UK. I asked a single lady of the permanent staff in the department, after knowing her for three weeks, if she'd like to join three of us for dinner on our one night off, hoping she'd know the area and a good place to eat. Next thing I knew, I was in the Boss's office being accused of sexual harassment. I hadn't touched her or offered anything more than dinner for four! It turned out that this woman had already had two Americans fired for the same thing in the past year! The western world, even then, had begun to go PC crazy!

Thankfully there were funny moments, some necessary to relieve the tension through lengthy, hard working shifts where lives were at stake. In the early days of the war, the USN rep. on the next desk had been very worried about an Iraqi submarine thought to have been loose and undetected in the Gulf waters. If true, this could have done untold damage to allied naval and merchant shipping. That story died a death but, three weeks later, a human intelligence (HUMINT) report (in signal format known as a flimsy) arrived from the CIA, as a result of an interview with a dissident Iraqi, entitled "UNDERWATER RUNWAYS"! Yes, you read it right the first time!

What became apparent was that this 'humla' had been working on a country palace just outside Baghdad for Saddam Hussein. The palace was surrounded by a huge bund-wall covering hundreds of acres with a causeway across the middle to the palace in its central point. The area in between had then been flooded so that there was only one access across this causeway to/from the palace. The humla reckoned that the Iraqis had built a secret, escape runway for Saddam underneath this flooded area. His premise was that all they had to do in an emergency was to pull out the plug exposing a private runway from which escape was possible! Laughable maybe, but typical of some HUMINT.

Thinking the Navy might have a laugh at this, I showed the flimsy to the USN rep, who, amid a fit of giggles, said that now he knew where this damned submarine had been all this time: obviously it was in the lake defending the palace! Now that's good intelligence work, putting numerous bits of info together to produce a "logical" picture. Two and two often makes five! We subsequently believed that the simple Iraqi humla had seen the causeway being built across the lake and had mistaken it for a runway!

Memorable events can recur. Echoing my frustration in Belize during the Falklands crisis, our predicament was now similar. Although we had CNN in

Figs 14. DIA Citations for the Gulf War

the corner of every room, broadcasting up-to-date war info, sometimes faster than intelligence agencies, we were receiving nothing about the RAF and our mates in the Gulf – only news on American forces. Even on secure lines back to the UK, people were reluctant to talk to us. Pooling information with a Canadian and a Australian (the only other foreigners in the DIAC) from the permanent staff, we managed to cobble together a semblance of what was happening amongst the allied forces.

This grew more necessary when the boys started getting shot down. It was difficult digging out names of those missing, most of whom I knew. Some had been in my peer group, others I had taught on the Weapons Employment Course. Most of the squadron commanders had been through the Department of Air Warfare and listened to my lectures: they were all familiar names. After all, the Air Force was much smaller than when I'd joined in the early '60s; everyone knows everyone else these days.

Much later, after the war, I was somewhat saddened by those who sought to profit from their incarcerations. John Nichol is still the 'talking head' when the media need a sound-bite, pontificating as though he were an expert on all aviation matters. In no way would I detract from the horrors that this crew went through as POWs, but (and it's a big but) they were inexperienced failures. They got shot down on their first ever mission before arriving at their first ever target, because mistakes were made. Hindsight wisdom comes easy but there were switchery errors running in to the target, compounded by, and contributing to their downfall, the most basic of mistakes: *they went around for a second attack!* This smacks of gross overconfidence: you utterly lose the element of surprise.

What of all those pilots and navs who carried on day after day, mission after mission, doing their jobs properly for the whole war, and who received nothing but a campaign medal? They are the real, silent heroes!

You've heard about and seen the American penchant for throwing medals at everyone for anything. When Roger and I left Washington to return home, General Carr's words to us on shaking our hands were that, by golly, we both deserved a medal and he would make damn sure we each got one! Some weeks later in the post, for what they are worth, were two citations (see Figs 14).

So, having worked entirely with the intelligence and ops staffs in Washington for the war, it's hardly surprising that the comments made below mostly come from my experiences there. Some can be said to be American viewpoints but I did also lecture extensively on the subject on my return home after the war.

Unequivocally the Iraqi invasion of Kuwait was a tragic, timely warning to us all that demonic aggressors still exist. The aggressor initially holds all the top cards. Hence, the defenders must be able to counter aggression swiftly and effectively. Therefore, for air forces, responsiveness and flexibility are of critical importance. The mere existence of this capability may deter aggression. Far better to deter aggression by early deployment than have to fight: the previous Kuwait deployment in 1961 is a perfect example from which we did not learn. Moving 45 Para and my Sqn (No.8 Sqn) into Kuwait International Airport in the first few hours directly from Bahrain, while re-inforcements arrived, put an instant stop to Iraqi incursions – end of problem. The Labour Government's decision to pull out of the Middle East in the late

1960s and '70s was the root cause of much that has happened there since.

Hence, the first lesson is to safeguard our current levels of air power responsiveness, if not to enhance them, and not, as Labour is doing yet again, to cut or diminish them.

During the Cold War we trained for over forty years for a European mainland battle. In the event, we were required to operate in a very different area, against a different type of enemy, with different allies. We deployed virtually the full spectrum of combat and support capabilities: the key to this success was our flexibility, though we couldn't deploy similar forces now.

Six months planning commenced in Aug '90, as three overall campaign objectives were named:

– *Immediate withdrawal of Iraqi forces from Kuwait*
– *Restoration of the Kuwaiti legitimate government*
– *Security and stability for the gulf region*

All three were achieved, the third being accomplished by the early cessation of military action, with subsequent containment using sanctions and air policing. Only since the second Gulf war of 2002 has the third objective become questionable. But back in '91, our forces were at As Samawah, only 150 unopposed kilometres from Baghdad. Should we have gone for Baghdad? No! That was not the main objective! Security and stability for the Gulf region was the prime requirement, which in turn equalled security and stability for Iraq. Pushing on to Baghdad in the second war and toppling the regime has produced nothing but instability across the whole region. Therefore, the first President Bush was correct in stopping when he did. Containment rather than victory is often a better policy. The problem now is with whom do you replace Saddam? Whomever, he has to be acceptable to all. He has to be acceptable to Saudi Arabia, Kuwait, Iran, Syria and Turkey, acceptable to the Kurds, Sunnies and Shiites, and acceptable to the major western nations, Russia, China and the UN et al. As the Americans have found to their cost, no such animal exists. If it hadn't been for the corruption of the UN's "oil for medicine" programme, Iraq might well have remained stable, contained, and without the necessity to topple Saddam. But what happens after he dies? We have seen already the in-fighting and instability that this has brought. They are the same as the Yemenis, and Afghans – when not fighting the British or Americans, they are fighting amongst themselves!

To succeed in that first Gulf war, it was felt necessary to topple the leadership around Saddam. To do that we needed to peel away some physical and psychological circles from around that leadership, viz:

–– *Defeat the military forces*
– *Use psychological warfare against the population*
– *Degrade the Iraqi infrastructure*
– *Destroy the key production facilities*

However, in facing the fourth largest army in the world, no account was taken of their quality, only their quantity. Sound familiar – Cold War assessments of the Warsaw Pact forces? The ground plan commenced with an enormous deception. A Marine landing was practised to give the impression the invasion was coming from the sea, while sixteen army divisions moved unnoticed 300miles West across the desert in two weeks. The air war was then used to soften up the region for a ground offensive, but there were some unexpected limitations, not least of which was the unusually bad weather over much of the region for long periods of time. This affected the intelligence gathering, particularly from satellites, which made the only all-weather recce assets, the RAF's Tornado GR1As indispensable.

Further unexpected problems occurred with the politically important hunt for the Iraqi's mobile SCUDS which diverted considerable weight of forces from their main tasks, and must be considered one of the least successful facets of the allied campaign.

Furthermore, the fact that the Iraqi Air Force did not fly could never have been envisaged, despite that portentous advice from Bangladesh! Two other points for which we were unprepared were the excellent Iraqi propaganda campaign, and the success of their massive Anti-Aircraft-Artillery (AAA). AAA has for many years had a bad name in western, military, analytical circles due to its expense, manpower requirements and lack of kills. But Iraqi AAA, larger than the whole WW2 AAA deployment, while not producing many kills, produced remarkable psychological success in forcing major changes to allied aerial tactics in order to avoid them – in particular, the RAF's slow realization to change from their traditional low-level role and into the totally unfamiliar medium level (ML): a classic case of too much doctrine and not enough flexibility.

Air power is primarily an offensive rather than a defensive instrument. The allies took the offensive in the air while the Iraqis chose to remain on the defensive. Why they chose a defensive stance may never be known. After all, their defensive posture led them to disaster, losing their airforce, achieving nothing, and launching no sorties in the final two weeks. We, therefore, operated over Iraq unchallenged. We need only to remember the diversion of allied assets necessary to find and destroy the SCUDS, to know that the initiative would have been wrested from the allies by even minor offensive air action on Iraq's part. Perhaps the facts that within six days their air defence system was knocked out, air force Generals had been assassinated, communications were down to 20% capacity, and Command-and-Control was almost non-existent, provide the answer.

Now, it may be considered that this war was entirely American. In Washington, certainly you wouldn't have known that anyone else was involved! But even America couldn't have won without the near unanimous support of the UN and the military and financial backing of most of the rest of the free world. Apparently, even the Irish sent a contingent to the Gulf, but the Mexicans didn't know what to do with them and sent them home!

When the Iraqis invaded Kuwait on 2nd Aug, air power was the only instrument available to the British Government which could get to the Gulf, IN TIME and with SUFFICIENT FORCE, to deter the threat of invasion of Saudi Arabia. Because of that, the RAF was from the outset at the forefront of the British effort. The RAF's contribution was second only to the USA in size and importance, both in the crisis and the conflict.

Within 48hours of the Government's decision to send large-scale forces to the Gulf, a squadron of F3 Tornado fighters arrived in Saudi Arabia and flew the first operational missions only two hours after arrival. However, the F3 lacked investment in electronic warfare equipment and therefore did not penetrate Iraqi airspace. One operational lesson learnt was that air defence aircraft must have as good an Electronic Counter-Measures suite as the attack aircraft they support.

Within two days, a Jaguar sqn, half a tanker sqn, and half a Nimrod Maritime Patrol sqn were also in theatre. By the start of the war we had in the Gulf:

18 x F3 Tornado fighters
46 x GR1/1a Tornado fighter-bombers/recce
17 x various tankers
3 x Nimrod MPA
12 x Chinook helicopters
19 x Puma helicopters
7 x C130 Hercules transports
1 x BAe 125 VIP transport
2 x Rapier surface-to-air missile sqns
4 x RAF Regiment Field Sqns

Seven thousand RAF personnel were involved, and overall we flew 6,100 missions, the largest number by any nation except the USA, and two and a half times as many as flown by the French.

OFFENSIVE OPERATIONS

The Tornado GR1 crews went to war in a difficult situation: the aircraft had been heavily modified, were flying at heavier weights than ever experienced, at night, often in bad weather, using Night Vision Goggles (NVGs) over unfamiliar terrain. There were many inexperienced crews on their first ever war missions against a supposed high level of enemy air defences. However, thanks to the JP233 airfield denial weapon, the Tornado made a particular, initial contribution to the offensive counter-air (OCA) campaign. The only other OCA aircraft in theatre was the F111 using the French Durandal runway-cratering rocket. The USAF crews really disliked Durandal because it meant flying at too high a level down enemy runways and, in the event, didn't use it. Hence, British Tornados flying at low level were initially tasked with suppression of twelve main Iraqi air bases.

All attack missions were packaged together with various support aircraft. F15 fighters flew fighter sweep and escort roles to clear away any Iraqi fighters, with F4G Wild Weasels providing Suppression of Enemy Air Defences (SEAD) using HARM anti-radiation missiles to close down enemy SAMs/AAA. EF-111A Ravens employed Electronic Counter Measures (ECM) to suppress the early warning radars, and all were controlled by AWACs. Typically, forty-three others supported a thirty-two attack aircraft package.

Despite this enormous support, attack aircraft still had to fly through intense AAA fire to reach their targets. Soon it was realised that simultaneous 'toss' attacks by other Tornados using 1000lb bombs against AAA clusters would help to clear the way in for the JP233-armed aircraft. Using Forward Looking Infra-Red (FLIR) and NVGs at night turned the darkness into day for the crews, but the systems were susceptible to blooming under the incandescent arrows of FLAK and tracer conditions. Also, when JP233 fires, it brightly lights up the underside of the aircraft as it flies down or across an enemy runway. At night that's the last place you would want to be lit up like a Christmas Tree! After four nights of JP233 attacks, air opposition had been effectively neutralized for the loss of four Tornados. Eight Iraqi main operating bases had been closed, whilst operations from several others had been markedly reduced.

Yet, if the lack of IAF missions had been appreciated earlier, we may never have needed to fly JP233 missions at all, though it must be stated that only one aircraft was lost on a JP233 mission, and that one went down after the target so the loss cannot be blamed on the weapon system. Despite being the RAF's most expensive weapons system, JP233 was just as unpopular among Tornado crews as Durandal had been among F111 crews, and for similar reasons. Both weapons were misused, having been designed for an eastern European environment. Indeed, the weapon has never been used since, and is no longer considered part of the Tornado's main armament inventory.

The severe dislocation inflicted on the Iraqi surface-to-air system and air defence fighter force in those first four nights allowed the majority of subsequent Tornado sorties to be flown in daylight, and at ML above the Iraqi AAA – the one Iraqi anti-air strength that remained throughout the campaign. Hence, the first ML GR1 sorties used free-fall bombs to attack large area targets such as fuel/ammo storage dumps and airfields, but to little effect. Their lack of accuracy showed up the earlier, poor decision not to deploy laser designator aircraft. Ten days after the war commenced, a major volte-face brought six Buccaneers equipped with Pavespike laser designators from the UK into the battle – the RAF's lofty reputation having been severely stained by then. Now accurate combined attacks using Buccaneer Laser Guidance for Tornado bombers were possible, allowing similar tactics and accuracies to those of the USAF.

Hence, within ten days of war, and after thirty-odd years of low-level operational doctrine in which the RAF had barely acknowledged the use of air space offensively above 200 feet agl, much of the basic offensive doctrine had been demolished and replaced with the ML doctrine of the USAF. Did we ever get it wrong!? Did my colleagues and I train at low level for nothing? Was it all a total waste of time? Did we lose aircraft and crews for nothing? Certainly the RAF had been somewhat blinkered for many, many years.

Immediately after the Gulf War, a seminar was organised at RAF College Cranwell in which, inter alia, all the Gulf squadron commanders gave presentations based on their personal experiences. One of them, the Jaguar Sqn Cdr, Wg Cdr Bill Pixton DFC AFC RAF commenced his lecture with a picture of an 8 Sqn Hunter over Aden in the 1960s, and the words: "Oh how I wish I'd listened to those old AFME Hunter pilots' war stories." Maybe I didn't tell my war stories well enough, but he and his Jaguar personnel learnt some major lessons the hard way about operating in the Middle East. For example, it took most of the Falklands War before the attributes of Laser Guided Bombs (LGBs) were realised, and for the Harrier to be so equipped. Nine years later, it took six months of planning and three weeks of war before the Buccaneer and LGB operations were again included, belatedly, in the RAF's Gulf War inventory. Kip Kemball was correct in his assertion that, *"a fully developed and defined air power doctrine* (which the air force has in the Air Warfare Centre and AP3000) . . . *mainly serves to constrain the imaginative use of air power."*.

The Coalition had a total of 1,317 attack aircraft in theatre plus 443 support aircraft, of which the RAF provided 70 combat aircraft. 1,220 attack sorties were flown in the first 24 hours, plus 300 support sorties, after which over 2000 sorties per day were sustained. We dropped 7,400 tons of guided weapons and 81,000 tons of unguided.

Iraq was hit by more sorties each day than had been flown against them in all the eight years of the Iranian war! Is it any wonder they didn't fly? They didn't know what had hit them! Forty-two Iraqi aircraft were shot down and over 160 destroyed on the ground excluding those not known within HAS interiors. The coalition flew 109,876 sorties for 38 combat losses, plus six accidents: an attrition rate of 0.074% against a planned figure of 5%, of which the RAF's contribution was 11,000 sorties with a 0.037% attrition. These loss rates continued the trend since WW2 of decreasing attrition rates: WW2 US-9.7%, Korea-2%, Vietnam-0.4%. Thirty-six UK personnel were killed out of 45,000 in the Gulf, seventeen on ops whilst forty-three were injured and eight missing.

Of the above, the RAF had 950 tasks put on 2838 aircraft[1]. 2044 weapons loads were tasked, some tasks being non-weapon ones such as recce, Pavespike or TIALD[2]. Fifty-five aircraft aborted on the ground, and 2479 aircraft were actually flown, of which 1482 were reported as a total success, i.e. hit the target.

482 aircraft aborted in the air – 273 due to bad weather – and seven aircraft were lost. I do not intend here to speculate any further on the loss rates or reasons, though some were due to deficient tactics or airmanship. The fatal accident of a JP233 mission flown by a brand new squadron commander with no operational experience on type, and Rupert Clark's shooting down while attacking in long line astern as number eight in a stream of twelve aircraft, were avoidable. The Iraqi "gunners" had had seven practice attempts before Rupert arrived in range! Two woeful examples of overconfidence.

The three least stealthy aircraft had the highest attrition rate: TORNADO lost six, AV8B and the A10 each lost five. The stealthiest aircraft, the F117a, not surprisingly had the lowest attrition of one. Seventy aircraft were damaged in battle, though the use of titanium plating round some cockpits saved many a pilot, mainly those in US A10s and Apaches.

Of the 2,838 RAF tasks, only 1,482 were successful: a 52 % success rate. While this may sound pretty low to the uninitiated, anything over 50% is actually considered quite good. If one takes out the bad weather aborts, then the success rate goes up to nearly 62%. i.e. only 38% were caused by some other unservicabilities in the aircraft or equipment, which seems rather high until you take into account the difficult conditions in which they were operating.

Of the 6,145 RAF weapons dropped or fired, over 4,962 were considered successful, and 338 were known to have missed the target. This gives a success rate of nearly 81%, which puts a whole different light on the success or failure of the campaign if one believes the figures. Perhaps we're into lies, damned lies, and statistics here, and attrition rates are *definitely* part of the latter, or is it called "spin" these days? When considering loss or attrition rates, the figure used seems to depend on who you are, and where you're coming from:

For example, imagine a force approximating that of the RAF during the Gulf War:

A total fighter/bomber force available	*150*
Aircraft deployed to the operational area	*60*
Sorties flown	*1,800*
Aircraft lost:	*6*

What is the attrition rate?

If you were the CinC with a force of 150 and lost six: your attrition rate is 4%, which is comfortable to live with.

If you were the Operational Commander in theatre having flown 1,800 sorties and lost six: your attrition rate is 0.003%, and you'd be very happy.

However, if you were the Wing Commander with 60 aircraft, losing six and writing to the lost airmen's relatives, you'd have lost twelve aircrew and had twelve letters to write, and your attrition rate would be 10% — *and you'd be really miffed!*

The figures above approximate to our position in the Gulf War. It is worth noting that six RAF Tornados were actually lost out of forty attack aircraft in theatre; this was 15% of the total Tornado force available.

One ironic outcome was that, after forty years of low level strike/attack, this doctrine was discarded within four days of war breaking out, when we were forced up to the ML. The ML doctrine had been heartily embraced by the USAF since their problems at LL in Vietnam. Why did we think we were different and knew better?

In the '60s, we had three squadrons of attack fighters permanently based in the Middle East. In 1991 it took the whole RAF attack force to mount four squadrons of Tornados and one squadron of Jaguars at war. It is frightening that we had nothing else left, and more so because we couldn't mount the same number again today. For a country with the fourth largest world economy, we are punching so far below our weight militarily that some enemy somewhere is going to take advantage of us, and probably sooner rather than later. It is not well known that we now have no air defence fighters permanently based south of Lincolnshire – is that how we defend our capital, seat of Government, Treasury, the Royal Family and 25million subjects in the Southeast? Especially after 9/11!

Before the Gulf War, the RAF had no ground attack pinpoint precision weapons – dumb bombs were still the order of the day. Hence the long lasting adage of the Weapons Employment Course, "Most Weapons Miss Most Targets Most of the Time"! Only in the past twelve years or so have we acquired the ability to hit accurately, and not before time!

We must now acquire the same accurate capability while able to stand off from the target, even at low level. Whatever comes into service to satisfy this stand-off requirement, the ordnance must be put on target for the least money commensurate with keeping the aircraft and crews out of the reach of the enemy. The most cost-effective solution would be one having the **largest** CEP (4 to 5m) needed to hit the **smallest** target (the HAS), combined with the **shortest** stand-off range (50Kms?) to ensure survival of the aircraft and crew from target defences.

NON-RAF ASPECTS OF THE AIR WAR

Of course, this viewpoint was garnered from Washington DC experience. Accordingly, it would be wrong not to mention some of the major non-RAF aspects of the air war, without which we might still be fighting today (perhaps we still are!). There was one unsuccessful, and three roaring success stories, the latter all involved with precision bombing.

One of the biggest headaches for all the allied forces, as previously mentioned, was the enormous effort eventually put into locating the mobile SCUDS with singular lack of success. We had discounted SCUD in the early days due to its lack of accuracy, but forgot that you don't need accuracy if targeting large areas such as towns or cities. Yet only one out of eighty SCUDS hit its target. The mobile SCUDS were hiding in road culverts, looked like Bedouin tents when static and camouflaged, and successfully surprised our strategic systems with their ability to fire and hide quickly throughout the war. Perhaps the best part of our anti-Scud ops was the Patriot success. Although some Scuds got through, there was a definite no fire decision if the Scud's trajectory was perceived as hitting bare desert – Patriot's success was partially due to an excellent misinformation campaign and, in any case, they're very expensive!

However, the clinical precision of our bombing using Laser, TV or IR guidance was the surprise success above all else in the Gulf. For comparison, in 1943, RAF Bomber Command placed 95% of its bombs within three miles of their targets! In other words, most missed, but was quoted at the time as "an extraordinary concentration"! In the Gulf, 90% were placed within FIVE FEET, thus minimizing collateral damage and unintended civilian casualties. This suddenly made air power more selective and a more politically useful tool. Since the demise of our V-force we had given strategic bombing little thought, but new, widely-available accuracies required a rethink of our offensive strategies.

The three most successful systems were TOMAHAWK, F117a and the newer Laser Guided Bombs (LGBs). It was the first operational use of cruise missiles and, because of its accuracy, Tomahawk was one of only two systems used over Baghdad, in order to minimize civilian casualties. Three aspects though, are worth a mention. Cruise missiles are comparatively slow at 0.8–0.9Mach, very predictable to defences, and rely on known good waypoints for accurate navigation. If your campaign has already destroyed a waypoint, such as a large building of military significance, the missile will be severely degraded in its terminal accuracy. In other words, very close co-ordination is required between the targeting cell and any cruise missile, mission-planning cell.

Nevertheless, the F117a stealth fighter was *the* system which won us the air war. It flew 10% of the total missions but achieved 90% of the total damage inflicted. Why? ACCURACY! Reverse that argument and the other 90% of sorties produced only 10% of the damage due to lack of accuracy, usually from lack of guided weapon capability, particularly with the F16s. The F117s were the only aircraft allowed to operate over Baghdad. Their single-aircraft sorties, using stealth techniques and a nil-radar, ML (above AAA), delivery profile gave the F117a a unique capability. Only one was shot down, the least attrition of all Gulf aircraft, while achieving much more than any other. Its capability, though, was achieved because of the third of our successful systems which it carried: the LGB.

The LGB – specifically GBU24/27(BLU109+PWIII) had greater success than any other weapon. This is a 2,000lb, improved penetration, bomb designed for hard targets, and fitted with a PW111 Laser guidance kit. With state-of-the-art, trajectory-shaped profile to obtain the correct impact angles/velocities for good target matching, this weapon is also capable of use from low level.

A larger 4,700lb version, known as the GBU28 and made from old eight-inch artillery barrels, was developed and used within only six weeks to obtain penetration of deep, command bunkers. After being dropped on trials, an inert version of this weapon was found over 100ft underground and still intact.

The three systems described: Tomahawk, F117A and the modern LGB penetrator, have two things in common which ensured their success. The first, as already mentioned, is ACCURACY. Accuracy is a major force multiplier. For example, you can use 32 x F16s with dumb bombs requiring 43 support aircraft, or 8 x F117s with GBU27 plus two support aircraft, or two x B2s with LGBs on their own. Each of those packages produces the same theoretical effect on the target. Which is more efficient?

The second is NIGHT/ALL WEATHER OPS. Our enemy was incapable of night/all-weather ops. Our accuracies were achieved at night, and also by Tornado in bad weather, sometimes totally blind. This gave us the ability to operate 24 hours a day, for half of which the enemy was grounded. Hence, this ability is fundamental for any future air conflict.

Finally, our same Jaguar Squadron Commander, Bill Pixton, complained that his crews had been forced to live in a 5-star hotel in Bahrain between missions. On the premise that you must train in peacetime exactly as you would operate in war, he felt that he and his crews required further training in the fine art of living in 5-star hotels! Their accommodation put ours in Washington to shame.

Some interesting observations on the Gulf War:

"This was the first time in history that a field army had been defeated by air power."

General McPeak – USAF Chief of Staff

"It is no longer realistic for the UK to plan major out-of-area operations without allied support." (Meaning US support)

UK Parliamentary Defence Committee

"THE GULF WAR IS BEHIND US NOW. WE MUST LEARN FROM IT AND, MORE TO THE POINT, BUILD FOR A PROSPEROUS AND PEACEFUL FUTURE." Air Marshal Shurdom – Chief of the Jordanian Air Staff

(Spoken directly to the author in conversation on the front steps of the RJAF HQ building, three weeks after the war – June 1991.)

The typical military mind:

'Then to the rolling Heav'n itself I cried,
Asking, "What Lamp had Destiny to guide
Her little Children stumbling in the Dark?"
And – "A blind Understanding!" Heav'n replied.'

Rubaiyat of Omar Khayyam
from Fitzgerald's first translation 1859

Notes
1. A single task can be for a formation of aircraft.
2. Pavespike and TIALD (Target Indicator and Laser Designator) are both target marking pods for the bombers. They can be used for self designation, but were often used on dedicated aircraft for other bombers.

Section Four

BELIZE –
THE LAST GUNBOAT

The Central American conglomerations
Are medleys of many human nations.
We'd have you believe that they're all liars
But most of them come straight from the Mayas.
Of Creole they speak, I am no fan
They always say, 'No big ting, Man.'

(The author – 1982)

Chapter Twenty-Seven

The Last Gunboat

BELIZE – NOVEMBER 1975

Little did I know, when I left Aden for Europe at the end of 1967, that I would have any more to do with Empire. If they'd called it British Honduras, from schoolboy stamp collecting days – then no problem, but I can remember we initially looked for Belize on a map of Africa! I was destined to act as the No.1(F) Harrier Squadron's Operations Officer and an extra pilot in Belize. So, 1 (F) Sqn and I flew out in November, for the first time at a week's notice, in response to much overt sabre rattling by Guatemala whose government, based on an ancient treaty that they had curiously misinterpreted, was now laying serious claim to southern Belize. In fact, they did not intend to overrun the country, even though when we arrived, we found the border town of San Ignacio partially evacuated[1].

We reaped the benefit of a simple, cheap country with a very affable, racially-mixed population living in harmony in those days. There were Mayan Indians, Creoles descended from African slaves, Carribs and East Indians, Mestizos from Amerindians and Spanish settlers, shipwrecked Garifuna and escaped slaves, together with whites of British, Spanish, German and Dutch origin, and a sizeable Mennonite farming community. One could even see ginger-haired, black Africans, and such was the racial harmony and political incorrectness at that time that once I heard half-a-dozen Negro-boys sitting on a wall in the town square, singing all eleven verses of the Ten Little Nigger Boys song! Indeed the only trouble we had with the locals was trouble in understanding them. Although English is the primary language, they switch between Spanish, Creole and English, often in the same phrase. For example: *"Bad ting neda gat owner"* = Bad things never have owners! How true!

Nevertheless, last among the locals are the rather seedy American expats, in stained white suits and panamas splitting at the brim. They add to the atmosphere of rot and decay, both physically and morally. There is often the sense that oddly sinister and rather noxious and notorious activities, probably to do with drugs, were being conducted in the back of little bars on the grimy side streets. I was conned by one of these Yanks once and the result gave me no end of grief, but that's a story for later.

Arriving in Belize was the beginning of a real lesson in survival. Dwellers in temperate zones seem to have only two perceptions of the tropics: happy island paradises or disaster-ridden banana dictatorships. Belize manages to

Fig 15. Belize's position in Central America

combine elements of both. This was a virtually unspoilt country, the size of Wales with the population of Cardiff. Extended political turbulence limited foreign investment in this undeveloped land of jungle, mangrove swamps, spectacular electrical storms, hurricanes and merciless, stifling, humid heat.

Travel is difficult in the extreme and, now that the hardwoods (mostly mahogany) have been stripped out, the secondary jungle is impassably dense. Indeed, this is where Papillon was shipwrecked after his escape from Devil's Island, and is known as part of The Mosquito Coast. Man defends a precarious foothold in resentful clearings, fighting back tangled undergrowth and vegetation of every genus, while an endless variety of screeching birds, biting insects, venomous spiders, scorpions, ants, crocodiles, flees, beetles, and Iguanas in every drain-pipe, conspire to end his fragile tenure. The snake and the Jaguar are masters here and malaria-carrying mosquitoes are king while we are the unwelcome intruders.

That any empire sprung up in this part of the world at all is a wonder; only failed pirates would ever have bothered to attempt to conquer this manifestly alien territory, and then not without the lucrative hardwoods to harvest.

The air in Belize hangs oppressive, especially just before the rainy season, and 170 inches of water fall each year. Standing under a thrice daily, warm shower (the water is never cold) in your flying suit is the only way to keep the salt and sweat stains away, while allowing a certain cooling of the body. To wear clothing here was intolerable, but to cast it aside was to scorch by day,

270

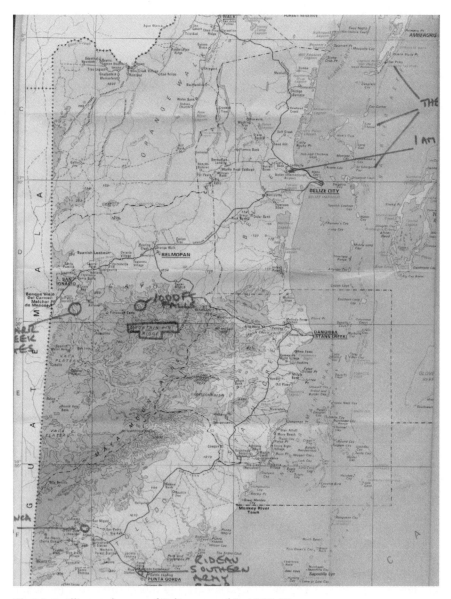

Fig 16. 1million scale map of Belize as used in 1975–82.

and expose an ample area to the ever-hungry mosquitoes and sand-flies by night. To venture outside by day without sunglasses was to be blinded by glare, and to stay inside with no air conditioning was to suffocate. But throughout the daytime, and particularly at dawn and dusk, came certain gnats, flees and sand-flies, extremely noxious, clever and persistent about one's wrists and ankles. Later among the deafening trip of evening crickets

271

POTTED HISTORY OF BELIZE

(ALTHOUGH BELIZE'S HISTORY IS OF INTEREST, IT IS THE RAF'S INVOLVEMENT IN BELIZE THAT HAS NEVER BEEN PUT TO PAPER. HENCE, I ONLY GIVE A SHORT POTTED VERSION HERE FOR THE SAKE OF COMPLETION.)

Later to become British Honduras, Belize has been successively dominated by the Mayan Indians, pirates, the Spanish and the British. The former have largely disappeared a thousand years ago and the first pirate attacks occurred in the 1600s.

4500BC	First Maya-speaking groups settle.
1511	First Spanish speaking contact with the Maya.
Early 1600s.	Piracy prevails. Henry Morgan, and his buccaneers used St.Georges Caye as one of their main bases from which to plunder Spanish ships in the Caribbean area.
1618	Spanish rule.
1630/40	Maya revolt against Spanish rule.
1638.	According to legend, the pirate, a Scot called Peter Wallace, built himself a temporary camp at the mouth of the Belize River, and enjoyed a lucrative career relieving Spanish ships of their cargo. These buccaneers started the first industry cutting hardwoods in the swamps, whilst Spain claimed sovereignty but never effectively colonized the place. The site where Wallace's camp had stood on the estuary's mouth became the most prominent of these settlements: Belize City.
1670.	Treaty of Madrid to restrict piracy. British military presence established. Belize City builds up on site of Wallace's settlement.
1718-98	Anglo-Spanish wars.
1786	1st British superintendent established.

1798	Battle of St Georges Caye. The settlers and slaves under the command of the British army, and with support from the Royal Navy of one schooner, soundly defeated a 32-ship Spanish invasion fleet.
1821	Mexico and other central American countries over-throw Spanish colonial government. Guatemala claims Belize from England, who claim they won it fair and square. Belize insisted it belonged to neither, and was ignored!
1859	Treaty between England and Guatemala defines borders, and this is the essence of the problems today. The treaty was left deliberately vague to fool the USofA, who were taking the Monroe Doctrine** seriously. So, the Guatemalans claimed under the treaty that they had sold roughly half of Belize - the northern half - to us while retaining the rest. We claimed that the treaty defined the borders as they existed at the time. In essence, Guatemala sold England land it never owned for money that we never paid! And that was still the argument that raged, causing the 1970s dispute and the consequent deployment of, inter alia, the RAF Harrier peace-keeping force in 1975 and 1977 to 1994.
1862	England declares Belize a Crown Colony called British Honduras.
1964	Granted autonomy as part of Empire shedding policy but not full independence. Reverted to original name of Belize.
1975	Harrier force deployed.
1977	Second Harrier deployment.
1981	21st Sep: Full independence granted.
1991–93	Guatemala agrees to recognize Belize.
1994	Harriers returned to UK.

**Monroe Doctrine suggested that all Americas were part of the USA's backyard for defence and economic purposes. USA did not want any other colonial power interfering in its back yard.

found a certain liberal, heathen deity in the shape of Late Bottled Nuval Port (LBNP), which frequently held seductive court in the Mess bar. Legend had it that copious LBNP – late-bottled meaning this year's vintage – was rough and potent enough to stop the 'mossi's' biting!

No one would invest in the country while the instability instilled by Guatemala continued. Hence, the infrastructure was ancient and a little shaky. There were only four so-called highways in the country: Northern, Southern and Western, with the Hummingbird Highway connecting the latter two. But for highway read "potholed and rutted tracks[2]", often washed away during the rains. There were less than a hundred miles of metalled roads, half in Belize City itself, ten miles of Northern highway to the airport, and thirty miles of Western highway to the new capital city.

When Hurricane Hattie destroyed Belize City in 1961, it sucked the corrugated iron roofs off the houses and imploded the walls. Tidal waves tossed streets into the sea. The coral reef gave in places and an offshore caye was cut in two by a channel thirty feet deep. Wind speeds in the system exceeded 120mph, and took eight hours to pass over the city, leaving little besides the Governor's mini-mansion and the Anglican Cathedral. The village where the population weathered it out, just inland next to the airport and on a bend on the northern highway, is now called, unsurprisingly – Hattieville!

After Hurricane Hattie, Belmopan was built. This new administrative capital, inland away from the hurricanes, must rate as the world's least significant capital city. In a country that boasts such lively village names as Roaring Creek, Double Head Cabbage, Teakettle, Big Eddy, Over-the-Top Camp, and Gallon Jug, then Belmopan is as dull as the Premier could make it. The grand creation of the long-running Premier, George Price of wooden Harrier fame, Belmopan had five main buildings in 1977, a mini-market, a cinema, a one-engine fire station, and a population at weekends of around seven hundred. A figure of fun and derision, Price was given the usual advice by the opposition newspapers, which was, *"Yu mouth no get stink if yu kip it shut!"*

To the South, Punta Gorda is the main metropolis and a prime target for the Guats. Yet it only runs to a grass airstrip, a whorehouse and five cafes! The only time I was there, the cafes were out of beer for a week because the liquor lorry from Belize City had gone off the dirt-track into a mangrove swamp, and the whores were away on holiday – and I'm sticking to that story!

The only real enterprise comes from the Mennonite community in the centre of the country at Spanish Lookout and Pilgrimage Valley. Here they have cleared the jungle and bush, and have immaculate farms. The women are in shawls and long blue cotton dresses, the men in white shirts and dark waistcoats, driving horses and carts, and the Bible their only entertainment in their spick and span, scrubbed, wooden houses. The yields are high for they put all their Puritanism and passion into their work. The only source of high quality, mahogany furniture comes from there – I have two mahogany rocking chairs and two rosewood folding chairs that are so well hand-made that they'll see my family for a few generations yet.

Along the reef off the east coast lie a scattering of unspoilt Palm-covered island Cayes with names such as Dead Man's Caye, Laughing Bird Caye, Man o'War Caye etc., many with a history of piracy. The northernmost is

Ambergris Caye, legendary haunt of Blackbeard. Its little village of San Pedro is where we headed on most weekends.

The entire economy is revealed by the drive from the airport into Belize City: a sawmill, a brewery (Belican) and soft drink plant, a jeans factory, a scrap-yard and between two and four whorehouses, depending on your definition of whore, with such wonderful names as *"Raul's Rose Garden"*!

The city has now been rebuilt using softwoods and corrugated iron. Each house had its own water barrel for catching the rain as there was no piped water. Any elegance and wealth left from the boom days of mahogany, with tall white rooms, hardwood floors and wide verandas, have disappeared over the reef. The mahogany is long gone, while there are now few verandas because there's little worth viewing.

Belize City today is an old colonial style town, crumbling in the heat and humidity, built out of wood with corrugated iron roofs, regularly battered by hurricanes and history and well off the beaten track. Its ramshackle wooden buildings lurch out over the water, are partially colonial – those few that survived the hurricanes – but their grandeur has faded adding to their quaint charm. It is typical of the old British Empire, and somewhere you imagine hasn't existed since the mid-1800s. The houses were mostly built on stilts on the edge of the Mangrove swamps where the Belize River estuary has deposited its long alluvial banks of sand and mud, which stick out into the warm shallow waters of the western Caribbean. Crossing this isthmus at right angles and open to the sea at both ends is the main open city-sewer. Welcome to Sweet Water Canal! People live in wooden huts with wooden outdoor loos over-hanging and depositing straight into the canal. The water was always sluggish, moribund, thick with dirt and debris, animated with Catfish, scavenging birds and the odd shark, and fed by the inexhaustible supply of torpid human detritus. It reaked for miles around and pervaded the market and everything else in the vicinity. Yet the locals live alongside it in a rudimentary shanty town. *(No Big Ting Man)* But it does look good on Kodak!

By comparison, a typical up-country village, Gallon Jug, was inspired by the local rum brew and has two shacks that hardly run to a single bottle, but it does have a Super Constellation aircraft fuselage used as a grain store. Quite remarkable, considering the plane had crashed eighty miles away at the airport and there are no proper roads!

To quote from the travel booklet, *"The Rough Guide to Belize"*: *"Set in neat fenced pastures, Gallon Jug, a little town near Orange Walk, is now home to one, Barry Bowen. Barry is, reportedly, now the richest man in Belize."* However, back in 1977, already worth a bob or two and owner of the Belican and only brewery and soft drinks plant in the country, Barry, a white Belizean, and I had some real escapades together – drinking his Belican beer of course! We had an excellent relationship as much because his Belican Brewery was immediately across the road from our C/D Harrier hide, and operationally we'd made provision for two more hides inside the brewery, and there were no end of volunteers for this job!

On one particularly boozy night, after becoming bored with the Mess cock-tail party where we met for the first time, and to which all the local bigwigs had been invited, Barry suggested a night flight out to San Pedro in order to put in some real drinking. Scott-Cowper, the Nova Scotia Bank Manager,

Dave Lott, my Flight Commander, Barry and I all slightly merry, sped off to Municipal Airport where, without any airfield lighting, we launched North in Barry's Cessna. Flying uncertainly and unsteadily in the dark, we threw it back at the ground on the caye's unlit sand airstrip, where we tried most of the bars on the beach that night. A free bed awaited in one of the beach hostels where, the following day, an enormous and very late but welcome breakfast finally found us before a lunchtime flight back. Welcome to Belizean hospitality, and a wonderfully unregulated free country!

BFB – BRITISH FORCES BELIZE

Although Belize was granted independence in 1981, the end of British rule did not end British involvement. Guatemala still contested Britain's 160year old claim to Belize, and continued to indicate that it would take by force what it couldn't win by treaty. Thus, within the independence treaty which returned Belize to the Belizeans lay a defence agreement providing for a small British garrison to remain in Belize as a deterrent force. Without such a deterrent force, Belize would have remained vulnerable to Guatemala. Against a Guatemalan force of 15,050 military personnel drawn from a population of 7.2 million people, Belize had had two partially-trained Belize Defence Force (BDF) companies (fewer than two hundred men) drawn from a population of only 145,000: hardly an army. As part of its military might, Guatemala's 14,000 man army included nine infantry battalions, a paratroop battalion and seven tanks. Its airforce was 450 strong, consisting of 10 Cessna A-37B ground attack fighter/trainers, 21 transports, 21 liaison aircraft, and a squadron of 16 helicopters. Opposing them, Belize has a couple of B&N Islanders.

The reality was simple: an arch left-wing regime in Cuba, an arch right-wing regime in Guatemala, with Belize caught in between. What better training ground for communist guerrilla infiltrations on the Guat's eastern border than Belize itself? It shares a whole one hundred and fifty mile common border with Guatemala: a border that, but for one unmetalled road, was solid secondary jungle. What the Guats really wanted was security on their western border with Belize; they really and rightly feared a left-wing Belizean government allowing any Cuban or other left-wing, guerrilla organisation to operate in the country. So, what stopped any troubles happening? Us! – the British Forces interposed between the two of them.

In Nov 75 the last gunboat departed our shores in the guise of six Harriers from 1(F) Sqn at RAF Wittering, together with some helicopters, a radar, and a few 40mm Bofors anti-aircraft guns. After reinforcement the British Forces there consisted of roughly 1,600 troops, and included two Army infantry battalions backed up our Harriers, helicopters and a Royal Navy frigate on call somewhere in the Caribbean. Later, whenever the Guats felt we were moving out (like UK did in the Falklands, and look at the disastrous consequences of that), leaving the border free for Cuban infiltration, all they had to do was a little more sabre-rattling and the Brits stayed another six months. Cuban communist guerrillas, operating from Belize into Guatemala, would have been the ultimate nightmare for the latter's right wing government. Hence, their sabre-rattling whenever they thought we would move out. As the

Overseas-Commitment Review Committee met every six months to extend or end any detachment, the Guats were on to a good thing here! This political analysis was proven by the enormous size of the Cuban delegation to the Belize Independence Day celebrations, but that came much later.

"We are here under an agreement to assist in training the BDF and assist Belize in defending itself against external aggression," to quote Brigadier A. C. Vivian, commander of British Forces Belize in the late '70s. *"The Belizean Government provides guidelines (training and defence) under the agreement. We are confined strictly to protecting the border areas. We are not concerned with internal affairs."* To protect the Belizean borders, we employed a mini-Rapid Deployment Force (RDF) – select elements from the British military operating independently and capable of sustaining a full combat situation.

Any spy relaying to the Guats the size of the RAF force in Belize would have been overpaid, no matter what he had charged. There were simply four of everything: four Harriers with four pilots (there were six of each initially), four Tigercat missile launchers and four x 40mm twin Bofors guns (both later replaced by four Rapier missile fire units), and four Puma helicopters with crews. The Army also had four Gazelle helicopters for observation and command and control. In total, this formed a 300 man air force, defending the country.

The only major airport in Belize is located nine miles outside Belize City. Despite the new capital, Belize City continued to be the centre of commerce; therefore, defence was designed to protect its airport without interfering with civilian air traffic. With Rapiers defending the airfield, backed up by a 24 hour surveillance radar, and Harriers for longer range defence, it was pretty secure.

Belize International is still the only airport in the country capable of handling a jet fighter. If it should be damaged, there would be no place for a conventional fighter to land. Hence, the use of the Harrier, which could divert if necessary to one of the many tiny, light aircraft landing sites dotted around the country. The airport also was of strategic importance since it had the only runway long enough to accept regular resupply and/or reinforcement aircraft from the UK. This remains the case today.

Flying the Harrier in Belize was different from Europe because of the potential threat. In UK or Germany we flew at low level and fast. The threat to the aircraft was from ground-to-air missiles or enemy fighters, but in Belize, the primary threat would have been small arms fire, so you flew high enough to avoid them. Even so, as in Aden, we were using a ground attack fighter for air defence without any proper air defence weapons, usable air-to-air gunsights or defensive capability. Operational training also required rethinking for the differing jungle operations (between the European theatre and Belize). Here we learnt to live rough in the jungle, as could be the case in actual battle conditions. Even so, just our very presence was more than enough to discourage any potential aggressor. Seeing our Harriers in the sky all the time reassured the local Belizeans of the RAF presence. Indeed, the Harrier was the most potent weapon system in Central America.

The role of the Harrier in an actual combat situation was essentially the same as it would have been in Europe: to destroy the enemy and his vehicles on the ground, cut the roads over which he must travel, and provide close-air-support for the ground forces. They also provided a modicum of air defence coverage which would have been handled elsewhere by air-to-air fighters. We were constantly intercepting Guatemalan DC-6s and C-47s intruding into Belizean airspace.

We didn't do any training that would put great stress on the Pegasus engine, as the hot weather would have quickly used up the engine's life. Since plenty of VSTOL practice was available in Europe, and most pilots rotated to/from Belize every eight weeks, we didn't practise this hot-end engine performance in Belize. Pilots only completed minimum-performance training tasks, such as vertical landings and 65% engine power landings to conserve engine life. Our primary operational training here consisted of weapons training, reconnaissance, forward air control, air defence interceptions and area familiarization, for all of which the pilots and the aircraft together averaged about sixty hours flying per month.

The Harriers were deployed around the airport, based in high-walled, camouflaged, revetted, double Hides, consisting of wood and corrugated tin walls filled with dirt, and a floor of perforated steel planking. In each concentrated complex, two hides are operational and a third hide can be used for reinforcement aircraft, if necessary. The hide complexes are self-contained units for operations, including defence, Mess and domestic facilities. We also provided our own defence if attacked, backed up by elements of the Belizean Defence Force, if required.

We had eleven enlisted technicians per Hide, consisting of nine junior ranks and two senior NCOs. The hide chief was a chief technician, who was either airframe or engine qualified. A Sergeant, always an armourer, supported him. Together they completed all our own first echelon maintenance. In the Wilkinson hangar was a third team engaged on second line maintenance as well, and a lot of problems did they have. The hangar itself was infested with Black Widow spiders, and was next to the Belize river, full of crocodiles. It was a sheet-metal hangar, which was stiflingly hot and humid in the incessant sun, so some of the engineering, such as engine changes, often had to be completed outside. Other surprising aspects were the effects of the climate on the various facets of the aircraft, the worst of which were the fuel tanks. There was a minute microbe in the atmosphere that at those temperatures became active in the fuel and then, ate the sealant compounds that sealed the tanks. Fuel leaks were interminable and beastly to repair.

The only defence the hides could not provide for the Harriers was against hurricanes. For that event we had contingency plans to fly out to Key West, Florida or Montego Bay, Jamaica. On the best military premise that any plan needed practising before the real thing happened, we were always requesting permission to practise this hurricane diversion plan; a weekend in Montego Bay after weeks of Mangrove swamps was extremely enticing! Needless to say, permission was never forthcoming!

Of the Rapier missile sites, one was always on 24 hour alert with a full crew standing by. They could detect an inbound aircraft twelve kms (seven-to-eight miles) out, and at heights up to 10,000 ft. We were constantly exercising the Rapier crews ourselves, and considered it a coup to sneak back to the airfield from a training flight without being "shot down" by them. They didn't miss often, I'm glad to say!

Also supporting us was Butcher Radar, an old, airfield ACR7 surveillance radar named after Flt Lt Ted Butcher who designed the site. Located at the edge of the airfield, the radar provided the Rapier crews with advance warning of any inbound aircraft, and was able to guide us into an attack position on any hostile aircraft. Air-to-air combat training in Belize included radar guided intercepts, something that was not practised by the Harrier squadrons in Europe. Butcher also provided us with a semi-automatic landing aid in bad weather, giving us range and azimuth directions to touchdown, while we looked after our own altitude, which depended on the range given. Unfortunately, the radar was usually blotted out in bad weather, exactly when we really needed to use it. However, it saved at least one pilot who was caught out in a torrential tropical downpour, but more of that later.

In summary, RAF Belize provided a small but extremely effective contribution to the overall defence of Belize, but the price was substantial for defending this smallest of the Central American countries. For the money spent, the British not only protected one of the earliest and longest-lived democracies in the New World from territorial aggression, but had access to a continuing source of training, not available in Europe, for jungle warfare, and could test their reinforcement procedures. There is no question the benefits outweighed the costs. The British forces also put an enormous amount into the local economy, and the troops certainly kept the whorehouses occupied.

I was one of the priority personnel sent out on the first of thirteen C130 Herculi to organise the place ready to receive the six Harriers and 12 C130's worth of specialist equipment. The C130s flew out from Wittering to Nassau, Bahamas for a quick crew change before a short dash into Belize, while the Harriers staged via Bermuda. Amazingly, the Americans (our closest ally?), would not let us overfly their airspace! They supported Guatemala on the basis that Cuba supported the new left wing Belizean government. This was yet another example of American humbug: our ally covertly but incessantly helping to bring down British colonialism.

Typical of my luck and of military planning, while all of us priority passengers left on the first Hercules, we were the last to arrive. Five hours after leaving Wittering, and half way across the Pond, the weather radar went unserviceable, and our C130 turned back into RAF Lyneham. Three hours later we took off again, landing finally at Nassau, Bahamas after a thirteen hour flight, but now the last in the stream of thirteen. Then to cap it all, we found that they had only pre-positioned twelve slip crews, so there was no crew available to take our aircraft on to Belize! By now it was late at night in Nassau, and we were even more astonished at the next act. Leaving all the passengers in a completely closed airport terminal building, the crew went off to a five-star hotel for their eight hours sleep. We sat on tubular metal chairs all night, in the semi-dark with no facilities whatsoever, waiting for them to return. When they did, we took off again, but not before a few choice words had been thrown, to arrive five hours later in Belize after a thirty-eight hour journey with no sleep, and little food or drink. In that state, we reinforced Belize! If the Guats had known at that time, they could have overrun us with the greatest of ease!

On arrival, we set to establishing a Harrier operations and engineering organisation, only to find that there was nothing with which to start, except an old round-topped, corrugated-iron, filthy Nissen hut with one or two tables and chairs obviously unused for years. Even our domestic quarters were tiny, double-bunked, open-partitioned-to-the-roof, unairconditioned, six-foot-square 'cabins'. Typically, no-one had anticipated our arrival or our requirements, and we started in our dazed state from scratch – that's the army for you: just a key to an old hut long disused! I shudder when I recollect organising our operations room. The GLO and I were moving a two-drawered, wooden, office table across the dusty room when, after putting it down, I opened one of the small drawers. A five-inch diameter, greeny-grey, jumping spider leapt out of the drawer on to my shoulder and immediately onto the wall! Instant fright! For the next five minutes, four of us careered around the room with brooms, smashing everything whilst trying to hit this hairy monster and avoid its leaps, but its jumping ability and anticipation were so great that we couldn't get near it. Of course, at the time, we were not sure whether it was poisonous, so were extremely reluctant to venture closer than a full broom's length: it had demonstrated a four-foot jumping ability! We finally delivered a fatal blow, but not before we'd stirred up years of dust and put quite a few dents in the various plasterboard walls! I never saw spiders like this in the Middle East, but developed a healthy respect for them ever since. We found out afterwards that they are *not* poisonous, but they do have a healthy bite!

Twenty minutes after an exhausting flight via Bermuda from the UK, the first two Harriers were airborne again, flagwaving over Belize City, and making their presence known along the border. In the event, the Guats stopped all invasion manoeuvres and the Belizeans were dancing in the streets, believing we'd saved them.

That uneventful detachment didn't last long, but what a contrast it had made from European operations. When a country's Prime Minister asks Harriers to beat up his capital city, you know you're certainly not in Europe! You also know you're part of the most popular organization in the region. It is unlikely you'll ever have another opportunity like this again!

Just before Christmas '75, a hurricane devastated Guatemala City and led to their government postponing any immediate claim on Belize. Seven weeks later, as everything then quietened down and we'd seen no Guats despite many border patrols, the Sqn came home again, only to find that this period was the lull before the storm.

FERRY TO BELIZE – July 1977

Another opportunity came, one that would last many years! Eighteen months later, the Guats forced us back to Belize again. The month was July 1977 and the Guats were really serious this time with troops on the border. Again it was a Wilson Labour Government, and his first reaction was that he *". . . had no mind to send a gunboat."* Nevertheless, he was persuaded eventually to send a small force, and for once I was involved in the pre-planning. Our AOC, AVM Donaldson, arrived unannounced at the Sqn to discuss plans for cross-border operations in Guatamala. As the Boss was away that day, Dave Lott and I sat in the Boss's office with the AOC and a large map of Guatemala, planning how we would attack their main airfields and aircraft. In deciding the tactics, the various weapon types that we'd need fell into place. From that step the logistics of air-lifting the right weapons out there became simpler.

In all my time as a weapons instructor, that was the only episode in the RAF where the big Boss came to ask our opinions, talk tactics and operations with us directly, before then implementing our advice. Though the same thing happened to me in SOAF with their COS, Air Marshal Bennett, eighteen years later, it was not the RAF way of doing things. In 1977 it was a refreshing change to use one's knowledge and experience to plan major international operations beforehand, and our opinion of Donaldson rose accordingly.

This time though, I was not only the Squadron Weapons Instructor, but a deputy Flight Commander as well. This 'lofty' status gave me the huge pleasure of flying one of the six Harriers from Blighty out to Belize. Unlike the first occasion in '75 when they flew via Bermuda with crews pre-positioned there to take the aircraft on straight away to Belize, we flew direct to Goose Bay in Labrador, night stopped, and flew on to Belize the following day. But it was never to be quite as simple as that!

To fly our little Harriers safely across the Pond required the addition of an in-flight refuelling probe and two enormous, underwing 330gallon ferry tanks on each aircraft. These tanks were so large that it was like driving a trimaran, and they made the aircraft extremely unstable longitudinally. At slow speed for take-off and landing and especially in any cross wind, the instability was at its worst. Add to this pilots who had little experience of flying under these conditions, together with the lack of any autopilot, and nav aids no use over the ocean, and it was never going to be straightforward. This was in the days before routine Atlantic crossings by fighters for various flag exercises. We did have an analogue, inertial-nav that stopped working when the moving map display film spool ran out in mid-Atlantic. Our only other aid, TACAN[3], with a maximum 200mile range from any ground beacon was of little use in the middle of this enormous Pond. So there was an occasional frisson of adrenalin accompanying this unusual ferry mission. My logbook records a total of 12hours,10minutes airborne, of which two hours were spent in cloud, and eight 20minute periods spent plugged into the tanker aircraft uplifting fuel.

We flew out from Wittering on 6 Jul 77, with ground crew and logistics in a Hercules following us down the route, initially over the North Sea off the Yorkshire coast, to rendezvous with the tankers for our first fuel uplift. Well, once clear of cloud, I'd never seen so many aircraft milling around since the FAA cocked up our Aden flypast in '67! There were tankers everywhere! Each flight of two Harriers had two tankers along with it. Each pair with its tankers was half an hour apart en route, and I was leading the third or rear pair with Henry de Courcier as my number two, or wingman.

As well as the en route tankers, there were six airborne spares whirling around over the North Sea; I think we had the whole tanker force up there to meet us. When I finally edged behind what I thought was my tanker for my first refuel, I had just lined up on the drogue and shoved the throttle forward to plug in, when his wing went down and I shot right over the top of him! Pure luck that we didn't touch! It transpired that it was a new OCU tanker crew, unused to operational tanking procedures, and they had lined up behind two other tankers, thus hitting wake turbulence at the critical moment. A great start to a very long flight!

In-flight refuelling is not the simple operation often described. After a number of stabs and misses, it is as well to move back and attempt the impossible – relax! Impossible because you're in the middle of the Atlantic, and if you don't make contact with the drogue, you're going one way only – downwards!

In between these refuelling bursts, formating on tankers for five hours at high level is almost mind-numbingly boring. Then, lulled into an upper airspace lack of focus, for an instant you look away from the Victor. When you look back he's disappeared! Gee, there goes my fuel, and my nav aids with him! Panic, panic . . . and then just as suddenly he hops back into your vision less than half a mile away! This happened so often, one almost got blasé about being in the middle of nowhere, with not enough fuel to make a landfall, and the siren-like, cold, blue North Atlantic welcoming you with whitecaps and immense, open rollers into a sea survival situation!

As the sop to survival, a NIMROD search and rescue (SAR) aircraft was tasked to accompany us. This guy had taken off before us, flown out to the mid-point or PNR[4], turned back and flown underneath us, turned back again on to his original flight path, retraced his flight and caught us up about half an hour before landing. Well, if it had been boring up to then, this four-engined, thirteen-crew aircraft arrived on frequency with, *"How'd ya like ya steaks doin'?"* and the banter started.

Eventually he said to me, *"You'll be landing before me won't you ?"* With my bum now numb after seven hours strapped to a Martin-Baker rocket ejection seat, I confirmed there was no way he was going in first! So he asked, *"Get the beers in for us, then ?!"* To which I stupidly replied, *"Yup!"* only to hear him cry, *"There's thirty-eight of us in here!"*

That night at Goose Bay cost me the biggest round of beer I've ever bought!

But we yet had to land there, and the weather and Canadian air traffic controllers were not about to help. In the '70s, it was still unusual to be flying IN-derived[5] true headings, instead of compass-derived, magnetic headings. In the UK this posed no problem: there were only four or five degrees difference. But in Goose Bay, much closer to the Magnetic Pole, the difference was a massive forty-five degrees! In our pre-flight planning we'd realised this, but no amount of radio explanation to the arrival radar controllers at Goose Bay was going to change their 'well-tried' system! Their acknowledgements led us to believe they understood the problem, so we duly let-down under their direction as a pair in close formation from 35,000ft to 200ft altitude in thick cloud all the way. Unfortunately, it was forty-five degrees off heading into the mountains! Yup, they were working magnetic, they'd always worked magnetic, and no young upstart Brit was going to tell them otherwise!

Half-way down, I started to get this pit-of-the-stomach intuitive feeling. It's that in-built survival mechanism, that sixth sense that somehow tells you it ain't all it's cracked up to be! We were descending into the mountains in thick cloud – no doubt about it!

A not insignificant fifty-five degree heading change made just ahead of the radar controller's, *"Where the hell are you going ?"* kept us clear. But just how close we got to those mountains, I would rather not know!

To make matters worse, on the final approach there was a howling cross-wind down to runway level, way outside our landing limits with these big underwing drop tanks aboard. The relief as we broke cloud to see the runway ahead of us was instantly tempered. As the ferry tanks' centre of gravity was so far back, at low speed we were starting to run out of forward stick control. Simultaneously we also had some 25 degrees of port drift on to maintain the centreline. Pretty much out of control, we hit the runway going sideways, ran off the side through the runway lights onto frozen tundra to plough the fields . . . slid back on again, and eventually skidded to a heart-rending stop! I don't know how Henry managed, or managed to miss me, but never in my life have I been so happy to be back on terra firma in one piece!

That night at Goose I bought that thirty-eight pint, round of beer, but I did get my own back, though purely by chance. My aircraft sprang a hydraulic leak that evening, and the other five aircraft went on to Belize on day two using a new set of support tankers, Hercules and Nimrods, and leaving me behind. That second day the weather was again atrocious, with solid cloud from 100ft to 30,000ft extending the whole way down the eastern seaboard of Canada and the USA.

Back at Goose, on day two, my aircraft was repaired and readied for the lone trip south on day three. This ensured that all the tanker and Nimrod crews, whose original part in the saga had been completed and were due to return direct to the UK, got all the way to Montego Bay, Jamaica for the weekend just to 'tow' me to Belize! Two tanker crews, two Hercules crews and a Nimrod crew were, that second night, buying me beers like they were going out of fashion!

Meanwhile, our other five Harriers had arrived in Belize in dramatic fashion – perfectly timed, less than an hour before the announcement in the House of Commons of their arrival. Led by Jeremy Saye, the pilots reported that as they flew over Belize City in formation, inbound to the airport, they could see the crowds running and dancing in the streets. They fell in love with our machine – The Harrier. Despite seeing all the other reinforcements arriving, the locals gave the aircraft the credit for saving their country. To quote the Belizean magazine Brukdown, *". . . it can jump, it can skip, it can hop. It can almost dance the reggae. It has class!"* The aircraft were turned round, armed up, and were ready to go within an hour of landing. The Guatemalans were abruptly stopped in their tracks, and The Gunboat was having its last fling!

Day three (8 July) in Labrador dawned bright and beautiful for me, with not a cloud in the sky. Up at 40,000ft after take-off we were treated to a panoramic view of the whole length of the eastern coast of the States, Cuba and Mexico. This was an exciting trip with a Nimrod number '55', alongside a 55 Sqn tanker, with my single-seater squashed in the middle.

The trip wasn't helped by the Yanks again refusing us over-flight rights. It's not well known that 'our biggest ally' wasn't up for this trip, supporting Guatemala instead! Hence, my own second day's flying was at least 200 miles out to sea down the eastern seaboard of the USofA! Abeam Key West one flies right into the Gulf of Mexico skirting left round the NW of Cuba where their SAM3 missile batteries' radars locked us up, before a final descent into Belize.

After two days and twelve-odd hours flying without an autopilot or navigation aids, the tanker took me to right overhead Belize City, circling there at 30,000ft until they heard me call on the ground, then departed east for Montego Bay. A low pass over the City en-route to Airport Camp ensued, only to find, after landing, that yet again I was totally blind. Five hours of cold soaking at high level does not prepare the aircraft for the hot, humid conditions of Central America. The moment the cockpit canopy was rolled back, everything misted up so badly it proved impossible to taxi! Welcome back to 1730N 8812W!

BELIZE – 1977 to 1981

So there I was back in Belize again, defending this last, tiny, but still cherished colony of the Empire. Did we notice any difference from 1975? Well, I did think the 'mossies' were even larger and more numerous!

Belize airport, together with HQ British Forces Belize, and RAF Belize, consisted of a single East/West 6,000ft tarmac runway, with a tiny dispersal, one hangar, a small airport building and tall control tower, all on the South side with the military camp to the North. Here was where we settled into our routine operations and training – two 2-ship missions every morning with the afternoon too hot for anything much but recovery, while living in the army garrison Mess, two to four men to a non-air conditioned room.

If you were anything to do with the RAF Harrier Force in 1975 or 1977, you were a little tin-pot god in Belize. The locals watched the army reinforce: a second battalion and some artillery. They watched a SAM missile battery being assembled to guard the airport and capital city. They watched the Caribbean Guard Ship come in. They saw the RAF Hercules and VC10s arrive, bringing in materiel, at the rate of two or three aircraft a day instead of once per week. But when they heard the five Harriers overfly Belize City in perfect close formation on 7 Jul 77, the locals were literally dancing in the streets, convinced they had been saved and, that day became a national holiday! Discos and bars in town were renamed "The Harrier", and likewise boats in the harbour. The locals fell in love with us. Even newborn babies and football teams were named Harrier.

The Boss (Wg Cdr Jerry Saye, later Air Cdre Ret'd) was in fact called back to the UK to brief the AOC on the situation only four weeks after arrival. Jerry Saye was one of the most operationally minded Bosses I've worked with. A measure of our popularity amongst the locals was shown on the day he was called back to the UK. An hour before take off for the UK he made the 'mistake' of rushing off downtown in his military Landrover, wearing his green regulation flying suit as we did out there, to buy some of the fantastic fruit available from the market – grapefruit were the size of footballs, and the sweet, soft avocados each were enough for four people.

Jerry arrived back loaded to the gunwales with fruit and vegetables dropping off this enormous pile in the back of the Landrover. It was like a scene drawn by Giles: the vehicle bucking over the pot-holed tracks and bits of fruit and vegetables flying off in all directions! Apparently, recognizing who he was, the stallholders had mobbed him, piled the Rover full of produce, and refused all payment. How I wish we had been that popular in the UK!

We had deliberately taken some Sqn silver with us to decorate the dining tables, and at our first formal dinner night Jerry was trying to massage army/air force relations. In his conversation with the Lt Colonel commanding the resident infantry battalion, 3rd Battalion the Anglian Regiment, was heard to guestimate that No 1(F) Sqn RAF had at least £100,000 pounds worth of Sqn silver. I can vividly remember the Colonel turning to him, looking down his nose and replying, *"The Regiment old boy, has so much silver, it costs us that much just to insure it!"*

As a further measure of the Harrier's popularity, there follows a remarkable, true tale, supported some twenty-four years later, when we re-met in the UK, by JJ Scott-Cowper, Belize's Area Manager of the Bank of Nova Scotia in 1977.

The resident British Army battalion at Airport Camp on this occasion was the 1st battalion King's Own Scottish Borderers (KOSBIs), a bunch of some five hundred lowland Scots. Along the roadside into downtown Belize City were a number of wooden shacks that actually were brothels including "The Continental Hotel". The Continental, known as "The Big C" to the troops, was a three-storey, wooden building on the outskirts of town, and was *THE* semi-official brothel; semi-official only in that every Thursday afternoon, our military doctors used to give the girls a "health" check, and pump them full of penicillin: a military policy based on the fact that you'll never stop the trade, so let's make it as safe as we can. After all, this was the year when Time Magazine had a front cover and long article all about this *new* disease called "Herpes"! Well, there's news for Time, in Belize this gave us one big laugh – there were far worse strains of VD, particularly of syphilis, some of which the western world had never heard of – and some of our groundcrew were certainly badly infected. Herpes – forget it!

Anyway, The Big C contained, besides some hard-bitten whores, a number of young, naïve, Mayan Indian girls who had come out of their up-country, jungle villages to make a few dollars for the family – SO I'M TOLD! One night, one of the Jock troopers conned one of the Mayan girls into letting him spend the whole night with her, instead of the usual ten minute trick, on the grounds that he was a Harrier Pilot! She – quite obviously – fell for this ruse in a big way!

The following morning, he paid her with a wodge of Embassy cigarette coupons, saying, *"If you take these round the local bank, they'll change them into Belizean Dollars for you!"* This she truly did, and after explaining herself at the bank's counter, was eventually ushered in to see the manager. Enter one JJ Scott-Cowper. JJ later became a good friend of mine, but at that time he was already a friend of the new CBF Belize: one Brigadier Vivian, ex Royal Welch Fusiliers, who had taken over from the Colonel. Rather disliking us 'light blue jobs'; there was little love lost between the Army and the Air Force out there in the Brigadier's days.

So Scott immediately rang the Brigadier to complain bitterly about the morals of Harrier Pilots! The Brigadier delights in yet another nail in the Air Force's coffin. The 'lack of morals' message didn't take long to wing its way down to us, becoming worse at every level of command until attaining its crescendo on reaching us!

Honour obviously had to be served! The following Thursday, two of us joined the doctors on their rounds of The Big C. We found the girl in question but, with little English on her side, and no Creole on ours, all we ever found out was that the culprit spoke with a Scottish accent! There were five hundred

KOSBI troops within ten-miles, but not a single Scottish Harrier Pilot within 6,000miles of the place! QED!

Needless to say, we paid her for her night's work out of sqn funds, and you'll find in the sqn accounts book a red-line entry that says, "For services rendered: .. . . . 50B$". Honour and popularity were both served and regained, in absentia. We wished the KOSBI trooper well, but it will remain the only time I've ever paid good money for it and, what's more, I never got it! Presuming that the KOSBIs have now disbanded, there's no chance of getting our money back. It could only have happened in Belize, but as they say out there: *"No big ting, Man!"*

There may have been a lack of love between us, but the Brigadier did make a good speech. His staff would research the dates of British battles that coincided with the date of his speech. His luck remained when, one day, our lifeline, the weekly VC10, ran off the side of the runway after landing. Sinking horribly into the swampy mud, the aircraft became hopelessly bogged down. The captain tried full power to extricate himself from an embarrassing situation, but only succeeded in ploughing huge trenches through the mud!

That night, unfortunately for us, there was a formal dinner night in the Mess, which just so happened to be the anniversary of the third battle of Ypres. Well, Brigadier Vivian waxed lyrical about the muddy trenches of Ypres being not dissimilar to those the Air Force had ploughed off the edge of *his* runway in the Belizean swamp! If you wore light blue that night, he made you feel tiny – very tiny! We had the last laugh – the Brigadier was returning to UK the following day on that very same VC10, which, of course, was badly delayed because of the effects of the Brigadier's mud!

During this period one of those Combined Services Entertainment (CSE) shows arrived from the UK to entertain the troops. Topping the bill was that excellent ad-libber, Jim Davidson. For the troops, the amazing sight to greet them on the CSE's arrival by helicopter, was the stripper. Clad in a tight, short, black leather tunic, this amazing brunette called Brandy de Frank, climbed down from the chopper, her long legs clad in thigh length shiny-black PVC boots, as the troops went wild! Yet it was Jim Davidson who stole the show. Situated on a makeshift stage in the car-park, he ad-libbed for over two hours, and I swear none of us has ever laughed so much before or since. It was a memorable night.

In this part of the world it was easy to come a cropper, especially out on the Cayes. Jungle and sea survival situations were never far away in that environment. I used to spend Tuesday evenings partnering the Air Commander (Brian Johnson) downtown Belize City playing bridge at JJ Scott-Cowper's house. During this period, I was introduced to a 60ish-year old Yankee who lived on his own, also downtown. The Yank invited me to be his guest for the day on a trip out to the Cayes the following Sunday in his motor boat. Seemed a good idea at the time: there were never enough boats for everyone wanting to visit the Cayes each weekend. So that morning I set off in the Sqn Landrover, dropped all my mates off at the main harbour for their regular Mess BBQ outing to the Cayes, saying I would pick them up at the end of the day. When

I drove into the Yank's house, I found not one but two US National Airlines stewardesses staying the weekend with him, the boat packed with four picnic lunches, and his boatman dismissed for the day. That hadn't been in the brief, but OK, sounded good to me, and we roared off to a tiny rock of a Caye, some twenty miles SE of the city, where they proceeded to strip off and go skinny-dipping! That was also new to me in front of strangers, but what followed was worse. Drying off, they started passing round a few reefers of cannabis which they continued to smoke all day, and I felt obliged to at least try one. This was the only time in my life I've ever tried drugs. The joint was so foul tasting I was nearly sick which, I'm sure had some bearing on what followed!

Soon it became obvious that our Yank was heavily involved with one of these stewardesses and the other was a friend brought along for the occasion thrown literally into my lap. Come the time to go home, we were a little late leaving. By now I was anxious that I would be late picking up the mates from the Mess Boat. Off we set, and so late that it was soon dark. At this juncture it became apparent that our American host, probably high on cannabis, had no idea how to navigate without his boatman. With no maps or nav-aids of any sort, he had only a small compass attached to the boat. Just imagine powering, totally blind, in the dark and at full throttle across the reef and shallow waters inside the reef, surrounded by Cayes, mangroves, reefs and rocks of various shapes and sizes. The trip was scary – and I don't scare that easily! I sat at the bow – closest to the crash – watching the black water for obstacles and land, only really seeing a few yards in front of me. We screamed along at what seemed like twenty-knots too fast with no lights of any sort in sight, least of all the glow from Belize City, seemingly oblivious to any danger. In retrospect, I believe that, besides the cannabis, the compass also wasn't calibrated because, after about an hour of this, I saw some lights. We arrived with me shaken and stirred, on the inner, western coast of Caye Chapel, some twenty miles NE of Belize City, forty odd miles from where we had set off, and forty-five degrees off track. Caye Chapel was due North along the length of the reef and there was no direct route on the map without bumping into any one of some fifty Cayes on the way! How we avoided a catastrophe, in their drug-inebriated state, I shall never know!

The lights of Caye Chapel blazed out from the only Hotel on the island, which was owned by a Kentucky, coal-mining baron, and known to be used as a drug running stop-off point for boats and aircraft– it had its own sand airstrip as well.

At this stage I had long given up any hope of making it back that night, and hoped the Mess boat guys had managed a lift with someone else. Already in trouble, I was now worried about getting back to start work on time in the morning. We finished up in two double rooms in this hotel, where this tall, dark hostess from Galveston, Texas, proceeded to lie on the bed stark naked and bade me make love to her. It was a unique experience!

We set off back at dawn, about 6am. My hope was that I would get back in time with my only problem buying the guys a beer for missing the pick up the previous evening. Then it happened! To cap it all, and half way back, we ran out of petrol! The engine came to a spluttering halt. I couldn't believe what this foolish Yank had done this time: there was no petrol in the auxiliary motor either! What a cock up – I was only a guest, but the only one going to be in real trouble.

Luckily there's precious little tide inside the reef. We just sat there, no paddles either, with the sun getting higher and hotter until, by pure luck, another motorboat with two locals on board came past. Even then they would have ignored us if this Yank hadn't suddenly produced a pistol and fired some shots into the air! We then persuaded our rescuers to tow us back the last ten miles to the Yank's jetty. Here, without waiting to say any good-byes, I hit the pier running, jumped into my Landrover and disappeared in a cloud of dust as fast as I could go. Even now, I thought, I was only going to be half an hour late, so no big deal. How wrong can you get?

Half-an-hour later, trying to walk into the Sqn Ops nonchalantly, I got a chorus of "Where the hell have you been?" The Air Commander wanted see me A S A P! I then got one of the biggest bollockings of my life. It turned out that when I had neither arrived to pick up the mates from the Mess boat, nor pitched up back at the Mess by mid-evening, they thought I was lost or in trouble on the reef. Consequently the Air Commander had ordered a full scale Search and Rescue Operation to find me! He not only scrambled two helicopters and diverted an RAF Hercules inbound from the UK to look for me in the dark, but also diverted a civilian BAC111 airliner, all of whom were searching for me. Meanwhile, I was out of communication, in bed on Caye Chapel with this drugged-up, American stewardess from Galveston!

In retrospect, things might have been better if they'd found me while out in the boat, but how would I have explained both the girls and the drugs? No one in the RAF out here, least of all the Air Commander, ever knew about the girls or drugs – as much of a surprise even to me! Leaving out the Air Stewardess's and drugs bits, I explained to him the rest of the sad and sorry story, whereupon he delivered his verdict: *"You are confined to camp for two weeks, except on Tuesday evenings when you will accompany me to Scott's house to play Bridge!"* Couldn't say fairer than that! I'd been stitched up a treat by a seedy Yank!

After the first few months, once we'd settled in, it became evident that drugs was still a major occupation and industry in that part of the world. The lack of real industry, besides some sugar cane and citrus fruit, produced the oft-told quote that we (the British Forces) were the second biggest contributor to the local economy. The first was drugs! They were all at it up to the highest in the land, from locally grown Khat to South American produce. Not only are various drugs grown overtly up-country but, more importantly, Belize is ideally situated as the last staging post for aircraft and boats to refuel on their way up to the United States from Colombia, Panama and most points South. In association with the US Drug Enforcement Agency (DEA), we began guarding against drug-smuggling, fast, patrol boats along the coast and Cayes, and searching for airborne drug smugglers refuelling at any of the up-country airstrips. A number of reconnaissance missions flown by both our helicopters and my Harriers were therefore paid for by the US DEA.

A major "success" took place when one of our Harriers, looking for drug running ships off the reef, found a boat off-loading boxes on to one of the smaller Cayes, and took some good aerial photography of the operation.

Subsequently, a troop of infantry scrambled in a Puma helicopter to capture the boat and found £30 million worth of best South American cocaine. The ship was then towed into Belize City harbour where the drugs were off-loaded into the police HQ compound.

A few days later, the pilots involved went downtown to make their legal statements to the police. Afterwards they had coffee in the Superintendent's office. Picture the first floor of an old, colonial, two-storeyed, green and white, balconied, wooden building. In the first-floor office sat the Superintendent, a rotund, jovial Negro. From the open French windows one could see the boxes of drugs in the compound, and the conversation obviously revolved around them.

"What's going to happen to the drugs now?", asked one of the pilots eventually.

The Superintendent looked round the assembled company, broke into a huge grin and said: "Smoke it, man, smoke it!!"

Sure enough, within a few weeks, the whole lot had seeped back into the local economy.

The Caribbean guard ship came into Belizean waters as she did from time to time. I was amused by the term the Navy used: 'Caribbean Guard Ship'. Here we have this tiny 2,000ton frigate guarding the whole Caribbean! Some capability! On this occasion in Oct '77, it was HMS Scylla which arrived. Scylla's Captain, a rather pompous little Welshman, was the most senior four-ringed Captain in the Navy at the time. In typical Navy tradition that meant that when this small frigate sailed past, even HMS Ark Royal had to dip its colours in respect! Everything in the Navy is done to excess on seniority, and therein lies the core of this next tale. Here we go again – trouble with the navy!

Every time the Guard Ship came into Belizean waters, we always arranged a morning of splash-target firing with her. This entailed her towing a target that produced a tall vertical wall of white-water at some fifteen to twenty knots on a long tow-line. The white-water, or 'splash' as it was known, could be seen from a long distance. This gave us our only opportunity to fire at a moving target for peacetime practice. Put another way, it was also great fun!

The QWI's task was to organize the morning's shooting. Accordingly I had signalled Scylla with our requests in the same manner used for all the previous frigates. The information in her signalled reply duly plotted on our chart produced astonishment that she was attempting to tow at those speeds between the shoreline and the barrier reef in badly-charted shallow waters. Once we'd pencilled in the safety traces for our guns and rockets, the danger area always included some inhabited caye or coastline, irrespective of her course. She should have known that!

What is not well known is that ball ammunition will ricochet off the sea's surface easily. In so doing, ricochets can fly down-range quite a few miles. The danger area, therefore, is much larger than might be supposed. Furthermore, the attendant ecological damage to the reef could not be countenanced. Not wanting to teach the Navy their business, I tentatively signalled back, pointing out our danger area problems. In return came a very short, sharp and unhelpful reply. To this I signalled yet again, suggesting a position outside the reef in deeper waters away from habitation where previous frigates had towed for us. In typical Navy fashion, the reply came back, *"I am not a previous frigate!"*

At that point communications broke down. That week I went to the Colonel's weekly O-group, the Commander British Forces (CBF) Belize's weekly organising meeting, and told my story. To my puzzlement he asked me for all the signal paperwork, and with a determined grin on his face, said he would resolve the problem. I found out afterwards that this snotty naval captain, being the equivalent rank as CBF but of higher seniority, had expected on arrival in Belizean waters to take over the command of British Forces Belize for the week. The Colonel had been having all sorts of trouble with this Captain long before my little splash-target affair had come to light, and had even had to signal the MOD asking just who the hell was in charge around here! Needless to say, later that week, Scylla towed for us in the correct 'previous frigate's' position and, though tempted, we only fired at the towed target, and the Colonel remained in charge!

As an adjunct to this tale, Scylla's captain was later promoted and retired as a Rear Admiral, while the next CBF was a Brigadier, a rank higher than a naval captain. This was not only because of the increase in force size due to the reinforcement, I would be surprised if the Scylla incident didn't have something to do with this upgrading! After all that, Scylla was very nearly The Last Gunboat[6].

In 1978 during my third detachment, and being the Squadron QWI, I was bowled yet another spinner. With our pilots there for months at a time, they desperately needed weapons' firing practise. Building your own air-to-ground firing range somewhere in the jungle to give the crews some weapons training was a tall order in Belize, with no roads, inhospitable swamps, and no manufacturing facilities for goods such as the twenty-five foot long, metal poles which were required for the strafe targets.

One morning the air commander and I set off in an Army Air Corps (AAC) chopper to look for a suitable area from the air. Previously I had seen what looked like a burnt out area of jungle, ideally situated, some thirty miles NW of the airfield, and conveniently away from any known habitation. This flat, two-square-mile area was on the east side of a long, narrow lake called New River Lagoon. So sprang up the newest RAF unit: RAF New River Lagoon, without any personnel or buildings, only a few target facilities, was one which the rest of the RAF knew nothing about! In fact, after the first week's firing, there were no facilities whatsoever! Here's what happened:

On landing in the chopper to survey the ground, we found the area just suitable. Most of the time it was under two inches of swamp water, but it generally consisted of sparsely scattered, long grass with the odd medium-sized, deciduous tree. Decidedly, there was no population or any form of habitation within ten to fifteen miles through the whole 360 degrees. There was the odd logging boat on the lagoon, but that was all. This meant we could use the Harrier's laser range finder through all points of the compass, an unheard of freedom in peacetime back home or anywhere else in Europe. So we decided to build the range there.

The plan was for me to have the targets made up, before our Puma helicopters would ferry them out, together with a party of Royal Engineers to erect them on the range. Whenever we were firing, we would use a small, army, Scout chopper with one Harrier pilot in the left seat to act as Range Safety Officer to clear all aircraft weapon attacks by radio.

Now came the amusing bit! We couldn't obtain any poles! We needed twenty-five foot long poles on which to stretch the hessian screens used for strafe targets, but nothing was available in Belize. Then we hit on the bright idea of using thick palm tree trunks; long, straight, thick and heavy, they were ideal.

Hence, one day we arrived at one of the local timber yards where we ordered eight palm trunks twenty-five foot long cut roughly to six inches square.

"Come back next week, man," was the reply!

Next week we went back again. Sure enough, there were a dozen palm trunks, roots, coconuts, branches, the lot lying on the ground of this timber yard. No, that's untrue . . . the coconuts had long gone!

"How many did ya say ya wanted, man?"

"Eight."

"Come back next week, man!"

Next week came round: the branches were off!

"Come back next week, man!"

The following week came round: the roots were off!

"Come back next week, man!"

A further week came round . . . miracles: they were ready! It had taken six weeks!

The rest of the plan went well, and the great day came for the first firing. We were going to train all week, then use the range once per month for a week at a time.

That first week was fine. Monday morning I sat in this hovering chopper, directing our aircraft. Everybody had a good time with some excellent bombing, rocketing and strafe training throughout the week, despite the fact that we had failed to see some of the small, practice-bomb impacts.

A month went by. On the Monday morning I went out in the chopper to check everything was set up for the next firing phase. Could we find the range? Could we, hell! This enormous, black, burnt out area of jungle had disappeared under four weeks of rapid growth of the secondary jungle. To a European, the rate of vegetation growth was phenomenal. Green again it was the same as the rest of Central America! About an hour later, having finally found the right area, we couldn't find the targets! Eventually, we decided to land and scout around on the ground. As the chopper's skids disappeared into two inches of water, then sank into the mud, I began to realise what the rainy season really meant out here! Scrambling out of the chopper in our flying suits and wellies into that mud must have been a sight, but we waded through the water and looked for those targets with no joy. They should have been obvious, 25 feet high, but there was nothing to be seen.

Suddenly, I stumbled to measure my full length in the water! I had fallen into a hole about two to three feet deep and the same diameter! As I scrambled out, covered in mud and soaked, I noticed these little, six-inch long, wiggly things. They were baby snakes! This was the only time in my life I could say I suddenly acquired the ability to walk on water – one of those "road-runner" dashes at Warp 9 . . . until I tripped into the next hole!

Later it became clear what had happened in the first week of bombing! We had been using 28lb slick, practice bombs in dive attacks. These had a one-pound smoke and flash spotting charge for plotting the fall of shot, set off on impact. We had missed many impacts simply because the ground was so swampy and soft that the bombs were sliding four to six feet underground before going off. In fact, there must be some still intact a long way under-ground that never went off at all! These little bomb craters filled with water were *the* ideal spot for mummy snake to lay her eggs! Suffice it to say that that was the last time we ever walked that range in the wet season!

Eventually we did find our targets. They were lying on the ground in the water, having been chopped down at ground level. The ropes and pulleys were long gone with only the old palm trunks left! So much for there being no locals! This just showed how much value was placed on anything manu-factured. The poles had been chopped down for the metal pulleys at the top!

Again, one felt this could only have happened in Belize! Nevertheless, looking at the serious and legal aspects of this story, this was the Empire at work again. We took a piece of land, a large piece, some 10,000 acres perhaps, and without so much as a by your leave, we built a firing range. We told nobody and received no authorization from any national or civilian source, before spending months intermittently firing bullets, rockets and dropping practice bombs onto that piece of ground. New River Lagoon itself is a beautifully unspoilt loch surrounded by the greenery of the jungle. Flooding may forbid development in that part of the bush, but can one imagine trying to take that sort of instant initiative in the UK?

As a sequel, the following month we strung the hessian screen between two trees, but it didn't last long against 30mm ammunition. Eventually we had the Puma choppers lift in a number of old scrap cars and bangers from one of the many downtown scrap yards. Buckets of brightly coloured paint were then thrown all over them, and from the air they made excellent targets with a much longer life expectancy, but ricochets were always a problem!

Operating from such primitive bases as Belize was always only going to be the remit of the Harrier. No other aircraft could survive the conditions of that part of the world without a fully modernized main operating base. Inspection of the Harrier Hide photos shows the water, mud and gravel, with tiny metal strip taxiways over which the aircraft had to pass. Any other jet would have bogged down within the first few yards. Even the Harrier's makeshift home shows nothing more than a muddy, camouflage-netted, primitive hide erected on mud and gravel. Only the Harrier's rough field capability allowed us to defend Belize, one of the last vestiges of our Empire.

It was this rough field capability that brought us to Belize in the first place, and was to put us in the vanguard of the country's Independence Day celebrations. On 21st September 1981 Belize became finally and fully in-dependent. All the Central American and Caribbean nations sent two or three man delegations. Cuba brought in a Cubanair, Russian-made TU154 airliner with one hundred and twenty delegates on board, a measure of the

66. Harriers over Belize
City Centre – 1977.

(© Crown Copyright/MOD)

67a & b. The Author,
intercepting Guatamalan
Air Force DC6s in NW
Belize - 27 Feb 81 and
13 Mar 81.
(© Crown Copyright/MOD)

68. Henry de Courcier in-flight
refuelling somewhere over the
North Atlantic on our way to
Goose Bay – 6 Jul 77.
(Photo taken by the Author)
(© Crown Copyright/MOD)

69. Belize International Airport, HQ British Forces Belize, and RAF Belize, built in a mangrove swamp, squashed between the Belize River to the South, and the coastline to the northeast. Northern highway running from Belize City in the east, to the Mexican border to the North, and Hattiville to the northeast. (Photo taken from 48,000feet in 1986. North to top of frame.)
(©Crown Copyright/MOD)

70. The VC10 bogged down, ploughing muddy trenches in the mud off the side of Belize runway.
(©Crown Copyright/MOD)

71a & b. Harrier taxying on rough ground, and Charlie/Delta Hides – Belize 1981.
(©Crown Copyright/MOD)

72a – c. The author and his No 1417 Flight Harrier XW921 'C' with his name on the side – RAF Belize – 1982.

73. A caption competition is warranted here! The author, hand on bum in flying kit, showing the AOC round Charlie/Delta Harrier Hides. AOC's PA in the foreground seems to be writing on my back! AOC's Annual Inspection – 1417 Flt, Belize, 20 Jan 82.

74a & b. The Flight's Snoopy Cartoon Bar dedicated to the Orange Baron.
(Apologies to, and Copyright of, Snoopy)

75. The Orange Baron himself! Belize 1982.

76a. My C/D Hide groundcrew being introduced to ACM Sir Keith illiamson, Chief of the Air Staff – author extreme right.

76b. The Belizean Prime Minister, Mr Price, shaking hands with the author on his visit to 1417 Flt.

76c. HRHs. My groundcrew being introduced to The Prince and Princess Michael of Kent. Author again extreme right with characteristic 'hand-on-bum' pose!

77a. The shallow Macal river passing Chaa Creek, Cayo District, Belize, 1982.

77b. Chaa Creek from the river – 1982

78a & b. Lucy's kitchen, Chaa Creek 1982. At the table: Army Adjutant, Archie Lund (SengO), Mavis Lund, Adjutant's fiancée, two local schoolteachers. Standing Mick Fleming, the owner.

79a & b. Roast beef Harriers for my dining out from 1417 Flight.

Belizean hard-wood Harrier model presented to the author by the personnel of 1417 Flight – 1982.

80a & b. 1417 Flight RAF Belize, 20 Sep 82, on hand-over of command to Sqn Ldr Dave Linney.

81. The Last Gunboat.
The final Harrier in 1417 Flight markings now acts as the gate guardian for Price Barracks (Our Airport Camp) alongside the runway of Belize International Airport.

importance to them of the Belizean government, the Belize/Guatemalan border, and confirmation of Guatemala's fears and consequent sabre-rattling. This tiny, Central American celebration, with no mention in the British media, ended the last British toehold on the American continent. From Cape Horn to Baffin Bay, 400 years of British rule finally ended.

We on the Harrier unit did have a problem that day. We had to keep all four aircraft serviceable and on standby because there were rumours that a Guatemalan air invasion may disrupt the celebrations. On the other hand, we were to provide the only fly-past for the salute on the main independence parade arranged outside the government buildings at the capital, Belmopan. The plan was that, if we hadn't been scrambled for a border incursion by the time of the flypast, we were to take off, conduct the fly-past on time and return to base. One minute before the fly-past start-up time we were scrambled, two for the southern border and two for the western, and I was leading one of the pairs. A hurried re-brief over the radio found us quickly airborne as a four-ship en route to Belmopan as fast as we could go, where we conducted the noisiest, fastest and shortest fly-past ever for any country's Independence parade! We hit Belmopan at a hundred feet in close formation at 550 knots and were through in a matter of seconds. The moment we passed clear of the government buildings we broke up into two pairs and, at full throttle with guns armed, flew to our respective border areas to take on the Guats' armada – from a pansy peacetime fly-past to a possible air battle in one easy move! Anticlimax followed when, after an hour's patrol, none of the expected armada had arrived anywhere near our border. Then, short of fuel, the two uneventful patrols returned to base.

Despite independence, the last presence of Empire would continue. In the South, the KOSBIs mounted patrols for a week or more though the thick jungle. The Pumas picked up soldiers with snakebites, bad sores and heat exhaustion from rough jungle clearings, while our Harriers continued to scream about overhead. From a hill-top observation post on the SW corner of the border, a Guatemalan army post down in the next valley, 300 yards away, could be continually watched. You could count up to fifteen Guat soldiers there, often finding every one of them asleep!

Back in the Big C, the young Mayan Indian girl of Embassy cigarette coupon fame was being pawed at by an off-duty soldier. While she moaned he pinched her harder until she jumped up screaming *"no, no . . . bastard!"* A bottle shattered in the sudden silence as the clientele stare. *"Jesus,"* says the girl, shrugging and smiling, *"you goddam dangerous in the bar – come upstairs!"*

Here was the universal military incident. But to Belizeans, the Harrier was something else. Calling out the Harriers, they would say in Belize, is like calling on James Bond. They reserve the deepest praise they know for it. *No mean ting, man!*

Notes

1. Belize, considered an Empire success, maintains its relationship with the commonwealth today, and, unlike Aden, it realized it couldn't protect itself and wanted us to stay.

2. Now all tarmaced – 2003.
3. TACAN - Tactical Air Navigation system - an aid providing distance from and bearing to ground beacons.
4. PNR - Point of no return.
5. IN - Inertial Navigation.
6. In March 2004, HMS Scylla was deliberately sunk off Cornwall to be used as an artificial diving reef.

Chapter Twenty-Eight

The Orange Baron

I took over my first real command in January 1982. The whole independent Harrier unit was all mine: No. 1417 Flight. One of various independent WW2 flights, 1417 was the only one to survive by the 1960s[1], and was the only independent fighter flight in the RAF at that time. It had reformed in the Middle East out of the disbandment of 683 Lancaster Recce Squadron at RAF Khormaksar, Aden in Sep 1953. The Lancs were later replaced by six photo recce Ansons and called 1417 Flt.

The Flight was then disbanded again with Meteors taking over the Aden recce commitment as part of 8 Sqn, but it subsequently reappeared as a separate Flight with the introduction of the Hunter FR10s in Aden. They continued recce operations until the withdrawal from Aden in 1967, and were then re-amalgamated into 8 Sqn at Bahrain. But what an amazing connection with my early times in the Empire – I had flown 1417 Flt's Hunter FR10s occasionally in Aden back in the early '60s while on 8 Sqn, and now here I was commanding the unit in the jungles of central America, some fifteen years later.

The Flight was divided into four parts: the HQ and officer staff, the Rectification section working in the Williamson Hangar – the only hangar in Belize, and the two operational, double, Harrier Hides known as Charlie/Delta and Foxy/Golf. These two Hides were totally self-sufficient.

1417 Flt rose again, this time from the ashes of 1(F) Squadron's continuous deployment in Belize. The constant rotation of squadron pilots from the UK had left 1(F) Sqn with a non-operational status within NATO, which was unacceptable. Hence, the Belizean burden was then shared amongst all the Harrier squadrons, each of whom provided one pilot for a six to eight week detachment, but with permanent groundcrew who were on six months unaccompanied postings. 1 (F) Sqn then withdrew, having been helped by the

Fig 17. No.1417 Flight Emblem as painted in red and blue on either side of the aircrafts' nose (without the writing!). Not many can have worn this Emblem with pride, as there were less than half-a-dozen pilots ever on the permanent posted staff.

295

RAF Germany Harrier squadrons for a short time, and 1417 Flight was reformed but with detached aircrew and a detached Boss. However, eventually even this solution was having a detrimental effect on the Harrier Sqns back home with both senior and junior pilots constantly rotating to Belize.

As part of this rotation I had myself been out in Belize on detachment six times previously, including twice during 1981. Then, while I was back in the UK that year the Flight lost two aircraft in avoidable Cat 5^2 accidents. The first, fatal, accident happened during a simulated rocket dive when control was lost due to a disconnected tail-plane linkage. The second was when an inexperienced pilot ran off the end of the runway on take-off because he forgot to put his flaps down, or use his nozzle stop to pre-select the take off nozzle angle, prior to the take-off run. He ejected safely, and the aircraft was written off in the Mangrove swamp on the side of the Belize River a hundred yards off the end of the runway. These two accidents, more than anything else, changed the Flight's organisation.

Both Boards of Inquiry remarked, inter alia, on the lack of control and supervision amongst rapidly rotating aircrews and COs. The obvious conclusion was to have a permanent CO supervising junior aircrew who stayed for longer periods. I was handed the first permanent CO job, and went out there with the difficult task of putting the Flight on a sound, supervisory footing – difficult only because the young first-tourists had traditionally looked on the six-week detachment as their annual, tropical, summer holiday.

1417's capability was encapsulated in the first sentence of what became my Flight Presentation to new army units arriving from the UK: "Welcome to 1417 Flight – the most potent weapon system, and greatest stabilizing influence, in Central America today!"

I arrived off the weekly RAF VC10 from Brize Norton via Washington Dulles at 1.30pm on a Tuesday. I had noticed during the flight that our AOC was on board but never gave it another thought! The weekly VC10 schedule was British Forces' Belize (BFB) lifeline. It was the only source of mail and spare parts, for us the only way in and out of the country, and more to the point, the only way home. It became quite famous locally because it was given a "magic/crap" rating by the radar crews, with the appropriate board being held up half-way along the runway for the Captain to see as he completed his landing run. The 'rools' were quite strict: in order to obtain a magic rating, the VC10 had to land on time (Rule 1), on the runway numbers (Rule 2) and without bouncing or producing any smoke (Rule 3). There ain't no rule 4!

Rule one was inviolate! Morale on the Base rose steeply with timing reports confirming that it was on time over the eighteen hours it was en-route from Brize Norton. The whole progress of the flight was monitored to the minute! The "magic/crap" rating system was eventually incorporated in the official Flying Orders for VC10 flights into and out of Belize! An unprecedented order incorporated from an unofficial wooden board with the two words painted back to back by our radar groundcrew: "Magic" or "Crap"!

So, Tuesday afternoon at 1.30, we landed in Belize on time with a 'magic' rating. But that was the only 'magic' of the next week! I found to my horror that my predecessor was boarding the same aircraft to go home, and it was leaving at 3pm. So with less than an hour's handover/takeover – I was in command!

Part way through the short handover briefing the reason for the AOC having been on board became apparent – it was the annual, AOC's bullshit-inspection the following day! No wonder my predecessor was so keen to depart – I'd been stitched up! Nevertheless, suffering from jet lag and knowing little about the present organisation, never mind the names of the groundcrew, I accompanied the AOC round 1417 Flt the following day in my best suitcase-crinkled KD uniform. I must have looked a real fool, especially trying to introduce people I didn't know!

He certainly knew that I was new because I have photos of the occasion, and he was very easy on me! Indeed, the flight groundcrews had done a sterling job and there was little found wanting. Undeniably, the operating situation here gave him more than enough to think about without worrying about the state of my uniform! Nevertheless, AOC's inspection on your first day in command is a real brute!

That was Wednesday.

Just before dawn on Thursday I was woken, startled by some sort of klaxon. The Commander British Forces, Brigadier Vivian, had called a full command alert exercise. It lasted until late on Friday night – *forty-eight hours on alert and still jet-lagged!*

I slept almost the whole weekend!

On the Monday, after bombing practice that morning, a SNCO and a flight line mechanic (FLIM) were injured while downloading a 4lb bomb. Its safety pin snagged on the lip of its box and the bomb detonated – bang in the middle of a Harrier hide and thousands of gallons of aviation fuel in pillow tanks: that is not a benign environment!

As is usual in the tropics, the crews were only wearing KD shorts and desert boots. The bombs themselves only have a 1lb smoke and flash spotting charge, but it was enough to badly burn both their chests and faces, and the FLIM was also thought to have lost an eye.

That was the end of my first week as CO!

Subsequently, a unit inquiry was convened and lasted two to three weeks. The outcome was that the SNCO would be charged with negligence. By this time, after visiting him in hospital, I found the FLIM to have recovered his eyesight – sighs of relief all round!

The accused had previously come to us with an excellent reputation, was very popular, and his contrition over wounding a mate was palpable for all to see. He was inconsolable. Hence, I then had a big fight over the charge with the Air Commander, Wg Cdr Peter "I tell the jokes" Dodworth, the only air authority above me in the country. He was adamant that he should hear the charge because his powers of punishment were greater than mine. I was equally adamant that the problem was on my unit, and I should, therefore, keep the whole thing in-house. This would greatly increase the morale of the groundcrews by seeing that justice was done swiftly, fairly and locally.

I had already decided that the charge would be met by the maximum fine and punishment available because anything less would not fit the crime, and anything more would require a remand for a hearing by the Air Commander; I was stuck between the rock and a hard place on this one!

Fortunately, the accused pleaded guilty and accepted my punishment, otherwise it would have had to have gone to a court martial. Then our Flight

Sergeant produced a real pearler: he gave such an eloquent plea in mitigation that I was forced in all fairness to reduce my punishment anyway. After the formalities, a friendly pep talk together with the Flt Sgt and a wee dram ensured the SNCO could put this behind him and resume his normally exemplary duties. I have a lot to thank the Flight Sergeant for, though: without his wisdom of many years, the outcome may have been very different. There's nothing to beat a competent SNCO – when he's on your side!

Another fight with the Air Commander ensued over showing too much leniency, but my view is that as we had to work and live together – and they didn't even know me properly yet – I had to be seen to be working for their welfare and discharging a difficult situation quickly, fairly and justly. It had been a minor slip in an exemplary career, no lasting damage had been done, and don't even start down the "what ifs?" road – that is no way to dispense justice. The future of the flight's morale was hanging on the result.

Having stumbled through my first eventful two weeks, at last I had time to review the supervisory problems that I'd inherited. Bearing in mind my briefing from the AOC, I obviously had to divest the young pilots of the idea that it was a summer holiday camp. I would be forced, therefore, to be harder on them than perhaps I would have liked. To help them realize the importance of their time in Belize, I instituted a formal letter system to their COs back home. I hoped that as each returned to Europe, an indication of his attitude and contribution should be put on record and included in his annual report. Perhaps that would help focus their minds!

As a prime example of the problems of flight supervision in Belize, the story of how I came closer than ever to losing an aircraft and also possibly a pilot, is worth telling. This young, full-of-himself, first tour pilot, who shall remain nameless as he still has a career of some sort, arrived to join the Flight. After the usual briefings and sector recce flights with me, I let him loose on his own to fly a Forward Air Controller (FAC) training mission at the far end of the Western Highway.

To understand this episode it may help to recall firstly the lack of aviation support facilities twenty-five years ago in Belize, and secondly, how we managed to circumvent local problems whilst still operating within the rules and regulations. The environment is pretty hostile to short-range, jet aviation and, yes, there's a Belizean Met Office, but it had 365 ways of saying the same thing! My best, and only, method of checking the weather before allowing flying was simply to climb on to the roof of the control tower – the tallest building – and do a quick 360 degree sweep, looking round as far as one could see, and if there were no fog, rain or tropical electrical storms in the vicinity, we got airborne. On the way back to our ops-room I then called in at the radar site and confirmed that there was no weather showing on their scope. This was the first and major part of my early morning routine on every flying day, and 99% of the time, sufficed for the safe flying of 45 minute sorties.

But in the rainy season, when enormous tropical storms could obliterate the airfield with little warning, then any weather approaching on radar was passed to us by the operator every half hour or when necessary, but even this often gave us only ten to fifteen minutes notice. However, they were capable of giving us a fairly agricultural radar approach to the runway if required. This was not the usual precision approach one could expect on properly equipped

European airfields. No, this was the old radar mentioned in the last chapter and still going strong, but which was blotted out by bad weather when you really needed it! But it was capable of giving steering directions if the pilot maintained certain descent heights which accorded with a three-degree glide-path self-interpreting altitude with the distance to go to the touchdown point (5miles=1500ft, 4miles=1200ft, 3miles=900ft etc.).

Our aircraft flew mostly at low level and usually it meant they were out of U/VHF radio contact if a weather recall was necessary. Hence, if in doubt the policy was simply not to launch as there was nowhere else within the country which could be used as a diversion. Of course, in extreme cases, there were a number of up-country and island, rough-ground, airstrips that could have been used in a dire emergency as long as one had a hover capability. Unfortunately though, if the main airfield was out with bad weather, it often meant that so were most of the up-country strips, and there was no way of telling.

Hence, I also insisted that all pilots copied their flight-route onto a fabloned map on the Ops Room wall, so that we knew where they were at all times. With all the swampy jungle with which to contend, and the pilots all dressed in green, any search and rescue attempt would have been severely hampered if we had not known the aircraft's rough location along its route. Deviations were not allowed as it was quite possible to crash into the jungle and leave no trace from above.

Meanwhile, for FAC work, we also had a short wave radio contact from our operations room directly with the FAC on the ground who was talking to the aircraft on UHF. We could use this to relay recall messages to the pilot. All these procedures allowed us to operate without the normal support facil-ities without too much trouble in the dry season. The wet season weather though often posed some serious safety problems.

On this particular day in the wet season there were a few cu-nimbs (storm clouds) around, but nothing threatening us, so I launched this new guy on his low level FAC training mission to the west. Thirty minutes after launch I was warned that a tropical storm had appeared on radar and was fast coming our way from the east out to sea. Unworried, I contacted the FAC on the short wave radio to recall our aircraft, only to be told that he had already left the FAC and was on his way home. This gave him about ten minutes transit time back to the base, enough time before the weather clamped, so there was no cause for alarm. End of problem, I thought. Far from it, as it happened!

Fifteen minutes later, as the storm was by then hovering off the eastern end of the airfield, I rang Air Traffic to see where he was, only to be told that there hadn't yet been any contact with him. By this time the storm was really close, visibility had dropped and tropical rain was pouring down. It looked as though the airfield would be out within five minutes so I ordered the radar to put out recall messages on all frequencies, including the two emergency frequencies of 243 and 121.5Mcs. Then, just as the airfield went out in bad weather, visibility down to 200yards, wind gusting nearly 40 knots and cloud base below 100feet in driving tropical rain, they contacted him thirty miles away on his way home, but he was replying 'short of fuel', and asking for a priority landing!

Radar then proceeded to give him vectors for a radar approach, although they could hardly see him because of the weather returns on the radar tube.

As he commenced his approach, I drove the half-mile down to the radar cabin to watch the screen from behind the controller. How he ever controlled an aircraft on that blotted out screen with only fleeting radar returns, I will never know.

The pilot never saw the runway, and we never saw him but we heard him go by overhead after missing his first approach. He went round again for a second attempt, now desperately short of fuel. By then the weather was atrocious with low, dark, scudding clouds, tropical rain blotting out visibility to less than a hundred yards and there was also a flooded runway to contend with, but, more to the point, it was way below his official approach limits. I then asked him via the controller what his fuel state was, and he reported about five or six minutes fuel remaining. At that point, I told him that if he didn't make it on this next approach, he was to head out to sea, and if he still could not see the ground and find somewhere to put it down, he was to eject.

I put the controller on the spot by uniquely ordering him (probably illegally) on this occasion to continue directing the aircraft all the way down right on to the runway, a procedure that is normally forbidden. The controller's orders stated that he must stop the talk down when the aircraft descends to its minimum legal descent height, which in this case was way above the cloud base for a white-rated pilot. I then stood behind him, leaning over with my hands on the back of his chair to get a clear view of the radar screen as the second approach got under way. The controller had turned him in very tight towards the runway at three miles instead of the usual eight miles and, knowing how much of his fuel was unusable, I was so sure he wouldn't make it that I was now shaking with both anger and anxiety.

The poor controller! My quaking was now so bad that he was forced to demand that I took my hands off the back of his chair as it was juddering so much he couldn't read the radar screen! Not that there was much to see anyway! The screen was completely obscured by weather returns, and only very occasional and momentary glimpses could be seen. In the end the pilot came way below his legal minimums, slowed down as only a Harrier can do, and glimpsed the flooded runway at the very last second. Watching from the door of the radar cabin, I saw him land safely, aquaplaning down a longer length of runway than normal, but finally coming to a stop after a few more heart stopping moments. If I was weak-kneed by now, the pilot's flying kit was brown!

He had about one and a half minutes of fuel remaining when he shut down, and we had both run out of adrenalin! I met him in this state as he climbed out of the aircraft. I thought I'd been angry before, but now listening to what he had to say, his excuses, I was so enraged that I had to go and cool down on my own before I hit him.

Apparently, he had decided on a whim to leave the FAC training early and beat up the beautiful Hummingbird Highway to the south before coming home. So not only could we not contact him, but he would have been nowhere near the planned route if we'd had to go searching for him.

We came within ninety seconds of losing an aircraft, and possibly the pilot, for the most stupid of reasons: a lack of flight discipline, never mind ignoring basic orders and flight safety procedures. But this, in retrospect, was typical of the attitude of the youngsters – it was a simple summer holiday for most of them and, of course, could have been just that if they'd adhered to normal and local flying regulations. They had never operated before outside the comfortable supportive environs of a main European airbase and couldn't understand how quick and easy it was to get into trouble. It was also the only time I'd ever taken a pilot round the back of the hangar and filled him in! He learnt about flying from that, and he's now a respected airline pilot!

My second example is, in my experience, quite unique. A major supervision problem came with a young pilot whom I'll call Joe. He had arrived with a long background of drunken, stupid acts, a most unusual situation in our professional world, but each time he'd been given another chance. Even the Navy had thrown him off their carrier and had had him flown home in disgrace, but again he'd been forgiven! In what I can only describe as a total lack of responsibility on the part of his previous COs and the personnel staff back home, no one had had the courage to cashier him and, consequently, he arrived with us a few months later. To be fair, Joe had partially reformed. He only drank after flying on Friday evenings, staying drunk until Sunday evening, then waking up on Monday morning to go back to flying cold-sober! He was never seen drinking during the normal working week.

However, one weekend he made a big mistake: he forgot to pick his enemy wisely! In a drunken state he decided to have a punch-up with the most capable army Sergeant in the garrison! Here we have an inebriated Flight Lieutenant picking a fight with an accomplished SNCO, and in the Sergeants' Mess to boot!

We – the other pilots and I – were called out late that Saturday night to remove him from the Sergeants' Mess, which we did and then put him to bed. Thirty minutes later, we were called out again. He had got up again and returned to the Sergeants' Mess to continue the fight!

Formal complaints from the Chairman of the Sergeants' Mess Committee I could deal with, and I basically banned Joe from the Mess bar 'til further notice, while awaiting the call from above. If that had been all we could have kept it in-house and no more would have been said. But on Monday morning after twenty-four hours of sulking in the bedroom he shared with the other pilots, instead of sober contrition, he turned up for work reeking of alcohol and insisting he was ready to fly. He then started to argue because I refused to authorize him to fly and took him off the flying programme that day. Continuing to protest that he was capable of flying, he became quite antagonistic and, at that point, I had to march him into my office and read him the riot act. He still refused to accept my decision and I had no alternative but to ground him until further notice.

The grounding put him into the longest, child-like sulk I've ever seen in a grown man which, if he had been on his own, I would have totally ignored. Unfortunately, as the junior pilots' domestic accommodation was a single, shared room with four beds in it, he was badly affecting the rest of the boys. By the end of Wednesday his sullen attitude and refusal to act normally had become totally unacceptable for an officer, never mind one on such a small unit as ours, and I tried everything I could to have him sent home. Unfortunately, I was unsuccessful as we had to maintain a full complement of pilots in the country to fly all the aircraft in case of an emergency deployment. I was therefore forced to reinstate him the following week, though he continued to be banned from the bar. Of course, by now, the whole episode had reverberated round the shared army/air-force camp and set back inter-service relations a long way. He should never have got away with it back in the UK, and especially after the débacle with the navy. If only someone had cashiered him earlier, as he deserved, this incident would never have happened. Sobering up later in life he is now, so I'm told, the chief pilot for a well known airline!

After those two incidents, I'd beware of travelling on civvy airlines!

Soon afterwards, I'd found a couple of 'lost' patrols in the jungle. This was quite a routine exercise. After weeks on jungle patrol, the soldiers often were unsure of their 'exact' position. By plotting from above their red smoke emanating purposely through the top of the jungle canopy, we could radio their position to them from above. Well, one jungle stream junction looks just like any other at ground level, so we have our uses! We agreed the score was even and a respectful truce ensued.

THE ADVENT OF THE ORANGE BARON

Things calmed down a bit after that, and we began trying to improve our "*esprit de corps*". The answer came in the unlikely guise of my flying suit! I'll explain . . .

An old friend from Aden days, Geoff Timms, had the only known 1417Flight Badge from those days, and he lent it to me to wear on my flying suit for the duration of my time as the CO. During my previous test flying tour, I had spent the odd day with British Aerospace (BAe) at Dunsfold, testing Harriers, where the BAe test pilots all flew in RAF style suits. However, theirs were better tailored, bright orange in colour, and they gave me one.

All RAF aircrew used their green flying suits as their normal daytime uniform, but I had decided that because of the search and rescue problem over the Belizean jungle, I would use the orange suit for all my flying there, though I wouldn't wear it as a normal daytime uniform. With the old 1417 Flight patch and the orange flying suit, unwittingly **The Orange Baron** was born! It certainly was most efficacious in lifting the spirits of these lads who toiled in such poor conditions, away from their homes and loved ones.

Throughout the Harrier hides, Snoopy and the Orange Baron cartoons sprung up everywhere. All of us were given Flight tee-shirts with our names on the back. Mine was presented to me with, not my name but, "The Orange Baron" (TOB) printed on it. The aircraft with my name had TOB on it. And so on and so on! The classic Snoopy, flying his kennel in leather flying helmet, was painted across the Charlie/Delta hide walls, together with his words, "Curse you, Orange Baron!"! It became the emblem of the Flight's existence and became their "symbol of affection", or was it mine?

The next project was to address the lack of decent toilet facilities for the Charlie/Delta hide crew. The other hide, Foxy/Golf, had always been accom-modated to some extent in the airfield's old fire station, a partially dilapidated set of wooden huts that at least had a proper toilet. But for five years Charlie/Delta had been using Elsan bogs placed in a tent on awful, swampy, or at best, muddy conditions. They really were dreadful for such a basic human requirement in what had now become semi-permanent accommodation: Portakabins had replaced their tents. Then one day, in looking for a solution, we came across a disused, box-bodied, army vehicle which we managed to purloin. Then the Royal Engineers were persuaded to rig up a proper, modern, flushing toilet inside and proper drainage outside. What a difference for the Charlie/Delta hide-crews that comfortable mobile bog on wheels made! The guys were much happier, morale increased and, more to the point, they felt it also right and proper that they should be shiting in an army vehicle!

There were two other aspects that I changed immediately, which I hoped would also add to the 'esprit de corps'.

The flying task was to achieve fifteen airborne hours per pilot per month, making roughly twenty missions each. The initiative, which served to concentrate the minds on efficient aircraft servicing, was to announce a 'long weekend' break at the end of the month if the task were completed early. That meant relaxing on the beautiful beaches of the cayes.

The second was end-of-month, competitive parties where I was expected to make a speech. Competitive because the hides had the wherewithal to produce a good party, with each alternately attempting to outdo the other! In my speeches, I would welcome those that had arrived during the previous month, then say goodbye to those leaving in the next month, and present them with Flight ties and plaques. As a grand finale, and for my sins, I was then customarily thrown into the emergency water supply tank . . . a cooling down which actually was welcome in the hot, humid atmosphere – don't tell that to the groundcrew!

But two facets bore on our ability to complete the task: one was the dreadful ambient conditions which produced a greater number of aircraft unserviceabilities than in Europe (same excuse as in Aden!), and a high sickness rate among the groundcrew, though various forms of VD contributed markedly!

The other was the long supply line for spare parts. If an aircraft went unserviceable needing a new part on a Monday, it was too late for the Tuesday VC10 resupply, and we had to wait eight days minimum for the VC10 the following week. This often produced a 'Christmas Tree' policy. A 'Christmas Tree' is an aircraft left in the back of the hangar, unserviceable, and used to provide spare parts for the others. Hence, we rarely had more than three serviceable aircraft at any one time, and often only two.

But if I'd ever needed something to pull the flight together, give it some focus, and produce a real sense of unity, I could not have found anything better than my simple orange flying suit! It, and its wearer, became the main love/hate object of the whole unit, and as long as I came to every end-of-month party prepared to be thrown into the water tank after my speech, honour was served on both sides.

"Curse you, Orange Baron!"
(With apologies to Snoopy)

A further major aspect of being the 'Boss' on a military unit comes with the pomp and ceremony. A favourite spot for overseas staff visits, RAF Belize had

303

its fair share in a short period. Besides the AOC, we had the Chief of the Air Staff, MRAF Sir Keith Williamson, pay a formal visit. He had forgotten I'd served under him on 2 Sqn when he was station commander at Gutersloh in '69.

Then came Mr Price, the Belizean Prime Minister, whose claim to fame in our eyes was that, on being shown round the Harrier aircraft, he tapped with his knuckles on the tailplane and then turned to the assembled company and said, "Oh, it's not wood then?"!

Finally, as the jewels in the crown, came HRHs Prince and Princess Michael of Kent. This royal visitation was a lovely day of pomp and ceremony including a full beating of the retreat by the resident Gordon Highlanders' Battalion band, and a formal luncheon for the senior officers and their ladies in the Mess. It was also a treat for our crews to watch the army continually repainting the curb-stones!

Such was the lazy environment in Belize that I came across a body in the Belize river and no one was in the least bit surprised. Late one Sunday morning, four of us had taken a small outboard motorboat from a jetty near the airport, along the Belize river, through the city, over the estuary to one of the cayes for a day's outing. Half-way through the city section, just before the swing bridge, I saw what looked like the inner, brown hairy shell of a coconut bobbing about just under the water's surface. As the coconut passed us, it became obvious that it was actually the top of a dark-haired person's head. Manoeuvring alongside, we grabbed the hair and towed it towards the bank where there was a small landing stage. A couple of locals on the stage, who had noticed the incident, helped us drag the body out of the water, and as we were heaving him out, the stench then hit us. Although I'd seen dead bodies before in sanitized situations, I had forgotten that a dead body relaxes and, when kept warm in tropical water, everything that could possibly leak out of every orifice does just that – it was a stinking, bloated, ichorous mess. It also became apparent that it was a young Mayan Indian man known to these locals. He had been high on Khat[3], probably also mixed with alcohol, the previous night – most nights so they said – and had not been seen since. High on some narcotic mixture, he'd obviously stumbled into the river and drowned. They were all shrugging their shoulders, as did a local policeman who arrived on the scene. However, having given him our names and addresses, we never heard another thing: isn't life cheap?

Varying the task to make it interesting was difficult for the airmen in the small, closed environment of Belize, but we did what we could. One day, during the dry season, we sent the engineers with all their equipment down the Western Highway to Holdfast, the western army camp near the Guatemalan border, which had a short grass airstrip alongside it. We then flew into and operated out of there for the day quite successfully, despite slightly soft ground. It proved we could do it during times of tension if required, but it would not have been possible during the rainy season. It also gave all the groundcrew another chance to see some other parts of the country outside their Harrier hides, Belize City and the local brothels!

We also organised an open day with drinks and food all laid on in the Charlie/Delta Hide, and invited all the army and local dignitaries to come and inspect our various displays. A Puma helicopter put on an amusing display for us, and I had to fly a Harrier display as the highlight of the afternoon. Unfortunately, at exactly the time of my display, a large cumulo-nimbus cloud came steaming past, just to the south of the airfield, causing appalling wind-gusts and turning the display into more of a survival exercise. I certainly wasn't able to put on the full display I'd practised, and it was rather a let down. At least the boys were able to show off their wares to the army, and perhaps the latter, for once, left with a better understanding and perception of the air force! Perhaps!

Of course, there were always unforeseen flying problems. Half-way through my time there my instrument rating expired. Naively expecting the authorities to grant an extension for a few months, I signalled the problem back to our HQ in UK, only to find myself on the next VC10 back home to renew my rating in a two-seater Harrier at Wittering. One of the Wittering Sqn Ldrs, Bruce Monk, came out to Belize to act as temporary CO for a week while I regained my rating. It must 'rate' as some sort of record, having to fly a 14,000mile round trip for a single flight in a two-seater Harrier!

For the whole of my time in Belize I was the only flight authorizing officer. The rest of the pilots were too junior, and no one else was allowed to authorize Harrier flights. It meant that if I wasn't there the Flight didn't fly. Hence, I couldn't take a day off at any time without grounding the Flight. An un-accompanied Boss of any unit, especially overseas in an isolated unit, with no friends of the same rank and discipline with whom to discuss professional or personal matters or indeed with whom to relax, needs a form of escape – a stress release mechanism. Now no one is indispensable, yet one needs to get away from the commensurate constant worry and nervous tension every now and again in order to unwind.

Then I found Chaa Creek. More a farm than a holiday retreat in its early days, Chaa Creek was the most relaxing place in the world. Although some will now know it as a well respected, environmentally-friendly, holiday desti-nation in western Belize, back in the early '80s Mick Fleming and Lucy Langan had only just started Chaa Creek and the place was very rough and ready. It was only an area of cleared jungle, rough pasture on a steep hillside over-looking the Macal river, with only two, open-to-air, sleeping cabins. Its kitchen was a thatched, open basha, and you had to walk across the rough-grass hillside to the only makeshift toilet and shower. It had a certain quaint silent charm. The welcome, the slow pace of life, and the home cooking, were worth every cent, and Lucy's black bean soup was to die for!

I used to spend the weekends there, and travelled on a Friday afternoon in my Landrover with a large cold-box full of Gin and tonics, soft drinks and ice along the western highway to the mile long track into Chaa Creek. The track then was almost impassable, one of the roughest I'd used, and I'd used some rough ones in the Middle East! It was so rough that for three weekends running, the Gin bottle broke in the cold box, *only the Gin bottle!* But then, after dark, Mick Fleming and I would start up the outboard of his ex-army, metal-skinned, open boat and bomb up this very shallow river. Regularly bottoming on the gravel banks, we'd eventually disgorge ourselves some eight miles away in the centre of the local town of San Ignacio. There we could repair to the local hostelry for a few well-earned pints before, suitably inebri-ated, an even madder roar homeward along the river in the pitch dark. How we missed so often all the obstructions in this shallow, narrow, winding river over those months of 1982 I shall never know, but it was thrilling, fun and a set of exhilarating experiences along that Macal river bed.

Then came the weekend of the recapture of South Georgia from the Argentinians at the beginning of the Falkland's campaign, and for once the Gin bottle remained intact. I'd also added a bottle of Champagne because I'd heard that week on the jungle grapevine that Lucy had had her second baby, a boy to be named Piers. We stood and toasted the birth and the Queen and British forces down south. It was a poignant moment, but here I could relax in a friendly, peaceful atmosphere away from the troops, and recharge my batteries ready for the Monday morning fray.

Twenty-one years later, I e-mailed Mick at Chaa Creek with every intention of revisiting. It never happened but I did receive a lengthy reply in which he makes mention of the retaking of South Georgia, our toasting of the birth of Piers and the Queen, and recalls my visits which, he jokes, ". . . helped to finance the growth of Chaa Creek and gave us the courage to continue . . . ".

The property, he tells me, "has changed out of all recognition – 21 rooms – two treetop suites . . . "! I often think, though, of those beginnings and how Mick literally hacked it out of the jungle in '82!

As my tour as the Boss was coming to a close, I started preparing for my next challenge. I'd been offered not one, but my choice of two, squadron commands in the UK, and naturally I was over the moon. Instead of 79 Sqn where I'd spent some time in 1967–68, but who were now in South Wales at Brawdy, I chose to take command of 63 Squadron at one of my favourite stations, RAF Chivenor in North Devon. Then the Argentinians muscled in on the act. The Falkland's crisis reared its ugly head, and my successor was sent south with the Falkland's Fleet, while I was left holding the baby in Belize. Indeed for the next few months, I had nothing but inexperienced first tourist pilots sent to 1417 Flight while all the experienced hands were either in or on stand-by for the Falklands. My posting was cancelled. I was extended in Belize TFN, and the rest of the boys went south and got the glory! I was devastated . . . and my career never recovered.

In a small community like Airport Camp Belize, nothing can be kept secret. Our first part in the Falklands build up was to refuel a 51 Squadron Recce Nimrod on its way out to Easter Island. Four weeks before the campaign really commenced, it had no flight plan but was to arrive at midnight one Tuesday night to be refuelled, and fly on overnight at very high level, outside any radar cover, across Guatemala/San Salvador and out into the Pacific. Only the unit commanders were told, but as the airport never ever opened at night, everyone on Base not only knew something different was about to happen, but after the various bars closed, they also turned out to watch! Every member of Airport Camp bordered the runway on both sides, most with a can or two of beer, watching the dark stealthy arrival and departure of this unique aircraft.

It arrived surreptitiously, straight in, out of the night and departed just as furtively, exactly as advertised; no doors were opened, and no one got in or out of it. It sat there, dark, silent, brooding and unmoving for forty minutes while the fuel was pumped into it. It then started up and left as quickly and as stealthily as it had arrived, disappearing South-westwards into the charcoal of the night sky, across central America, without invitation or advertisement.

During the build up to retaking the Falklands, my Flight was all ready to go. We made the incorrect assumption that as the nearest Air Force fighter unit to the Falklands, we would be the first to be sent down there. All the aircraft were made serviceable. Long range ferry tanks and in-flight refuelling probes, unused since our arrival in Belize back in 1977, were reinstalled and flight tested. By 1st April I was able to report that we were fully serviceable and ready to go.

It was not to be. We had our own problems during the Falklands campaign. Imagine that the two most extreme right wing regimes, Argentina and Guatemala, were in cahoots. Imagine also the world headlines if our Harriers, who were winning world headlines and glory in the south, were to be blown up in Belize? What a coup for the Argentinians. This created a major defence problem, which turned into a large guarding task for our groundcrew. Twenty-four hours per day for many weeks we had to mount armed guards on all our aircraft and installations.

We purloined every ISO container in Belize, and built double storied container, defensive rings around each aircraft to protect them from small arms and intruders. We jealously guarded those rings, with our resident army battalion and the Belize Defence Force mounting outer guard rings in ever increasing circles, out as far as any possible mortar range from the aircraft.

We still thought we'd be the first to be sent south, as we could easily have flown that distance with the aid of a single VC10 tanker, probably over-flying Honduras, staging via Ecuador, and on to the south of Chile, perhaps to Punta Arenas prior to Stanley. Indeed, our Harrier office at the Ministry of Defence initially told John Knott, The Secretary of State for Defence at the time, in a face to face briefing, that we would be the best bet, not only because of our geographical position, but simply because it meant not having to de-assign a NATO squadron for the task. All looked well until the Foreign Office, probably acting on intelligence information received, refused to sanction any use of the Belize defence force in any way whatsoever. We couldn't understand why, until the guarding problem cropped up. Soon after, it all became clear when the rumour went round that an army patrol had picked up and captured a couple of Argentinian agents crossing the Belizean/Guatemalan border. Apparently, their sole target was exactly what we had feared – my Harriers. It seems that the two countries, Guatemala and Argentina, were indeed co-operating, and those potential world headlines loomed larger.

The Falklands campaign was extraordinarily successful, particularly the air battle, despite the weather conditions, but we also had a lot of luck. It is not the business of this book to pontificate about the Falklands campaign as the author did not participate – we had our own Belizean problems. Accordingly, to assuage all our successful guarding efforts, we were stood down for a well-earned rest once the Falklands were retaken. This was for all of us in Belize, however, a frustrating time. There was little news from the few ad-hoc sources available, and therefore it was very difficult to keep up with the detail of the campaign in the South. Additionally, I must have been the nearest available, senior, Harrier pilot, current on the aircraft, not to have taken part, and after all the years of training, it was yet another personal disaster: wrong place, wrong time!

*   *   *

You may remember from Chap 27, there were strains of VD, particularly of Syphilis, of which the western world had never heard – and some of my groundcrew were certainly badly infected. Indeed, back in the early days of 1(F) Sqn detachments, a couple of airmen died from Syphilis after being 'casevaced' back to The RAF Institute of Tropical Medicine at RAF Halton. On the bright side, the VD problem has to be put in context. Napoleon's army that invaded Russia in 1812 was said to have 80% of his soldiers with VD. Our doctors in Belize finally let me into their confidences: between 15 and 20% of my groundcrew at any one time had some form of VD! I suppose, since Napoleon's day, we should consider that some sort of progress!

I made the mistake soon after arriving of attending the dentist's morning clinic where one sat in a row of chairs along the medical centre corridor waiting one's turn. On the opposite side of the corridor was another medical queue, in which were two or three of my groundcrew. So conversation was engaged: Me – "I've got a filling needs replacing, what's your problem 'Smithy'?" I caused a lot of red faces that morning, finding out later that this was the clap clinic!! It could only have happened in Belize, but once again, as they say out there: "No big ting man!"

With the VD problem came the classic dilemma with which an overseas commander has to deal – fraternization with the native women. When overseas and unaccompanied, it is axiomatic that everyone lives together on the base, so when a member of the groundcrew shacks up with a native girl downtown, it becomes a supervision problem. If this had been an ordinary airman, that would have been easy to deal with. But what do you do with a SNCO who started living away from base with a Mayan 'Lady', who swore blind he was deeply in love with this Indian girl and, who had a large family back in the UK!? Allow one to get away with it, especially one who's supposed to be setting an example, and chaos reigns. Well, after much head-scratching, he eventually solved the problem himself. After twice being warned as to his conduct, and still continuing to live downtown with this Mayan girl, he was put on the next plane home to UK to look his wife in the eyes!

Since 1975 I had flown many missions policing the airspace of Belize, including their Independence Day flypast in Sep 1981. The boys and the SNCOs of the flight gave me a wonderful send-off dinner at Foxy-Golf Harrier Hide, our own chefs having put together an excellent cold buffet using lobsters and strips of roast beef made up into the shape of Harriers with my name on the side (see photo). It was an emotional tribute that I'll never forget, and for once, words failed me when it came to making my final speech that night. Even more of a surprise was the beautifully carved mahogany Harrier model they had commissioned from one of the many craftsmen downtown as a leaving present (see photo).

What is oft said in military circles is so true: there is nothing so rewarding as having your own front-line command. Even better is to have one of the few overseas fighter commands. The groundcrews were a splendid bunch whose spirit could never be engendered in a UK environment. Nevertheless, on this sad departure from Belize for the final time, besides the demise of The Orange Baron, I felt that once again my wings had flown over yet another retreat and

308

withdrawal from Empire. I'd served seven separate detachments, adding up to over two years, and spanned more than seven years. I'd flown 217 missions, of which more than half – 120 were as the CO, and perhaps, just perhaps, if Barry Bowen ever reads this, he'll invite me back for a few final ice-cold Belicans. As always, they await the next hurricane with increasing trepidation. Maybe they'll call it Hurricane Harrier after defending the country for twenty years and saving it twice in the 1970s. Long after the last gunboat claimed back the Falklands for the British Empire, 1417 Flt was still policing peaceful Belize.

But more was to come – yet another fly-past. This time though it was a surprise fly-past flown especially for me by the four Harriers I had handed over the previous day. It was a great ending and I was extremely sad to be leaving. It was a poignant moment as the Harriers in box-four, close formation dipped overhead as I prepared to board the Hercules that was to fly me on the three-day plod via Fort Bragg and Gander, back home. There can be very few occasions in the modern Air Force when a lowly Sqn Ldr on departure receives such a tribute as his own fighter fly-past. It was a very moving moment and one that will remain with me always. Even in front of my own groundcrew who had come to see me off, though hopefully hidden by the inevitable tropical rain, I cried.

> " 'Tis all a chequer-board of Nights and Days
> Where Destiny with Men for Pieces plays:
> Hither and thither moves, and mates, and slays,
> And one by one back in the Closet lays."
>
> "With Them the Seed of Wisdom did I sow,
> And with my own hand labour'd it to grow:
> And this was all the harvest that I reap'd-
> 'I came like Water, and like Wind I go.'"
>
> (Rubaiyat of Omar Khayyam)

Notes
1. No.1453 Flt was later re-activated as the Tornado F3 flight in the Falklands.
2. Cat 5, the most severe of five categories of RAF accidents, usually meaning an aircraft write-off, not necessarily fatal.
3. Khat: A local mildly narcotic herb chewed by the natives, and identical to that used by the Arabs of Aden.

Epilogue

Between 1991 and 1993, Guatemalan President Serrano agreed to recognize Belize. Diplomatic relations were established but still no final agreement was signed. But it was enough and in 1993, 1417Flt once again disbanded, hopefully not for the last time. With this final withdrawal from Belize, the country was now able to defend itself against all but the most determined. Nearly twenty years had elapsed since our first deployment in 1975.

After leaving the service I continued to work for the MOD in a number of capacities. Initially, I became a defence consultant for the, then, Defence Research Agency at Farnborough airfield working on future weapons effectiveness and battle damage assessment. I then moved to the Air Warfare centre at RAF Waddington working with the Command Research Team before moving back to flying again. I continued test and trials flying as Chief Pilot at DRA West Freugh in the Southwest corner of Scotland.

At both Waddington and West Freugh, there are WW2 honours boards in their main operations buildings. I did not know before I joined both these organisations but, my Father's name is on both boards: "Sgt J Bain DFM 21 Sep 1941" (the Gazetted date).

Would I encourage my son to join up these days? No chance! The services have lost their way in looking after their personnel. All support services have been privatised, and we all know what that means. By taking away the medical, support, training and facilities so necessary to fight a war, the politicians and senior officers have left the ordinary serviceman with an enormous burden of extra stress. They should be ashamed of themselves. There are organisations that offer invaluable help to the serviceman, but it is striking that they are ALL CHARITIES – NOT ONE OFFICIAL BODY AND NO PROPER SERVICE MEDICAL FACILITIES! At times I can understand countries whose officer class finally flip and send tanks onto the streets against ministeral corruption and government spin.

Annex A

Table of the author's operational missions in South Arabia 1965 to 1967:

DATE	MISSION	REMARKS
6 Nov '65	Flagwave – Al Mithaf – 2 aircraft	Flagwaves were for showing our strength and threatening further action
19 Dec '65	Flagwave – Am Surrah – 2 ac	No 2
2 Feb '66	Op. Strike – Wadi Yahar – 4 ac	Fired 12 rockets
4 May '66	Flagwave – Wadi Markhah – 2ac	No 2
4 May '66	Op Strike – Wadi Tiban – 2ac (No2 to the Boss – reported in local papers and RAF News)	Fired 9 Rkts, 420 rnds of 30mm – 13killed, 5 wounded
2 Aug '66	Border Patrol – Beihan – 2ac	Yemeni Migs came across Border at Beihan, and shot up the village of Nugub. This started 3 x daily patrols and Beihan a/f landings, putting 2ac on QRA at Beihan from dawn to Dusk.
12 Aug '66	Border Patrol – Beihan – 2ac	
13 Aug '66	Border Patrol – Beihan – 2ac	
23 Aug '66	Border Patrol – Beihan – 2ac	
24 Aug '66	Border Patrol – Mukeiras – 2ac	
27 Aug '66	Border Patrol – Beihan – 2ac	No 2
1 Sep '66	Border Patrol – Beihan – 2ac	No 2
18 Sep '66	Border Patrol – Beihan – 2ac	No 2

DATE	MISSION	REMARKS
22 Sep '66	Border Patrol – Beihan – 2ac	No 2
28 Sep '66	Border Patrol – Mukeiras – 2ac	No 2
7 Oct '66	Top cover for SAS Operation – 2ac	No 2
9 Oct '66	Flagwave – Al Mithaf – 2ac	Leader
17 Oct '66	Top Cover –SAS Op at Dhala	No 2
22 Oct '66	Border Patrol – Beihan – 2ac	Leader
24 Oct '66	Border Patrol – Beihan – 2ac	No 2
28 Oct '66	Border Patrol – Beihan – 2ac	Leader
3 Nov '66	Border Patrol – Beihan – 2ac	No 2
8 Nov '66	Flagwave – Dhala – 2ac	Leader
7 Dec '66	Border Patrol – Beihan – 2ac	No 2
9 Dec '66	Border Patrol – Beihan – 2ac	Leader
18 Dec '66	Border Patrol – Beihan – 2ac	No 2
28 Dec '66	QRA scramble – Op. Strike – Awabil – 4ac **NIGHT ATTACK**	No 2 – 6 Rkts fired
29 Dec '66	Border Patrol – Beihan – 2ac	Leader
9 Jan '67	Border Patrol – Beihan – 2ac	Leader
12 Jan '67	Op Strike – Wadi Bana – 4ac	No3
14 Jan '67	Border Patrol – Beihan – 2ac	Leader
15 Jan '67	Border Patrol – Beihan – 2ac	Leader
16 Jan '67	Border Patrol – Mukeiras – 2ac	Leader
19 Jan '67	Border Patrol – Beihan – 2ac	No 2
12 Feb '67	Flagwave – Tor Al Baha – 2ac	No 2
15 Feb '67	Border Patrol – Beihan – 2ac	Leader
25 Feb '67	Border Patrol – Beihan – 2ac	Leader
1 Mar '67	Flagwave – Mukeiras – 2ac	Leader
6 Apr '67	Border Patrol – Beihan – 2ac	Leader
12 Apr '67	Top cover – Habilayn Convoy	Leader
14 Apr '67	Border Patrol – Beihan – 2ac	Leader
24 Apr '67	Firepower demo – Beihan – 2ac	Leader 12Rkts, 420Rnds 30mm
26 Apr '67	Top cover –Habilayn convoy – 2ac	Leader
27 Apr '67	Border Patrol – Mukheiras – 2ac	Leader
2 May '67	Firepower demo – Beihan – 2ac	Leader12 Rkts, 420Rnds 30mm

DATE	MISSION	REMARKS
4 May '67	Top cover- cordon and search op – Dhala – 2ac	Leader
8 May '67	Flagwave – Khora	Leader
18 May '67	Flagwave – Zamahk, Eastern Aden Protect-2ac	Leader
20 May '67	Firepower Demo – Dhala – 4aircraft	Leader – 6Rkts fired
23 May '67	Border Patrol – Dhala – 2ac	Leader
24 May '67	Op Strike – Wadi Bana – 4aircraft	Leader 6Rkts, 420Rnds 30mm
30 May '67	QRA Scramble – Jebel Lahmahr – 2ac	Leader
7 Jun '67	Border Patrol – Dhala – 2ac	Leader
22 Jun '67	Air Defence QRA scramble – Mukeiras – 2ac	Leader – Comet 2 Signals Cmd
28 Jun '67	Patrol Dhala and Habilayn – 2ac	Leader
11 Jul '67	Border Patrol – Dhala – 2ac	Leader
15 Jul '67	Border Patrol – Perim Island to Am Riga –2ac	Leader
20 Jul '67	Firepower Demo – Al Khabb – 2ac	Leader
20 Jul '67	QRA Scramble – to Aqqan – 2ac	Leader
23 Jul '67	Border Patrol – Khora – 2ac	Leader
1 Aug '67	Border Patrol – Mukeiras – 2ac	Leader
8 Aug '67	Border Patrol –Perim to Am Riga – 2ac	Leader
10 Aug '67	Top cover – Habilayn Op – 2ac	Leader
15 Aug '67	Border Patrol – Mukeiras to Beihan – 2ac	Leader
16 Aug '67	Armed Recce – Al Kirsh – 2ac	Leader – 40 terrorists – 2 bullet holes in my aircraft
17 Aug '67**	Top cover – Al Kirsh – 2ac	Leader – last mission

** On the 9 Sep 67, I left Aden for good, flying my Hunter FGA9 XG255 en route to Amman via Jeddah to deliver the aircraft to the Royal Jordanian Air Force.

Annex B

Record of Service

RAF South Cerney – No 1 ITS	Apr-Sep 62
RAF Leeming – No 3 FTS	Nov 62 – Oct 63
RAF Valley – 4 AFS	Oct 63 – Aug 64
RAF Chivenor – 229 OCU	Aug 64 – Mar 65
RAF Khormaksar – 8 Sqn	Mar 65 – Jul 67
RAF Khormaksar – 43 (F) Sqn	Aug 67
RAF Muharraq – 8 Sqn	Sep 67
RAF Chivenor – 79 Sqn	Oct 67 – Apr 68
RAF Gutersloh – 2 (AC) Sqn	Apr 68 – Jun 69
RAF West Raynham – 54 and 4 (AC) Sqns	Jun 69 – Mar 70
RAF Wittering – 4 (AC) Sqn	Mar – Jun 70
RAF Wittering – HCT(Harrier Conversion Unit)/20 sqn	Jul – Oct 70
RAF Wildenrath – 20 Sqn	Oct 70 – Feb 72
RAF Wittering 223 OCU (Fighter Recce Instructors Cse)	Nov 71
RAF Wildenrath – 3 (F) Sqn	Mar 72 – Nov 73
RAF Wittering – 233 OCU (incs: MOD(Air) OR26 – Link-Miles Worthing – 11 mths, and first 1(F)Sqn Belize detachment – Nov 75)	Nov 73 – Jun 76
RAF Wittering – 1(F) Sqn (incs: QWI Course – 3mths on 233 OCU, Feb-May 77 and Belize: Jul/Aug 77 – Oct/Nov 77 – Feb/May 78)	Jun 76 – May 79

RAF Wittering – Unit Test Pilot/Wing Weapons Officer (incs Belize dets: Feb/Mar 81 and Sep 81)	May 79 – Jan 82
RAF Belize – OC 1417 Flight	Jan – Sep 82
RAF Cranwell – Dept of Air Warfare	Sep 82 – Jan 86
RAF Wyton – Flt Cdr No. 1 PRU	Jan 86 – May 87
RAF Cranwell – Dept of Air Warfare	Jun 87 – Oct 94
Defence Research Agency – Farnborough/ Waddington	Oct 94 – Dec 97
Chief Pilot – DERA West Freugh	1998

Annex C

Types Flown

Jet

Jet Provost Mks 3 and 4

Gnat T Mk1

Hunter F6, T7, FGA9, FR10, T67(SOAF), K68(SwissAF)

Javelin Mk T2

Lightning Mk 4**

Jaguar T2**

Harrier Mk GR1, 1a, T2, T2a, GR3, T4

Canberra B2, T4, PR9**

Tornado GR1**

Phantom RF4C (USAF)**

Hawk T1

Hawker-Siddeley HS125**

Turbo-prop

Pilatus Turbo Porter PC6/B2-H2

Tucano Mk 1

Jetstream T Mk 2**

Piston

Varsity T Mk 1**

Dakota C4**

Britten-Norman Islander BN2a**

Beech 55 and 95**

Dove HS04**

Cessna 150, 172, 180, 182, 185, 206

Chipmunk T10, Mk 21 and 22

Fuji

Grumman Traveller

Piaggio PA31

Cherokee 140

Helicopter

Whirlwind Mk 10

Puma C1**

** Twin engine
Italics: not as first pilot

Bibliography

(This is intended to be a list of those books on which I have drawn during my research, and to indicate my debt to their authors, as well as providing suggestions for further reading.)

1. *"Flight from the Middle East"* – by Air Chief Marshal Sir David Lee GBE CB RAF(Ret'd).
2. *"The Big Show"* – by Pierre Clostermann DFC FAF
3. *"Masirah – Tales of a Desert Island"* – by Colin Richardson
4. *"A Mad World – My Masters"* – by John Simpson
5. *"Introduction to Geopolitics"* – by General Augusto Pinochet (English translation from the Spanish by Liselotte Schwarzenberg Matthei 1981)
6. *"The Last Post – Aden 1964 to 1970"* – by Julian Padget
7. *"Last Sunset"* – by Stephen Harper
8. *"A History of Britain 3 – 1776–2000 The Fate of Empire"* – by Simon Schama
9. *"Empire-How Britain made the modern world"* – by Niall Ferguson
10. *"Hope and Memory: Lessons from the Twentieth Century"* – by Tzvetan Todorov, translated into English by David Bellos
11. *"Air Power"* – by Stephen Budiansky
12. *"The Devil's Dictionary"* – by Ambrose Bierce
13. *"Hudibras"* – by Samuel Butler (1612 – 1680)
14. *"The Malayan Emergency 1948–1960"* – Ministry of Defence, June 1970.
15. *"The Rickshaws of Bangladesh"* – by Rob Callagher.
16. *"Return to Aden"* – by Peter Richards
17. *"A brief History of Time"* – by Stephen Hawkings
18. *"The Elegant Universe"* – by Brian Greene
19. *"Empire of the Stars"* – by Arthur I Miller
20. *"Hawker Aircraft since 1920"* – by Francis K Mason
21. *"The Time of my Life"* – by Dennis Healey
22. *"The Collapse of British Power"* – by Correlli Barnett
23. *"The Effects of Nuclear Weapons"* – Glasstone and Dolan *(Dept of Army*[US Army] *Pamphlet 50-3)*
24. *"Last Take-off – a Record of RAF Aircraft Losses 1950 to 1953"* – edited by Wg Cdr Colin Cummings
25. *"RAF Historical Society – Journal 18 – 1998"*
26. Four x *RAF Form 414: Pilots Flying Log Books 1962–1998* – of Sqn Ldr C J Bain RAF(Ret'd)